FALSE FRIENDS
OF FATIMA

Christopher A. Ferrara

Good Counsel Publications
Pound Ridge, New York

First Edition June 2012

ISBN: 978-0-9815357-5-3

To contact the publisher write or call:

Good Counsel Publications
P.O. Box 203
Pound Ridge, New York 10576-0203
United States of America
1-800-954-8737

To purchase extra copies retail or wholesale
or to get the supplements mentioned in this book:

In USA:
St. Joseph's Books
2711 Elmwood Avenue
Kenmore, New York 14217

In Canada:
Catholic Books
P.O. Box 693
Crystal Beach, Ontario
L0S 1B0

www.fatimashoppe.org

Printed in Canada

Table of Contents

About the Author

Christopher A. Ferrara is an attorney who serves as President and Chief Counsel for the American Catholic Lawyers Association, a religious organization dedicated to the defense of the rights of Catholics by way of litigation, public discourse and debate. Mr. Ferrara is also a widely published author on Catholic issues whose writings have appeared in *The Latin Mass* magazine, *The Remnant* newspaper, *Christian Order*, *The Fatima Crusader* magazine, the *Catholic Family News*, and in his regular Internet column, *Fatima Perspectives*. He is the author of *Liberty: the God that Failed*, *The Secret Still Hidden* and *EWTN: A Network Gone Wrong*. Mr. Ferrara and his wife, Wendy, reside in New Jersey; they have six children.

Preface

FOR EACH OF US
FATIMA MUST BE OUR FIRST PRIORITY

Section I

EMBRACING THE WHOLE PROPHETIC TRUTH OF FATIMA WILL MAKE YOU FREE AND SAVE YOUR LIFE AND YOUR SOUL

Fatima is about the truth. Our Lady came to Fatima to put an end to satan's empire. Lucifer—the former angel of light, by his rebellion against God, became satan—the devil. This enemy of mankind bases his reign of darkness over this world on the *lie*. To him the lie is "sacred", because it is by lying to men and women who in turn believe his lies that they thus enslave themselves to his will. The lie is the very foundation of his entire kingdom on this earth.

Jesus tells us in St. John's Gospel that the devil "was a murderer from the beginning: and he stood not in the truth, because truth is not in him. When he speaketh a lie, he speaketh of his own: for he is a liar, and the father thereof." (John 8:44)

The Blessed Virgin Mary came to Fatima to crush the serpent's head. We know that She will triumph because She has told us, "In the end, My Immaculate Heart will triumph. The Holy Father will consecrate Russia to Me, and she will be converted, and a certain period of peace will be granted to the world."

In the end, truly, She will crush the serpent's head, just as God the Father foretold in the Garden of Eden: "I will put enmities between thee and the Woman, and thy seed and Her seed: She shall crush thy head, and thou shalt lie in wait for Her heel." (Genesis 3:15)

The devil, however, will not be defeated until his lies against Fatima are exposed and overthrown. The truth is simple. The lies are many, and there is more than one method to suppress and distort the truth about Fatima.

One method is to conceal the truth by not allowing people to know about Fatima, especially children and young people, as well as those first entering the Church who do not know much about their faith. The topic is simply never introduced to them. They are not given the opportunity to learn about the apparitions, the Message, the promise and the prophecies. This concealment, it should be noted, has been accomplished through a *de facto* moratorium on Fatima in Catholic publications and media (radio and television).

Another method is to suppress the truth about Fatima by lying to those who have heard at least something about it. In this case the lie is presented to the newly initiated, and even to the very knowledgeable, in such a subtle manner that the lie goes undetected. Crafting such a lie takes a great deal of skill. Moreover, the liar has to be seen as a friend of Fatima in order for the lie to be widely accepted and believed.

This book is about unmasking the leading false friends of Fatima, so that you will know the truth about Fatima and pass it on to others. Our Lady, at Fatima, warned us that Russia would spread its errors throughout the world unless and until it is properly consecrated in the manner that She prescribed: in a solemn and public ceremony by the Pope, together with all the Catholic bishops of the world, to Her Immaculate Heart.

Contrary to the omissions, the half-truths and the outright lies— as we have demonstrated time and time again over the years—the Consecration of Russia has not been done. In this book, that fact is proven once again. It is also a fact that Russia continues to spread its errors throughout the world.

The errors of Russia certainly include Communism (an error which is still spreading today, even if it appears to have been defeated in Russia), but they are not limited to this one particular evil. The errors of Russia also include the errors of Freemasonry (from which Communism was born), Zionism and many others still. These ideologies (or religions, more precisely) stand against Our Lord Jesus Christ, true God and true Man. They are opposed to His Gospel, His Church and His Blessed Mother Mary.

What is difficult for some people to realize is how the errors of Russia could have spread to and within the Catholic Church. Here we must remember the example of the Apostle Judas, who betrayed Jesus Christ unto His death.

Judas was only able to betray Our Lord by virtue of his position as an Apostle. Similarly, those "Judases" who betray Fatima can do so only as a result of their position of rank within the Church.

This brings us to a question that naturally comes to mind when reading this book: "Why is it that the Vatican Secretary of State— not just one of them, but three of them in succession—has opposed Our Lady of Fatima and taken a stand against Her Message? All three (Cardinals Casaroli, Sodano and Bertone) have used their power, position and prestige to fight against the full Fatima Message.

A more complete answer is given in this book, but it is worth mentioning here that the Secretariat of State, in 1962, reached a secret agreement with the Communist rulers of Russia. That agreement is known as the Metz Pact, or, simply, the Vatican-Moscow Agreement. Even to this day, in 2012, this agreement is not widely known or publicized, but it is still in effect. Furthermore, the agreement has never been repudiated or denied by the Vatican, and the worst of its terms are actually hidden in plain sight. Anyone who seeks to know the truth can easily learn about the Metz Pact. *The*

Fatima Crusader has published important articles on this matter over the years, and reprints of these indispensable works are available from the publisher. (See "Further Suggested Reading" on page 277.)

By this agreement, the Vatican Secretary of State, since October 1962, has agreed not to condemn the errors of Russia. This policy, which is still in place today, is fundamentally and therefore directly opposed to Our Lady of Fatima's specific condemnation of the errors of Russia.

As a result of this agreement, the Second Vatican Council, which, it was claimed, would address the most pressing concerns of humanity in its day, deliberately chose not to condemn Atheistic Communism, even though Communism was the biggest problem mankind faced at the time. Of course, Communism is still among the world's foremost problems half a century later.

The Metz Pact has been wrongfully imposed on much of the Church because many religious do not realize that *no one* has the authority to order bishops, priests and lay people to remain silent in the face of Communism or any other error against God and the teachings of His Church. God is the author of all human authority and He would never authorize anyone to uphold, by way of silence, errors against Himself, Our Lady, the Church and the legitimate rights of human beings in general, and of each man specifically.

The Cardinal Secretary of State, even if he were to claim that he was acting under direct orders from the Holy Father himself, does not possess the authority to order anyone not to expose, explain, denounce and warn against the error of Russian (or for that matter, Chinese, Cuban, etc.) Communism. It is obligatory on the part of the Pope and the hierarchy of the Catholic Church to denounce this error.

This obligation is solemnly taught by Pope Pius XI in his Encyclical on Atheistic Communism. He issued this stern warning against Communism in 1937:

> See to it venerable Brethren, that the Faithful do not allow themselves to be deceived! **Communism is intrinsically evil**, and no one who would save Christian civilization may collaborate with it in any undertaking whatsoever. Those who permit themselves to be deceived into lending their aid towards the triumph of Communism in their own country, will be the first to fall victims of their error. And the greater the antiquity and grandeur of the Christian civilization in the regions where Communism successfully penetrates, so much more devastating will be the hatred displayed by the godless.

To maintain silence when confronted with the error of Communism is an evil. Pius XI taught this truth in the same encyclical:

In the face of such a threat the Catholic Church could not and does not remain silent. This Apostolic See, above all, has not refrained from raising its voice, for it knows that its proper and special mission is to defend truth, justice and all those eternal values which Communism ignores or attacks.

Pius XI also wrote a little further on:

Yet, despite Our frequent and paternal warnings, the peril [of Communism] only grows greater from day to day because of the pressure exerted by clever agitators. Therefore, **We believe it to be Our duty to raise Our voice once more, in a still more solemn missive**, in accord with the tradition of this Apostolic See, the Teacher of Truth, and in accord with the desire of the whole Catholic world, which makes the appearance of such a document but natural. We trust that the echo of Our voice will reach every mind free from prejudice and every heart sincerely desirous of the good of mankind. We wish this the more because Our words are now receiving sorry confirmation from the spectacle of the bitter fruits of subversive ideas, which We foresaw and foretold, and which are, in fact, multiplying fearfully in the countries already stricken, or threatening every other country of the world.

Hence, We wish to expose once more, in a brief synthesis, the principles of Atheistic Communism as they are manifested chiefly in Bolshevism. We wish, also, to indicate its method of action and to contrast with its false principles, the clear doctrine of the Church, in order to inculcate anew and with greater insistence, the means by which Christian civilization, the true *civitas humana*, can be saved from the satanic scourge, and not merely saved, but better developed for the well-being of human society.

To further enunciate why such a policy of silence is morally reprehensible, consider the following lesson. The bishop—every bishop—is a watchman. That is the actual meaning of the word "bishop" in Greek. We entrust our safety to the watchmen (the soldiers hired to man our outposts) to sound the alarms if they see the enemy approaching. But if the watchmen sleep on the job, so that they do not see the enemy coming, or if the watchmen strike a bargain to look the other way when they see the enemy at the gates, either way the people are not aroused from their slumber and are attacked without warning. In such instances, they have been betrayed by their watchmen.

For the Vatican to orchestrate a deal so as not to sound the alarm at the "approach" of the errors of Russia is a betrayal of the faithful.

As God said to the prophet Ezekiel:
"...if the people of the land take a man ... and make him

a watchman over them: And he see the sword coming upon the land, and sound the trumpet, and tell the people: Then he that heareth the sound of the trumpet, whosoever he be, and doth not look to himself, if the sword come, and cut him off: his blood shall be upon his own head. He heard the sound of the trumpet and did not look to himself, his blood shall be upon him: but if he look to himself, he shall save his life. And if the watchman see the sword coming, and sound not the trumpet: and the people look not to themselves, and the sword come, and cut off a soul from among them: he indeed is taken away in his iniquity, but I will require his blood at the hand of the watchman." (Ezek. 33:2-6)

Of course, this scriptural teaching about the duties of a watchman is absolutely true, and is obviously applicable to the Pope and the bishops. They must sound the alarm. If they do not, they betray us and become answerable before God.

Pope Benedict XVI has promised more transparency in the recent Vatican leaks scandal (Jan. 2012 - May 2012). Similarly, the secret Vatican-Moscow Agreement needs to be (1) publicly admitted; (2) repudiated; and (3) the intellectual damage repaired through proper education of the bishops, priests and laity. To clarify and elaborate on this third point, anti-Communism has not been taught in the seminaries since the Second Vatican Council in 1962. The result is that current-day bishops and priests are ignorant in what should have been a vital aspect of their formation. As a consequence, Fatima has been removed from our schools, our pulpits, our Catholic press, from the Second Vatican Council and from the counsellors of our bishops, their bishops conferences, and Papal Nuncios, etc., and the laity, for their part, do not even know to ask for what has been taken away from them.

Disclosure and reparation are of the highest priorities for the Church. In the meantime, since Providence has seen to it that this widespread error (i.e., our shepherds have neither denounced nor explained the error of Communism) has been brought to your attention by this book, you should take the time to inform yourself. Do not be deceived by the half-truths, the lies, the gross omissions and suppressions of truth proffered by the last three Vatican Secretaries of State.

Jesus said, "I am the way, and the truth, and the life," (John 14:6) and the Church applies the following words of Sacred Scripture to Our Lady: "I am the Mother of fair love, and of fear, and of knowledge, and of holy hope. In Me is all grace of the way and of the truth: in Me is all hope of life and of virtue." (Eccl. 24:24-25)

While the devil is a murderer and a liar from the beginning, Our Lord and Our Lady give witness to the truth: "And you shall know the truth: and the truth shall make you free." (John 8:32) Always remember that the lie enslaves you. You must not let yourself be deceived, and you must not deceive yourself. As Pope Benedict XVI said on May 13, 2010: "He deceives himself who thinks the prophetic mission of Fatima is concluded."

Because the Fatima requests are the definitive solution to defeating the devil and his agents, we must unmask satan's lies and expose his lying cohorts who are working feverishly against Our Lady's message of world peace. The only path to that peace and the salvation of countless souls is through exact obedience to Our Lady of Fatima's solemn requests. We know that the victory of Our Lady over satan—that is to say, Her victory over the errors of Russia—will not be the result of some other message, of some other apparition that has not been approved by the Church.

One of the more sophisticated techniques, or lying tricks, the devil uses to draw good people away from Fatima (and other Church-approved Marian apparitions) is for himself to appear as Our Lady. For example, when the Blessed Virgin came to St. Bernadette at Lourdes in 1858, the devil impersonated Her at 16 or more apparition sites near the French town of Lourdes. St. Paul tells us that "Satan himself transformeth himself into an angel of light." (2 Cor. 11:14) In the case of Lourdes, the devil transformed himself into the appearance of Our Lady to distract people and pull them away from the true message that Our Heavenly Mother was then giving to St. Bernadette.

We know from the careful consideration of Our Lady's words that Fatima cannot ever be replaced by any other so-called apparition which pretends to be the continuation of Fatima. Our Lady was very clear when She said: "If My requests (i.e., those requests that She made at Fatima on July 13, 1917) are heeded (i.e., are obeyed by those to whom She put the requests), Russia will be converted and there will be peace; if not, she will spread her errors throughout the world, causing wars and persecutions of the Church. The good will be martyred, the Holy Father will have much to suffer, various nations will be annihilated."

The conditions are unequivocal. They absolutely do not rely on some future apparition. They rest only upon the fulfillment of the Fatima requests. These conditions, above all, concern the release and publication of the full Third Secret of Fatima, the proper Consecration of Russia and the promise to promote the Five First Saturdays devotion.

Why is this book so important at this time? After 35 years of my life, doing everything I can to bring the truth of Fatima to the attention of Catholic priests (I have 160,000 out of 409,000 total Catholic priests on my mailing list), and after writing to 5,000 bishops about ten times a year for the past 25 years, I have come to the realization that, unless the lies against Fatima are exposed, and unless those "Judases,"—those lying false friends of Fatima—are unmasked, the lies against Fatima will prevail and the devil will win in the near term. It is not only conceivable, but highly probable that 2 to 5 BILLION people will suffer violent deaths in the next five years, because Our Lady predicted that "various nations will be annihilated". Many of those same souls who will perish, if all comes to pass, will go to hell for all eternity.

I beg you to inform yourself. Do not be deceived by the devil, or by his agents, or by the "useful idiots" who allow themselves to be deceived and, as a result, go about deceiving others.

I beg you to read, intently, every page of this book. If you think the author is mistaken on any point, please write to the publisher or to *The Fatima Crusader*. You will be given further material to prove the point and to answer any specific question.

If too many people refuse to inform themselves and take appropriate action to implement the whole Fatima message in their lives, horrible consequences will befall the entire world. If you inform yourself and act upon this information, Our Lady will protect you in the upcoming conflict.

For those of us who survive beyond what appears to be World War III and the ensuing reign of the Antichrist, we must persevere and cling to Our Lady's words of hope: "In the end, My Immaculate Heart will triumph. The Holy Father will consecrate Russia to Me, and she will be converted, and a certain period of peace will be granted to the world."

Section II

FATIMA'S PROPHETIC TRUTH MORE URGENT AND NECESSARY THAN EVER

The Kingdom of God, which is the Holy Roman Catholic and Apostolic Church, is compared by Our Lord to a field in which seeds are sown. The farmer and his helpers sow good seed in anticipation of a bountiful harvest, but while they are sleeping an enemy enters the field and sows bad seed. The good seed springs up, but is often choked out by the weeds.

This is the situation in the Catholic Church today. The good seed—the Faith of all time, the seed of the Word Incarnate—has been sown in the hearts of the faithful by baptism, and by the sound doctrine and dogma handed down by the Apostles in Sacred Scripture and Sacred Tradition. This "Deposit of the Faith" is explained and defined by the dogmatic definitions of the twenty dogmatic Ecumenical Councils of the Church before the year 1960—a very fateful year for the Church and the world, as the Third Secret of Fatima warns.

Since the Second Vatican Council, which had been announced in 1959—the year before the Secret was to have been revealed by order of the Blessed Virgin Mary, but was suppressed instead—the devil and his fallen angel cohorts have managed to sow bad seed in the field of the Church, just as the parable foretells.

They have done so by infiltration, employing human followers of various ranks and commitment to the devil's ends. Unfaithful priests and bishops—how the world delights in the spectacle!—have brought public scandal to the Church.

Over the past half-century, the hearts and minds of many who still consider themselves the faithful the world over have been corrupted by ideas, attitudes and desires which are contrary to the Gospel and to the dogmas, doctrines, practices and observances that make up the fullness of the Catholic Faith.

We know from Sacred Scripture that all of God's revelations to mankind, the Deposit of Faith of all the truths He revealed for our salvation, are not to be found *only* in the Bible.

We have the teaching of St. John's Gospel: "But there are also many other things which Jesus did, which, if they were written every one, the world itself, I think, would not be able to contain the books that should be written." (John 21:25)

St. Paul tells the Corinthians: "And the rest I will set in order when I come." (1 Cor. 11:34)

Obviously, the entire Deposit of Faith is not written in the Bible. Pope Leo XIII points out that if the Fathers of the Church agree unanimously on a certain point, it is because they learned it from the Apostles. Thus, the unanimous teaching of the Fathers binds us all to believe that teaching is a part of the Deposit of Revelation—even if it is not in the Bible itself. Obviously, that teaching is part of Sacred Tradition.

To be precise, Sacred Tradition with a capital T means all the truths that God has revealed to us in a supernatural manner but are not found explicitly in Sacred Scripture. As the First Vatican Council declared definitively, citing the Council of Trent: "supernatural revelation, according to the belief of the universal Church, as declared by the sacred council of Trent, is contained in written books and unwritten traditions…"[a]—that is, the books of the Bible and the oral teaching of the Apostles handed down to us.

Thus the twin sources of authentic Revelation are the Holy Bible and Sacred Tradition.

It is the duty of the Church to preserve and pass on to each generation the Sacred Deposit of Faith, that is, to pass on all the Sacred Scriptures—the Bible—as well as all Sacred Tradition, whole and entire with no mixture of falsehood in it.

---

[a] Denzinger 787.

The role of the Catholic Church's Magisterium (from the Latin word *magister,* meaning "teacher") is to explain what the Bible and Tradition means. It is not the role of the Magisterium to reveal new doctrine, as the First Vatican Council teaches infallibly.

Nor is every word that comes from a Pope or a Council part of the Magisterium, but only that teaching is bound to be believed which is solemnly defined by the Extraordinary Magisterium or which is taught by the Ordinary and Universal Magisterium.

But the Catholic religion is not merely a set of truths to be believed, as vital as these are for salvation. It is also a great ensemble of received and approved practices, devotions and observances—above all, the received and approved rite of Mass in Latin, whose origins go all the way back to the Apostles themselves. Hence, for example, Pope Pius IV prescribed a profession of Faith which declares: "It behooves us unanimously and inviolably to observe the ecclesiastical traditions, whether codified or simply retained by *the customary practice* of the Church."[b]

These "ecclesiastical traditions" support, affirm and reinforce belief in the revealed truths that are necessary for our salvation. Communion on the tongue while kneeling, for example, affirms and reinforces belief in the Real Presence of Our Lord in the Holy Eucharist. So, to be good Catholics and to properly practice our Catholic religion, we must believe with our heart and profess with our tongue all of the Catholic Faith—which consists of all the truths that God has revealed to us in the Deposit of Faith, on the one hand, and to observe all the practices and observances handed down through the centuries which surround and protect those truths, on the other hand.

To tamper with the latter in the name of "reform" or "updating" of the Church is to threaten the adherence of the faithful to the former: *lex orandi, lex credendi*—the law of prayer is the law of belief. Hence, if one wishes to undermine belief in the Real Presence of Christ in the Holy Eucharist, one need only give the appearance of "authorizing" Communion in the hand, passing out the consecrated Hosts as if they were pieces of mere bread, rather than what they actually are: the most sacred and precious Objects on earth.

Now, some of the Catholic faithful, praying the Rosary daily as Our Lady of Fatima requested again and again, have seen the danger to Tradition—to our Faith—and have been more successful in immunizing their hearts, minds and wills from "the smoke of Satan"—*the very words of Pope Paul VI* concerning what he saw invading the Church after the Second Vatican Council. It was then that both the truths of revelation and the practices and observances surrounding them were already under fierce attack. But many others have not been so fortunate.

---

[b] Denzinger 995-996.

As St. Paul teaches us in Sacred Scripture, when a false idea or teaching reaches a critical level of acceptance among members of the Church, a party or faction will emerge around it. His epistle to the members of the Church at Corinth is precisely a warning against factions or schisms in the Church whose effects are disastrous locally, and even universally.

The most famous example in Church history of an error being accepted as truth throughout most of the Catholic world is the Arian crisis, during which Saint Athanasius almost singlehandedly held onto the Catholic Faith whole and entire and successfully passed it on to future generations, while some ninety percent of the bishops had fallen into the error of Arianism, which denied the true divinity of Christ.

St. Athanasius was even "excommunicated" for a time by Pope Liberius in 357 A.D.. Yet it is St. Athanasius who was shown to be in the right and is today proclaimed a Doctor of the Church and a canonized Saint, while Pope Liberius was the first Pope from 33 A.D. until 357 A.D., an age filled with martyr-popes, *not* to be canonized.

Today, we see the Church divided on a scale similar to that of the Arian crisis, but over much more than one divine truth. We have modernists, neo-modernists, progressives, liberals, and deniers of papal infallibility or some other dogma or doctrine. Between them all, however, they either deny, or undermine, or soften, or abandon, almost every element of the Faith.

Pope Benedict XVI himself is forced to admit this. As he declared in his homily just before the papal conclave that elected him:

> How many winds of doctrine have we known in recent decades, how many ideological currents, how many ways of thinking…. [T]he thought of many Christians has often been tossed about by these waves—flung from one extreme to another: from Marxism to liberalism, even to libertinism; from collectivism to radical individualism; from atheism to a vague religious mysticism; from agnosticism to syncretism and so forth. Every day new sects spring up, and what St. Paul says about human deception and the trickery that strives to entice people into error (cf. Eph. 4:14) comes true.
>
> Today, having a clear faith based on the Creed of the Church is often labeled as fundamentalism. Whereas relativism, that is, letting oneself be "tossed here and there, carried about by every wind of doctrine", seems the only attitude that can cope with modern times. We are building a dictatorship of relativism that does not recognize anything as definitive and whose ultimate goal consists solely of one's own ego and desires.[1]

---

[1] Homily at Votive Mass for Election of a Pope, April 18, 2005, http://www.vatican.va/gpII/documents /homily-pro-eligendo-pontifice_20050418_en.html

The people who generate these "winds of doctrine" and belittle adherence to the Creed as "fundamentalism" form a kind of loose and sometimes even unconscious alliance, to which they more or less adhere depending on how "conservative" or radical their strain of "progressive" Catholicism might be. The author of this book refers to this alliance as "the party of the innovators." Opposed to the party of the innovators is what the author calls the party of Tradition. These are simply Catholics who cling to the Faith whole and entire, for which the ultimate standard is the defined dogmas of the Church.

This means holding on to the *explanation* of those dogmas (and the rest of the Faith) by all the Popes and Councils who taught for 1,962 years before Vatican II. It means, as well, holding on to the traditional practices and customs of the Catholic Church, which reinforce belief in her doctrines and dogmas.

In the midst of the present-day struggle for the salvation of souls, we see that many souls have been placed in peril by following various "winds of doctrine" and modern attitudes. These departures from the Faith are often fostered by the very priests and bishops—some one-third of them, as a famous prophecy of the Book of the Apocalypse foretells[2] (Apoc. 12:3-4)—who are supposed to be their shepherds on the journey to eternal life.

In fact, those bad clergy are really the sowers of bad seed and the wolves in sheep's clothing Our Lord warned would come. The victims of bad clergy are now enmeshed in sin; and even if they sense this, they cannot see how to escape from a mentality the Pope rightly describes as one "whose ultimate goal consists solely of one's own ego and desires." Contraception, abortion, and divorce are part of the web in which they are entangled. Yet, Jesus Christ is their Savior, Who could unentangle them if they would but completely accept His teaching and His gentle ways.

So, two parties or camps have emerged in the Church since Vatican II: a vast party that has more or less departed from the Faith, like the vast majority of the bishops during the Arian crisis, and a minority party that clings to it, like Saint Athanasius and his small remnant of Catholic faithful. And that is why Our Lady came to Fatima in 1917.

Pope John Paul II, speaking at Fatima before 500,000 pilgrims in 2000, declared before the whole Church that "The message of Fatima is a call to conversion, alerting humanity *to have nothing to do with the 'dragon' whose 'tail swept down a third of the stars of heaven, and cast them to the earth'* (Ap. 12:4)." In what many believe was a veiled indication of the true meaning of the Third Secret, the Pope was making an allusion to the work of the devil, who manages to corrupt

---

[2] Cf. Chapters 7 and 9.

some of the clergy by bad doctrine—in our time, Modernism, which the author explains—and bad morals.

The devil drags down "a third of the stars of heaven," traditionally understood to mean consecrated souls, priests and bishops. The devil's insidious influence, combined with the lack of a fervent prayer life, cause these clergy to fall, little by little, into an abyss of corruption, and then into heresy, schism and even outright apostasy. The scandals that, consequently, have convulsed the Church in recent years need not be elaborated here.

This is why it is so necessary to be able to identify and oppose with truth what this book calls "the false friends of Fatima." For the Message of Fatima is a prophecy for our time, and the voice of prophecy is a guide, a vitally important guide, that the faithful *should not, must not* despise. As St. Paul teaches:

> "Do not extinguish the spirit. Do not despise prophecy. Test all things and hold fast to that which is good." (1 Thes. 5:19-21).

Why does God send us prophets if we already have His revelation in the Bible and the teaching office of His Church? Saint Thomas Aquinas, the greatest of all the Doctors of the Church, explains:

> The prophets who foretold the coming of Christ could not continue further than John, who with his finger pointed to Christ actually present. Nevertheless as [Saint] Jerome says on this passage, *"This does not mean that there were no more prophets after John.* For we read in the Acts of the Apostles that Agabus and the four maidens, daughters of Philip, prophesied." ...
>
> [A]t all times there have not been lacking persons having the spirit of prophecy, *not indeed for the declaration of any new doctrine of faith, but for the direction of human acts.*[3]

Note well, Saint Thomas teaches that *at all times* God sends prophets, not to announce new doctrines, but to *direct human acts.* This is necessary because the Church is constantly under attack by the devil, who corrupts Judases among the clergy and the laity—and there but for the grace of God go any one of us! The faithful need a sure guide to direct their actions in confronting the *concrete circumstances* that confront the Church in a given age, and always in a time of crisis when the wrong actions will mean disaster, but the right ones will stay the divine wrath.

Our Lady of Fatima warned that Russia would spread her errors throughout the world. In 1962, Russia negotiated the Vatican-Moscow Agreement, in which the Vatican itself promised to remain silent regarding the errors of Russia. To this day, the Vatican-Moscow Agreement is still in effect and is enforced by the Secretary of State of

---

[3] *Summa Theologica,* II-II, Q. 174, Art. 6, ad. 3.

the Vatican. Until Russia is consecrated by the Pope and the bishops in the manner Our Lady of Fatima requested, Russia will continue to spread her errors. And as long as the Vatican-Moscow Agreement is not repudiated, the Vatican Secretary of State will enforce it.

Thus, it should not be surprising that the leading false friend of Fatima is the Vatican Secretary of State. Presently, that position is occupied by Cardinal Bertone. Before him, it was Cardinal Sodano and before him, Cardinal Casaroli.

For those souls who do not ardently seek the truth; for those souls who do not make knowing, loving, seeking and defending the truth their first priority, it is easy to see how they can be deceived and being deceived themselves, deceive others.

"He deceives himself who thinks the prophetic mission of Fatima is concluded." (Pope Benedict XVI)

We may very well have entered into that time foretold by Our Lord in St. Matthew's Gospel, when "Even the elect would be deceived if that were possible."

That is why we need the Message of Fatima in this time of unprecedented scandal and confusion in the Church. Our Lady—the ultimate Prophetess, as She is the Mother of God—came to Fatima "to direct human acts" in order to avert disaster for the Church and the world. Her directions include warnings about dangers that threaten the Church and the whole human race as we endure a growing storm *that has shaken the faith and practice of hundreds of millions of Catholics*. And God will not be mocked.

Jesus, foreseeing the coming collapse of faith and discipline in the Church, sent His Mother, the prophetic guide par excellence, to prescribe the means for avoiding it: the Consecration of Russia to Her Immaculate Heart and the revelation of the Third Secret of Fatima, in its entirety, for the safety of the Church and all of humanity. In aid of these things, Our Lady also prescribed the praying of the Rosary every day, other mental prayer, doing penance for sin, and the practice of the Five First Saturdays devotion. These are directions for human acts in our time of great peril.

Some reduce the Message of Fatima to just a personal encouragement to prayer, piety and penance. But, there is more to the Message of Fatima than just these appeals to individuals to keep the Ten Commandments and pray the Rosary and other indicated devotions. The Message is also directed to the leaders of the Church—that is, the Pope, the bishops and the priests—to apply and fulfill special commands given to them.

The requests for personal devotion are certainly not spoken enough about from our pulpits, our Catholic schools, our Catholic press and so forth. Rather this part of the Message of Fatima is generally treated by silence or just mentioning it once in a while, whatever minimum will pass by the faithful. But these requests for personal piety are not contradicted and combatted over and over again like the requests, the commands of Jesus and Mary for the Consecration of Russia and for the release of the whole Third Secret to the faithful in our time.

The devil knows that obedience to these two requests will end his empire here on earth and so he astutely uses various strategies to prevent this obedience. One of his best weapons against the full Fatima Message is to use the technique of false friends of Fatima who are used to get ignorant and badly informed, well-intentioned persons to follow them into joining their faction against Our Lady's real requests.

These false friends mislead the unsuspecting into error about the Consecration of Russia, about the Third Secret and about Our Lady's whole purpose for coming to Fatima in the first place. This book unmasks that very sly technique of the devil and it identifies leading persons who are false friends of Fatima. The author has written other booklets exposing other false friends and these booklets are available from the publisher as well. (See "Further Suggested Reading" on page 277.)

As this book demonstrates, there are false friends of Fatima who profess to embrace the Fatima event, to hold it in the highest esteem, while they are in the act of burying those elements of the Fatima prophecy, especially the Third Secret, which warn of the "winds of doctrine" and other confusions and corruptions that would carry the Catholic faithful away from the refuge of truth, from what Pope Benedict calls "a clear faith based on the Creed of the Church."

Many of these false friends of Fatima may even believe that they possess the clear faith of which Benedict speaks, but "adapted"— their favorite word—to the "modern world"—their favorite phrase— along with the Fatima event itself.

Sincere or not, the false friends of Fatima seek to lead us astray. If not opposed and defeated, they will lead the Church and the world into disaster—not only a massive loss of life on earth, including quite possibly your own life and the lives of your loved ones, but, infinitely worse, the loss of eternal salvation for countless souls—perhaps even your own, and those of the ones you love most dearly.

"If My requests are granted," said Our Lady of Fatima, "many souls will be saved and there will be peace." If the requests are ignored, however, Russia "will spread her errors throughout the world, causing wars and persecutions of the Church. The good will be martyred; the Holy Father will have much to suffer; various nations will be annihilated."

On these pages you will see that the currently reigning Pope had suggested again and again that we are facing the very consequences of which Our Lady of Fatima warned. Yet he has been impeded in addressing this emergency by the means Our Lady of Fatima prescribed: the Consecration of Russia and the full disclosure of the Third Secret of Fatima. Those who impede him are found in high places in the Vatican, and are joined by their facilitators below. They are all numbered among those we call the false friends of Fatima, and they must be seen and opposed for what they are.

In the August-September issue of the *Inside the Vatican* magazine, editor Robert Moynihan shared some reminiscences of his late friend, Archbishop Pietro Sambi, who died in July 2011. Archbishop Sambi was Papal Nuncio to the United States, and thus a key attaché of the Vatican Secretariat of State under Cardinal Bertone—the leading figure among the false friends of Fatima. Archbishop Sambi even personally escorted Pope Benedict XVI on his visit to America.

One of the memories Moynihan mentions is a discussion he once had with Archbishop Sambi. This discussion regarded "the Third Secret of Fatima, the allegations that the Vatican has not published the entire text of the Third Secret as revealed to Sister Lucy, and the response of Cardinal Tarcisio Bertone, the Vatican Secretary of State, in a book where Bertone states that there is nothing more to be revealed." At the mention of this issue, Archbishop Sambi did something quite extraordinary:

> Sambi said, "Excuse me." He got up, went out of the room, and came back with a book. "Here," he said. "Do you know this book? You should read it." It was Christopher Ferrara's *The Secret Still Hidden*. "Wait," I said. "You are the Pope's representative in the US, and you are urging me to read a book that questions what the Secretary of State wrote?" Sambi replied: "All I am saying is that there are interesting things worth reading in this book. And in the end, we are all after the truth, aren't we? The truth is the important thing..."[3a]

Thus, even a high-ranking member of the Vatican Secretariat of State was willing to listen to the truth about the Third Secret of Fatima; he took the time to read a book demonstrating that his superior was involved in covering up that truth, even though the author holds no office or prestigious position in the Church. For the truth *is* the important thing. And that is why this book was written.

Father Nicholas Gruner
Friday, July 13, 2012
95th Anniversary of Our Lady's Message
that humanity is at a crucial crossroads:
either world peace or enslavement and annihilation.

[3a] Robert Moynihan, *Inside the Vatican,* August-September 2011.

Introduction

THE SCENE BEFORE US

"The very future of the world is at stake." These are not the words of the latest failed prophet of the mass media, predicting the end of the world on a certain date. Rather, they are the words of the Roman Pontiff Benedict XVI in his Christmas message to the Roman Curia in 2010.

In that dramatic address, the Pope compared the scene confronting humanity today with the state of the Roman Empire in the midst of its fall: "The sun was setting over an entire world. Frequent natural disasters further increased this sense of insecurity. There was no power in sight that could put a stop to this decline."[4] Today as well, Benedict warned, "moral consensus is collapsing, consensus without which juridical and political structures cannot function. Consequently, the forces mobilized for the defense of such structures seem doomed to failure…"

After nearly fifty years of inexplicable optimism concerning "the modern world" inaugurated by the Second Vatican Council, the Pope returns to the gravely pessimistic line of his preconciliar predecessors, including the admonition by Pius XII in an encyclical on Catholic missions issued eleven years before the Council began:

> Venerable Brethren, you are well aware that almost the whole human race is today allowing itself to be driven into two opposing camps, for Christ or against Christ. The human race is involved today in a supreme crisis, which will issue in its salvation by Christ, or in its dire destruction.[5]

Nor has Pope Benedict confined himself to an assessment of the condition of the secular world. For since the Council an entirely new situation has developed *within* the Church, a situation Benedict famously described as "a continuing process of decay" when he was still Cardinal Ratzinger.[6] Now, speaking as Pope, the former Cardinal Ratzinger has expressed alarm before the entire universal Church concerning "a grave crisis of the sense of the Christian faith and of belonging to the Church."

On this occasion the Pope announced the creation of a new pontifical council whose specific task will be "promoting a renewed evangelization in countries where the first proclamation of the faith already resounded… but which are going through a progressive

---

[4] Benedict XVI, CHRISTMAS GREETING TO THE ROMAN CURIA, December 20, 2010.

[5] Pius XII, *Evangelii Praecones* (On the Promotion of Catholic Missions), n. 70.

[6] *L'Osservatore Romano*, November 9, 1984.

secularization of society and a sort of 'eclipse of the sense of God'..."[7] Benedict was referring to what his predecessor had already decried publicly as nothing less than "silent apostasy" throughout a once-Christian Europe.[8]

Here too the currently reigning Pope shatters the post-conciliar "optimism" about the Church and the world, abandoning the myth of a great post-Vatican II "springtime" for the Church. He evokes instead the almost panicked admission of Pope Paul VI in the immediate aftermath of the Council—an admission without precedent in the annals of the pronouncements of Roman Pontiffs:

> By some fissure the smoke of Satan has entered into the temple of God: there is doubt, uncertainty, problems, unrest. Doubt has entered our consciences, *and it has entered through the windows which were meant to have been opened to the light.* This state of uncertainty reigns even in the Church. It was hoped that after the Council there would be a day of sunlight in the history of the Church. *Instead, there came a day of clouds, of darkness, of groping, of uncertainty.* How did this happen? We will confide Our thoughts to you: there has been interference from an adverse power: *his name is the devil...*[9]

After Vatican II *the smoke of Satan* entered the Church, afflicting her human element with doubt, uncertainty, problems and unrest. Paul VI himself admitted this in his very capacity as Roman Pontiff, placing the diagnosis beyond any claim of "traditionalist" exaggeration.

And now Pope Benedict further confirms the diagnosis. Indeed, speaking as Cardinal Ratzinger he admitted much earlier that "Developments since the Council seem to be in striking contrast to the expectations of all, beginning with those of John XXIII and Paul VI. Christians are once again a minority, *more than they ever have been since the end of antiquity....* What the Popes and the Council expected was a new Catholic unity, and instead one has encountered a dissension which—to use the words of Paul VI—'seems to have passed over from self-criticism to *self-destruction.*'"[10]

But how did this happen? Once again a Pope himself provides the decisive admission. Speaking only eight years after the Council, Paul VI declared: "the opening to the world [at Vatican II] became *a veritable invasion of the Church by worldly thinking.* We have perhaps

---

[7] Cf. Vespers Homily, June 28, 2010.

[8] John Paul II, *Ecclesia In Europa* (2003), n. 9.

[9] Paul VI, *Insegnamenti*, Ed. Vaticana, Vol. X, 1972, p. 707.

[10] In Joseph Ratzinger and Vito Messori, *The Ratzinger Report* (San Francisco: Ignatius Press, 1986), p. 29.

been too weak and imprudent."[11] But how did *that* happen? What explains an "opening" of the Church to the world, the invasion of the Church by worldly thinking, and all the disastrous consequences that have followed? Here we enter into the mystery of the greatest prophecy of our age—the Message of Fatima—recognized as such by the same Popes who admit the ecclesial and civilizational crisis.

Christopher A. Ferrara
Good Friday, 6 April 2012

Anniversary of the day on which, as the Second Vatican Council declares, "the Jewish authorities and those who followed their lead pressed for the death of Christ..." *Nostra Aetate* (1965).

---

[11] Address of November 23, 1973, in Romano Amerio, *Iota Unum*, trans. Fr. John P. Parsons (Kansas City: Sarto House, 1996), pp. 9-10.

Chapter 1

A Two-Party Conflict

"The Appeal of Our Lady of Fatima is so deeply rooted in the Gospel and Tradition that the Church feels herself bound by this message."[12] Thus declared Pope John Paul II at Fatima on May 13, 1982, during a pilgrimage to the Fatima shrine in gratitude to Our Lady of Fatima for having intervened to save him from the assassin's bullet—as the late Pope devoutly believed—a year to the day earlier, on the very anniversary of the first Fatima apparition. In so declaring, the Pope definitively rejected the attempt by some, including those whose conduct is the subject of this book, to categorize the Message of Fatima as a mere "private" revelation.

Clearly alluding to that part of the Message which Catholics know as the Third Secret, the Pope further declared: "The successor of Peter presents himself here also as a witness to the immensity of human suffering, a witness to the almost *apocalyptic menaces looming over the nations and mankind* as a whole."[13] Two years later, Cardinal Ratzinger, the Pope's doctrinal right-hand man, revealed that the Third Secret speaks of "dangers *threatening the faith* and the life of the Christian and therefore of the world."[14]

On May 13, 2000, speaking again at Fatima during the Mass for the beatification of two of the three Fatima seers, Jacinta and Francisco Marto, the Pope linked the threat hanging over humanity to a threat hanging over the Church herself. Citing Chapter 12, verse 4 of the Book of the Apocalypse, commonly interpreted as a reference to the fall of consecrated souls—priests, nuns and religious—from their exalted states, the Pope warned: "The message of Fatima is a

---

[12] "Il contenuto dell'appello della Signora di Fatima è così profondamente radicato nel Vangelo e in tutta la Tradizione, che la Chiesa si sente impegnata da questo messaggio." Homily at the Fatima Shrine, May 13, 1982, http://www.vatican.va/holy_father/john_paul_ii/homilies/1982/documents/hf_jp-ii_hom_19820513_fatima_it.html.

[13] Ibid. ("Il successore di Pietro si presenta qui anche come testimone delle immense sofferenze dell'uomo, come testimone delle minacce quasi apocalittiche, che incombono sulle nazioni e sull'umanità.")

[14] *Jesus* magazine, November 11, 1984, p. 79. See also Father Paul Kramer, *The Devil's Final Battle*, pp. 33, 274-276 (also at http://www.devilsfinalbattle.com/ch4.htm, http://www.devilsfinalbattle.com/appendix.htm); "Published Testimony: Cardinal Ratzinger (November 1984)" at http://www.fatima.org/thirdsecret/ratzinger.asp; Frère Michel de la Sainte Trinité, *The Whole Truth About Fatima*, Vol. III: *The Third Secret* (Buffalo, New York: Immaculate Heart Publications, 1990), pp. 822-823; "Cardinal Ratzinger Speaks on: The Third Secret of Fatima", *The Fatima Crusader*, No. 18 (Oct.-Dec. 1985), pp. S4ff (also at http://www.fatimacrusader.com/cr18/cr18pgS4.asp); *The Fatima Crusader*, No. 37 (Summer 1991), p. 7 (http://www.fatimacrusader.com/cr37/cr37pg6.asp); and *The Fatima Crusader*, No. 64 (Summer 2000), p. 118 (http://www.fatimacrusader.com/cr64/cr64pg28.asp).

call to conversion, alerting humanity to have nothing to do with the 'dragon' whose 'tail swept down a third of the stars of heaven, and cast them to the earth' (*Rv* 12:4)."[15]

As we shall see, this was John Paul's way of alerting the Church and the world to that part of the Secret yet to be revealed: a text accompanying the enigmatic vision of the "Bishop dressed in White" whose impending publication on June 26, 2000 was announced during the beatification proceedings at Fatima by the Vatican Secretary of State, Cardinal Angelo Sodano.

This text would explain how the white-clad bishop in the vision— apparently (but not certainly) a future Pope—comes to be executed by a band of soldiers on a hill outside a ruined city filled with dead bodies, followed by the execution of bishops, priests, religious and members of the laity.

This text would contain the words of the only one who could explain the vision with infallible surety, including whether it indeed depicts the fate of a future Pope: the Lady who conveyed it to the seers of Fatima, the Blessed Virgin Mary. It is this text those we shall call the false friends of Fatima have labored to conceal from the Church and the world, keeping it "well hidden" in the Vatican, as the famed Italian Catholic intellectual Antonio Socci has put it.[16]

A Secret Still Hidden

The world knows—even Hollywood knows[17]—that on October 13, 1917, some 70,000 souls witnessed the Miracle of the Sun at the Cova da Iria. In this country field outside the Portuguese village of Fatima, the three Fatima seers, Lúcia dos Santos (known to the Anglophone world as Lucy) and her cousins, Jacinta and Francisco Marto, had been receiving a series of apparitions by the Blessed Virgin on the 13th of each month since May. At precisely the moment pre-announced by Lucia—noon, solar time—the Miracle that authenticated the apparitions for even the skeptical began.

Over the next twelve minutes the sun danced in the sky, threw off a stunning array of colors that transformed the landscape, and then plunged toward the terrified crowd, instantly drying the muddy field and the clothing of the rain-drenched witnesses before the phenomenon ended with the sun returning to its normal place in

---

[15] "Apostolic Journey of His Holiness John Paul II to Fátima, May 12-13, 2000, Homily of His Holiness Pope John Paul II, Beatification of Francisco and Jacinta Marto, Shepherds of Fatima", at www.vatican.va/holy_father/john_paul_ii/travels/documents/hf_jp-ii_hom_20000513_beatification-fatima_en.html.

[16] Antonio Socci, "Bertone in the 'Wasp's Nest' of the Polemics," *Libero*, June 2, 2007 ("he [Cardinal Bertone] demonstrated (involuntarily) that as a matter of fact the explosive part of the 'Third Secret of Fatima' exists yet is well hidden....").

[17] Cf. *The Miracle of Our Lady of Fatima*, Warner Brothers (1952), http://en.wikipedia.org/wiki/The_Miracle_of_Our_Lady_of_Fatima.

the sky. The amount of solar energy involved in that feat would have incinerated everyone present, but not a soul was harmed. Quite the contrary, at the same moment numerous miraculous cures and—hardly surprising!—instantaneous conversions took place among the witnesses.

As the Bishop of Leiria-Fatima, D. Jose Alves Correia da Silva, wrote shortly afterwards: "This phenomenon, which was not registered in any astronomical observatory, and could not, therefore, have been of natural origin, was witnessed by people of every category and class, by believers as well as unbelievers, journalists of the principal daily papers, and even by people kilometers away, a fact which destroys any theory of collective hallucination."[18]

One of those remote witnesses was none other than the poet laureate of Portugal, Afonso Lopes Vieira, who, having forgotten about the apparitions at Fatima, was dramatically reminded of them by the solar phenomenon he observed from his veranda, 25 kilometers distant from the Cova.[19]

What was the Message the Virgin authenticated by this absolutely unprecedented display of heavenly power, the Message that John Paul II declared binding upon the Church? When Our Lady came to Fatima in 1917 from that heavenly realm which stands outside and above time, She foresaw the situation that confronts us now.

For Her, the crisis in the Church and the world lamented by Paul VI, John Paul II and Benedict XVI was an already present event. With that crisis in view, the Virgin conveyed to the three seers, Lucia, Jacinta and Francisco, a "Great Secret" in three parts during Her apparition of July 13, 1917.

The first part of the Great Secret is a vision of hell:

> Our Lady showed us a great sea of fire which seemed to be under the earth. Plunged in this fire were demons and souls in human form, like transparent burning embers, all blackened or burnished bronze, floating about in the conflagration, now raised into the air by the flames that issued from within themselves together with great clouds of smoke, now falling back on every side like sparks in a huge fire, without weight or equilibrium, and amid shrieks and groans of pain and despair, which horrified us and made us tremble with fear. The demons could be distinguished by their terrifying and repulsive likeness to frightful and unknown animals, all black and transparent. This vision lasted but an instant. How can we ever be grateful

[18] John De Marchi, *Fatima from the Beginning* (Fatima: Edicoes: Missoes Consolata, 1950), p. 140.
[19] Ibid., p. 142.

enough to our kind heavenly Mother, who had already prepared us by promising, in the first Apparition, to take us to heaven. Otherwise, I think we would have died of fear and terror.[20]

But the "Lady in white" did not simply leave the three children in their state of terror. She immediately explained the vision the children had just seen, and then provided the second part of the Great Secret:

> We then looked up at Our Lady, who said to us so kindly and so sadly:

> "You have seen hell where the souls of poor sinners go. *To save them*, God wishes to establish in the world devotion to my Immaculate Heart. If what I say to you is done, many souls will be saved and there will be peace. The war is going to end: but if people do not cease offending God, a worse one will break out during the Pontificate [reign] of Pius XI.[21] When you see a night illumined by an unknown light, know that this is the great sign given you by God that he is about to punish the world for its crimes, by means of war, famine, and persecutions of the Church and of the Holy Father. To prevent this, I shall come to ask for the consecration of Russia to my Immaculate Heart, and the Communion of reparation on the First Saturdays. If my requests are heeded, Russia will be converted, and there will be peace; if not, she will spread her errors throughout the world, causing wars and persecutions of the Church. The good will be martyred; the Holy Father will have much to suffer; various nations will be annihilated. In the end, my Immaculate Heart will triumph. The Holy Father will consecrate Russia to me, and she shall be converted, and a period of peace will be granted to the world."[22]

The content of the first two parts of the Message, conveyed with so few words, is staggering in its scope and theological richness, and in its implications for the Church and the world: Innumerable souls will be lost for eternity; the world will be punished by war, famine,

---

[20] Congregation for the Doctrine of the Faith, *The Message of Fatima* (Vatican City: Libreria Editrice Vaticana, 2000) (*Message*), p. 13; photo-reproducing in its entirety and quoting from Lucia's handwritten text in her Third Memoir.

[21] As can be seen from the handwritten text photo-reproduced in *Message*, the Vatican translation of Lucia's original Portuguese arbitrarily substitutes "*Pontificate* of Pius XI" for Lucia's "*reign* of Pius XI" ("*renado* de Pio XI")— one of many signs of the "modern" and "ecumenical" attitude of what we call here the false friends of Fatima, who have militated against the authentic Fatima message since Vatican II, as will be apparent from the rest of this discussion.

[22] *Message*, p. 16.

and persecutions of the Church and the Pope. Yet these calamities can be avoided by establishing in the world devotion to the Immaculate Heart—through the Communion of reparation on the First Saturdays, among other things—and by consecrating Russia to the same Immaculate Heart. And then, nothing less than a terrible ultimatum from Heaven itself: "If my requests are heeded, Russia will be converted, and there will be peace; *if not*, she will spread her errors throughout the world, causing wars and persecutions of the Church. The good will be martyred; the Holy Father will have much to suffer; *various nations will be annihilated*." Finally, however, a promise of God's mercy:

> "In the end, my Immaculate Heart will triumph. The Holy Father will consecrate Russia to me, and she shall be converted, and a period of peace will be granted to the world."

We know, of course, that every one of the calamities the Virgin predicted in the first two parts of the Great Secret (except the ultimate "annihilation of nations") did in fact happen: World War I ended, World War II ravaged the globe, Russia spread its errors—including international Communism—throughout the world, there were persecutions of the Church, the good were martyred and the Holy Father had much to suffer. The fulfillment of these predictions verifies the authenticity of the Message even more effectively than the Miracle of the Sun, for the very nature of true prophecy is that it unerringly predicts what comes to pass.

True to Her word, Our Lady did come to ask for the Consecration of Russia. On June 13, 1929 at Tuy, Spain, She appeared again to Sister Lucy during a great and sublime vision representing the Blessed Trinity. She told Lucy that "The moment has come for God to ask the Holy Father to make, in union with all the bishops of the world, the consecration of *Russia* to My Immaculate Heart. By this means, He promises to save *Russia*." That simple request, deemed authentic by a series of Popes, has been at the heart of the undying controversy arising from the decision of certain "advisors" to Pope John Paul II to avoid at all costs any mention of Russia in the act of consecration, producing the utter absurdity of a "consecration of Russia" designed specifically *not to consecrate Russia* in particular.

But what of the third part of the Great Secret, commonly known simply as the Third Secret of Fatima? In her Fourth Memoir recording the apparitions, Sister Lucia declared that she would write of everything "With the exception of that part of the Secret which I am not permitted to reveal at present..."[23] But, after restating the

---

[23] Frère Michel de la Sainte Trinité, *The Whole Truth About Fatima*, Vol. II: *The Secret and the Church* (Buffalo, New York: Immaculate Heart Publications, 1990), p. 37.

first and second parts of the Great Secret as already set forth in her Third Memoir (August 1941), Sister Lucia added to the integral text the words which have, ever since, been at the heart of the Third Secret controversy:

> "In Portugal, the dogma of the faith will always be preserved etc.[24] *Tell this to no one.* Yes, you may tell Francisco."[25]

The reference to the preservation of dogma in Portugal, having no evident connection to the first two parts of the Great Secret, could only pertain to a dogmatic crisis *outside* of Portugal, which in turn could only be explained in further words of the Virgin to be found in the place Lucia had indicated with her telltale "etc." It is there, in the content of those missing words, that we would find the link between a crisis in the Church and a crisis in the world—the same two-fold crisis Pope Benedict now laments.

And indeed it would be none other than Pope Benedict himself who would declare on May 11, 2010 that in the Third Secret

> are indicated *future realities of the Church* which are little by little developing and revealing themselves... Thus it is true that beyond the moment indicated in the vision, it is *spoken*, it is seen, the necessity of *a passion of the Church that naturally is reflected in the person of the Pope; but the Pope is in the Church, and therefore the sufferings of the Church are what is announced....*
>
> As for the novelty that we can discover today in this message, it is that *attacks on the Pope and the Church do not come only from outside, but the sufferings of the Church come precisely from within the Church*, from sins that exist in the Church. This has always been known, but today we see it *in a really terrifying way*: that the greatest persecution of the Church *does not come from enemies outside, but arises from sin in the Church.*[26]

---

[24] *"Em Portugal se conservera sempre o doguema da fè etc."*

[25] Francisco had only seen, but not heard, the Virgin during the apparitions.

[26] The full text in Italian: "Oltre questa grande visione della sofferenza del Papa, che possiamo in sostanza riferire a Giovanni Paolo II sono indicate realtà del futuro della chiesa che man mano si sviluppano e si mostrano. Cioè è vero che oltre il momento indicato nella visione, *si parla*, si vede la necessità di una passione della chiesa, che naturalmente si riflette nella persona del Papa, ma il Papa sta nella chiesa e quindi sono sofferenze della chiesa che si annunciano. Il Signore ci ha detto che la chiesa sarà per sempre sofferente, in modi diversi fino alla fine de mondo. L'importante è che il messaggio, la risposta di Fatima, sostanzialmente non va a situazioni particolari, ma la risposta fondamentale cioè conversione permanente, penitenza, preghiera, e le virtù cardinali, fede, speranza carità. Così vediamo qui la vera e fondamentale risposta che la chiesa deve dare, che noi ogni singolo dobbiamo dare in questa situazione. Quanto alle novità che possiamo oggi scoprire in questo messaggio è anche che non solo da fuori vengono attacchi al Papa e alla chiesa, ma le sofferenze della chiesa vengono proprio dall'interno della chiesa, dal peccato che esiste nella chiesa. Anche questo lo vediamo sempre ma oggi lo vediamo in modo realmente terrificante che la più grande persecuzione alla chiesa non viene dai nemici di fuori, ma nasce dal peccato nella chiesa." Transcript by Paolo Rodari, http://www.ilfoglio.

Thus, the Third Secret would appear to have two parts: the vision of the "Bishop dressed in White" and the Virgin's explanation of the vision in Her own words. This would correspond exactly to what we see in the first two parts of the Great Secret: a vision—the vision of hell—and the Virgin's explanation of it: "You have seen hell, where the souls of poor sinners go. To save them..."

That Sister Lucia's "etc" held the place for words of the Virgin which belong to the Third Secret was confirmed in 1952, when an Austrian Jesuit, Father Joseph Schweigl, was sent by Pius XII to interrogate Sister Lucia in her convent at Coimbra. The interrogation took place on September 2nd of that year. While bound not to reveal the precise contents of Sister Lucia's statements regarding the Secret, Schweigl did make the following statement: "I may not reveal anything with regard to the Third Secret, but I am able to say that it has two parts: One part concerns the Pope. The other part is the logical continuation—though I may not say anything—of *the words*: 'In Portugal, the dogma of the Faith will always be preserved etc.'"[27]

To this testimony must be added that of Canon Casimir Barthas (a renowned Fatima expert), who interrogated Sister Lucia concerning the Third Secret on October 17-18, 1946. Barthas likewise reported: "The text of *the words of Our Lady* was written by Sister Lucia and enclosed in a sealed envelope."[28] Further, no less than Cardinal Ottaviani, then Secretary of the Holy Office, interrogated Lucia in 1955 concerning the Secret, later revealing that "She wrote on *a sheet* of paper [*folha* in Portuguese] *what Our Lady told her* to tell the Holy Father."[29] Ottaviani read the Secret himself and can hardly have been mistaken in his reference to what Our Lady *told* Lucia to *tell* the Holy Father.

So, it was clear very early on that the Third Secret of Fatima has two parts, one of which presents the *spoken words* of the Virgin Mary embraced within Sister Lucia's "etc". But, as we shall see, it is precisely those spoken words which assorted false friends of Fatima assure us do not exist, even though it is obvious that they must exist.

Fatima Versus a New "Orientation" of the Church

The Message of Fatima, understood in a traditional Catholic

---

it/palazzoapostolico/2675, confirmed by this author, who watched the video of the Pope's remarks.

[27] *The Whole Truth About Fatima*, Vol. III, p. 710.

[28] Quoted in Laurent Morlier, *The Third Secret of Fatima* (Éditions D.F.T., 2001), p. 196.

[29] Remarks during the Fifth Mariological Conference in the great hall of the Antonianum in Rome, February 11, 1967; quoted in Alonso, *La Verdad sobre el Secreto de Fatima*, p. 65. Cardinal Ottaviani's phrase "to tell the Holy Father" appears to be an extrapolation of his, which if anything would highlight the importance of the Secret. In any case, the Cardinal confirms the hard fact that the Secret contains words of the Virgin Mary.

sense, cannot be reconciled with decisions that have been taken since the Second Vatican Council to change the entire "orientation" of the Catholic Church. This is the "opening to the world" whose ruinous effects upon the faith and discipline of the human element of the Church Pope Paul lamented too late to avert them, leaving both John Paul II and Benedict XVI to lament the resulting disaster in the Church and in the larger world, culminating in Benedict's warning that the very future of the world is now at stake.

The Message of Fatima—in line with all of Catholic Tradition, as John Paul II affirmed—speaks clearly and dramatically of the fundamental elements of the Catholic Faith: death, judgment, Heaven and hell; the necessity of conversion to the Faith for the salvation of souls, and in particular the necessity of the conversion of Russia to avert calamities in our time; the infinite power of grace, producing miracles in the world; the necessity of devotion to the Immaculate Heart of Mary, the Virgin Mother of God; the need to make reparation to God for offenses against His divine law; and the centrality of the Holy Eucharist as a means of reparation for sin (hence the Communions of Reparation on the Five First Saturdays called for by Our Lady of Fatima).

During and after the Council and the opening of the Church to the world, however, the Catholic verities that the Fatima message affirms by the prophecy of the very Mother of God have been abandoned as "triumphalism" by innovators in the Church, who have pursued instead a policy of "aggiornamento" (updating) of the Church and "dialogue" with the world and with the members of any and all religions or no religion at all, thus placing the evangelizing Church Militant of pre-conciliar times into the ecclesial equivalent of a coma. This is why the current Pope is reduced to calling for the re-evangelization even of the once-Catholic peoples of Western Europe. The implicit admission is that the West has entered into a state of neo-paganism.

The same innovators have also presided over a totally unprecedented "liturgical renewal" which the great liturgist, Msgr. Klaus Gamber—writing with the approval of no less than Cardinal Ratzinger—has described as "the destruction of the Roman Rite,"[30] meaning the traditional Latin Mass which, in a providential course correction, Pope Benedict released from its "captivity" under a non-existent "ban" with his Motu Proprio *Summorum Pontificum* (2007).

Pius XII's Fatima Prediction

---

[30] Klaus Gamber, *Reform of the Roman Liturgy* (San Juan Capistrano, Calif.: Una Voce Press, 1993), p. 97.

It is no coincidence that the incalculably destructive work of these innovators was foreseen by the future Pope Pius XII precisely in light of the Message of Fatima. Speaking only thirty-one years before the Council began in 1962, the future Pope made this Fatima-related prophecy of a coming catastrophe in the Church:

> I am worried by the Blessed Virgin's messages to little Lucia of Fatima. This persistence of Mary about the dangers which menace the Church is a divine warning against *the suicide of altering the faith, in her liturgy, her theology and her soul….* I hear all around me *innovators* who wish to dismantle the Sacred Chapel, destroy the universal flame of the Church, reject her ornaments and make her feel remorse for her historical past….
>
> A day will come when the civilized world will deny its God, *when the Church will doubt as Peter doubted.* She will be tempted to believe that man has become God. In our churches, Christians *will search in vain for the red lamp* where God awaits them. Like Mary Magdalene, weeping before the empty tomb, they will ask, "Where have they taken Him?"[31]

Neither the first two parts of the Great Secret of Fatima, nor the vision the Vatican would claim in 2000 is the entire third part or the Third Secret, say anything of coming suicidal alterations in the Church's liturgy, theology and very "soul." That the future Pope related this prophecy of disaster to the Message of Fatima all but compels the deduction that he must have learned something of the contents of the Third Secret as intimated by Lucia's reference in her fourth Memoir to a dogmatic crisis outside of Portugal. And what he learned cannot be a wordless vision standing alone, like the one published in 2000, but rather *words of the Virgin* by which She conveyed "a divine warning against the suicide of altering the faith, in her liturgy, her theology and her soul."

In any event, what Pius XII foresaw in light of Fatima came to pass in the years following his death in 1958. No one can seriously deny the radical and unprecedented changes in faith, liturgy and theology which have afflicted the Church since the end of the Council in 1965. These changes, it must be said immediately, have never actually been imposed on the universal Church by the Church's authoritative teaching office or Magisterium as exercised by the Pope alone or the Pope presiding over an ecumenical Council. For in truth, Vatican II did not change, and could not change, one iota of the doctrine of the Faith. As the Magisterium solemnly declared at the *First* Vatican Council, "the Holy Spirit was not promised to the Successors of Peter

---

[31] Msgr. Georges Roche, *Pie XII Devant L'Histoire* (Paris: Editions Robert Laffont, 1972), pp. 52, 53.

that by His revelation they might disclose new doctrine, but that by His help they might *guard* the revelation transmitted through the apostles and the deposit of faith, and might faithfully set it forth."[32]

Nor has the Church any power to abolish her own received and approved rite of Mass. As the future Pope Benedict rightly declared seven years before he ascended to the Chair of Peter: "the Church, throughout her history, has never abolished nor forbidden orthodox liturgical forms, which would be quite alien to the Spirit of the Church."[33] Thus, Pope Benedict declared in 2007 that "the traditional Latin Mass was never juridically abrogated [abolished] and, consequently, in principle, was always permitted."[34]

The post-Vatican II work of ecclesial "auto-demolition" has been accomplished entirely by means of a false appearance of binding official changes created by the very innovators whose program Pius XII foresaw, acting in the name of a pastoral Council whose ambiguous documents created openings for their "updating" of the Faith. It is those very ambiguities that have prompted Pope Benedict to call for a "hermeneutic of continuity" between Vatican II and the traditional teaching of the Church. But the very need for a "hermeneutic of continuity" between *an ecumenical Council* and the Church's constant teaching indicates a grave problem the Church has never before encountered.

Today, indeed, we understand quite well why the Virgin specifically directed that the Third Secret was to be revealed to the world by the Cardinal Patriarch or the Bishop of Fatima no earlier than 1960—an order Sister Lucia inscribed on the *two* sealed envelopes which contain the Secret in its entirety. The Secret will be "more clear" (*mais claro*) in 1960, Sister Lucia explained.[35] And indeed by 1960 the Second Vatican Council had been convoked, setting the stage for the ecclesial earthquake from which the Church is still reeling, while the West succumbs to "silent apostasy" (John Paul II) and "the very future of the world is at stake" (Benedict XVI).

As this book makes its appearance, the Church is witnessing a struggle to uncover the Secret still hidden and to accomplish what Our Lady of Fatima prescribed for the salvation of souls and the good of all humanity: the Consecration of Russia. That struggle involves

---

[32] Denzinger, 1836.

[33] Address to Pilgrims Gathered in Rome on the Occasion of the 10th Anniversary of the Motu Proprio "Ecclesia Dei."

[34] "Letter of His Holiness Benedict XVI to the Bishops on the Occasion of the Publication of the Apostolic Letter 'Motu Proprio Data' Summorum Pontificum on the Use of the Roman Liturgy Prior to the Reform of 1970", at www.vatican.va/holy_father/benedict_xvi/letters/2007/documents/hf_ben-xvi_let_20070707_lettera-vescovi_en.html.

[35] *Documentation Catholique*, March 19, 1967, Col. 542; cited in *The Whole Truth About Fatima*, Vol. III, p. 725.

two parties that have been contending for the very soul of the Church ever since the "opening to the world" led to the "invasion of the Church by worldly thinking," to recall the astounding admission of Paul VI: the party of Catholic Tradition on the one hand, in continuity with all that the Church has handed down in her doctrine and practice through the centuries, including Marian devotion and piety, and, on the other hand, the party of innovation, modernization, liberalization, adaptation, indeed revolution in the Church.

For the sake of convenience let us refer to the two parties, respectively, as the party of Tradition and the party of the innovators, whose baneful emergence Pius XII foresaw from his "Fatima perspective." We do not propose here a strict division of the Church after Vatican II into these two camps, for human beings are far more complex than that. Allegiances cross Party lines even in secular politics, and it would not be fair to say, especially in times of confusion like these—times of "diabolical disorientation," to use Sister Lucy's famous phrase—that all Catholics are simply one or the other. That the Church has been divided along these lines since Vatican II, however, is undeniable, as the following pages should confirm even for the skeptical. This in itself is an unprecedented development in the Church. But within each constituency there are determined leaders, game followers, uncertain stragglers, and many who are simply ignorant of what is at stake.

We propose, rather, a description of the basic *orientations* of those who, within each constituency, are today actively engaged in contending over the future of the Church in the light of Fatima. It is our burden here to show that within the party of the innovators we will find those who falsely present themselves as favorable to the Fatima event. They do so because they know that the Fatima event commands the respect of so many of the faithful, who see that the apparitions have the weight of Tradition, a public miracle, papal approbation, and the witness of the Mother of God behind it. Like the Pharisees who persecuted Our Lord, they have calculated that they cannot place their own respectability at risk by attacking directly the object of their hidden contempt or disbelief.

These innovators pose as friends of Fatima even as they seek to consign the Fatima event to oblivion, because its meaning is at war with their orientation as progressives who believe the Church has been permanently "updated" since the Council and can never return to her "pre-conciliar" state. To admit the imperatives of the Message of Fatima is to turn back from the road they have followed. This they cannot allow—absent a special grace from God that would illuminate their folly in a way they cannot ignore.

Chapter 2

THE BATTLE LINES ARE DRAWN

Within thirty years of the dramatic prophecy of the future Pius XII, inspired by "the Blessed Virgin's messages to little Lucia of Fatima" concerning "the dangers which menace the Church," the innovators he saw all around him were unleashed to do their work of destruction. But how exactly did the party of the innovators whose triumph Pius XII foresaw achieve their triumph? Did they suddenly appear out of nowhere and overrun the Church? Or was Pius XII aware of realities indicating, even on a human level, a growing danger that would explain the "persistence of Mary" about dangers to the Church? The question cannot be answered without reference, first of all, to the influence of that worldwide society known as Freemasonry.

The Role of Freemasonry

One need not descend into the fever swamps of conspiracy theory to know that before 1960 the Popes issued more condemnations and warnings about the plotting of the Freemasons against the Church than on any other single subject in Church history. On this point, one cannot fail to consider the specific papal involvement in making known the *Permanent Instruction of the Alta Vendita*, a Masonic document that mapped out an entire plan for the infiltration and corruption of the Catholic Church by "innovators" in the 20th century.[36]

The *Alta Vendita* was the highest lodge of the Carbonari, an Italian secret society with links to Freemasonry and which, along with Freemasonry, was the subject of papal condemnations.[37] While it has become fashionable since Vatican II to scoff at the existence of conspiracies against the Church, the secret papers of the *Alta Vendita*, including the *Permanent Instruction*, are crucial historical evidence of just that. The renowned Catholic historian Father E. Cahill, S.J., who was hardly a "conspiracy nut," notes in his work *Freemasonry and the Anti-Christian Movement* that the *Alta Vendita* was "commonly supposed to have been at the time the governing center of European Freemasonry."[38] In fact, the Carbonari were most active precisely in Italy, the heart of the Church, and France, the "eldest daughter" of the Church.

---

[36] Cf. John Vennari, *The Permanent Instruction of the Alta Vendita* (TAN Books and Publishers, 1999).

[37] *The Catholic Encyclopedia,* Vol. 3, (New York Encyclopedia Press, 1913) pp. 330-331.

[38] Rev. E. Cahill, S.J., *Freemasonry and the Anti-Christian Movement*, (Dublin: Gill, 1959) p. 101.

By what must have been a providential intervention, the *Instruction* fell into the hands of Pope Gregory XVI, that fierce opponent of "modern liberties," including unlimited "freedom of speech" and "freedom of conscience," which he called "that delirium."[39] The *Permanent Instruction* was later published at the request of Blessed Pope Pius IX by Cardinal Cretineau-Joly in his work *The Roman Church and Revolution*.[40] With his brief of approbation of February 25, 1861 (addressed to the author) Pius IX guaranteed the authenticity of the *Instruction* and the other Masonic papers, but he did not allow disclosure of the real names of the *Alta Vendita* members implicated in the documents. Pope Leo XIII had likewise requested publication of the *Instruction*. The full text of the *Instruction* is also contained in Msgr. George E. Dillon's book, *Grand Orient Freemasonry Unmasked*.[41] When Pope Leo XIII was presented with a copy of Msgr. Dillon's book, he was so impressed that he ordered an Italian version to be completed and published at the Pope's own expense.[42] Both Popes so acted, no doubt, because they knew that infiltration and corruption of the human element of the Church was far from impossible. And, as we have seen, Pope Pius XII knew this as well and indeed prophesied precisely such a development: "the day will come when the Church will doubt as Peter doubted," to recall his exact words.

In his book *Athanasius and the Church of Our Time* (1974), Bishop Rudolph Graber, another objective and quite unimpeachable authority writing after the Second Vatican Council, quoted a prominent Freemason who declared that "the goal (of Freemasonry) is no longer the destruction of the Church, but to make use of it by infiltrating it."[43] Indeed, according to the very promises of Christ, the Church is indefectible—incapable of being destroyed. But this indefectibility did not preclude Freemasonry's design to use men within the Church's structure as instruments of "renewal," "progress" and "enlightenment," thereby furthering its own vision of the world. That vision would require at least the Church's practical accommodation to the world as Freemasonry would have it—hence the very "opening to the world" at Vatican II, followed by "a veritable

---

[39] Gregory XVI, *Mirari vos* (1832), n. 14.

[40] 2nd volume, original edition, 1859, reprinted by Circle of the French Renaissance, Paris 1976; Msgr. Delassus produced these documents again in his work *The Anti-Christian Conspiracy*, DDB, 1910, Tome III, pp. 1035-1092.

[41] Msgr. George E. Dillon, *Grand Orient Freemasonry Unmasked*, (Palmdale, California: Christian Book Club) pp. 51-56 (full text of *Alta Vendita*).

[42] Michael Davies, *Pope John's Council*, (Kansas City, Missouri: Angelus Press, 1992) p. 166.

[43] Bishop Rudolph Graber, *Athanasius and the Church of Our Time*, (Palmdale, California: Christian Book Club, 1974) p. 39.

invasion of the Church by worldly thinking," as Paul VI observed with dread.

Bishop Graber introduces the Masonic worldview with the concept of *synarchy*:

> What we are faced with here is the sum-total of the secret forces of all the 'orders' and schools which have joined together to set up an invisible world government. In the political sense, synarchy aims at the integration of all the financial and social forces which the world government, under socialist leadership naturally [following the logic of their false principles], has to support and promote. Catholicism, like all religions, would consequently be absorbed into a universal syncretism. Far from being suppressed, it would be integrated, a course which is already being steered in the principle of fellowship between clerics [of various religions].[43a]

The *Permanent Instruction* is essentially a strategy to enlist the human element of the Church in achieving this *synarchy*—a strategy of amazing audacity and cunning. The document describes a process that will take many decades to complete. Those who drew up the document knew that they would not live to see its fulfillment. They were inaugurating a work that would be carried on by succeeding generations of the initiated. As the *Instruction* declares: "In our ranks the soldier dies and the struggle goes on."

The strategy laid out in the *Instruction* is simply the dissemination of Masonic-liberal ideas not only throughout society, which was a given, but also within the Catholic Church. In other words, the "invasion of the Church by worldly thinking" that Pope Paul witnessed immediately after the Council. The aim was that laity, seminarians, clerics and prelates would absorb progressive principles and be made ready to accommodate themselves to "the modern world." In time, a new mentality among Catholic clerics would be sufficiently widespread that priests would be ordained, bishops consecrated, and cardinals created whose thinking was in step with the modern thought rooted in the "Principles of 1789"—i.e., the principles of the French Revolution: pluralism, the equality of all religions, separation of Church and State, unbridled freedom of speech, and so forth. It must be stressed that the clerics involved in this attitudinal transformation *need not themselves be Freemasons*, even if certain of those directing the transformative process—essentially a change of public opinion and practice within the commonwealth of the Church—would indeed be members of "the Craft."

Eventually, the *Instruction* predicted, even a Pope would be elected who would lead the Church on the path of "enlightenment and renewal" without being himself a Freemason. Such a Pope would

---

[43a] *Athanasius and the Church of Our Time*, p. 33.

be merely the product of the new intellectual climate in the Church. The end result would be what the *Instruction* calls "a Pope according to our needs" and a hierarchy won over to the ideas of liberal Catholicism, *all the while believing themselves to be faithful Catholics*. These liberalized Catholic leaders would no longer be opponents of the errors of liberalism condemned by Pope after Pope before Vatican II, but rather would seek to "baptize" them into the Church in a great reconciliation with "the modern world." Catholic clergy and laity would march together under the banner of "enlightenment," all the while believing that they were marching "under the banner of the Apostolic keys."

No doubt with the *Permanent Instruction* in mind, Pope Leo XIII, writing in his landmark anti-Masonic encyclical *Humanum Genus* (1884), called upon Catholic leaders to "tear away the mask from Freemasonry, and to let it be seen as it really is".[44] The publication of the documents of the *Alta Vendita* was an obvious step in "tearing off the mask." Lest there be any claim that we have mischaracterized the *Permanent Instruction*, we now quote from it at considerable length. What follows is not the entire *Instruction*, but the section which contains the elements we have just summarized. The reader should compare what follows with the predictions of the future Pope Pius XII in view of the Message of Fatima, noted in the previous chapter:

> The Pope, whoever he is, will never come to the secret societies; it is up to the secret societies to take the first step toward the Church, with the aim of conquering both of them.
>
> The task that we are going to undertake is not the work of a day, or of a month, or of a year; it may last several years, perhaps a century; but in our ranks the soldier dies and the struggle goes on.
>
> We do not intend to win the Popes to our cause, to make them neophytes of our principles, propagators of our ideas. That would be a ridiculous dream; and if events turn out in some way, if cardinals or prelates, for example, of their own free will or by surprise, should enter into a part of our secrets, this is not at all an incentive for desiring their elevation to the See of Peter. That elevation would ruin us. Ambition alone would have led them to apostasy, the requirements of power would force them to sacrifice us. What we must ask for, what we should look for and wait for, as the Jews wait for the Messiah, is *a Pope according to our needs* ...
>
> With that we shall march more securely towards the assault on the Church than with the pamphlets of our brethren in France and even the gold of England. Do you want to know the reason for this? It is that with this, in order to shatter the high

---

[44] Leo XIII, *Humanum Genus* (1884), (Rockford, Illinois: Tan Books and Publishers, Inc., 1978) p. 18.

rock on which God has built His Church, we no longer need Hannibalian vinegar, or need gunpowder, or even need our arms. We have the little finger of the successor of Peter engaged in the ploy, and this little finger is as good, for this crusade, as all the Urban II's and all the Saint Bernards in Christendom.

We have no doubt that we will arrive at this supreme end of our efforts. But when? But how? The unknown is not yet revealed. Nevertheless, as nothing should turn us aside from the plan drawn up, and on the contrary everything should tend to this, as if as early as tomorrow success were going to crown the work that is barely sketched, we wish, in this instruction, which will remain secret for the mere initiates, to give the officials in charge of the supreme Vente some advice that they should instill in all the brethren, in the form of instruction or of a memorandum ...

Now then, to assure ourselves a Pope of the required dimensions, it is a question first of shaping him ... for this Pope, a generation worthy of the reign we are dreaming of. Leave old people and those of a mature age aside; go to the youth, and if it is possible, even to the children ... You will contrive for yourselves, at little cost, a reputation as good Catholics and pure patriots.

This reputation will put access to our doctrines into the midst of the young clergy, as well as deeply into the monasteries. In a few years, by the force of things, this young clergy will have overrun all the functions; they will form the sovereign's council, they will be called to choose a Pontiff who should reign. And this Pontiff, like most of his contemporaries, will be necessarily more or less imbued with the Italian and humanitarian principles that we are going to begin to put into circulation. It is a small grain of black mustard that we are entrusting to the ground; but the sunshine of justice will develop it up to the highest power, and you will see one day what a rich harvest this small seed will produce.

In the path that we are laying out for our brethren, there are found great obstacles to conquer, difficulties of more than one kind to master. They will triumph over them by experience and by clear-sightedness; but the goal is so splendid that it is important to put all the sails to the wind in order to reach it.

You want to revolutionize Italy, look for the Pope whose portrait we have just drawn. You wish to establish the reign of the chosen ones on the throne of the prostitute of Babylon, *let the Clergy march under your standard, always believing that they are marching under the banner of the apostolic keys.*

You intend to make the last vestige of tyrants and the oppressors disappear; lay your snares like Simon Bar-Jona; lay them in the sacristies, the seminaries, and the monasteries rather than at the bottom of the sea: and if you do not hurry,

we promise you a catch more miraculous than his. The fisher of
fish became the fisher of men; you will bring friends around the
apostolic Chair.

You will have *preached a revolution in tiara and in cope*,
marching with the cross and the banner, a revolution that will
need to be only a little bit urged on to set fire to the four corners
of the world.[45]

The Rise of Liberal Catholicism

As just shown, the goal of Freemasonry was not to destroy the
Church, which the Masons knew was impossible, but to neutralize
and *instrumentalize* her—that is, to make her human element an
instrument for the advance of Freemasonic goals. *Here nothing more
would be required than to convert traditional Catholics into liberal
Catholics.* A liberalized hierarchy would readily lend itself to the
work of establishing the Masonic ideal of a "new world order" (*novus
ordo seclorum*)—a pan-religious "brotherhood" in which the Church
abandons her claim to be the sole ark of salvation and ceases her
opposition to the forces of the world.

Now, whether or not this process of the liberalization of the
Catholic can be attributed to the plans of the *Alta Vendita*, there is
no question that, just as its *Instruction* predicted, the process has
occurred. It began in the 19th century, by which time society had
become increasingly permeated with the Masonic liberal principles
of the French Revolution. Even in the mid-1800s this program
was already causing great damage to the Faith and the Catholic
commonwealths of Europe. The notions of pluralism, religious
indifferentism, a democracy founded on the idea that all authority
comes from the people rather than God, false notions of liberty,
separation of Church and State and other novelties were gripping
the minds of post-enlightenment Europe, infecting statesmen
and churchmen alike. This was not some inevitable historical
development, but rather a grave threat to the Church. And the Popes
of the time acted accordingly.

Liberal Catholicism Condemned

The Popes of the 19th and early 20th centuries waged war
against these dangerous trends. With a presence of mind rooted
in the unchanging certitudes of the Faith, these Popes were not
deluded by modernity. They knew that false principles—which is to
say evil principles—no matter how "reasonable" they are made to
appear, cannot bear anything but evil fruits, including heresy and
apostasy—indeed, the "silent apostasy" John Paul II would lament

---

[45] Msgr. Dillon, *Grand Orient Freemasonry Unmasked*, pp. 51-56.

in the first years of the 21ˢᵗ century. Like commanding generals who recognized their duty to hold their ground at all cost, these Popes aimed powerful cannons at the errors of the modern world and fired incessantly. The encyclicals were their cannonballs, and they never missed their target.

The most devastating blast came in the form of Blessed Pope Pius IX's monumental *Syllabus of Errors*, which he appended to his encyclical *Quanta Cura* (1864). When the smoke cleared, all involved in the battle were in no doubt as to where the battle line had been drawn. In the *Syllabus*, Blessed Pius IX condemned the principal errors of the modern world, not because they were modern, but because they were rooted in pantheistic naturalism and, therefore, were incompatible with Catholic doctrine, as well as being destructive to society.

The teachings in the *Syllabus* were counter-liberalism, and the principles of liberalism were counter-syllabus. This was clearly recognized by both the liberal and the Catholic parties. Father Denis Fahey referred to this showdown as "Pius IX vs. the Pantheistic Deification of Man."[46] Speaking for the other side, the French Freemason Ferdinand Buissont declared likewise, "A school cannot remain neutral between the *Syllabus* and the *Declaration of the Rights of Man*."[47]

Yet the 19th century saw a new breed of Catholic who sought a utopian compromise between the two. These men looked for what they believed to be "good" in the principles of 1789 and tried to introduce them into the Church. Many clergymen, infected by the spirit of the age, were caught up in a net that had been "cast into the sacristies and into the seminaries" by Freemasonry. These men came to be known as Liberal Catholics. Blessed Pope Pius IX regarded them with absolute horror, declaring that they were the "worst enemies of the Church." In a letter to the French deputation headed by the Bishop of Nevers on June 18, 1871, Pius IX declared:

> That which I fear is not the Commune of Paris—no—that which I fear is Liberal Catholicism ... I have said so more than forty times, and I repeat it to you now, through the love that I bear you. The real scourge of France is Liberal Catholicism, which endeavors to unite two principles as repugnant to each other as fire and water.[48]

The Rise of Modernism

---

[46] Father Denis Fahey, *Mystical Body of Christ in the Modern World*, (Dublin, Ireland: Regina Publications, 1939) Chapter VII.

[47] Ibid., p. 116.

[48] In Father Michael Muller, *The Catholic Doctrine* (Benzinger, 1888), p. 282.

Nevertheless, the numbers of liberal Catholics steadily increased. The crisis reached a peak around the turn of the century when the liberalism of 1789 that had been "blowin' in the wind" swirled into the tornado of Modernism, which Pope Saint Pius X would condemn as "the synthesis of all heresies." Father Vincent Miceli described Modernism's "trinity of parents": "Its religious ancestor is the Protestant Reformation ... its philosophical parent is the Enlightenment ... its political pedigree comes from the French Revolution."[49]

What is meant by "Modernism"? Modernism is a synthesis or combination of all the errors of Liberal Catholicism into a comprehensive philosophical and theological system whose effect is to undermine the integrity of the entire Catholic Faith. While a complete examination of the vast Modernist system of thought is far beyond the scope of this book, it suffices for our purposes to say that, by various subtle errors, the Modernist denies or undermines the divinity and divine revelation of Christ, the founding of the one true Church by Him, and the absolute immutability of Catholic doctrine (which the Modernist claims can "evolve" according to changing circumstances). The Modernist also embraces and promotes the liberal notions of "free speech" and "freedom of conscience." Above all, he promotes the error of religious indifferentism, which holds that all religions are more or less good and praiseworthy because they all arise from a so-called "religious sense" in man. This error, of course, implicitly denies the reality of Original Sin by suggesting that all men can find true religion—or at least true enough religion—in the various creeds they have invented and thereby obtain sanctifying grace and salvation without need of Baptism, the Catholic Faith or the sacraments of the Catholic Church.

Modernism Condemned

Pope St. Pius X, who ascended to the Papal throne in 1903, recognized Modernism as a most deadly plague that must be arrested. St. Pius X waged war on Modernism by systematically isolating, defining and condemning its many erroneous propositions. In particular, St. Pius X issued a monumental encyclical against Modernism (*Pascendi*) and a *Syllabus* of Modernist errors (*Lamentabili*). In his encyclical *Pascendi* this great Pope wrote: "There is no part of Catholic truth which they leave untouched, none that they do not strive to corrupt." In the same encyclical he called Modernism "the synthesis of all heresies," declaring that the most important obligation of the Pope is to insure the purity and integrity

---

[49] Father Vincent Miceli, *The Antichrist*, (Harrison, New York: Roman Catholic Books, 1981) p. 133.

of Catholic doctrine, and that if he did nothing, then he would have failed in his essential duty.[50]

But St. Pius X did not stop there. A few years after *Pascendi*, recognizing that the Modernists had to be crushed before they rose up and caused havoc in the Church, this sainted Pope issued his letter *Sacrorum antistitum*, which mandated the Anti-Modernist Oath to be sworn by all priests and teachers. He oversaw the purging of Modernists from the seminaries and universities and excommunicated the stubborn and unrepentant. St. Pius X knew that nothing less than the very nature of the Church was under attack by these ecclesial termites, who in their audacity were now acting openly for the overthrow of Catholic dogma and Tradition. Writing of the "Modernist as Reformer" the Pope outlined their entire program for a transformation of the Church:

> [I]n all Catholicism *there is absolutely nothing on which it [Modernism] does not fasten.*
>
> Reform of philosophy, especially in the seminaries: the scholastic philosophy is to be relegated to the history of philosophy among obsolete systems, and the young men are to be taught modern philosophy which alone is true and suited to the times in which we live.
>
> Reform of theology; rational theology is to have modern philosophy for its foundation, and positive theology is to be founded on the history of dogma.
>
> As for history, it must be for the future written and taught only according to their modern methods and principles. Dogmas and their evolution are to be harmonised with science and history....
>
> Regarding worship, *the number of external devotions is to be reduced,* or at least steps must be taken to prevent their further increase...
>
> Ecclesiastical government requires to be reformed in all its branches, but especially in its disciplinary and dogmatic parts....
>
> The Roman Congregations, and especially the Index and the Holy Office, are to be reformed....
>
> The ecclesiastical authority *must change its line of conduct in the social and political world*; while keeping outside political and social organization, *it must adapt itself to those which exist* in order to penetrate them with its spirit.[51]

St. Pius X effectively halted the spread of Modernism in his day. It is reported, however, that when he was congratulated for

---

[50] Pope Pius X, *Pascendi Dominici Gregis (On the Doctrine of the Modernists),* September 8, 1907.

[51] *Pascendi*, n. 38 (paragraph breaks added).

eradicating this grave error, he immediately replied that, despite all his efforts, he had not succeeded in killing the beast but had only driven it underground. He warned that if Church leaders were not vigilant, it would return in the future with a vengeance. And St. Pius X's prediction has indeed come true, like that of Pius XII only thirty years before the Council began.

The Modernist Breakthrough at Vatican II

A little-known drama that unfolded during the reign of Pope Pius XI demonstrates that the underground current of Modernist thought was alive and well in the immediate post-St. Pius X period. Father Raymond Dulac relates that at the secret consistory of May 23, 1923, Pope Pius XI questioned the thirty Cardinals of the Curia on the timeliness of summoning an ecumenical council. In attendance were illustrious prelates such as Merry del Val, De Lai, Gasparri, Boggiani and Billot. The Cardinals advised against it. Cardinal Billot warned: "The existence of profound differences in the midst of the episcopacy itself cannot be concealed ... [They] run the risk of giving place to discussions that will be prolonged indefinitely." Boggiani recalled the Modernist theories from which, he said, a part of the clergy and of the bishops are not exempt. "This mentality can incline certain Fathers to present motions, to introduce methods incompatible with Catholic traditions." Billot was even more precise. He expressed his fear of seeing the council "maneuvered" by "the worst enemies of the Church, the Modernists, who are already getting ready, as certain indications show, to bring forth the revolution in the Church, a new 1789."[52]

The Cardinals were right. In discouraging the idea of a Council for such reasons, they showed themselves more adept at recognizing the "signs of the times" than all the post-Vatican II theologians combined. Yet their caution may have been rooted in something deeper. They may also have been haunted by the writings of the infamous *illuminé*, the excommunicated Canon Roca (1830-1893), who preached a coming revolution and Church "reform" and predicted in amazingly precise detail the subversion of the Church that would be brought about *precisely by an ecumenical council*.

In *Athanasius and the Church of Our Time*, Bishop Graber quotes Roca's prediction of a "newly illuminated church" that would be influenced by the "socialism of Jesus."[53] In the mid-19th century, Roca predicted that "The new church, which might not be able to retain anything of Scholastic doctrine and the original form of the

---

[52] Raymond Dulac, *Episcopal Collegiality at the Second Council of the Vatican*, (Paris: Cedre, 1979) pp. 9-10.

[53] Graber, *Athanasius and the Church of Our Time*, p. 34.

former Church, will nevertheless receive consecration and canonical jurisdiction from Rome." Roca also, amazingly enough, predicted the liturgical "reform" after Vatican II: "[T]he divine cult in the form directed by the liturgy, ceremonial, ritual and regulations of the Roman Church will shortly undergo a transformation *at an ecumenical council,* which will restore to it the venerable simplicity of the golden age of the Apostles in accordance with the dictates of conscience and modern civilization." Roca foretold that through this council will come "a perfect accord between the ideals of modern civilization and the ideal of Christ and His Gospel. This will be the consecration of the New Social Order and the solemn baptism of modern civilization."

In short, this future council would usher in the triumph of the Masonic plan for subversion of the Church—a reality reflected in admissions concerning the critical condition of the Church post-Vatican II by Paul VI, John Paul II, Cardinal Ratzinger, Pope Benedict XVI, and innumerable other priests, prelates and theologians of the post-conciliar epoch—including, as we shall see, no less than Monsignor Guido Pozzo, appointed Secretary of the Pontifical Commission Ecclesia Dei by Benedict XVI precisely in order to facilitate a restoration of the traditional Latin Mass overthrown after the Council.

The Vatican-Moscow Agreement

The new "orientation" of the Church that emerged after the Council and has been carried out in its name is not limited to a doctrinal or liturgical "updating" whose horrendous results are obvious. The new orientation extends as well to the Church's relation with the powers of the world according to the new "spirit of dialogue." Recall here the plank in the program of the "Modernist as Reformer" noted by Saint Pius X in *Pascendi*: "the ecclesiastical authority *must change its line of conduct in the social and political world*; *it must adapt itself to those which exist* in order to penetrate them with its spirit." This "opening to the world" would not bring about the penetration of the world by the Catholic spirit, as the Modernists had disingenuously promised, but rather precisely the opposite: the invasion of the Church by worldly thinking that Paul VI bemoaned but did little or nothing to repel.

As part of the "opening to the world," just before the Council's commencement there would be an explicit betrayal of the mission Our Lady had launched with Her request for the Consecration and conversion of Russia—a request in keeping with the Church's staunch opposition to the errors of Communism, which at the time of the Council were indeed spreading throughout the world as She had predicted at Fatima. In the spring of 1962, in Metz, France, Cardinal Eugene Tisserant had a meeting with none other than Metropolitan Nikodim of the Russian Orthodox Church—a KGB operative, as were the other Orthodox prelates. At this meeting Tisserant and Nikodim negotiated what came to be known as the Metz Pact, or more popularly, the Vatican-Moscow Agreement. The existence of the Vatican-Moscow Agreement is an irrefutable historical fact attested to in all of its details by Monsignor Roche, who was Cardinal Tisserant's personal secretary.[54]

In substance, the agreement was that Pope John, according to his fond wish, would be "favored" by the attendance of two Russian Orthodox observers at the Council. In return, the Catholic Church would agree that the Council would refrain from any condemnation of Soviet Communism or Soviet Russia. In essence, the Council would compromise the moral liberty of the Church by pretending that the most systematized form of evil in human history did not exist—even though, at the very moment the Council opened, the Soviets were persecuting, imprisoning and murdering millions of Catholics, just as Our Lady of Fatima had warned in 1917.

Its liberty thus constrained in a bargain with Communists, the very Council that proclaimed "the duty of scrutinizing the signs of the times and of interpreting them in the light of the Gospel"[55] failed even to mention Communism. By this failure the Council departed from the teaching of Popes Leo XIII, Blessed Pius IX, Saint Pius X and Pius XI, who reminded the Church that she could not refrain from condemning this incomparable evil:

> This all too imminent danger, venerable brethren, as you have already surmised is Bolshevistic and atheistic Communism which aims at upsetting the social order and undermining the very foundations of Christian civilization. In the face of such a threat the Catholic Church *could not and does not remain silent.* This Apostolic See above all has *not refrained from raising its voice* for it knows that its proper and special mission is to defend truth, justice and all those eternal values which Communism ignores or attacks.[56]

And yet the Council that purported to read "the signs of the times" would say not one word about an evil ideology which, at that very moment in history, was "upsetting the social order and undermining

---

[54] *See* Jean Madiran, "The Vatican-Moscow Agreement," *The Fatima Crusader,* Issue 16, September-October, 1984, p. 5. *See also* articles at pages 4, 7, and 11 in *The Fatima Crusader,* Issue 17, February-April, 1985 and Atila Sinke Guimarães, "The Metz Pact," *Catholic Family News,* Sept. 2001.

[55] *Gaudium et Spes,* n. 4.

[56] Pope Pius XI, *Divini Redemptoris,* Encyclical on Atheistic Communism, March 19, 1937.

the very foundations of Christian civilization." On October 12, 1962, two representative priests of the Orthodox church debarked from a plane at Fiumicino Airport to attend the Council. The Council began with Orthodox observers watching over its proceedings in order to verify compliance with the Vatican-Moscow Agreement. The written intervention of 450 Council Fathers against Communism was mysteriously "lost" after being delivered to the Secretariat of the Council, and Council Fathers who stood up to denounce Communism were politely told to sit down and be quiet.[57]

Obviously, given the Vatican-Moscow Agreement, the Consecration of Soviet Russia to the Immaculate Heart to effect its conversion would be absolutely out of the question. On this point alone, the "new orientation" of the Church that emerged after Vatican II was already radically in conflict with the Message of Fatima. And so it has been ever since the meeting in Metz, which marked the beginning of the conciliar and post-conciliar pursuit of *Ostpolitik*, the policy by which the Church has ceased all condemnation and opposition to Communist regimes in favor of "dialogue" and "quiet diplomacy."

The two most famous architects of *Ostpolitik* were Archbishop Agostino Casaroli, employed by the Vatican Secretariat of State under John XXIII and elevated to the cardinalate and the office of Secretary of State under John Paul II, and Cardinal Achille Silvestrini, a top-ranking Vatican diplomat under Secretary of State Casaroli. Casaroli would be succeeded by Cardinal Angelo Sodano, who would continue the *Ostpolitik* throughout his tenure, as would his successor Cardinal Tarcisio Bertone. The policy continues to this day, as we see with the Vatican's studious avoidance of any condemnation of the vicious persecution of the "underground" Church in Red China. It is no coincidence that both Sodano and Bertone, as we shall see, have pursued a parallel policy of "decommissioning" the Message of Fatima, and in particular its imperative of the Consecration of Russia to the Immaculate Heart, which is quite irreconcilable with a "New World Order" of democratic pluralism—the great Masonic dream—whose erection is now facilitated even by Vatican prelates in their diplomatic relations with the United Nations and other worldly powers, including Russia itself.

The "Reform" of the Curia

In 1967-68, by order of Pope Paul VI in his apostolic constitution *Regimini Ecclesiae Universae*, the Roman Curia underwent its own "reform" in a dramatic restructuring. The

---

[57] A complete account of this debacle is found in *The Rhine Flows into the Tiber,* Father Ralph Wiltgen, (New York: Hawthorne, 1967; TAN, 1985) pp. 272-278.

restructuring was actually designed and implemented by the then Vatican Secretary of State, Cardinal Jean-Marie Villot. The aim was to eliminate, as much as possible, what the party of the innovators would call "the old monarchical model of the Church" in favor of the "new model of collegiality."

Before the Second Vatican Council, the Curia was indeed plainly structured as a monarchy. The Pope was the Prefect of the Holy Office, while the Cardinal in charge of the day-to-day business of the Holy Office was the Pro-Prefect (second-in-command), reporting directly to the Pope. The other dicasteries were of lower rank and, while having their own authority and jurisdiction,[58] were subordinate to the Holy Office, with the Holy Office directly under the Pope. This arrangement was entirely in keeping with the Divine Constitution of the Church. The Pope, the Vicar of Jesus Christ on earth, was at the head of the chain of command over which he wielded his authority either directly or through the Holy Office.

Long before Gorbachev announced his program of *perestroika* in the Soviet Union, the Church underwent its own *perestroika* in the Vatican. Under the "reform" engineered and carried out by Villot, the Holy Office was renamed, becoming the Congregation for the Doctrine of the Faith (CDF)—the name "Holy Office" being far too old-fashioned for the party of the innovators. Far more significant, however, the renamed Holy Office lost its supreme position in the Curia. The Cardinal Secretary of State was placed above all the other Vatican dicasteries [departments], including the CDF. Worse, *the Pope was no longer Prefect of the CDF*, which would now be under a Cardinal Prefect organizationally subordinated to the Secretary of State. In sum, with the approval of Paul VI—one of the many imprudent decisions that would leave him weeping over the state of the Church during his last days—Villot "enhanced the powers of the Secretary [of State], *placing him over all the other departments of the Roman Curia*." For good measure, Paul approved "abolishing the ancient office of Chancellor of the Holy Roman Church and merging its functions into those of the Secretary."[59] The party of the innovators could hardly allow the continued existence of anything so "archaic" as a Chancellor of the *Holy Roman Church*.

The net result of this sweeping administrative "reform" was to sever in practice, but not spiritually, the Pope's direct control over the daily governance of the Church. Under this bureaucratic

---

[58] The principle which requires that authority be exercised at the lowest possible level to avoid tyranny through excessive centralization of government. For example, the budget of a town should be determined by the town Fathers, not by the state or federal government.

[59] Cf. "Cardinal Secretary of State," http://en.wikipedia.org/wiki/Cardinal_Secretary_of_State.

rearrangement, Vatican ecclesiastical decisions would tend inevitably toward the pragmatic and the self-serving, rather than the requirements of truth and justice. St. Thomas Aquinas tells us that the first fruit of error is injustice, as error is the lack of a truth that should be there. The "reform" of the Curia provided a perfect framework for the isolation of Vatican decision-making from the objective norms of truth and justice that were inherent in the "old monarchical model" with its direct governance by the Vicar of Christ. Thus, now no longer under the Pope's "oppressive" monarchical hand, Vatican policies would no longer necessarily be determined by those norms, but rather by what the Vatican department in question deemed politically expedient. The immense implications of this development for the Fatima event, the Church, and the world as a whole will be drawn out on the following pages.

The "Reform" of the Liturgy

In the name of the Council's document on the liturgy, *Sacrosanctum Concilium*, Paul VI—the same Pope who wondered how the smoke of Satan had "entered into the temple of God"—authorized something totally without precedent in the 2000-year history of the Church: the creation of a new rite of Mass that would be presented entirely in the vernacular and would be stripped and "simplified" in comparison with the traditional rite.

Pope Paul himself openly admitted that his new rite was a novelty that represented a startling and bewildering break with the past. As he declared in his audience address of November 19, 1969:

> We wish to draw your attention to an event about to occur in the Latin Catholic Church: the introduction into the liturgy of the *new rite* of the Mass.... This change has something astonishing about it, something extraordinary. This is because the Mass is regarded as *the traditional and untouchable expression of our religious worship and the authenticity of our faith*. We ask ourselves, *how could such a change be made*? What effect will it have on those who attend Holy Mass? Answers will be given to these questions, and to others like them, arising from this *innovation*.

In his audience address of November 26, 1969, only a week later, Pope Paul could not have been more explicit in his intention to depart from the Church's ancient liturgical tradition:

> We ask you to turn your minds once more to the *liturgical innovation* of the new rite of the Mass.... A new rite of the Mass: *a change in a venerable tradition that has gone on for centuries*. This

is something that affects our hereditary religious patrimony, *which seemed to enjoy the privilege of being untouchable and settled*.... We must prepare for this many-sided inconvenience. It is the kind of upset caused by every *novelty* that breaks in on our habits.... So what is to be done on this special and historical occasion? First of all, we must prepare ourselves. This *novelty* is no small thing. We should not let ourselves be surprised by the nature, *or even the nuisance,* of its exterior forms. As intelligent persons and conscientious faithful we should find out as much as we can about *this innovation.*

Pope Paul's description of what he had decided to do regarding the traditional Latin liturgy would be impossible to believe if he had not said it publicly and for the historical record:

> It is here that the greatest newness is going to be noticed, the newness of language. No longer Latin, but the spoken language will be the principal language of the Mass. The introduction of the vernacular will certainly be *a great sacrifice* for those who know the beauty, the power and the expressive sacrality of Latin. *We are parting with the speech of the Christian centuries; we are becoming like profane intruders in the literary preserve of sacred utterance.* We will lose a great part of that stupendous and incomparable artistic and spiritual thing, the Gregorian chant. We have *reason indeed for regret, reason almost for bewilderment.* What can we put in the place of that language of the angels? *We are giving up something of priceless worth.* But why? What is more precious than *these loftiest of our Church's values?*[60]

Pope Paul's answer to his own question—"But why?"—is even more astonishing:

> The answer will seem banal, prosaic. Yet it is a good answer, because it is human, because it is apostolic. Understanding of prayer is worth more than the silken garments in which it is royally dressed. Participation by the people is worth more— particularly participation by modern people, so fond of plain language which is easily understood and converted into everyday speech.

As purely factual matter, there was no evidence whatever to support Pope Paul's claim that his liturgical innovations were necessary to accommodate a supposed need of "modern people" for "plain language." As Cardinals Ottaviani and Bacci observed in their famous Short Critical Study of the new rite in 1969 (which later came

---

[60] The authors of *The Pope, the Council and the Mass* actually cite this text in an appendix in support of their claim that the new Mass is not novel. Comment would be superfluous.

to be known as *The Ottaviani Intervention*), the people themselves had never asked for and did not want this change: "If the Christian people expressed anything at all, it was the desire (thanks to the great St. Pius X) to discover the true and immortal treasures of the liturgy. They never, *absolutely never*, asked that the liturgy be changed or mutilated to make it easier to understand. What the faithful did want was a better understanding of a unique and *unchangeable* liturgy—a liturgy *they had no desire to see changed*."[61] In fact, when the liberal German bishop William Duschak of Calapan proposed in a speech during Vatican II that there be a new rite of Mass in the vernacular, he was asked whether his proposal had originated with the people he served. Duschak replied: "No, *I think they would oppose it*. But if it could be put into practice, I think they would accept it."[62]

And Bishop Duschak, it must be noted, was only suggesting that a new vernacular rite be implemented on an experimental basis *alongside* the traditional Latin rite, not in place of it. The *de facto* abolition of the traditional Mass would have been unthinkable to the vast majority of Council Fathers. In fact, when Cardinal Browne expressed to his fellow Council Fathers the fear that if the Council allowed the vernacular into the liturgy the Latin Mass would disappear within ten years, he was greeted with incredulous laughter. But as Fr. John Parsons notes: "The pessimistic reactionary proved to be more in touch with the flow of events than the optimistic progressives."[63]

The creation of the New Mass was placed under the direction of Monsignor Annibale Bugnini, who had been Secretary of the Pontifical Preparatory Commission on the Liturgy, which drafted *Sacrosanctum Concilium*. After the Council, Pope Paul appointed Bugnini as Secretary of the Consilium for the Implementation of the Constitution on the Liturgy. The result was the imposition of a new Missal and the purported "ban" of the old, which Pope Benedict has declared non-existing in restoring the old Missal to universal use. As Benedict admitted when he was Cardinal Ratzinger: "The prohibition of the missal that was now decreed, a missal that had known continuous growth over the centuries, starting with the sacramentaries of the ancient Church, introduced *a breach of the liturgy whose consequences could only be tragic*."[64] In a further devastating admission, he wrote this by way of introduction to Msgr. Klaus Gamber's withering critique of the New Mass: "In the place

---

[61] Ottaviani and Bacci, *The Ottaviani Intervention*, p. 32.

[62] Wiltgen, *The Rhine Flows into the Tiber*, p. 39.

[63] Fr. John Parsons, "Reform of the Reform? [Part II]," *Christian Order*, December 2001. Fr. Parsons is a diocesan priest in Australia and a renowned Catholic scholar. His bishop has not, to our knowledge, accused him of "private judgment."

[64] Cardinal Ratzinger, *Milestones – Memoirs 1927–1977* (San Francisco: Ignatius, 1998), p. 146.

of liturgy as the fruit of development came fabricated liturgy. We abandoned the organic, living process of growth and development over centuries, and replaced it—as in a manufacturing process— with a fabrication, a banal on-the-spot product."[65] As Gamber himself explained in the work the future Pope Benedict XVI endorsed:

> there has never actually been an actual break with Church tradition, as has happened now, and in such a frightening way, where *almost everything the Church represents is being questioned*..... At this critical juncture, the traditional Roman rite, more than one thousand years old and until now the heart of the Church, was destroyed... We can only pray and hope that the Roman Church will return to Tradition and allow once more the celebration of that liturgy of the Mass which is well over 1,000 years old.[66]

Today, Pope Benedict can hardly deny what he admitted as Cardinal Ratzinger: "I am convinced that the ecclesial crisis in which we find ourselves today depends in great part on the *collapse of the liturgy*, which sometimes comes to be conceived 'as if God does not exist': as if it no longer matters whether God is there and is seen and heard in it. But if in the liturgy there no longer appears the communion of the faith, the universal unity of the Church and of her history, where does the Church appear in her spiritual substance?"[67]

In July of 1975, with liturgical collapse already spreading everywhere, Paul VI suddenly removed Bugnini, now an Archbishop, from office, disbanded the Congregation for Divine Worship over which he had presided, and packed him off to Iran to serve out his days as a Papal Nuncio. Stunned by the suddenness of his fall from a position of total command over the Roman liturgy, Bugnini mused in his autobiography about what could have caused it. Here he freely admits that a cardinal advised him of the "existence of a 'dossier' which he had seen on (or brought to?) the Pope's desk which proved that Bugnini was a Freemason."[68] While Bugnini denied he was a Mason—as a member of a secret society could he have admitted it?—he noted that "the silence of the official organs of the Holy See was interpreted as proof that the 'rumors' were well founded."[69]

Was Bugnini in fact a Mason? Evidently, Paul VI was sufficiently convinced of it, for why else would he have removed Bugnini and disbanded his Congregation within days of receiving the evidence?

---

[65] Gamber, *The Reform of the Roman Liturgy*. Excerpts from Cardinal Ratzinger's preface to the French-language edition appear on the back cover.

[66] Ibid., pp. 98-99, 109, 113-114.

[67] Joseph Ratzinger, *My Life*, p. 115.

[68] Annibale Bugnini, *The Reform of the Liturgy: 1948-1975* (Collegeville, Minnesota: The Liturgical Press, 1990), p. 91.

[69] Ibid., p. 92.

In any case, the "liturgical reform" and the vast upheaval it has caused in the Church—the tragic consequences Cardinal Ratzinger admitted—has more than fulfilled the platform of the Masons (already they had published internally to their Masonic brethren what they wanted the Catholic Church to have in its new Mass, which comes very close to the Novus Ordo) and the program of the Masons and of the Modernists, of "the Modernist as Reformer" noted by Saint Pius X: "Regarding worship, the number of external devotions is to be reduced, or at least steps must be taken to prevent their further increase..."

The "Reform" of the Index

The *Index Librorum Prohibitorum* ("List of Prohibited Books") was first created in 1559 and later administered by the Holy Office, with the most recent edition being issued in 1948, only fourteen years before the Council. For the centuries of its existence, the Index was a warning to the faithful against heresy and immorality in the rapidly expanding world of the printed word. More than that, it was the basis for proceedings aimed at compelling Catholic authors to defend their works and, if they failed to maintain a defense, to conform what they had written to faith and morals or withdraw it from publication.

In keeping with the Curial reform and its abolition of the Holy Office, however, Paul VI did away with the Index. In his Motu Proprio *Integrae Servandae*, which authorized the conversion of the Holy Office into the Congregation for the Doctrine of the Faith, there was no reference to the Index. In response to queries about whether the Index was still in existence, the Congregation, on June 14, 1966, announced that while the Index maintained its "moral force" as a warning against heresy and immorality, it would no longer have any legal force as the grounds for penalties or proceedings, nor would it ever be updated. The Index had thus ceased to exist as part of the Church's ecclesiastical law.

Thus, yet another plank in the program of "the Modernist as Reformer", condemned by Saint Pius X in *Pascendi*, had been implemented: "The Roman Congregations, *and especially the Index and the Holy Office, are to be reformed....*"

Vatican Admission of a Modernist Resurgence

Today, no less than Msgr. Guido Pozzo, Secretary of the Pontifical Commission "Ecclesia Dei," which is in charge of restoring the traditional Latin Mass to its rightful place in the Church, is constrained to admit that the ecclesial catastrophe Paul VI bewailed after the Council continues, and that its occurrence is related specifically to Modernism as condemned by Saint Pius X: "Unfortunately, the effects as enumerated by Paul VI have not disappeared. *A foreign way of thinking has entered into the Catholic world*, stirring up confusion, seducing many souls, and disorienting the faithful. There is a 'spirit of self-demolition' that pervades modernism..." The post-conciliar crisis in the Church, he observed, involves a "para-Conciliar ideology" that "proposes once more *the idea of Modernism, condemned at the beginning of the 20th century by St. Pius X*."

Msgr. Pozzo's reference to a "para-*Conciliar* ideology" traces the crisis to where it first erupted anew: at the Second Vatican Council. Pozzo exonerates the Council documents themselves, but he admits that the Council provided the occasion for the emergence of the "para-Conciliar ideology" that "proposes once more the idea of Modernism" and "a 'spirit of self-demolition' that pervades modernism..." thus necessitating the unprecedented "hermeneutic of continuity" Pope Benedict XVI has called for. Of course, no other Council in the history of the Church has been accompanied by such a development. And that development was predicted by none other than the Freemasons, as we have seen.

Yet not only Msgr. Pozzo, but the entire Vatican apparatus seems impotent to address the very disaster whose occurrence is admitted. This mysterious incapacity, this "diabolical disorientation" in the Church, as Sister Lucy called it, is clearly bound up with what the Third Secret must predict with its yet-to-be-revealed references to what Pope Benedict described in 2010 as "future realities of the Church," and "attacks on the Pope and the Church... precisely from *within* the Church..."

The Two Parties and Their Relation to Fatima

Around the developments we have just sketched coalesced the two parties we mentioned in the Introduction: the party of Tradition and the party of the innovators. That Pius XII foresaw their conflict in light of the Message of Fatima—likely the Third Secret in particular—would explain what that very Message would stand in the way of the program of innovation itself. And this in turn would explain why the conciliar Popes—John XXIII and Paul VI—suppressed the Third Secret despite the world's expectation that it was to be revealed in 1960 in keeping with the Virgin's order. This is not to say that these Popes were themselves intent on destructive innovation, but rather that they were intent on allowing the Council to proceed—not seeing, or refusing to see, that the Council would unleash exactly what Pius XII feared in view of Fatima: "dangers which menace the Church" and "the suicide of altering the faith in her liturgy, her theology, and her soul."

The Italian intellectual Antonio Socci, at first a skeptic of "Fatimist" claims regarding the Third Secret but then a confirmed believer, has been quite unsparing in his criticism of the refusal of Pope John and Pope Paul to reveal the Secret. Speaking of John XXIII, he writes of Sister Lucy's astonishing request for permission to speak to the world about the Message of Fatima, followed by Pope John's silencing and isolation of the visionary:

> We are in the first days of January 1959. It is not yet clear today how and why Sister Lucia, usually very reserved and submissive, would immediately after the election of John XXIII (on October 28, 1958) think of an initiative as sensational as a radio message to the world. The year 1960 had not yet arrived. What was she afraid of? What did she know? What urgency did she feel? It would never be known. Because in the first days of January 1959 an alarmed summit met in the Vatican and, faced with the prospect that the visionary of Fatima would reveal to the world something the Madonna had said, by the will of the Pope there issued the prohibition on the sister, and her substantial isolation from the entire world.[70]

Socci further recounts that when it was suggested to Pope John that he read the Third Secret, his attitude was "'No, wait.' First he wanted to announce the convocation of Vatican Council II, almost as if to place before Heaven a *fait accompli*." The Council, Socci notes, could have been a great event for the good of the Church "if precisely that solemn assembly had made the consecration requested at Fatima, as sought by a petition of 510 bishops, and if the Third Secret had been revealed." But it was not to be. John XXIII "was worried and had stubbornly wished to postpone the reading of the Secret in case it contained something that advised against that announcement [of the Council]. Evidently, Roncalli wanted to take that enormous decision for the Church without being 'influenced' by the Mother of Good Counsel, without being illuminated by the Queen of the Apostles, without being assisted by the Mother of God, by the Mother of Divine Grace, by the Help of Christians."[71]

The Secret, Socci continues, was to be revealed to the world in 1960. But "the message of the Queen of Prophets not being to his liking," Pope John "decided to do exactly the opposite: He decided to bury the message and not to give any explanation, either to the Church or to the world."[72] Specifically, as recounted by his still-living personal secretary, Archbishop Loris F. Capovilla: "The Pope hesitated, then decided: 'I have seen it, I have read it, we will reseal it.' He dictated to me a text to write on the envelope: I give no judgment.

---

[70] Antonio Socci, *The Fourth Secret of Fatima* (Fitzwilliam, New Hampshire: Loreto Publications, 2006), p. 195, citing Marco Tosati, *Il Segreto Non Svelato* ["The Secret Not Revealed"], pp. 45-49.

[71] Socci, *The Fourth Secret of Fatima*, p. 195.

[72] Ibid., p. 196.

He deferred to others: to a commission, to a congregation, or to his successor." That envelope has never been revealed to the world by the Vatican, and its non-production is key evidence for the existence of a missing text of the Secret. After Pope John's decision to reseal and bury the text he read, we encounter the infamous Vatican-initiated press release of February 8, 1960, filled with hints of a text in which *spoken words of the Virgin* in the form of a letter—never revealed— would explain the ambiguous vision of the "Bishop dressed in White" published in 2000:

> According to Vatican sources (February 8, 1960), the Secret of Fatima will never be disclosed.
>
> It has just been stated, in very reliable circles of the Vatican, to the representatives of United Press International, that it is most likely that *the letter* will never be opened, in which Sister Lucia wrote down *the words* which Our Lady confided as a secret to the three little shepherds in the Cova da Iria.
>
> As indicated by Sister Lucia, *the letter* can only be opened *during the year 1960*.
>
> Faced with the pressure that has been placed on the Vatican, some wanting the letter to be opened and made known to the world, *others, on the supposition that it may contain alarming prophecies, desiring that its publication be withheld*, the same Vatican circles declare that the Vatican has decided not to make public Sister Lucia's letter, and to continue keeping it *rigorously sealed*.
>
> The decision of the Vatican authorities is based on various reasons: 1. Sister Lucia is still living. 2. The Vatican already knows the contents of *the letter*. 3. Although the Church recognizes the Fatima apparitions, she does not pledge herself to guarantee the veracity of *the words* which the three little shepherds claim to have *heard* from Our Lady.[73]
>
> In these circumstances, it is most probable that the Secret of Fatima will remain, forever, under absolute seal. (A.N.I.)[74]

Socci's commentary continues with the observation that John XXIII inaugurated the Council in October 1962 "with a discourse that remains celebrated for its infelicitous irony concerning the children of Fatima: 'To us it seems necessary to disagree with these prophets of doom who are forever forecasting calamity, almost as if the world end were imminent.'" That is, the Fatima seers themselves had been rejected as "prophets of doom," although Pius XII had certainly taken them quite seriously. "Evidently," writes Socci, "Roncalli felt that

---

[73] Francisco heard Our Lady's words indirectly from Lucia, who had been given permission by Our Lady to tell him, as revealed in the Fourth Memoir: "Yes, you may tell Francisco."

[74] *The Whole Truth About Fatima*, Vol. III, pp. 578-579.

his 'prophetic spirit' was much more acute than that of the 'Queen of Prophets.' In fact, he announced a splendid springtime for the Church, and we have seen that a dark and freezing winter arrived."[75] Indeed we have.

Respecting the Vatican-Moscow Agreement, Socci observes what will be thematic here: that "The message of Fatima evidently was felt to be profoundly embarrassing by one who was preparing to agree to what he thought to be a masterpiece of diplomacy and ecumenism: a pact with the Kremlin to have two Russian Orthodox observers at the Council, guaranteeing to that regime, in exchange, that the Council would not formulate any condemnation of Communism or the Soviet system.." And no one has been more acute than Socci in his assessment of this fundamental prudential blunder in favor of the party of the innovators:

> Beyond the judgment (the worst possible) that one must give to this compromise of the "moral liberty" of the Catholic Church and of the Council itself, and moreover in return for a mess of pottage (two orthodox observers well-chosen and controlled by the KGB), one remains horrified in the face of a Council—what is more, a "pastoral" council, and thus one occupied with the historical reality of the Church—that pronounces itself on everything, but does not proffer a single word on the ideology of a regime that since 1917 had realized (and was still realizing in those years) on a planetary scale the most immense and bloody work of eradication, extermination, and persecution of the Church in its bimillenial history. Pius XII was attacked furiously for years because, according to his critics, he did not formulate clear and public condemnations of Nazism during the war (which is, however, untrue). But John XXIII has received only applause for having contracted this "silence" with the Kremlin. How is this explained? [76]

How indeed *is* this explained? There is no explanation beyond that "diabolical disorientation" of which Sister Lucy would speak again and again in her private correspondence after the Council.[77] As for Paul VI, whose astounding public lamentations over the Council's results we have already noted, he read the Third Secret

---

[75] Ibid., p. 197, quoting Allocution at the opening of Vatican Council II, *Gaudet Mater Ecclesia* (October 11, 1962).

[76] Ibid., pp. 197-198.

[77] For example: "There is a diabolical disorientation invading the world and misleading souls…. [T]he devil has succeeded in infiltrating evil under the cover of good, and the blind are beginning to guide others…. And the worst is that he has succeeded in leading into error and deceiving souls having a heavy responsibility through the place which they occupy… They are blind men leading other blind men… [They] let themselves be dominated by the diabolical wave invading the world…." Quoted in excerpts from letters, *The Whole Truth About Fatima*, Vol. III, pp. 758-760.

in 1963, within days of his election as Pope in the midst of the Council, only to reseal the envelope and bury it as his predecessor had done.[78] And history records his refusal even to meet with Lucia, now the last surviving Fatima visionary, during his visit to Fatima in 1967: "Address yourself to your bishop," he insisted before the television camera as she begged to speak with him. Pope Paul, revealed his confidant Jean Guitton, "had a sort of generic aversion for visionaries. He maintained that, since revelation is complete, the Church has no need of these things, to which one must not give an exaggerated importance."[79]

Having buried the Third Secret as his predecessor had done, Pope Paul failed to foresee that triumph of the party of the innovators, both doctrinal and liturgical—the same triumph Pius XII had predicted with the aid of the Message of Fatima, and which Paul unleashed with his approval of the "reforms" whose effects he lived to regret. Writes Socci:

> It was precisely Montini—the Pope according to whom "the Church does not have need" of the extraordinary assistance of the Madonna and can do without Her maternal aid—who shortly thereafter had to recognize dramatically that, within a few years of the Council's conclusion, the Church was in the process of "auto-demolition." Paul VI even shouted out desperately his apocalyptic feeling that "from somewhere or other, the smoke of Satan has entered the temple of God." Then he added bitterly: "It was believed that after the Council there would come a day of sunshine in the history of the Church. Instead there came a day of clouds, tempests, of darkness....
>
> However, it was seen quite clearly who had opened the door to the world and to the "smoke of Satan." In fact, he persisted in error: The most devastating of the errors was the traumatic "coup d'etat" by a "minority revolution" that imposed the liturgical reform (with its thousand abuses), hailed by Paul VI but clearly not blessed by God. The prohibition of the millennial Latin liturgy of the Church was effectuated by a decision that contravened even the documents of the Council.[80]

Socci points to testimony from a most unexpected source: the Modernist theologian Henri de Lubac who, notes Socci, "even took part in the [Modernist] cause" after the Council. De Lubac freely

---

[78] Cf. Christopher A. Ferrara, *The Secret Still Hidden* (Pound Ridge, New York: Good Counsel Publications, 2008), p. 190: "'I will also do as much,' responded Pope Montini. The envelope was resealed and I don't know if it was spoken of further." Quoting transcript of video interview of Capovilla, broadcast on the Telepace network, September 21, 2007.

[79] Interview with Stefano Maria Paci in *30 Giorni* ["30 Days"], March 1990.

[80] Socci, *The Fourth Secret of Fatima*, p. 200.

admitted that:

> The drama of Vatican II consists in the fact that instead of
> having been conducted by saints, as was the Council of Trent, it
> was monopolized by intellectuals. Above all it was monopolized
> by certain theologians, whose theology started off with the
> preconception of updating the faith according to the demands
> of the world and to emancipate it from a presupposed condition
> of inferiority with respect to modern civilization. The place of
> theology ceased to be the Christian community; that is, the
> Church became the interpretation of individuals. In this sense
> the post-conciliar period represented *the victory of Protestantism
> within Catholicism*.[81]

Socci asks, as we ask: "The victory of Protestantism within
Roman Catholicism? Is this not already an apocalyptic event?"
And Socci concludes as we do respecting the results of that search
by the Council and the conciliar Popes for the "signs of the times"
without the aid of Our Lady of Fatima, who provided the greatest
sign of all. Noting the pious exhortations to Marian piety in certain
pronouncements by both Pope John and Pope Paul, Socci writes:

> In fact the true sign of the times, although misunderstood
> and unheeded, was Mary at Fatima. That Roncalli and Montini
> in particular indicated entirely different signs of the times to
> the Church, trying to "bury" the true sign of the Message of
> Mary and to elude its assistance, leads one to think that these
> teachings of the Popes are the judge of their own historical
> deeds. Fatima, therefore, *is a great sign of contradiction that
> makes evident a kind of blinding of the pastors.*[82]

Fatima, as a sign of contradiction, points the way back to a
safe harbor following the "apocalyptic event" of "the victory of
Protestantism within Catholicism" so astonishingly admitted by
one of the most prominent Modernists of the post-conciliar epoch
(evidently in a mode of regret). Hence, whatever the subjective
intentions of particular bishops in attendance, many of whom did
not anticipate its calamitous results (while others indeed planned
them), it is clear that the Second Vatican Council is the event that
divided the true from the false friends of Fatima and all that Fatima
represents for the course of the Church and the fate of humanity.
Thus oriented as to the plot lines of the drama that is Fatima, we are
now in a position to assess the role of some of its major antagonists.

---

[81] "The true Council and who has betrayed it," *Il Sabato*, July 12-18, 1980.
[82] Socci, *The Fourth Secret of Fatima*, p. 204.

Chapter 3

CARDINAL SODANO AND THE PARTY LINE

What has been the overall effect of the sudden, unprecedented and quite dramatic changes in the Church that began after Vatican II? Here—with due allowances for the inadequacies inherent to all analogies—it would be helpful to consider that the process bears an eerie resemblance to what was called at the time "the Adaptation" of the Russian Orthodox Church to the demands of the Stalinist regime.

The "Adaptation" of the Catholic Church

Stalin's subversion of the Orthodox Church is certainly among the developments in Russia foreseen by the Virgin of Fatima. This is precisely why She came to call for the consecration of Russia to Her Immaculate Heart: so that Russia would embrace the one true religion and the one true Church, not the schismatic Orthodox Church founded in a rebellion against Rome when it left the Mystical Body of Christ a millennium ago, thus losing divine protection against Russian Orthodoxy's total Adaptation to Stalinism.

The Orthodox Adaptation began officially when the Metropolitan Sergius of the Russian Orthodox Church published an "Appeal" in *Izvestia* on August 19, 1927. The Appeal of Sergius, as it came to be known, set forth a new basis for the activity of the Russian Orthodox Church. The Russian layman Boris Talantov described this as "an Adaptation to the atheistic reality of the U.S.S.R." In other words, the church had to find a way of living, so the argument goes, with the "atheistic reality" of Stalinist Russia. So Sergius proposed what came to be known in shorthand as the Adaptation.

The Adaptation consisted first and foremost of a false separation between the so-called spiritual needs of man, the purely religious needs of man, and his socio-political needs. In other words, following the Masonic principle of separation of Church and State, the church was to satisfy the purely religious needs of the citizens of the Soviet Union but without touching on the socio-political structure that had been erected by the Communist Party.

The Adaptation required a new administration of the church in Russia according to guidelines which were set forth after the appeal of Sergius was published. Basically this came down to an agreement not to criticize the official ideology of the Soviet Union under Stalin. And this would be reflected in all of the activities of the church. Any church opposition to the Soviet regime would henceforth be considered a deviation from pure religious activity and a form of counter-revolution to be crushed immediately.

In effect the Orthodox Church, through its silence, became an arm of the Soviet state. In fact, Sergius would go on to defend this betrayal and even call for the condemnation and the sentencing to concentration camps of his own fellow Orthodox for so-called counter-revolutionary activities. Talantov, who condemned the whole Adaptation, described it this way: "In actual fact all religious activity was reduced to external rites. The church preaching of those clergymen who held strictly to the Adaptation was totally remote from life and therefore had no influence whatever on hearers. As a result of this, the intellectual, social and family life of believers, and the raising of the younger generation, remained outside church influence. One cannot worship Christ and at the same time in social and family life tell lies, do what is unjust, use violence, and dream of an earthly paradise."[83]

This, then, is what the Adaptation involved: The church would be silent about the evils of the Stalinist regime. It would become a purely "spiritual" community "in the abstract", would no longer voice opposition to the regime, would no longer condemn the errors and lies of Communism, and would thus become the Church of Silence, as Christianity behind the Iron Curtain was often called.

The Appeal of Sergius caused a split in the Russian Orthodox Church. The real believers, who rejected the Adaptation, denounced the Appeal and remained attached to the Metropolitan Joseph rather than Sergius, were arrested and sent to concentration camps. Boris Talantov himself would eventually die in prison, a political prisoner of the Stalinist regime. The Church of Silence was effectively transformed into an organ of the KGB, with all the imprisoned or executed Orthodox clerics replaced by KGB operatives.

Shortly before Talantov died in August of 1967, he wrote as follows concerning the Adaptation:

> The Adaptation to atheism implanted by Metropolitan Sergius has concluded (been completed by) the betrayal of the Orthodox Russian Church on the part of Metropolitan Nikodim and other official representatives of the Moscow Patriarch based abroad. This betrayal irrefutably proved by the documents cited must be made known to all believers in Russia and abroad because such an activity of the Patriarchate, relying on cooperation with the KGB, represents a great danger for all believers. In truth, the atheistic leaders of the Russian people and the princes of the Church have gathered together against the Lord and His Church.[84]

---

[83] "The Moscow Patriarchate and Sergianism" by Boris Talantov, from *Russia's Catacomb Saints*, (St. Herman of Alaska Press, Platina, California, 1982) pp. 463-486.

[84] "The Moscow Patriarchate and Sergianism: An Essay by Boris Talantov," found at www.orthodoxinfo.com/ecumenism/cat_tal.aspx.

Here Talantov refers to the same Metropolitan Nikodim who would later induce the Vatican to enter into the Vatican-Moscow Agreement, under which (as we showed in Chapter 2) the Catholic Church was committed to a pact of silence concerning the evils of Communism, and in particular Soviet Communism. Thus, the same Orthodox prelate who betrayed the Orthodox Church to the Kremlin was instrumental in an agreement by which the Catholic Church was likewise betrayed. At Vatican II, Pope John, the Secretary of State, Cardinal Casaroli, and his emissary Cardinal Tisserant, cooperating with Nikodim, agreed that the Catholic Church, too, would become a Church of Silence.

In consequence, since the Council the Catholic Church has almost everywhere unquestionably fallen silent not only as to the errors of Communism—which the Church has almost completely ceased condemning, even in Red China, which viciously persecutes the Church—but also as to the errors of the world at large. We recall that in his opening address to the Council, Pope John freely admitted that the Council (and most of the Church after him) would no longer condemn errors but would open herself to the world in a "positive" presentation of her teaching to "men of good will." What followed, as Pope Paul VI himself admitted, was not the hoped-for conversion of "men of good will" but what Paul VI himself called "a veritable invasion of the Church by worldly thinking." In other words, to the extent that this is possible in the Catholic Church—which can never completely fail in her mission—there has been a kind of Sergian Adaptation of Roman Catholicism.

The Party Line on Fatima

If, as Antonio Socci says, the Message of Fatima is "a great sign of contradiction that makes evident a kind of blinding of the pastors" during the unprecedented crisis that now afflicts the Catholic Church, then no element of that Message could be more of a sign of contradiction than the Consecration of Russia to the Immaculate Heart of Mary. Here, in that one simple request of the Madonna of Fatima, we have practically every element of the "old" and "triumphalistic" Catholicism that was supposedly superseded after the "opening to the world" and the conciliar *aggiornamento* Pope Paul was forced to admit had been a disaster.

And so, just as the Communist Party dictated a Party Line containing whatever official lies were necessary to advance the Communist cause—including the lie that the Sergian Adaptation of the Russian Orthodox Church was what the Orthodox really wanted—so would the Vatican Secretary of State dictate a Party Line on the "Adaptation" of Fatima. What precisely do we mean by Party Line? A Party Line is the "official" version of the truth—in reality a pack of lies—that everyone who belongs to the Party is expected to believe and to propagate under pain of expulsion, ostracization or worse. The Party Line generally consists of a Big Lie—in this case, as we shall see, the reduction of Fatima to a prophecy already fulfilled and a mere call to prayer and penance. In support of the Big Lie one finds an assortment of supporting lies sufficient to persuade the uninformed public that no further inquiry into the truth of the matter is necessary, that the "official" version must be true. In this case, as we shall see, the supporting lies consist of the propositions that Fatima involves a mere "private revelation" which the faithful can take or leave at their pleasure, that Russia was "consecrated" without mention of Russia, and that the Third Secret pertains only to events of the 20th century, culminating in the failed attempt on the life of John Paul II in 1981. Further, Party members and those who enable them dutifully parrot the Party Line as the "official" substitute for the truth. Here we will see how the Party Line on Fatima, dictated from on high by the Vatican Secretary of State, has produced a lockstep conformity of opinion among all the false friends of Fatima, both low and high, whose statements are to be examined on these pages. This absolute uniformity of opinion is no coincidence; it is imposed from the top.

Now effectively the "prime minister" of the Church thanks to the "reform" of the Roman Curia, and in control all the major levers of Vatican administration, the Secretary of State was uniquely positioned to impose a Party Line that requires an Adaptation of the Fatima event to comport with the overall Adaptation of the Church, including *Ostpolitik*. The Adaptation of Fatima was deemed necessary because the Consecration of Russia and the related prophecies of its miraculous outcome embody exactly what the supposed "new orientation" of the Church since Vatican II cannot abide:

- that the Pope and bishops of the Catholic Church have the power to convert a non-Catholic nation by a single public act;

- that this power—the power of divine grace—has been given to the Catholic Church alone to wield in this miraculous manner;

- that the Russian people are in need of the grace of conversion, which only the hierarchy of the Catholic Church—not the Russian Orthodox hierarchy—can obtain for them by this singular act;

- that the Russian people, including their Orthodox clergy, are called to reunite with Rome as members of the Catholic Church upon their miraculous conversion;

- that this miracle of conversion will be a testament to the intercession of the Virgin Mary, Mediatrix of All Graces, whose Immaculate Conception is a defined dogma of the Catholic Faith and of no other religion;

- that the Triumph of the Immaculate Heart of Mary upon Russia's consecration and conversion will mean a worldwide and uniquely Catholic devotion to the Immaculate Heart;

- that this Triumph, and the resulting period of peace granted to the world, will thus be a triumph for the Catholic Church as well.

All of this, of course, is quite intolerable to the party of the innovators, intent as they are on the program of "dialogue," "ecumenism," and *Ostpolitik* inaugurated at Vatican II. Thus the Secretary of State would usurp authority to "manage" the Fatima event according to his requirements and those of the party of the innovators in general. We will see that, quite curiously, the Secretary has even arrogated to himself the authority to "interpret" the Third Secret of Fatima—an interpretation that binds no one. His office has no pastoral or teaching authority over the universal Church or even so much as a single diocese; yet from him would emanate the Party Line on Fatima. Before we examine its elements, a few words about the career of Vatican Secretary of State Cardinal Angelo Sodano, first enforcer of the Party Line, are appropriate. We need to place in perspective the utter incongruity of this man's involvement in the custody of the precious Message our Mother brought to us from Heaven.

An Ecclesiastical Politician

Former Vatican Secretary of State Cardinal Angelo Sodano provides a prime example of how the office of the Vatican Secretary of State commingles worldly concerns with what should be purely spiritual affairs over which a functionary of the Vatican city-state ought to have no jurisdiction. It was none other than Sodano who was instrumental in protecting for decades the now-infamous Marcial Maciel Degollado, head of the Legionaries of Christ, who molested boys, fathered children out of wedlock, abused drugs, and engaged in financial improprieties throughout his long career as an immensely successful ecclesiastical entrepreneur. As *America* magazine has observed: "The key Vatican figure in protecting Maciel in the 1980s and 1990s was Cardinal Angelo Sodano, the all-powerful secretary of state [sic] under John Paul II and now Dean of the College of Cardinals."[85] All-powerful indeed—so powerful that he took control of the Message of Fatima, although, as we shall see, Providence confounded his attempt to neutralize it. The respected Catholic pro-life website Lifesitenews.com summarized the evidence of Sodano's complicity in the Maciel scandal as presented in an exposé in *National Catholic Reporter*:

> Maciel developed a close relationship with Angelo Sodano, who served as Pope John Paul's Secretary of State, effectively the Vatican's Prime Minister, from 1991 to 2006.... The Legion hired Sodano's nephew as consultant when they built their flagship institution, Regina Apostolorum University in Rome.... [M]uch later, efforts to reveal Maciel's machinations and sexual improprieties were actively blocked by "pressure from Maciel's chief supporter, Cardinal Angelo Sodano." Berry reports that after nine former members of the Legion who claimed to have been sexually abused by Maciel filed a canonical case against the founder with the Congregation for the Doctrine of the Faith in 1998, Sodano "pressured" Cardinal Ratzinger to halt the proceedings.[86]

By late 2004, however, the future Pope Benedict XVI would put an end to the scandal. After a Vatican ceremony in November 2004 during which John Paul II honored Maciel, "Ratzinger broke with Sodano and ordered a canon lawyer on his staff, Msgr. Charles Scicluna, to investigate. Two years later, as Pope Benedict, he approved the order that Maciel abandon ministry for a 'life of penitence and prayer.'"[87] Maciel died shortly thereafter. Despite his deep involvement in the Maciel scandal, Sodano left office without consequences in 2006 to be succeeded by Cardinal Bertone, becoming Dean of the College of Cardinals. The journal *First Things* rightly observed that "Cardinal Sodano has to go. The Dean of the College of Cardinals [is]... an ongoing embarrassment to the Church he serves."[88] Yet to this day, Sodano remains Dean of the College of Cardinals. This, then, is the man who maintained the Party Line on Fatima first dictated by Cardinal Casaroli in July-August 1989, which has been carried forward unswervingly by his successor, Cardinal

---

[85] Austen Ivereigh, "Will Sodano Resign Over Maciel?", *America*, April 13, 2010, http://www.americamagazine.org/blog/entry.cfm?entry_id=2749.

[86] Hilary White, "Sodano's 'Head Should Roll': Report Reveals Close Ties Between Vatican Cardinal and Disgraced Legion," Lifesitenews.com, April 14, 2010, http://www.lifesitenews.com/news/archive/ldn/ 2010/apr/1004140.

[87] Jason Berry, "Money paved way for Maciel's influence in the Vatican," *National Catholic Reporter*, April 26, 2010, http://ncronline.org/news/accountability/money-paved-way-maciels-influence-vatican?page=2.

[88] Joseph Bottum, "The Cost of Maciel," *First Things*, May 12, 2010, http://www.firstthings.com/onthesquare/2010/05/the-cost-of-father-maciel.

Bertone. The result is a mockery of the Fatima event and grave injustice to the Church and the world.

The Elements of the Party Line on Fatima

In its original iteration, the Party Line was this: There is to be no consecration of Russia, for this would offend the Russian Orthodox, causing a setback for ecumenism, while challenging the Moscow regime, causing a setback for *Ostpolitik*. Fatima, then, was to be reduced to a generic call to prayer, penance and personal piety rather than a heavenly plan for the conversion of Russia, the Triumph of the Immaculate Heart, and a period of peace won for the world by Mary's intercession. The Pope was to be dissuaded from any explicit mention of Russia in any ceremony he might attempt in compliance with what Our Lady of Fatima had prescribed. This is the Big Lie concerning Fatima.

In support of the Big Lie is the underlying proposition that, in any event, the Fatima apparitions are merely a "private revelation" that can safely be ignored by the faithful and the leadership of the Church. According to this element of the Party Line, the Message of Fatima is merely "a help which is offered, but which one is not obliged to use."[89] We must dispense immediately with that foolhardly contention.

By its very terms the Message is not "private," but rather is addressed to the whole world, even if the Virgin Mary chose to deliver it to three children. Accordingly, Lucia pleaded with "the Lady in white" "to work a miracle so that everybody will believe that You are appearing to us," for the local anti-Catholic authorities and other critics were mocking the apparitions and suggesting that the children were liars and fakes. In fact, at one point Lucia and her cousins were literally kidnapped and carted off to jail by the Freemasonic mayor of nearby Ourem, seat of the local judicial district. The children were threatened with torture and death if they did not recant what they had seen and heard in the Cova. All three refused to do so, and the mayor released them after two days of captivity.[90] To silence the critics and persecutors of the children, the Lady promised that on the 13th of October, the date of the last apparition at the Cova, "I

---

[89] Cf. *The Message of Fatima*, n. 2, http://www.vatican.va/roman_curia/congregations/cfaith/documents/rc_con_cfaith_doc_20000626_message-fatima_en.html.

[90] This incident is abundantly documented in the historical sources, both secular and religious. *See e.g.*, Frère Michel de la Sainte Trinité, *The Whole Truth About Fatima*, Volume I: *Science and the Facts* (Buffalo, New York: Immaculate Heart Publications, 1989) pp. 214-231; and "The Seers Kidnapped (August 13-15, 1917)", at http://fatima.org/essentials/opposed/seerkidn.asp.

will perform a miracle for all to see and believe."[91] And, as we have seen, on October 13, 1917, a crowd of 70,000 people assembled in the rain-drenched Cova to witness the first pre-announced public miracle in the history of the world, and the first miracle Heaven had ever deigned to grant in answer to a challenge by the Church's enemies: the Miracle of the Sun.

Since those dramatic days in the Cova, the Message Lucia and her two cousins received from the Madonna has been treated as worthy of belief by a series of Popes. Pope John Paul II, who attributed his escape from death on May 13, 1981 to the intervention of Our Lady of Fatima (on the very anniversary of the first Fatima apparition) definitively removed the Fatima apparitions from the category of the so-called "private revelation" by a series of papal acts. The Pope beatified Jacinta and Francisco in May 2000, proclaiming February 20th as their Feast Day, elevated the Feast of Our Lady of Fatima on May 13th to the altars of every Church in the world by ordering its inclusion in the Roman Missal, and declared at Fatima in 1982 that "The appeal of Our Lady of Fatima is so deeply rooted in the Gospel and the whole of Tradition that the Church feels herself bound by this message."[92] Moreover, the Fatima prayers ("O my Jesus, etc.") have been incorporated into the Rosary, while the Five First Saturdays devotion is practiced throughout the entire Church.

In view of these facts and circumstances, Socci has best summed up the approach any Catholic should take to the Message of Fatima: "The Fatima event has received on the part of the Church—which in general is very cautious concerning supernatural phenomena—a recognition that has no equal in Christian history.... It is really impossible—after all this—to continue to speak of a 'private revelation' and of the relative importance of the Message."[93] It is not only impossible but completely irrational and indeed reckless to dismiss the Fatima message, and the Third Secret in particular, as a "private revelation," a mere "help" that one "is not obliged to use." Any reasonable Catholic, and even a non-Catholic inclined to believe in supernatural phenomena, should be prepared to agree that the Message of Fatima is in a category by itself. So much, then, for the "private revelation" canard.

---

[91] In *The Whole Truth About Fatima*, Vol. I, pp. 180-181.

[92] "Il contenuto dell'appello della Signora di Fatima è così profondamente radicato nel Vangelo e in tutta la Tradizione, che la Chiesa si sente impegnata da questo messaggio." *Sermon at the Sanctuary of the Virgin of Fatima*, May 13, 1982, at http://www.vatican.va/holy_father/john_paul_ii/homilies/1982/documents/hf_jp-ii_hom_19820513_fatima_it.html.

[93] Socci, *Fourth Secret*, p. 17.

Now, the existence of the Party Line on Fatima first became apparent to the general public in 1982. On May 13 of that year— the first anniversary of the failed attempt on his life—Pope John Paul II, acting alone, consecrated the world but *not Russia* to the Immaculate Heart in an attempt to comply with the Virgin's request for the Consecration of Russia. Then, on March 25, 1984 the Pope conducted a consecration ceremony in Saint Peter's Square from which any mention of Russia was again omitted. Why the failure to mention Russia? Answer: it had been ruled out by the Party Line.

In the November 2000 issue of *Inside the Vatican*, a leading Cardinal, identified only as "one of the Pope's closest advisors" (it was, in fact, Cardinal Tomko) expressly admitted that today "Rome fears the Russian Orthodox might regard it as an 'offense' if Rome were to make specific mention of Russia in such a prayer, as if Russia especially is in need of help when the whole world, including the post-Christian West, faces profound problems ..." By "Rome" the Cardinal did not mean the universal Church, but rather certain members of the Vatican bureaucracy as coordinated by the Secretary of State as "prime minister" of the Church. The same Cardinal-advisor added: "Let us beware of becoming too literal-minded."

Later, Bishop Paul Josef Cordes would reveal the twin aims of the Party Line on Fatima: avoiding any "offense" to the Russian Orthodox and any "provocation" of the regime in Moscow:

> I recall that [Pope John Paul II] thought, some time before [the Consecration], of mentioning Russia in the prayer of benediction. *But at the suggestion of his collaborators he abandoned the idea*. He could not risk such a direct provocation of the Soviet leader. The Pope also decided not to mention Russia directly *out of sensitivity to the Orthodox bishops* he had invited to join in the consecration prayer. So for good reasons, he followed the discreet approach of Pope Pius XII and of the bishops at the Second Vatican Council, where he [John Paul II] himself was very prominent.[94]

This "discreet approach at the Second Vatican Council" was none other than the Vatican-Moscow Agreement, already discussed, by which the Council had shamefully agreed to remain silent about the evils of Soviet Communism in exchange for the attendance of two Orthodox "observers."

Once the substitute ceremonies of 1982 and 1984 were out of

---

[94] Father Andrew Apostoli, *Fatima for Today: the Urgent Marian Message of Hope* (San Francisco: Ignatius Press, 2010), p. 251. This work, as we shall see, is a prime example of a production by the false friends of Fatima. It actually negates any element of urgency in the Message of Fatima, reducing it to prayer and personal piety in keeping with the Party Line.

the way—all mention of Russia having been "safely" avoided on the advice of men who thought themselves more prudent than the *Virgo Prudentissima*—the word came down from the Vatican that the subject of Russia's consecration was now to be considered closed. Frère Francois de Marie des Anges, an historian of the Fatima event, recounts that in 1988 "[A]n order came from the Vatican addressed to the authorities of Fatima, to Sister Lucy, to diverse ecclesiastics, including Father Messias Coelho, and a French priest [evidently Father Pierre Caillon] very much devoted to Our Lady, ordering everyone to cease pestering the Holy Father with the Consecration of Russia." Fatima devotee Father Caillon confirmed the issuance of this order: "An order came from Rome, obliging everyone to say and think: 'The Consecration is done. The Pope having done all that he can, Heaven has deigned to agree to this gesture.'"[95]

Sister Lucia's contrary testimony

This command to adhere to the Party Line ignored a lifetime of testimony by Sister Lucia about the necessity of an explicit consecration of Russia by name in a public ceremony conducted jointly by the Pope and the Catholic bishops of the world. As Socci notes: "precisely this lack of a specific object (Russia)" is why Sister Lucia "has repeated a thousand times… that there has not been a response to the request of the Virgin."[96] Moreover, before and after the 1982 and 1984 ceremonies Sister Lucia insisted that Our Lady had requested nothing less than the explicit public consecration of Russia by the Pope and the bishops and that, accordingly, a consecration of the world would not comply with the Virgin's request. We note here some keynotes of that testimony:

1946: On July 15, 1946 Sister Lucia gave the following testimony to the eminent author and historian, William Thomas Walsh, as recounted in his seminal history of the Fatima apparitions, *Our Lady of Fatima,* which sold over one million copies:

> Lucia made it plain that Our Lady did not ask for the consecration of *the world* to Her Immaculate Heart. What She demanded specifically was the consecration of *Russia.…* She did not comment, of course, on the fact that Pope Pius XII had consecrated the world, not Russia, to the Immaculate Heart in 1942. But she said more than once, and with deliberate emphasis: "What Our Lady wants is that the Pope and all the bishops in the world shall consecrate Russia to Her Immaculate Heart on one special day. If this is done, She will convert Russia

---

[95] *Fatima: Tragedy and Triumph,* pp. 189-190.

[96] Socci, *The Fourth Secret of Fatima,* pp. 29-30.

and there will be peace. If it is not done, the errors of Russia will spread through every country in the world."[97]

1952: In *Il Pellegrinaggio della Meraviglie*, published under the auspices of the Italian episcopate, we read (as noted earlier) that the Virgin Mary appeared to Sister Lucia in May 1952 and said: "Make it known to the Holy Father that I am always awaiting the Consecration of Russia to My Immaculate Heart. Without the Consecration, Russia will not be able to convert, nor will the world have peace."[98] Thus, *ten years* after Pope Pius XII's 1942 consecration of the world, Heaven itself informed Sister Lucia that Russia will not be converted, nor will there be peace, unless and until that nation is consecrated by name specifically.

1982: Thirty years later Sister Lucia's testimony remains unchanged. On May 12, 1982, the day before the attempted 1982 consecration, the Vatican's own *L'Osservatore Romano* published an interview of Sister Lucia by Father Umberto Maria Pasquale, a Salesian priest, during which she told Father Umberto that Our Lady had never requested the consecration of the world, but *only* the Consecration of Russia:

> At a certain moment I said to her: "Sister, I should like to ask you a question. If you cannot answer me, let it be. But if you can answer it, I would be most grateful to you … Has Our Lady ever spoken to you about the consecration of **the world** to Her Immaculate Heart?"
>
> "No, Father Umberto! *Never!* At the Cova da Iria in 1917 Our Lady had promised: *I shall come to ask for the Consecration of Russia …* In 1929, at Tuy, as She had promised, Our Lady came back to tell me that the moment had come to ask the Holy Father for the Consecration of **that country** (Russia)."[99]

Sister Lucia confirmed this testimony in a handwritten letter to Father Umberto, which the priest also published. (See photographic reproduction of the pertinent section of Sister Lucia's letter on next page.) A translation of the letter reads:

---

[97] William Thomas Walsh, *Our Lady of Fatima* (New York: Image-Doubleday, *Imprimatur* 1947), p. 221 (emphasis in the original).

[98] *Il Pellegrinaggio della Meraviglie*, p. 440, Rome, 1960. This same work, published under the auspices of the Italian episcopate, affirms that this message was communicated to Pope Pius XII in June. Also, Canon Barthas mentioned that apparition in his communication to the Mariological Congress of Lisbon-Fatima in 1967; see *De Primoridiis Cultus Marianae, Acta Congressus Mariologici-Mariana In Lusitania Anno 1967 Celebrati* (Rome, 1970), p. 517; see also *Fatima: Tragedy and Triumph*, pp. 21 and 37.

[99] *L'Osservatore Romano*, May 12, 1982.

Reverend Father Umberto, in replying to your question, I will clarify: Our Lady of Fatima, in Her request, referred *only* to the consecration of Russia ... — *Coimbra 13 IV - 1980 (signed) Sister Lucia*

1983: On March 19, 1983, at the request of the Holy Father, Sister Lucia met with the Papal Nuncio, Archbishop Portalupi, a Dr. Lacerda, and Father Messias Coelho. During this meeting Sister Lucia confirmed that Pope John Paul's consecration of 1982 *did not fulfill the requests of Our Lady*:

In the act of offering of May 13, 1982, *Russia did not appear as being the object of the consecration.* And each bishop did not organize in his own diocese a public and solemn ceremony of reparation and consecration of Russia. Pope John Paul II simply renewed the consecration of the world executed by Pius XII on October 31, 1942. From this consecration we can expect some benefits, but not the conversion of Russia.[100]

On this occasion Sister Lucia flatly concluded: "The Consecration of Russia *has not been done as Our Lady had demanded it.* I was not able to say it because I did not have the permission of the Holy See."[101]

---

[100] *Fatima: Tragedy and Triumph,* p. 165. See also "Sister Lucy's Recent Authorized Statements", *The Fatima Crusader,* Issue #13-14, Oct.-Dec. 1983, p. 3 (http://www.fatimacrusader.com/cr13/cr13pg03.asp); and "Fatima May 13, 1982—What Actually Happened? Was Russia Consecrated to the Immaculate Heart of Mary?", *The Fatima Crusader,* Issue #16, Sept.-Oct. 1984, pp. 22-23 (http://www.fatimacrusader.com/cr16/cr16pg22.asp).

[101] Reported within an article by Father Pierre Caillon of Centre Saint Jean 61500

1984: On Thursday, March 22, 1984, three days before the consecration of the world at issue, the Carmel of Coimbra was celebrating Sister Lucia's seventy-seventh birthday. She received on that day, as was her custom, her old friend Mrs. Eugenia Pestana. After extending good wishes to her Carmelite friend, Mrs. Pestana asked: "Then Lucia, Sunday is the Consecration?" Sister Lucia, who had already received and read the text of the Pope's consecration formula, made a negative sign and declared: "That consecration cannot have a decisive character."[102]

1985: In *Sol de Fatima*, the Spanish publication of the Blue Army, Sister Lucia was asked if the Pope had fulfilled the request of Our Lady when he consecrated the world the previous year. Sister Lucia replied: "There was no participation of all the bishops, *and there was no mention of Russia."* She was then asked, "So the consecration was not done as requested by Our Lady?" to which she replied: *"No.* Many bishops attached no importance to this act."[103]

1987: On July 20, 1987 Sister Lucia was interviewed quickly outside her convent while voting. She told journalist Enrique Romero that the Consecration of Russia has not been done as requested.[104]

One could cite more of Lucia's affirmations that the 1984 consecration of the world (and that of 1982) did not fulfill Heaven's conditions, but the point is made.[105] We will consider in due course Cardinal Bertone's contention that during private, unrecorded "interviews" Sister Lucia abruptly changed her testimony on this matter.[106]

In any event, one would think it beyond debate that a consecration of Russia needs to *mention* Russia. As Dr. David Alan

Sees, (Orne) France. This article was published by the monthly periodical *Fidelite Catholique*, B.P. 217-56402, Auray Cedex, France. English translation from *The Fatima Crusader*, Issue #13-14, Oct.-Dec. 1983, p. 3 (http://www.fatimacrusader. com/cr13/cr13pg03.asp); see also *The Fatima Crusader*, Issue #16, Sept.-Oct. 1984, pp. 22-23 (http://www.fatimacrusader.com/cr16/cr16pg22.asp).

102 *Fatima: Tragedy and Triumph*, pp. 167-168; see also "The Requests of Our Lady of Fatima Are Being Deliberately Hidden," *The Fatima Crusader*, Issue #31-32, March-May 1990, pp. 28-42, 54-55 (http://www.fatimacrusader.com/cr31/cr31-32pg28. asp).

103 *Sol de Fatima*, September 1985.

104 This testimony of Sister Lucia was reported in the early August (1987) edition of *Para Ti* published in Argentina. See "Sister Lucy States: 'Russia Is Not Yet Properly Consecrated'", *World Enslavement or Peace ... It's Up To the Pope*, Father Nicholas Gruner (Fort Erie, Ontario: The Fatima Crusader, 1989), pp. 212-213; also online at http://www.worldenslavementorpeace.com/e6cp10.asp.

105 For more testimony, see Chapter VI of *Fatima: Tragedy and Triumph*.

106 *But see, e.g.*, Christopher Ferrara, "A New Fatima for the New Church," *The Fatima Crusader*, Issue #75 (Winter 2004), pp. 65ff (also at http://www.fatimacrusader. com/cr75/cr75pg08.asp) for a thorough treatment of this subject.

White has put it, attempting to consecrate Russia without mention of Russia is like "publishing a recipe for beef stew that never mentions beef." As should be apparent from the rise of Vladimir Putin as the militaristic, neo-Stalinist dictator of Russia—a development even the *New York Times* has noticed[107]—Russia has not converted, which can only mean that the Consecration remains undone.

And, in fact, Pope John Paul II never made any official declaration that the Consecration had been effected by him. Quite contrary, as many sources have noted, during the 1984 ceremony in Saint Peter's Square, the Pope stated before hundreds of thousands of witnesses that Our Lady was *still awaiting* the explicit Consecration of Russia to the Immaculate Heart, referring pointedly to "those peoples for whom You Yourself *await* our act of consecration and of entrustment." Hours after the ceremony, speaking to a vast crowd in Saint Peter's Basilica, the Pope clearly alluded to the inadequacy of what he had done earlier that day: "We have been able to do all this according to *our poor human possibilities* and the measure of human *weakness*, but with immense confidence in Your maternal love and immense confidence in Your maternal solicitude."[108]

Consequently, if the Fatima message is taken seriously, as it ought to be, the world remains under the Virgin's ultimatum: consecrate Russia or face the annihilation of nations and the eternal loss of countless souls.

---

[107] *See, e.g.,* "With Tight Grip on Ballot, Putin is Forcing Foes out of Parliament," *New York Times,* October 14, 2007 (detailing the moves by which Putin has created an authoritarian one-party regime in Russia like that of "the old days.").

[108] *Avvenire,* March 27, 1984; cf. *The Devil's Final Battle,* Chapter 8.

Chapter 4

THE BLUE ARMY SURRENDERS

Founded in 1946 by Father Harold V. Colgan, a parish priest in Plainfield, New Jersey, the Blue Army had done good work in circulating throughout the world petitions for the Consecration of Russia up until the 1970s. The Blue Army had been instrumental in promoting disclosure of the Third Secret in 1960, the year the Virgin had indicated as crucial to the meaning of the Secret. The organization had even mounted a network television show whose theme was the coming disclosure of the Secret, "Zero, 1960," that was carried by over 100 stations and deemed worthy of a "star" rating in *The New York Times*. And it was Blue Army spokesman John Haffert who expressed the dismay of the Catholic faithful when Pope John XXIII suppressed the Secret instead of revealing it to the world:

> 1960 came and went and the Pope to whom the Secret had been entrusted did not make it public. He did not even make known the fact that he had opened it. The silence from Rome lay heavily on all of us. People began to murmur that Fatima must have been a fake, that there was no secret, that the 1960 secret was a 'hoax' [By 1964] the effect of the long silence concerning the 1960 Secret still seemed to hang over us like a pall.[109]

Yet, despite Sister's Lucia's overwhelming testimony on the necessity of an explicit consecration of Russia, including the testimony which had appeared in the above-noted edition of the Blue Army's own Spanish-language magazine in 1985, by that year the Blue Army had surrendered to the dictates of the Party Line.

The turning point appears to have come in August 1981, during the international assembly of Blue Army delegates at its world headquarters in the *Domis Pacis* Hotel in Fatima. Father Nicholas Gruner was in attendance as one of the two delegates from Canada, and he recounts how the procedural rules were violated in order to facilitate the election of Bishop Constantino Luna as President of the worldwide organization: "The numbers of delegates was arbitrarily halved from 52—two from each country represented—to only 26, and I was thus eliminated as one of the two delegates from Canada. Over my protest, and that of Father Alonso, the official Fatima archivist for sixteen years, Bishop Luna was swept into office. And that was the beginning of the end for the Blue Army."[110]

In the July-August 1982 issue of *Soul* magazine, the Blue Army

---

[109] *The Whole Truth About Fatima*, Vol. III: *The Third Secret*, by Frère Michel de la Sainte Trinité, English ed., Immaculate Heart Publications, 1990, p. 600.

[110] Interview by author, April 3, 2012.

floated a patently fabricated "exclusive interview" with Sister Lucia, by an anonymous interviewer, in which she purportedly agreed that Pope John Paul's consecration of the world in 1982 had effected the consecration of Russia because Russia is part of the world. By that logic, a consecration of the world would "consecrate" every specific thing in existence on the planet, even though the very meaning of the word consecration connotes the singling out of a *particular* object for sacred purposes: "'Consecration' is used in the Catholic Church as the setting apart for the service of God of both *persons and objects*."[111] As the Blue Army would have it, by consecrating the world, John Paul II set apart everything from Brooklyn to bananas for the service of God. But Our Lady of Fatima came to earth to call for the setting aside of one particular nation, Russia, for service to God by means of Russia's conversion. And Sister Lucia had said so repeatedly.

Father Gruner's apostolate exposed the interview as a fake in a series of articles in *The Fatima Crusader* magazine citing, among other things, the decisive testimony of Sister Lucia to the Papal Nuncio that the 1982 ceremony had failed to comply with Our Lady's request, noted in the preceding chapter. The Blue Army was forced to beat a hasty retreat. In the March-April 1986 issue of *Soul*, the Blue Army itself published Lucia's testimony to the Nuncio, but without admitting that that very testimony had exposed its prior "exclusive interview"—never retracted—as a fabrication.[112] Having implicitly conceded the falsehood, however, the Blue Army promptly adopted another: that the 1984 consecration of the world had effected the Consecration of Russia. But Sister Lucia had explicitly denied this as well, as the testimonies cited in the preceding chapter demonstrate.

Ostpolitik versus Fatima

In 1984 the then U.S. President of the Blue Army, Bishop Jerome J. Hastrich, announced a key development in the Vatican-directed campaign to "sanitize" the Message of Fatima by stripping it of its prophetic elements, especially the conversion of Russia, and reducing it to a call for *personal* prayer and sacrifice directed to *individual* spiritual advancement. In the March-April issue of *Soul* magazine Hastrich declared that instead of praying for the

---

[111] "Consecration," http://en.wikipedia.org/wiki/Consecration.

[112] *See The Fatima Crusader*, Issue #20 (June-July 1986): "The Plot to Silence Our Lady, Part I: Disinformation Tactics Against Fatima Exposed"; "The Plot to Silence Our Lady, Part II: The Organization's Smear Campaign Gets Worse." *The Fatima Crusader*, Issue #22 (April-May 1987): "The Vatican-Moscow Agreement has Silenced Our Lady"; "The Blue Army Leadership has followed a deliberate policy of falsifying the Fatima Message." *The Fatima Crusader*, Issue #31-32 (March-May 1990): "The Plot (To Silence Our Lady) Thickens." *The Fatima Crusader*, Issue #35 (Winter 1990-91): "The Fatima Consecration Hoax"; "The Conspiracy Against the Consecration of Russia Continues."

conversion of Russia "We are rather to pray that members of the Blue Army would so pray and fast that they themselves might be thoroughly converted ... to pray for the 'conversion' of Russia may seem like waving a red flag in front of a bull ... and so it might be more prudent to pray for peace in the world ..."[113] With this change in orientation, the Blue Army ceased to be an army, an extension of the Church militant dedicated to the cause of Fatima, and became instead the quietest association for personal piety it now is, under the name "World Apostolate of Fatima." That the change was motivated by the Vatican's *Ostpolitik* was placed beyond doubt by the bishop's observation that "We might pray explicitly for Russia if we wish to do so, but in our *public* message we should ... avoid upsetting the *delicate balance of international affairs which the Holy See is trying so hard to control and direct.*" Here was Exhibit A for the claim that the merely human and patently errant policy of *Ostpolitik* had collided head on with Heaven's plan for peace as enunciated by the Virgin of Fatima. And so it has been from the beginning of that ill-starred human policy, which has thwarted Russia's consecration to this day.

By 1986, under the Vatican-controlled guidance of Bishop Luna, the Blue Army was promoting a worldwide "Apostolate of the Two Hearts"—meaning the Sacred Heart of Jesus and the Immaculate Heart of Mary. This seemed worthy on its face, but it was actually part of the process we are examining here: the abandonment of the Consecration of Russia and the Third Secret as "too controversial" for the Vatican bureaucracy in its pursuit of "ecumenism," "dialogue," and, of course, *Ostpolitik*, and the consequent reduction of the Message of Fatima to personal piety and devotion confined to the domain of the Church. In an article on the subject by Hamish Fraser, the renowned ex-Communist and Catholic convert to the Faith, explained how the seemingly worthy "Two Hearts" initiative was actually designed to insure the failure of the Church to accomplish the mission Our Lady launched at Fatima by severing devotion to the Sacred and Immaculate Hearts from the Consecration of Russia:

> Whereas hitherto the campaign for devotion to the Sacred Hearts of Jesus and Mary was given special urgency by the Sacred Heart's own Message to Sister Lucy that no initiative can possibly expect to be fruitful unless envisaged as a means of glorifying the Heart of His Immaculate Mother, and that *only by Russia's consecration to that Heart and by no other means is it possible to obtain Russia's conversion and world peace*, the new "Apostolate of the Two Hearts" will be an apostolate *in vacuo* [in

---

[113] In Father Paul Leonard Kramer, "The Blue Army Leadership has followed a deliberate policy of falsifying the Fatima Message," *The Fatima Crusader*, Issue #22 (April-May 1987), http://www.fatimacrusader.com/cr22/cr22pg26.asp.

a vacuum] desirable as a thing in itself no doubt, but no longer directly related to the life and death realities which confront our contemporaries.

A more effective recipe for failure could therefore scarcely be devised.[114]

Responding to the argument by John Haffert that this new, pietistic Fatima apostolate was necessary because even certain bishops had expressed opposition to the "confrontational" and most un-ecumenical consecration and conversion of Russia, Fraser wrote:

> The "logic" of this non sequitur would seem to be that the only effective means of confronting the enemy is by *refusing to do so*, by instead seeking to persuade him that we are not really in earnest concerning the Message of Our Lady of Fatima, and by assuring him that he has nothing whatever to fear from this manifestly "non-political" apostolate, which in any case is scarcely likely to be taken seriously by anyone, least of all those whom it had hitherto been unable to rouse even by the unadulterated Message of the Queen of Heaven....
>
> Incredibly, it appears to be John Haffert's hope that whereas so many bishops cannot stomach the Message of Fatima, they may be expected to support this new Apostolate which has been so effectively defused both politically and spiritually.[115]

By 1988-89 not only the Blue Army but other major Fatima apostolates that had maintained that the consecration of Russia was not yet accomplished were reversing themselves. In conformity with the Party Line—which in fact they had never been bound to follow—they now declared that the 1984 ceremony fulfilled the desires of Heaven. Sad to say, even Father Caillon soon afterwards changed his testimony and began to maintain that the 1984 ceremony had fulfilled the Virgin's requests for the consecration of Russia even though mention of Russia had been deliberately avoided precisely so that the Russian Orthodox and the Moscow regime *would not think that Russia had been consecrated.*

It was also at this time that typewritten and computer-generated letters, purportedly from Sister Lucy—who never used a computer— began to circulate. Typical of the manifestly incredible letters was the one dated November 8, 1989, to a Mr. Noelker, which contains the statement by "Sister Lucy" that Pope Paul VI consecrated the world to the Immaculate Heart during his brief visit to Fatima in 1967—a consecration that never happened, as Sister Lucy certainly

---

[114] Hamish Fraser, "The Fourth Secret," *The Fatima Crusader*, Issue #37, p. 15, http://www.fatimacrusader.com/cr37/cr37pg15.asp.

[115] Ibid.

knew because she witnessed the entire visit.[116] The Noelker letter would become the Vatican's sole documentary evidence that even Sister Lucy had reversed herself and now "agreed" that Russia was consecrated in 1984 without mention of Russia.

And so the Blue Army, once a foremost friend of Fatima, became foremost among its *false* friends. The Blue Army even ceased to be an Army, reinventing itself as "The World Apostolate of Fatima," whose neutralization of the Fatima message has recently reached an extreme that could scarcely have been imagined before the Second Vatican Council: the transformation of the Fatima prophecies into an "inter-religious" program for the peaceful co-existence of all religions in a pluralistic world. We discuss this horrendous development in Chapter 14, where we will see that, having laid down its arms and surrendered, the former Blue Army has descended to treason against the cause of Fatima—all the while uttering pious sentiments of Fatima devotion.

---

[116] For a good treatment of the falsehood of the Noelker letter, see Mark Fellows, "This Present Darkness", Part II, *Catholic Family News,* Sept. 2000.

Chapter 5

THE SECRETARY OF STATE
TARGETS FATHER GRUNER

As of 1989 only one major Fatima apostolate stood firm in opposition to the Party Line: the Fatima Center in Canada, headed by Father Nicholas Gruner, whose eyewitness account of the turning point for the Blue Army we have already noted. Ordained in Avellino, Italy in 1976, but given permission by his bishop to reside in Canada, Father Gruner built a Fatima apostolate that was among the world's largest and most influential by the time the Party Line had been handed down from within the Vatican apparatus. The Fatima Center's flagship publication, *The Fatima Crusader* magazine, had been instrumental in debunking the computer-generated notes attributed to Sister Lucy, including the patently bogus Noelker letter, to the consternation of Father Fox and the Blue Army, which had been promoting the Party Line and the "letters from Lucy" as the end of the story of Russia's consecration.

By 1989 Father Gruner's bishop in Italy was receiving what the bishop called "worried signals from the Vatican Secretary of State"[117] concerning Father Gruner's activities in opposition to the Party Line, especially his promotion of the Consecration of Russia, which was perceived to be at odds with Cardinal Casaroli's *Ostpolitik*. By 1994 Fr. Gruner was encountering fierce opposition to his work from within the Vatican bureaucratic apparatus controlled by Secretary of State Sodano. This is the same bureaucracy that has hosted Vatican dinners with Mikhail Gorbachev,[118] supported the godless, pro-abortion International Criminal Court to the dismay of pro-life activists around the world,[119] and explicitly renounced any effort to

---

[117] Letter from the Bishop of Avellino to Father Gruner, dated May 29, 1989.

[118] News of June 27, 2000 press conference. "Gorbachev Helps Introduce Casaroli Memoirs", *Catholic World News*, June 27, 2000. See also photograph published in *Catholic Family News*, January 2001, p. 13 showing Gorbachev at the Vatican delivering a lecture to the Pope and world politicians during the "Jubilee of Politicians".

[119] "Vatican Supports International Criminal Court With Symbolic Donation: Pro-lifers Around the Globe Dismayed," *Life Special Report*, July 5, 2002: "Pro-lifers around the globe were dismayed Monday at the Vatican's welcoming of the establishment of the International Criminal Court (ICC). Archbishop Renato Martino, the Vatican's representative at the United Nations issued a statement in support of the ICC and noted that the Vatican had contributed a symbolic donation of $3,000 [30 pieces of silver, adjusted for inflation—c.a.f.] to the ICC trust fund set up by UN Secretary General Kofi Annan."

make converts among the Russian Orthodox.[120]

Recognizing that Father Gruner had every right under Church law to advocate his views on the Fatima message, the Sodano apparatus devised what it thought was a foolproof plan to silence this inconvenient priest by indirection. In 1994 Father Gruner's recently appointed Italian bishop in Avellino was pressured to order him to leave Canada and "return" to Avellino, Italy, where he had been ordained back in 1976, unless he found a new bishop to incardinate him.[121] Sodano's apparatus then took steps to prevent any other bishop in the world from incardinating Father Gruner, even employing papal nuncios—ambassadorial representatives of the Vatican city-state attached to the Secretariat of State—for the task of dissuading bishops from incardinating Father Gruner. At the end of this devious process, the plan was to announce (through the Bishop of Avellino) that since Father Gruner had "failed" to be incardinated by another bishop, he must return to Avellino within 30 days (abandoning his entire life's work) or he would be "suspended" for "disobedience."[122] But Sodano did not foresee at least two developments.

First, despite all efforts to block it, the Archbishop of Hyderabad agreed to incardinate Father Gruner. The Archbishop issued a formal decree of incardination declaring that "evil forces have conspired to destroy your [Father Gruner's] work of love" and that "bureaucratic forces cannot stifle God's work."[123] In subsequent canonical proceedings, the Sodano apparatus (speaking this time through the Congregation for the Clergy) arbitrarily asserted that the incardination in Hyderabad was *tamquam non extans*—"as if non-existent"—and that Father Gruner must still return to Avellino or be "suspended" for "disobedience" since he had "failed" to be incardinated elsewhere. The Archbishop of Hyderabad, rejecting this arbitrary claim, strongly reaffirmed his decree of incardination with a new decree, after examining all the pertinent documents and finding no defect in the incardination.[124]

---

[120] See, Vatican-negotiated *Balamand Statement* (1993), which declares that because of "radically altered perspectives and thus attitudes" engendered by Vatican II, the Catholic Church will train new priests "to pave the way for future relations between the two Churches, passing beyond *the outdated ecclesiology of return to the Catholic Church*." See also, Francis Alban and Christopher A. Ferrara, *Fatima Priest*, Chapter 13, "The Balamand Connection", Fourth Edition (Pound Ridge, New York: Good Counsel Publications, 2000), pp. 188-194.

[121] "Incardination" means the formal attachment of a secular (diocesan) priest to a particular diocese. It derives from the Latin word for "hinge."

[122] Letter from the Bishop of Avellino, May 16, 1996, Protocol #102/96.

[123] Archbishop of Hyderabad, November 4, 1995.

[124] Second decree of the Archbishop of Hyderabad, March 10, 1999: "Having reviewed the documents … I am satisfied that my decree of 4 November 1995 incardinating Father Nicholas Gruner into the Archdiocese of Hyderabad is valid and effective

Second, since Father Gruner had been living in Canada with the permission of the Bishop of Avellino since 1978, under Italian law it was legally impossible for him to return to Italy even if the order to return were just and valid. The bishop had never taken any steps to obtain proper permissions for a foreign priest to enter an Italian diocese, including an entry visa supported by written commitments that the bishop provide financial support, medical coverage and pension—for a priest who had been absent, with his permission, for more than 16 years and had not received one penny of support from Avellino in all that time. The Bishop of Avellino ignored two written requests from Fr. Gruner for an explanation of how he could be expected to "return" to Avellino without any visa or guarantees of financial support as required by Italian immigration law.[125]

Neither the Bishop of Avellino nor the Apostolic Signatura (the Church's highest canonical tribunal to which Father Gruner appealed) ever responded to Fr. Gruner's notification that the Archbishop of Hyderabad considered Fr. Gruner to be incardinated in that archdiocese.[126] The Bishop of Avellino himself had expressed no real interest in Father Gruner's "return" to Avellino, which would involve legal work and substantial expense for the lifetime support and maintenance of a foreign-born priest whose services the bishop had never needed. The bishop was but a pawn in a canonical chess game contrived by the Sodano apparatus. But the game had become moot after Father Gruner's incardination in Hyderabad.

Nevertheless, one must take note of the sheer injustice of what Sodano had attempted in defense of his Party Line. In essence, Father Gruner had been punished for nothing. He had been declared "suspended" by the Bishop of Avellino—*not* by any Vatican official— for "failing" to be incardinated elsewhere, when in fact he had been incardinated elsewhere. Even more insulting to one's sense of justice is that those who declared Fr. Gruner's "failure" to be incardinated

---

... After due discernment, I am convinced that I am acting correctly though I was partly misled by influential people. I strongly feel that the good work he is doing in spreading devotion to the Immaculate Heart of Mary should not be hampered ... through undue canonical or juridical pressures. May Jesus Christ be praised!"

[125] Father Gruner's letters of October 7, 1999 and September 17, 2000 to the Bishop of Avellino. The bishop has never answered these requests and to this day has failed to take the necessary legal steps—which *only the bishop* can take—for Father Gruner's "return" to Avellino under Italian immigration law. That the bishop has done nothing in this regard, even though Fr. Gruner has twice pointed out the bishop's duty to act, demonstrates that the bishop hasn't the least interest in Fr. Gruner's "return," but rather is only playing along with the canonical game contrived by Fr. Gruner's adversaries in the Vatican apparatus.

[126] Father Gruner's letter of August 16, 1999 to the Bishop of Avellino states: "I send to you with this letter a copy of the decree regarding my incardination dated 10 March 1999 in virtue of which I must consider myself, with all the effects, incardinated in the Archdiocese of Hyderabad ..."

were the very ones who had attempted to block his incardination anywhere in the world besides Avellino, and had then arbitrarily asserted that even the valid incardination in Hyderabad—which Fr. Gruner had obtained despite their interference—was "non-existent."

Having failed in his bid to canonically imprison Father Gruner in Avellino, Italy for the rest of his life, Cardinal Sodano abandoned the effort. But the Party Line endured to be imposed from above and promoted below.

Bishop da Silva was entrusted with the Third Secret of Fatima which contained the words of Our Lady. Her words followed the "etc" in the phrase "In Portugal the dogma of the faith will always be preserved etc." Sister Lucy put in the "etc" to hold the place for the rest of Our Lady's words. The words of Our Lady were written down by Sister Lucy under obedience to Bishop da Silva, placed in an envelope and delivered to the bishop on June 17, 1944. Bishop da Silva took Sister Lucy's envelope containing Our Lady's words in the Third Secret and placed that envelope into a larger envelope, on which he wrote:

Este envelope com o seu conteudo sera entregue a Sua Eminencia O Sr. Cardeal D. Manuel, Patriarca de Lisboa, depois da minha morte.
Leiria, 8 Dezembro de 1945
† Jose, Bispo de Leiria.

This envelope with its contents shall be entrusted to His Eminence, his Lordship Cardinal Don Manuel [Cerejeira], Patriarch of Lisbon, after my death.
Leiria, December 8, 1945
† Jose, Bishop of Leiria.

This photograph appeared in the January 3, 1949 edition of *Life* magazine. (See page 79.)

Chapter 6

CARLOS EVARISTO:
EARLY HERALD OF THE "NEW FATIMA"

In the very midst of Cardinal Sodano's failed campaign from on high to consign Father Gruner to oblivion in Avellino, a rather mysterious layman suddenly emerged to promote the Party Line from below. At a time when Sister Lucy had been "gagged" for more than 30 years by orders from the Vatican and precluded from having any visitors (outside her family and people she had known before 1960) without prior Vatican approval, one Carlos Evaristo of Portugal, a self-styled "journalist, historian and interpreter," came forward in 1993 to make the astonishing claim that he had conducted two "interviews" with Lucy in the convent at Coimbra on October 11, 1992 and October 11, 1993.

Evaristo published the interviews in the form of two pamphlets, entitled *Two Hours with Sister Lucy* and *It All Started with Two Hours with Sister Lucy*. The pamphlets ignited tremendous controversy because in them Sister Lucy is reported as having flatly contradicted a whole series of statements she had made over the previous 75 years regarding the Message of Fatima and its implications for the Church and the world. Before discussing the purported interviews in detail, it would be best to summarize the circumstances which surrounded their production and publication.

Two Hours with "Sister Lucy"

According to Evaristo, on October 11, 1992 he spent two hours interviewing the seer, during which she had contradicted all of her public and private statements over the past *75 years* concerning the Consecration of Russia to the Immaculate Heart of Mary, the conversion of Russia, and the Third Secret of Fatima.

Evaristo's pamphlet hewed perfectly to the Sodano Party Line: In it, we read that the "new" Sister Lucy, contrary to everything she had said in some 75 years worth of prior correspondence, conversations and published remarks, was now saying that Russia had been consecrated to the Immaculate Heart of Mary in 1984, that Russia was "converting," that "conversion" does not mean embracing the Catholic Faith, and that the Third Secret of Fatima was not meant to be revealed to the faithful in 1960.

The credibility of *Two Hours with Sister Lucy* (*Two Hours*) was immediately cast into doubt by a manifestly absurd "detail" with which Evaristo embellished his account: "Carlos Evaristo, who was sitting closest to Sister Lucy and directly in front, *held Sister Lucy's hands for most of the two hour interview.*"[127] Sister Lucy was a cloistered nun who is not even permitted to see her blood relatives alone. The claim that she held hands for two hours with a strange man she had never met before was laughable on its face and impossible to believe.

Equally impossible to believe was the "interview" as a whole. In fact, it was so unbelievable that the only other Portuguese-speaking witness to Evaristo's alleged encounter with "Sister Lucy," Father Francisco Pacheco (a lawyer as well as a priest), publicly disavowed the pamphlet in its entirety:

> I was the official translator of this meeting, which lasted two hours. I categorically affirm that the booklet entitled *Two Hours with Sister Lucy* published by Carlos Evaristo **contains lies and half-truths and is not to be believed**. When I was first shown a copy in January 1993, I immediately contacted Carlos Evaristo and I personally told him **not to publish this booklet because of the gross lies that he had put in it** ... I trust that this will end the confusion caused by Carlos Evaristo and his **notorious pamphlet**.[128]

Besides Father Pacheco, two other witnesses were present during the alleged 1992 "interview," but neither of them spoke Portuguese. Anthony Cardinal Padiyara and Bishop Francis Michaelappa, both from India, were in Fatima to attend a Marian conference at the invitation of Father Nicholas Gruner's Fatima apostolate, and they went along with Evaristo and Father Pacheco to the convent at Coimbra. Afterwards, Cardinal Padiyara would attest only that he had been present during the "interview," which was conducted entirely in a language he did not understand. As for Bishop Michaelappa, he not only refused to vouch for the authenticity of the "interview," but joined Father Pacheco in demanding that Evaristo not publish it.

Why did Father Pacheco publicly repudiate *Two Hours*, and why did both he and Bishop Michaelappa demand Evaristo refrain from publishing? The answer was supplied by Evaristo himself. In a fax transmission to Coralie Graham, editor of *The Fatima Crusader*, Evaristo admitted that the statements he had attributed to "Sister Lucy" contain: "... contradictory and unlogical (*sic*) things which at times seem almost *craziness*."[129]

In the same fax Evaristo further admitted: "The dialogue was not recorded at the time. *No notes were taken*."[130] As if to demolish

---

[127] Carlos Evaristo, *Two Hours with Sister Lucy*, First Ed., Jan. 1, 1993, p. 8.

[128] Letter of Father Francisco Pacheco, O.C.C. Postal, 60.033-790-Fort-CE-Brazil, published in *The Fatima Crusader* magazine, Issue No. 46, January 1994, p. 15.

[129] Fax from Evaristo to Coralie Graham, 23 November 1992, p. 2, paragraph (i).

[130] Ibid., par. (g).

any remaining vestige of credibility in the "interview", Evaristo even concedes that because his memory is unreliable, the "transcript" of the "interview" did not reflect his own memory but was "reconstructed"(!) from the memory of others: "Although I may have a *bad memory* this *reconstruction* of what was said was not largely made by me. *I only typed it*."[131]

This was a devastating admission, because if the "transcript" was not based on Evaristo's own memory of what "Sister Lucy" allegedly said, and if Father Pacheco, the only other Portuguese-speaking witness, repudiated the "transcript" because it "contains lies and half-truths and is not to be believed," then the only possible sources for the "transcript" are Cardinal Padiyara and Bishop Michaelappa, *neither of whom speaks a word of Portuguese.*

Yet, nowhere in *Two Hours* was the public ever told that the "transcript" of the "interview" with Sister Lucy is not really a transcript at all, but a "reconstruction" from the memories of people who could not even speak the interviewee's language!

Evaristo Tries Again

Following massive public criticism of the ridiculous statements attributed to "Sister Lucy" in *Two Hours,* Evaristo reemerged with a second pamphlet, entitled *It All Started with Two Hours with Sister Lucy.* The sequel simply republished the original fabricated "transcript," but this time attempted to buttress it with another purported "interview" that allegedly took place on October 11, 1993—a year to the day after the first interview. In this second interview the remarks attributed to Lucy were briefer and vaguer than those in the first "interview," and she did not repeat her remarks about the Third Secret of Fatima not being meant for the faithful. In contrast with the original pamphlet, justly ignored by the press, the 1993 version received considerable publicity in 1998, including coverage on a Spanish television show and articles in the periodicals *Christus* (of Portugal) and *Gente* (of Italy). That the sequel acquired such publicity made a refutation of its glaring incredibility a matter of considerable urgency.

Evaristo claimed that the second interview was audio and video-taped in the presence of himself and eight other witnesses who allegedly attended, including a Cardinal. The alleged audio and video tapes have never, however, been made available to the public. He further claimed that this second interview was conducted on *one hour's notice* to the Mother Prioress of the Convent, after the Cardinal (His Eminence Ricardo Cardinal Vidal of Cebu, Philippines)

---

[131] Ibid., par. (i).

spontaneously decided that a group of nine people, including Evaristo, should jump into cars and pay Sister Lucy a visit late at night with a video camera and a tape recorder! We are told that this hastily assembled crowd and its equipment was admitted into a cloistered convent at *10:30 p.m.* to interview an 86-year-old nun who would normally be asleep at that hour and could have no visitors in any event without prior Vatican approval.

As with the first interview, the reader is asked to believe that "Sister Lucy" now contradicted everything she had said publicly and privately about the Message of Fatima for more than 75 years before she spoke to Mr. Evaristo and his witnesses. Oddly enough, although a Cardinal and *seven* other witnesses were supposedly in attendance at the 1993 spontaneous late-night interview of "Sister Lucy," Evaristo's pamphlet does not contain any attestations by these alleged witnesses that the "transcript" of the 1993 interview accurately reflected what "Sister Lucy" supposedly said on that occasion.

We cannot here draw any final conclusions about which theory best explained the incredible "retractions" contained in these two "interviews" of "Sister Lucy." It is not necessary for our purposes to determine whether "Lucy's" repudiation of her own statements was attributable to treachery on the part of Evaristo or whether the woman in nun's garb he allegedly interviewed at the convent in Coimbra was an imposter (as some have implausibly theorized), or whether it was indeed Sister Lucy who said the things attributed to her, but only as the result of duress, obedience to the suggestions of her superiors, or the effects of declining mental acuity combined with the suasion of others. No matter which scenario is chosen, the conclusion is the same: Sister Lucy was betrayed by those who were promoting her "retractions." We do not here establish as fact a particular scenario for this betrayal, but demonstrate only that a betrayal must have occurred because the statements attributed to "Lucy" in both "interviews" are plainly unworthy of belief, for these reasons:

First of all, they contradict the Message of Fatima itself, which, as Cardinal Ratzinger has noted, "three Popes have already recognized in the most solemn manner possible and have wholeheartedly taken part in this devotion";[132]

Second, they contradict Sister Lucy's own repeated prior statements about the Message and its meaning over a period of seventy-five years before the Evaristo "interviews";

Third, they contradict the evidence of our own senses regarding

---

[132] *The Catholic Counter-Reformation in the XXth Century*, October 1996, #289, p. 6.

the drastic moral and spiritual deterioration of the world since the papal consecration of the world (but not Russia specifically) in 1984, and the supposed "fall of Communism" thereafter.

Now let us examine more closely the evidence that destroys the credibility of both pamphlets, above all the purported statements of "Sister Lucy."

Indices of Deception

The most obvious problem with *Two Hours* is that it deceptively presented as a *verbatim* transcript what was nothing more than a "reconstruction" of what Sister Lucy allegedly said, a "reconstruction" not based on Evaristo's own memory, but on the memory of "witnesses" who do not even speak Portuguese. *Two Hours never mentioned this crucial fact,* but rather led the reader to believe that "Sister Lucy" was being quoted word-for-word.

Only in the sequel pamphlet, *It All Started with Two Hours with Sister Lucy* (*It All Started*), did Evaristo finally admit that what he had originally presented to the public as a verbatim transcript was a fictitious reconstruction: "This [the first interview] *is not a literal translation.* It is a *conceptual* translation. The language used in this document is *based* on the actual Portuguese dialogue ..."[133]

What did Evaristo mean by a "conceptual" translation? What did he mean when he said that the translation was "based" on the "actual Portuguese dialogue"? And why did he fail to inform the public in the first place that his much-vaunted "interview" of "Sister Lucy," which had caused so much controversy and even outrage around the world, contained only *concepts* and not her actual words? That a "conceptual" reconstruction of a conversation was presented to the public as a *verbatim* transcript should be enough to discredit *Two Hours* entirely, along with any further products by its author. The republication of the admittedly fabricated "interview" in *It All Started* did nothing to improve its credibility.

Putting aside, for the moment, Evaristo's fatal admission that the original "interview" was a fabrication, the reader is now invited simply to consider, in themselves, the words which Evaristo ascribed to his 1992 version of "Sister Lucy," who dutifully parroted the Sodano Party Line.

"Lucy" on the Consecration of Russia

> **"Sister Lucy":** Yes, yes, yes ... The consecration of Russia was already partially done. Pope Pius XII made it in 1942 on October 31, but it lacked union with all of the bishops of the world, which Pope John Paul finally managed to unite in 1984.

---

[133] *It All Started with Two Hours with Sister Lucy*, p. 4.

Evaristo: So this consecration [1984] was then accepted by Our Lady?

"Sister Lucy": Yes![134]

How are we to reconcile what Evaristo now *admits* was a fabricated "transcript" with all of Sister Lucy's prior statements to the effect that neither the 1982 consecration nor the 1984 consecration fulfilled Our Lady's request? See Chapter 3. Recall, for example, Sister Lucy's September 1985 interview in *Sol de Fatima*, the Blue Army's official publication in Spain:

> **Question:** John Paul II had invited all the bishops to join in the consecration of Russia, which he was going to make at Fatima on May 13, 1982, and which he was to renew at the end of the Holy Year in Rome on March 25, 1984, before the original statue of Our Lady of Fatima. Has he not therefore done what was requested at Tuy?

> **Sister Lucy:** There was *no participation of all the bishops* and there was *no mention of Russia*.

> **Question:** So the consecration was *not done* as requested by Our Lady?

> **Sister Lucy:** *No.* Many bishops attached no importance to this act.

Sister Lucy's statements in the *Sol de Fatima* interview are completely consistent with all of her other prior statements about the requirements for a valid Consecration of Russia to the Immaculate Heart of Mary: (a) that it be done solemnly and publicly by the Pope, (b) in union with all the world's bishops, and (c) with *specific mention* of Russia. And that is precisely what Sister Lucy told the Papal Nuncio to Portugal, Most Rev. Sante Portalupi, when he met with her on March 21, 1982, to discuss how the Consecration which the Pope had planned for May 13 of that year should be carried out: "Sister Lucy explained that the Pope must choose a date upon which His Holiness commands the bishops of the entire world to make, each in his own Cathedral and at the same time as the Pope, a solemn and public ceremony of Reparation and Consecration of *Russia* ..."[135]

Even Evaristo admits in *It All Started* that the 1982 consecration was insufficient because "there was no participation by the bishops, making it *invalid*."[136] Indeed, how could the Pope consecrate Russia

---

[134] Ibid., pp. 8-9.

[135] Father Pierre Caillon in *Fidelite Catholique*, April 1983, B.P. 217-56402, Auray Cedex, France.

[136] *It All Started with Two Hours with Sister Lucy*, p. 59.

without even *mentioning* Russia? The notion offends logic and common sense. Yet the "Sister Lucy" who allegedly spoke to Carlos Evaristo in October 1992, following the Party Line, offered this curious explanation, which contradicted everything she had said before:

> **Evaristo:** But does not Russia have to be specifically mentioned, and did not Our Lady say this?

> **"Sister Lucy":** The Pope's intention was Russia when he said "those peoples ..." in the text of the 1984 consecration ... God knew that the Pope's intention was Russia and he meant "Russia" in the consecration. What is important is his intention, *like when a priest has the intention to consecrate a Host.*

But as "Sister Lucy" should be expected to know, the mere unspoken intention to consecrate a Host does not suffice to bring about the transubstantiation of mere bread into the Body (and Blood) of Christ. That is precisely the point: The priest must *say aloud certain specific words*—"This is My Body"—in order to carry out Our Lord's command at the Last Supper. *Absolutely no other words will do in their place.*

In the original pamphlet, *Two Hours*, Evaristo avoided mentioning a critical fact that demolishes the claim that "those peoples" are just as good as the crucial word "Russia": After Pope John Paul had said the words "those peoples" while reciting the 1984 consecration in St. Peter's Square, he spontaneously added the following words to the prepared text: " ... whose consecration and entrustment by us You are *awaiting*." While the added phrase does not appear in the prepared text printed before the 1984 consecration of the world, it does appear in the report of what the Pope actually said in *L'Osservatore Romano*.[137] As the Pope's spontaneous addition to the text establishes, "those peoples"—the peoples of Russia— *were still awaiting* Consecration to the Immaculate Heart on March 25, 1984. Russia was *not* consecrated in St. Peter's Square on that date because, for whatever reason, the Pope had determined that a

---

[137] Cf. *L'Osservatore Romano*, April 2, 1984 (English edition) where it is reported on pages 9-10 (or the March 26-27, 1984 Italian edition, on pages 1 and 6) that the Pope consecrated *the world*. There was absolutely no mention of Russia anywhere in the 1984 Act of Consecration. In fact, we find the following passage in Section 1 of the Act of Consecration, as published in *L'Osservatore Romano*: "Embrace, with the love of the Mother and Handmaid of the Lord, this human world of ours, which we entrust and consecrate to You, for we are full of concern for the earthly and eternal destiny of individuals and peoples. In a special way we entrust and consecrate to You those individuals and nations which particularly need to be entrusted and consecrated." It is *after* this passage that we find, in Section 2 of the Act of Consecration, the following spontaneously inserted words: "Enlighten especially the peoples whose consecration and entrustment by us *You are awaiting*." [emphasis added]

Consecration of Russia *by name* was not expedient.

This is confirmed beyond doubt by a report in *Avvenire*, the Italian Catholic Bishops' newspaper, which notes that several hours *after* His Holiness had recited the act of consecration, he again addressed Our Lady of Fatima, this time inside St. Peter's Basilica, stating in the presence of 10,000 witnesses: "We wished to choose this Sunday for the act of entrusting and consecration of the world ... of all peoples, especially those who have a very great need of this consecration and entrustment, of those peoples of whom You Yourself are **awaiting** our act of consecration."[138]

So, hours *after* His Holiness had recited the 1984 act of consecration in St. Peter's Square, he clearly understood that Russia ("those peoples") was *still awaiting* consecration to Mary's Immaculate Heart, and that he had yet to perform the act. And, as we have shown in the quote above, in September 1985 Sister Lucy publicly stated in *Sol de Fatima* magazine that the 1984 consecration ceremony *did not fulfill Our Lady's request*.

In any case, it should be obvious that when God commands the public consecration of a particular thing, it means that this particular thing must be *mentioned* to the public. A public consecration of Russia which does not even *mention* Russia is, therefore, no public consecration at all, but a mere private and unspoken wish. One might as well claim that the Pope could publicly consecrate Russia to the Immaculate Heart of Mary by merely thinking to himself—"I consecrate Russia."—while strolling in the Vatican gardens! The very notion is ridiculous. Yet it was precisely this ridiculous notion that was adopted by the "new" Sister Lucy of Evaristo's pamphlets:

> **Evaristo:** But doesn't Our Lady want Russia to be specifically mentioned?

> **"Sister Lucy":** *Our Lady never requested that Russia be specifically mentioned by name (!).* At the time I didn't even know what Russia was. We [all three Fatima seers] thought she was a very wicked woman. (!)

Are we now to believe, after all these years, that when Our Lady came to Fatima to request the Consecration of Russia to Her Immaculate Heart, She did not care whether Russia was even *mentioned*? Does it seem likely that the Queen of Heaven would neglect to make it clear to the seers of Fatima that Russia is a *nation*, not some "wicked woman"? We know that this cannot be true simply on the basis of Sister Lucy's statement to Father Fuentes, the Vice Postulator of the cause of Jacinta and Francisco, on December 26, 1957:

---

[138] *L'Avvenire*, March 26, 1984.

Father, the Most Holy Virgin is very sad because no one has paid any attention to Her Message, *neither the good nor the bad*. The good continue on their way, but without giving any importance to Her Message. Tell them, Father, that many times the Most Holy Virgin told my cousins Francisco and Jacinta, as well as myself, that many nations will disappear from the face of the earth. She said that **Russia** *will be the instrument of chastisement chosen by Heaven to punish the whole world if we do not beforehand obtain the conversion of that poor* **nation**...[139]

This statement alone establishes beyond all dispute that the seers of Fatima understood that the very essence of the Message of Fatima requires the conversion of the *nation* of Russia as a sign of God's grace at work in our time.

What is more, in the course of *four* detailed memoirs about the apparitions at Fatima, Sister Lucy had never indicated the slightest confusion about the meaning of the word "Russia." Nor can we find *anything* Sister Lucy wrote or said to anyone in the world before Evaristo's 1992 "interview" which would suggest that the Fatima seers did not understand, from the very beginning, that Russia is a nation singled out by God for a special act of consecration that would bring about the conversion of that nation and peace in the world.

But the new "Sister Lucy" produced by Evaristo was now claiming that the Fatima seers were all ignorant of the most basic meaning of what Our Lady told them, and that Heaven itself did nothing to disabuse them of their ignorance! This, of course, was completely impossible. Therefore, something was amiss at the convent in Coimbra. In any case, it was absurd that an act as important as the Consecration of Russia to the Immaculate Heart of Mary—an act specifically commanded by Our Lord Himself through His Blessed Mother—should now, for the sake of the Party Line Evaristo was promoting, become the subject of a worldwide guessing game in which the faithful are left to argue about the meaning of the vague phrase "those peoples." Is *this* how the Church of God carries out God's command? With an equivocation? We are certainly permitted to demand why, in Heaven's name, Russia was *not* mentioned specifically in 1984 so as to end all doubt about the matter. What possible impediment could there have been to the simple utterance of one word—"Russia"? Of course, we know the answer to that question: the impediment was Cardinal Sodano's Party Line on Fatima, now being promoted by a layman who enjoyed a rather mysterious easy access to the seer.

No wonder Evaristo himself admitted that there are

---

[139] *The Whole Truth About Fatima*, Vol. III: *The Third Secret*, English Ed., by Frère Michel de la Sainte Trinité, 1990, Immaculate Heart Publications, U.S.A., pp. 504-505.

"contradictory and unlogical things which seem almost craziness" in these "two hours with Sister Lucy"—two hours which he himself conceded (however belatedly) were "reconstructed" from the "memory" of witnesses who did not even speak Lucy's language!

"Lucy" on the Conversion of Russia

Now, if Catholics believe anything, they believe that their Church is the sole ark of salvation and that (inculpable invincible ignorance aside) *conversion* to the one true religion is objectively necessary for the salvation of souls. As Our Lord Himself warned us just before He ascended into Heaven: "He that believeth and is baptized shall be saved: but he that believeth not shall be condemned." [Mark 16:16]. When Our Lady came to Fatima She brought with Her a divine warning and a divine promise, with the promise being contingent upon *conversion* to the one true religion:

> You have seen hell, where the souls of poor sinners go. To *save them,* God wishes to establish in the world *devotion to My Immaculate Heart* ... If what I say to you is done, many *souls will be saved*, and there will be peace ... In the end, My Immaculate Heart will triumph. The Holy Father will consecrate *Russia* to Me, which *will be converted*.

In the context of the Message of Fatima, conversion can obviously mean only one thing: embrace of the Catholic Faith. The Catholic Church has defined three times *ex cathedra* that outside the Church there is no salvation:

Ex cathedra: There is but one universal Church of the faithful, outside of which no one at all is saved. (Pope Innocent III, the Fourth Lateran Council, 1215)

Ex cathedra: We declare, say, define, and pronounce that it is absolutely necessary for the salvation of every human creature to be subject to the Roman Pontiff. (Pope Boniface VIII, the Bull *Unam Sanctam*, 1302)

Ex cathedra: The most Holy Roman Catholic Church firmly believes, professes, and preaches that none of those existing outside the Catholic Church, not only pagans, but also Jews and heretics and schismatics, can have a share in life eternal; but that they will go into the eternal fire which was prepared for the devil and his angels, unless before death they are joined with her; and that so important is the unity of this ecclesiastical body that only those remaining within this unity can receive an eternal recompense for their fasts, their almsgivings, their other works of Christian piety and the duties of a Christian soldier. *No one,* let his almsgiving be as great as it may, **no one**, even if he pour out his blood for the name of Christ, can be saved, unless he remain within the bosom and the unity of the Catholic Church. (Pope Eugene IV, the Bull *Cantate Domino*, 1441)

In view of these pronouncements, anyone who says there is salvation outside the Catholic Church is denying a dogma of the Faith. In one way or another, all of the souls in Heaven enter as members of the Catholic Church.[140] Therefore, when Our Lady said that Russia will be converted, She can only have meant a conversion to the Catholic Faith. Nothing less than that could constitute a true conversion, because the Catholic religion is the religion established by God Himself in the Person of Christ.

Now, it is manifest that God did not establish the Russian Orthodox Church, whose doctrines differ very significantly from the doctrine of the Catholic religion He established. For example, the Russian Orthodox Church rejects: the Papal primacy; the teaching of the Catholic Church on divorce and remarriage; the Catholic teaching that the Holy Spirit proceeds from the Father and the Son together, not simply from the Father; Catholic doctrine on Purgatory; and the Catholic dogma of the Immaculate Conception of Mary.

On this last point of doctrine, God has ordained that souls are to be *saved* by devotion to the Immaculate Heart of Mary, whose Immaculate Conception was infallibly defined by Blessed Pius IX in 1854. Obviously one must believe in the Immaculate Conception as an object of faith in order to have a devotion precisely to Mary's Immaculate Heart—that is, one must be Catholic, since the doctrine of the Immaculate Conception of Mary is unique to the Catholic Church, which is the one and only Church founded by God for the salvation of souls.

Further, if "in the end, My Immaculate Heart will triumph," as Our Lady prophesied at Fatima, then Our Lady must be recognized by *nations* as well as individuals for what She is—and first of all by Russia. Thus the conversion of Russia can only mean that Russia will become a Catholic nation, because the Russian Orthodox religion does not admit as a doctrine that Mary was immaculately conceived and free from all sin whatsoever during Her earthly life.

---

[140] The Church's teachings on invincible ignorance, baptism of desire and baptism of blood are beyond the scope of this book. Nevertheless, it ought to be maintained that all those who enter Heaven have achieved in some way a conscious, explicit desire to belong to the Catholic Church and to submit to her authority, even if this occurs only at the moment of death. To deny this is to turn the doctrine of "no salvation outside the Church" into an empty formula—the very thing that Pius XII condemned in his encyclical *Humani Generis*. To hold, as the Modernists do, that Heaven is peopled by "anonymous Christians" who were oblivious to the truth until after death, makes a mockery of God's grace and denies the necessity of explicit Faith for salvation.

From all this it follows that *without the conversion of Russia to the Catholic Faith, the Message of Fatima is completely and utterly meaningless.* Indeed, if Russian Orthodoxy were acceptable to God, He would not have sent His Mother to Fatima in 1917 to speak of the conversion of Russia, when it was already an Orthodox nation. But what did this strange new "Sister Lucy" who appears on the pages of Evaristo's admittedly fabricated "conceptual transcript" have to say on the all-important subject of the *conversion* of Russia through devotion to the Immaculate Heart? It defies belief:

Evaristo: Has the conversion of Russia then taken place?

"Sister Lucy": Yes. The news speaks for themselves (*sic*).

Yes, the "news" did speak for itself; but the news did not tell Sister Lucy that Russia was converting. On the contrary, the "news" revealed that Russia was becoming a neo-Stalinist dictatorship under Vladimir Putin, that it led (and still leads) the world in the per capita rate of abortions, that Moscow is a center of the worldwide child pornography "industry," and that the Russian population is declining at the rate of 700,000 per year on account of abortion and early death from alcoholism and other diseases, and violence inflicted upon Russians by Russians.

There were a few other important items missing from the "news" filtering into the convent that housed the new "Sister Lucy": that euthanasia was being legalized around the world, and that human cloning will soon follow. Then there was the news that all the nations of the world were moving toward a "New World Order" in which contraception, abortion on demand, divorce and homosexual relations are viewed as "rights," while the Church's moral teaching is defied by politicians and mocked by the mass media. The new "Sister Lucy" also seemed ignorant of the news that wars and persecutions of Catholics around the world, especially in Russia and China, were on the increase since 1984.

Considering the following item in Evaristo's 1992 "conceptual" interview with "Sister Lucy," we might wonder whether it was "news" or pure fantasy that "Sister Lucy" was receiving in the convent at Coimbra:

"Sister Lucy": [T]hat man in Russia, unknowingly was an instrument of God in the conversion …

Evaristo: What man? Gorbachev?

"Sister Lucy": Yes, and when he visited the Holy Father in Rome, he knelt at his feet and asked pardon for all the crimes he had committed in his life.

There was one small problem with this bit of "news." *The Vatican denied that it ever happened.* Commenting on a Spanish television report about this alleged revelation by Sister Lucy, the Pope's spokesman, Joaquin Navarro-Valls, declared as follows: "Gorbachev did not ask for forgiveness from the Pope... Mikhail Gorbachev did not kneel before the Pope and beg forgiveness for his sins, as supposedly stated by Sister Lucy... It is neither true *nor plausible* ..."[141]

The same could be said of Evaristo's productions as a whole! Here the maxim "false in one, false in all" would seem to apply. If it could be shown that the new "Sister Lucy" had uttered at least one thing which "is neither true nor plausible," as the Vatican itself declared, then Evaristo's entire "interview" of this strange new "Sister Lucy" would, in prudence, have to be rejected. All the more so, in view of Evaristo's admitted technique of presenting fabricated "conceptual" translations as *verbatim* transcripts.

In any case, the truth of the matter was that after his meeting with the Pope at the Vatican, during which he repented of absolutely nothing, Mr. Gorbachev returned to his chairmanship of the globalist Gorbachev Foundation, which busily promotes reduction of the world's population by several *billion* people through a strict regime of contraception and abortion. Of such horrors is the "conversion of Russia" made, according to the new "Sister Lucy."

"Sister Lucy" on the Meaning of Conversion

Evaristo's "Sister Lucy" also had an entirely new idea about what "conversion" really means. It went along with her entirely new idea about what the "Consecration of Russia" really means. Here was what the new "Sister Lucy" had to say about the new meaning of conversion:

> **Evaristo:** But is the conversion of Russia not interpreted as the conversion of the Russian people to Catholicism?
>
> **"Sister Lucy":** *Our Lady never said that.* There are many misinterpretations around. The fact is that Russia, the communist, atheist power, prevented the people from carrying out their faith. *People now have an individual choice to remain as they are or convert.* This they are now free to do, and many conversions are in fact taking place ...

Our Lady never said that? Here the Evaristo's "Sister Lucy" drove a dagger through the heart of the Faith. She declared that Our Lady did not come to earth at Fatima to seek souls for the Church of which She is the Mother, but rather "an individual choice to remain as they are or convert"! Our Lady of Fatima becomes Our Lady of Religious

---

[141] *Contre-Reformation Catholique,* March 1998; a similar denial by the Vatican was also reported by *Catholic World News Service* on March 2, 1998.

Liberty! So, the miracle to be produced by the Consecration of Russia and the triumph of the Immaculate Heart of Mary would not be the salvation of many millions of souls through reception of the precious gift of the Catholic Faith, but only American-style pluralism: whatever religion floats your boat. No serious Catholic could be expected to believe the indifferentist drivel attributed to the last surviving Fatima seer, who actually saw the Mother of God six times in the Cova da Iria and was horrified to see the many souls burning in hell for all eternity because of their "individual choice."

Had "Sister Lucy" not considered that long before the 1984 "consecration" the entire Western world had been exhibiting the consequences of "individual choice"? The "individual choice" to kill babies in the womb; the "individual choice" to contracept; the "individual choice" to divorce; the "individual choice" to indulge in pornography or homosexual relations; and even the "individual choice" to become a Catholic, if one happened to be among the few so inclined in our increasingly amoral commercial civilization. Did this mean that the West had "converted" before Russia did, according to "Sister Lucy's" new definition of the word? Did the triumph of the Immaculate Heart of Mary mean nothing more, in the end, than the spread of religious and moral indifferentism to another country?

We cannot fail to note that even this worldly "miracle" of "individual choice" had yet to occur in Russia at the time Evaristo's "Lucy" was receiving wide publicity in 1998. On the contrary, Russia had just enacted a law forbidding the Catholic Church to seek converts among the Russian people and limiting the freedom of the Church even to exist in "that poor nation." So Russia was not even a liberal democracy as of 1998, let alone a Catholic country; and the situation in Russia has only deteriorated since then. *See* "What Conversion?" in Chapter 14.

And where were these "many conversions" the new "Sister Lucy" imagined were taking place all over Russia? Like the fabled repentance of Gorbachev on his knees before the Pope, they were pure fantasy. In all of Russia even today there are only 300,000 Catholics. *Catholics in Russia are outnumbered by Muslims ten-to-one.* In fact, there are far more converts to Islam than to Catholicism. Even worse, there were at least 500,000 Catholics in Russia at the time of the Russian Revolution—significantly more than today—and today there are fewer Catholic parishes in Russia than there were in 1917! Thus, the Church has been *losing ground* in Russia since it began "converting" in 1984.[142]

Still worse, since the 1984 "consecration of Russia" proselytization by Catholics has not only been forbidden by the law of Russia, but

---

[142] "The Catholic Church in Russia," *The Catholic Faith,* March/April 1998, p. 2.

by the Vatican itself: In 1993 at Balamand, Lebanon, around the time Evaristo claimed to have interviewed the seer, Vatican officials negotiated a joint statement with the Russian Orthodox Church. The Balamand Statement declares that in Russia "there is *no question of conversion of people from one Church to the other* in order to insure their salvation"; that the return of the Russian Orthodox to the Catholic Church is an "outdated ecclesiology", and that the Catholic Church will exclude "for the future *all proselytization* and all desire by Catholics for expansion at the expense of the Orthodox Church."[143] This, of course, was quite in keeping with Cardinal Sodano's Party Line, which had already prevented the Consecration by name for the very reasons indicated by the Balamand accord: the Party Line forbids Russia's conversion. At Fatima, Our Lady spoke of the conversion of Russia; but at Balamand, Vatican officials agreed that *the conversion of Russia is no longer permissible.* But Evaristo's "Lucy" was claiming that Russia had been "converting" since the 1984 ceremony!

Compare this abysmal situation with the *true* miracle which occurred in Mexico after the apparition of Our Lady of Guadalupe in 1531: some nine million Mexicans—virtually the entire nation—converted to the Catholic Faith within nine years. And in Portugal itself the apparitions of Our Lady at Fatima worked a similar miracle, causing the Masonic-Socialist government of that nation to topple and the Reign of Christ the King to be reestablished in that nation within nine years of the Miracle of the Sun at Cova da Iria.

But those were the days when conversion meant conversion. Today, in the midst of an ecclesial crisis without parallel, many words have lost their meaning—even the words of the Queen of Heaven at Fatima. Just as Monsignor Pozzo has observed (*see* Chapter 1), in the Church today we see that the poison of Modernism, condemned by Pope St. Pius X as "the synthesis of all heresies," has seeped into the thinking of many, even prelates. And now, according to Evaristo's conceptual testimony, it had corrupted the testimony of the "new" Sister Lucy of Fatima. In true Modernist fashion the new "Sister Lucy" used all the traditional words—consecration, conversion, peace—but invested them with false new meanings that were the antithesis of their true meanings. Thus did Evaristo's "Sister Lucy" serve the Party Line of the Vatican Secretary of State, of which Evaristo was an early lay herald.

In Evaristo's Lucy we see also a perfect example of the Modernist confusion between faith and politics in the post-conciliar Church, where Vatican diplomacy and *Ostpolitik* seem to have taken

---

[143] Pontifical Council for Christian Unity Information Service, N. 83, 1993 (II), pages 95-99.

precedence over the propagation of the Faith for the salvation of souls from hell, which is not even mentioned any longer. This confusion between faith and politics, between the supernatural and the natural orders is what led the new "Sister Lucy" of the Evaristo pamphlets to declare that the granting of a mere appearance of "individual choice" by a still-godless civil government was a supernatural miracle of "conversion."

What sort of "Sister Lucy" was it, then, who could look upon the awful developments in Russia and the world since 1984 and see in them the *fulfillment* of the promises of Our Lady of Fatima? It was a Sister Lucy we had never known; a Modernist Sister Lucy whose strange new words made a mockery of everything she had said before. It was a Sister Lucy sent to give us a New Fatima for the New Church the Modernists would have us believe emerged like a butterfly from a chrysalis at the Second Vatican Council. A New Fatima which heralds neither conversion nor triumph, but a pathetic accommodation to the worldly wisdom of a dying world: "People now have an individual choice to remain as they are *or* convert." A conversion of Russia without conversion to the Catholic Faith. What an insult to Our Lady of Fatima. And what an infinite insult to Him who sent Her.

The New "Lucy" on the Third Secret of Fatima

We have seen that when Sister Lucy placed the Third Secret of Fatima into a sealed envelope in 1944 and sent it to the Bishop of Leiria-Fatima, she made him promise that it would definitely be opened and *revealed to the world* either at her death or in 1960, whichever would come first, "Because the Blessed Virgin wishes it so" and in that year the Secret "will seem clearer" (*mais claro*). We know that in 1960 the whole Catholic world awaited disclosure of the Secret. There was even an American television show entitled "Zero 1960", whose theme was the expected disclosure of the Secret. But, as we have seen, it was not to be, because in February 1960 the Vatican announced through a Portuguese press agency that the Secret had been suppressed by Pope John and would probably "remain forever under absolute seal."

As the post-conciliar debacle unfolded over the next 35 years, a growing number of Catholics became convinced that the Third Secret must have predicted what would happen after the Council, and that this is why Sister Lucy had said the Secret "will be clearer" by 1960. By 1960 the Second Vatican Council had been announced. How sad it is to see that in 1992, at the convent in Coimbra, the "Sister Lucy" of the Carlos Evaristo pamphlet would turn her back on this aspect, too, of the Message of Fatima.

Evaristo: But didn't Our Lady say that it [the Third Secret] was to be revealed to the public by 1960, at the latest?

"Sister Lucy": Our Lady never said that. Our Lady said it was for the Pope.

Our Lady never said that? But as we now know, not only did Our Lady say that, She dictated a precise order to the effect which the real Sister Lucy recorded in her own handwriting on the outside of *two sealed envelopes* pertaining to the Secret in its entirety. For the *Pope*? More nonsense: The order of the Virgin recorded by the real Lucy on the outside of the two envelopes said the envelopes were to be opened by the Bishop of Fatima or the Cardinal Patriarch of Lisbon.

And what of Sister Lucy's statements to Canon Galamba, Canon Barthas, the Patriarch of Portugal and Cardinal Ottaviani, all to the effect that the Third Secret of Fatima, like the first two Secrets, was meant for the *whole world*? What of the outer envelope photographed for *Life* magazine [Jan. 3, 1949]; the envelope on which Bishop da Silva had written: "This envelope with its contents shall be entrusted to His Eminence Cardinal Manuel (Cerejeira), Patriarch of Lisbon, after my death" (see photo on page 62)—the very Cardinal who publicly confirmed that the Secret would be opened and read to the world in 1960! What of the Vatican's *refusal* in 1944 to accept delivery of the text of the Secret supposedly meant for the Pope? What of Cardinal Cerejeira's declaration in 1960, when Pope John ultimately suppressed the Secret, contrary to all expectations: "I affirm categorically that I was not consulted." And, finally, what of the Vatican's own 1960 press release, which announces the suppression of the Secret, but does *not* give as a reason that the Secret was "meant for the Pope."

Throughout all these events, and for decades thereafter, the real Sister Lucy had never even suggested that the Third Secret of Fatima was meant only for the Pope. No, it was meant for us, and the whole Catholic world knew it. Indeed, before the Blue Army became the instrument of the Party Line along with the new "Sister Lucy," its leader, John Haffert, expressed the disillusionment of Catholics everywhere over the unexpected suppression of the Secret:

> 1960 came and went and the Pope 'to whom the Secret had been confided' did not make it public ... The silence from Rome lay heavily on all of us. People began to murmur that Fatima must have been a fake, that there was no Secret, that the 1960 Secret was 'a hoax' ... [in 1964], the effect of the long silence concerning the 1960 Secret still seemed to hang over us like a pall.[144]

---

[144] *The Whole Truth About Fatima*, Vol. III: *The Third Secret*, by Frère Michel de la Sainte Trinité, English ed., Immaculate Heart Publications, 1990, p. 600.

At the convent in Coimbra in 1992 the "Sister Lucy" presented to the world by Carlos Evaristo completely rewrote the Message of Fatima. That is why Evaristo was forced to admit privately that this new "Sister Lucy" had uttered "contradictory and unlogical things which at times seem almost craziness," that his memory was bad, and that the whole "interview" was a "reconstruction" based on the memory of others who did not even speak Portuguese. But in 1993 Evaristo would tell the world, in his great sequel, that the illogical and crazy things he had "reconstructed" the year before were the purest truth.

The Second "Interview" Less of the Same

As our discussion of the 1992 "interview" should make clear, its publication proved to be a severe embarrassment to Evaristo. Hence his second attempt in 1993 to corroborate the capitulation of the last surviving seer of Fatima.

But here we have not more of the same, but *less* of the same. The 1993 "interview" is only half the length of the 1992 "interview"—one hour. Also, the 1993 interview conspicuously omits any discussion of "Sister Lucy's" alleged statement in 1992 that the Third Secret of Fatima was meant for the Pope, not the faithful at large.

The 1993 "interview" does contain in substance a repetition of "Sister Lucy's" alleged statements in 1992 that Russia was consecrated in 1984 according to the wishes of Our Lady, and that Russia is now "converting". On this occasion, however, Evaristo resorts to blatantly leading questions in order to prod "Sister Lucy" into giving the answers which would buttress the plainly incredible interview of 1992:

> **Evaristo:** So it is true that the consecration is done *right*? *true*?
>
> **"Sister Lucy":** Yes, it is true ... it is done ...
>
> **Evaristo:** And Russia *has started to convert, no*?
>
> **"Sister Lucy":** Yes, it has started to convert ... the word ... conversion. We should not give ears to those people who say otherwise ... The word conversion ... to convert ... indicates a change. A conversion is a change.
>
> **Evaristo: *Yes*.**
>
> **"Sister Lucy":** A change from evil ... It does not indicate that all evil will disappear but just a conversion from evil to good ...

More on the New Meaning of "Conversion"

As we can see from the above quotation, in the second pamphlet "Sister Lucy" continues to insist that the conversion of Russia does

En brisant les scellés des appartements privés, le Pape découvre les instruments du travail qui l'attend, ceux de Pie XII, et le coffre aux secrets de l'Eglise

Photo from *Paris-Match* magazine (Issue No. 497, October 18, 1958), showing the wooden safe in the papal apartment of Pius XII in which a text of the Third Secret was safeguarded. The text in this safe was *not* the text in the Holy Office archives.

not require conversion to the Catholic Faith. She will now settle for a supposed "conversion from evil to good." That cannot possibly be the authentic testimony of the last surviving Fatima visionary. Father Joaquin Alonso, probably the foremost Fatima expert of the 20th century, had many face-to-face encounters with Sister Lucy. In 1976 he wrote:

> ... we should affirm that Lucia always thought that the *'conversion'* of Russia is not to be limited to the return of the Russian people to the Orthodox Christian religions, rejecting the Marxist atheism of the Soviets, but rather, it refers purely,

Shortly after his amiable meeting with Agostino Cardinal Casaroli, architect of *Ostpolitik* and the new ecumenism, Evaristo emerged from the convent at Coimbra with a new "ecumenical" message from Fatima. What inference can we draw from this strange coincidence?

plainly and simply to the total, integral conversion of Russia to the one true Church of Christ, the Catholic Church.[145]

Why is Our Lady of Fatima so insistent on the *conversion* of Russia? The answer is what we have already noted: that the Catholic Church has thrice defined as infallible dogma that there is no salvation outside the Church. Christ did not found His Church for nothing, or to serve as an optional "body of believers." He founded it for one purpose: to sanctify souls and save them from hell, through the grace He won for all men on the Cross.

And we know that Our Lady came to Fatima precisely to obtain the salvation of souls: "If My requests are granted *many souls will be saved*." From which it obviously follows that many souls will be lost if Her requests are not granted, for otherwise the request would have been pointless. In this context the word "conversion" as used in the Message of Fatima cannot possibly mean anything other than a conversion to Catholicism and thus membership in the Catholic Church. It is nonsensical, therefore, to argue that by "conversion" the Mother of God—who is also known by Catholics under the title Mother of the *Catholic* Church—meant that Russia would embrace the *Orthodox* religion following the "fall of Communism" in 1991. The Mother of the Catholic Church did not come to Fatima to announce the "conversion" of Russia *to a state of schism from Rome*. What is more, Russian Orthodoxy was already the predominant religion in Russia when Our Lady appeared at Fatima. Therefore, according to this argument, Russia would already have been "converted" in 1917 and Our Lady of Fatima's statement that Russia *"will be* converted" would have been senseless.

But according to Evaristo's "Sister Lucy," Russia, a land of abortion on demand and vicious discrimination against the Holy Catholic Church, is now *good*? And what about the rest of the world, in which 600 million babies have been slaughtered by abortion since the 1984 "consecration of Russia"? Is the rest of the world now undergoing this "conversion from evil to good" as well? Or was the whole world *already* good, given the new meaning of "conversion" invented by the new "Sister Lucy"?

Russia has *"started* to convert"? Has it "started" to spare the lives of its unborn children? Has the world at large "started" to halt the holocaust of abortion? Is the world today more good or less good

---

[145] *La Verdad sobre el Secreto de Fatima, Fatima sin mitos,* Father Joaquin Alonso, (2nd edition, Ejercito Azul, Madrid, 1988) p. 78. English translation by Joseph Cain. Original Spanish reads: "... *podriamos decir que Lucia ha pensado siempre que la conversión de Rusia no se entiende solo de un retorno de los pueblos de Rusia a la religion cristiano-ortodoxa, rechazando el ateismo marxista y ateo de los soviets, sino que se refiere pura y llanmente a la conversion total e integral de un retorno a la unica y verdadera Iglesia, la catolica-romana.*"

than it was before the "conversion" of Russia "started" in 1984? Of course, we know the answers to these questions, even if the new Modernist version of "Sister Lucy" does not.

The new "Sister Lucy" tells us that conversion "does not indicate that all evil will disappear". Does not conversion require at least that a nation *stop killing its own children in the womb*? Has "Sister Lucy" forgotten that in 1917, not even communist Russia permitted abortion? Are we now to believe that Russia is "converting" when it is guilty of a routine daily slaughter of innocents which not even the Bolsheviks permitted at first?

Can "Sister Lucy", the sainted seer of Fatima, really be unaware that more innocent lives have been taken by abortion since the 1984 "consecration of Russia" than were claimed in all the wars in the history of the world, including all the wars spawned by Communism, which is only one of Russia's errors? When "Sister Lucy" tells us that not *all* evil will disappear after the conversion of Russia, does she mean to say that a "conversion from evil to good" can coexist with legalized[146] abortion?

We can only be outraged that the "Sister Lucy" presented to us by Mr. Evaristo would apply the word "conversion" to a state of affairs in which the civil authorities of nations around the world, including "converted" Russia, have decreed that children in the womb are not human beings and may be exterminated at will. We can only be sickened by this pollution of the purity of the Message of Fatima.

But the 1993 model of the new "Sister Lucy" has even more to say on the strange new notion of conversion which she introduced for the first time in 1992:

> **"Sister Lucy":** "The Holy Father will consecrate Russia to Me [Our Lady] which will convert" ... and a conversion is a change of a path of evil to good ... "and there will be some time of peace."

So, Russia is now on the *path to goodness*? And the West too? What exactly do we see on this path to goodness which the new "Sister Lucy" discerns in world events since 1984? We see, first of all, the European Union with its universal abortion on demand, contraception, "legalized" euthanasia, divorce, pornography, prostitution, "gay rights" and empty Catholic churches. If this is the "path of evil to good", what, God forbid, would constitute the path of good to evil? Sacred Scripture solemnly admonishes "Woe to you that call evil good, and good evil: that put darkness *for* light, and light *for* darkness: that put bitter for sweet, and sweet for bitter." [Isaias

---

[146] We judge a man by his habits—we judge a society by its institutions. Legalized abortion is an institution—a bad institution. Therefore, the nation is not converted as long as its laws on legalized abortion stand.

5:20] Yet that is precisely what the new "Sister Lucy" has done in Mr. Evaristo's little pamphlet.

We must conclude, therefore, that it could not possibly be the Sister Lucy we know and believe who utters these abominable things. The Sister Lucy who saw the Mother of God at Fatima and the vision of hell Our Lady permitted to her, would never *in any sense* use the word "conversion" or "good" to describe the unprecedented evil which exists in Russia and the rest of the world today.

The New Meaning of Peace

At Fatima, on July 13, 1917, Our Lady promised absolutely: "In the end, My Immaculate Heart will triumph, the Holy Father will consecrate Russia to Me, Russia will be converted and a period of peace will be given to mankind."

And what of the "period of peace" which Our Lady promised as the fruit of the conversion of Russia? If we have had "a period of peace" since 1984, then how does one explain the incessant war on the unborn, which has claimed 600 million innocent victims since then, or the constant eruption of local and regional conflicts around the globe over the past 27 years, including those in Iraq and Afghanistan? This is peace? But here too Evaristo's "Sister Lucy" found new meanings for old and well understood words:

> **"Sister Lucy":** But this peace to which the Virgin refers in the prophecy refers to wars and persecutions that the errors of atheist Communism were causing all over the world ...

> **Evaristo:** This is important to get straight ... as this is why many people do not comprehend and think that world peace is to be instantaneous ...

> **"Sister Lucy":** The Virgin spoke of a peace from wars promoted by errors ... by the errors of atheist Communism in the whole world ... Atheism, yes ... and therefore it is the greatest heresy that exists and it spreads from atheist Communism ... it could have been a Communism that wasn't atheist ... But it refers to atheist Communism that was producing many wars in the whole world.

> **Evaristo:** Why is there no peace in Russia today? Why?

> **"Sister Lucy":** Because the wars that exist now are practically not derived from atheism but are civil wars.

So, the new "Sister Lucy" tells us that the peace of the Reign of Mary following the conversion of Russia and the Triumph of Her Immaculate Heart means only that there will no longer be *atheist* wars, but all other wars will continue unabated!

A Friendly New Atheism

But does not atheism still exist in the world today? Are not wars still being fomented by *atheists* around the globe? The new "Sister Lucy" had an answer to this question as well: You see, the atheism of today is a kinder, gentler atheism which does not seek to destroy the Holy Catholic Church! Read it for yourself:

> **"Sister Lucy":** ... atheism still exists but I think *it is no longer the atheism that wanted to destroy the Faith, the Church, God*, and everything that is supernatural.

So, the Faith is no longer threatened by atheism! Here a strange new "Sister Lucy" jettisoned much of the New Testament! St. Paul tells us in Hebrews (11:6), "He who comes to God must believe that God exists and that He rewards those who seek Him." Therefore, atheists will go to hell precisely for their atheism. Did Our Lord Himself not say that those who are not with Him are against Him? Therefore, atheism makes one an enemy of Christ. Did St. Paul not teach that the atheist stands condemned as an enemy of God because he has closed his mind and heart to the evidence of God in nature (Romans 1:18-21) which even a man without faith can see? Is not atheism the very creed that the devil himself promotes? How, then, could atheists be anything but a threat to the Church, given that they are, by definition, her enemies by the very fact that they are enemies of Jesus Christ and followers of Satan's doctrine?

Seeing that atheists are enemies of Jesus Christ, Who is the Head of the Catholic Church, and realizing that atheists follow the lead of Satan, how is it possible for any one, even the new "Sister Lucy," to claim that modern-day atheists are not a threat to the Church?

And if this new, kinder atheism no longer seeks to destroy the Church and the supernatural, why is the world today steeped in the death and destruction of both body and soul in godless materialistic societies, which kill babies in the womb by the millions? The new "Sister Lucy" had no answer, because the new "Sister Lucy" was not asked such embarrassing questions. Her questioner, Mr. Evaristo, was evidently interested in preserving the credibility of his new and improved "Sister Lucy", whose nonsensical comments had caused him so much trouble when he first introduced her to the world in his pamphlet of 1992.

This new kind of atheism described by the new "Sister Lucy" must be seen as symptomatic of the general process of apostasy within and without the Church in the post-conciliar period. The destruction of the Roman liturgy, the overturning of our most cherished ecclesial traditions, the loss of vocations, wretched catechisms, the decline in the life of prayer in individuals and communities, have all combined to erode the integrity and the militancy of the Faith.

Did not Our Lord warn us in Sacred Scripture that "you are the salt of the earth but if the salt loses its flavor, of what use is it? It is good for nothing except to be thrown out and trampled underfoot." (Matthew 5:13). This new message of Fatima has no salt and is good for nothing. Only a Catholic who has lost the traditional faith could find it palatable. And for millions of young Catholics today, the new message of Fatima will be palatable only because they have never been fed by the faith of the ages in the first place. These millions of Catholics are the victims of the "new" Church of the post-Vatican II era, with its new message of Fatima—a Church which seems determined to bury its own past.

In view of this pathetic new "message" of Fatima, which has replaced the authentic one since the days of Evaristo's pamphlets, should we not entreat Rome with all the more urgency to reveal the suppressed Third Secret of Fatima? Cardinal Ratzinger told us in November 1984 that the Third Secret refers to the "dangers which menace the faith and the life of the Christian and therefore (menace) the life of the world."[147] And indeed if Christians no longer salt the earth with a fervent faith, what will stay the wrath of God? What will keep Christians who have lost their salt from being trampled underfoot, as Our Lord warned? Many believe that the revelation of the Third Secret would deliver us from the current apostasy, which clearly includes Mr. Evaristo's saltless version of the Fatima message.

Yet Another Fantasy

At the end of the 1993 interview, the new "Sister Lucy" offered another observation about world events which brings to mind the Vatican's dismissal of her fantastic story about Gorbachev's repentance on his knees before the Pope:

> **"Sister Lucy":** But when [in 1984] we were at the beginning of a nuclear war and all of a sudden (*sic*), those projects for war that the nations had ... From one moment to another at the moment when the Holy Father made the consecration, those projects of war ... Everything changed! and (*sic*) these projects of war ... changed into projects of peace! ... These were projects to terminate everything that have now changed into projects to liberate! ...
>
> **Evaristo:** Then, has the era of peace come, now that the Consecration of Russia has been accomplished and that Communism has collapsed?
>
> **"Sister Lucy":** The consecration of 1984 prevented an atomic (nuclear) war *that would have occurred in 1985* ...

---

[147] *Jesus* magazine, November 11, 1984.

It is very strange indeed that after "Sister Lucy" speculated that a nuclear war would have occurred in 1985 if not for the 1984 "consecration" *not one question was posed* concerning this remarkable "revelation." Was not Evaristo concerned about where Sister Lucy had acquired her purported knowledge of a nuclear war narrowly averted? Yet Evaristo seemed averse to learning anything about this during the 1993 "interview". This is most curious. Perhaps Evaristo realized that, like the conversion and repentance of Gorbachev, this "revelation" would not bear much scrutiny and was best left unexamined. At any rate, one searches one's memory in vain for any recollection of news stories in 1985 about the imminence of nuclear war between the United States and Russia. Nor does anyone with even a modicum of knowledge about world events over the past 27 years believe for a moment that Russia has stopped producing weapons of mass destruction and turned her energies to "projects to liberate"!

And what "projects of liberation", exactly, was the new "Sister Lucy" referring to? Was she not aware that Russia was (and still is) the chief supplier of weaponry to Communist China,[148] where the Catholic Church has been forced underground and bishops and priests are arrested for the "crime" of being Catholics in union with the Holy See? Was the new "Sister Lucy" unaware that Russia still possesses enough nuclear weapons to destroy the entire world several times over, and that Russian missiles by the thousands remain "on alert" in their silos? In fact, in January 1995 Russia came within *minutes* of a nuclear launch against the United States in response to a false warning on its early warning radar following a missile launch from Norway.[149] U.S. Senator Sam Nunn has warned publicly that Russia's and America's nuclear weapons are on a "hair trigger" alert—meaning fueled and ready to launch at any moment—and that the danger of nuclear war through human error or misjudgment is greater than it ever was during the "Cold War".[150] None of these hard facts about the state of the world seems to have

---

[148] *See* "Israel Second Only To Russia In Providing Arms To China," Carol Giacomo, Reuters, 8-31-02.

[149] As the Wikipedia entry notes: "This event resulted in a full alert being passed up through the military chain of command all the way to President Boris Yeltsin, who was notified immediately and the 'nuclear briefcase' (known in Russia as *Cheget*) used to authorize nuclear launch was automatically activated. It is reported that President Boris Yeltsin activated his 'nuclear keys' for the first time in his tenure. No warning was issued to the Russian populace of any incident; it was reported in the news a week afterward." Cf. "Norwegian Rocket Incident," http://en.wikipedia.org/wiki/Norwegian_rocket_incident.

[150] Cf. Congressional Record—Senate, March 6, 2003 at p. 5402. ("We have literally thousands of missiles on hair-trigger alert... We risk the lives of millions of people over what may turn out to be a simple miscalculation.")

penetrated the Convent at Coimbra, where the new "Sister Lucy" tells us, through Mr. Evaristo, of a world at peace, on the path of conversion to goodness. Yet we know that the world described by the new "Sister Lucy" is not the world we inhabit. It is a fantasy world, where apostasy is conversion, evil is good, and war is peace.

The New Message of Fatima

It would be well to summarize, in conclusion, the new message of Fatima which proceeds from the new meanings given to its key words by the new "Sister Lucy" who spoke to us from the pages of Mr. Evaristo's pamphlets:

- The *consecration* of Russia does not mean that Russia needs to be mentioned.

- The *conversion* of Russia does not mean that Russia will embrace the Catholic Faith, or indeed any religious faith at all. It means only that Russia will grant "individual choice," just like the godless pluralistic societies of the West. Nor does the *conversion* of Russia mean that Russia will stop killing babies in the womb or grant true liberty to the Catholic Church.

- The *peace* which Our Lady promised at Fatima if Russia were converted means only the cessation of wars caused by atheism, but all other wars will continue unabated.

- The *atheism* of today is not an enemy of the Holy Catholic Church.

The careful reader will notice that what this new, Modernist message of Fatima promises us is nothing more than a world *in exactly the same condition in which we see it today*—a world of godless, pluralistic societies which murder unborn children in the womb by the millions, refuse to recognize Christ the King or His Queen Mother, and reject the teaching authority of the Holy Catholic Church. Yes, by some amazing coincidence, the new message of Fatima in the Evaristo pamphlets jibes perfectly with the *status quo* of the emerging New World Order.

By another amazing coincidence, the new message of Fatima also serves perfectly the *Ostpolitik* and "ecumenical brotherhood" being promoted with abandon by certain Vatican bureaucrats, who no longer speak of such things as hell, conversion, and the triumph of the Immaculate Heart of Mary. Some light is shed on this coincidence when we consider that Mr. Evaristo has boasted of his kind treatment by Cardinal Casaroli, chief architect of the new Vatican policy toward Communism and the world's false religions. At Fatima, Mr. Evaristo could be seen in a gesture of friendship with his highly placed friend in the Vatican. Perhaps this explains how an obscure layman who was a total stranger to Sister Lucy could gain unprecedented access to the last surviving seer of Fatima, while mere Catholic archbishops and bishops were forbidden to speak to her without permission from Cardinal Ratzinger or the Pope himself. [See photo on page 81.]

So, according to the new, improved, politically correct message of Fatima, the Triumph of the Immaculate Heart and the Reign of Mary become nothing more than universal pluralistic democracy in a non-Catholic "civilization of love" which the Vatican itself is promoting. All is well. But all is not well. The world grows more rebellious, the signs of the coming Apocalypse more evident, by the hour. Something is terribly wrong with the world. And something was terribly wrong at the convent in Coimbra.

Was it Sister Lucy de Jesus, the last surviving Fatima seer, who spoke to Carlos Evaristo on October 11, 1992, and again on October 11, 1993? It does not matter. For even if the voice did belong to her, the words did not. They are surely not the words of Heaven entrusted to the saintly little girl at the Cova da Iria in 1917; the little girl who was shown the fires of hell and told of the great chastisement that was fast approaching.

This new message of Fatima simply cannot be accepted in good conscience by anyone who holds fast to the traditional Catholic Faith, or indeed to what Sister Lucy herself declared over and over again for a lifetime before her alleged encounters with Mr. Evaristo. We see in the new message of Fatima heralded by Evaristo—promoting from the bottom what had been decreed from the top—all the confusion and self-contradiction of the arch-heresy of Modernism, which says one thing but means quite the opposite. We see, in fact, precisely what Mr. Evaristo himself admitted was present in the statements of the new "Sister Lucy": "contradictory and unlogical things which at times seem almost *craziness*."[151]

At Fatima Our Lady warned that "if My requests are not granted ... various nations will be annihilated." In a world which seems intent precisely on annihilating itself, which moves ever closer to the divine chastisement it so richly deserves, not only faith but *prudence itself* dictates that we reject what Mr. Evaristo and certain elements in the Vatican apparatus have presented to us as the words of "Sister Lucy" of Fatima. Sister Lucy is no longer with us, but the counterfeit "Message of Fatima" attributed to her—never by her own direct testimony but only through the plainly incredible accounts of others—remains in effect as the Party Line on Fatima. We would be fools to believe it.

---

[151] Evaristo to Coralie Graham, November 23, 1992, fax transmission.

Chapter 7

THREE FALSE FRIENDS
AND THE THIRD SECRET

On June 26, 2000 the Vatican published the famous vision of the "Bishop dressed in White," giving the impression that the vision constituted the whole of the Third Secret of Fatima. Tellingly, Sister Lucia was not even permitted to watch the internationally televised press conference on television. Sister Maria do Carmo, custodian of Sister Lucia's convent in Coimbra, told *Corriere della Sera* that "We watch TV, but only in exceptional cases. The press conference on the Secret of Fatima is not such." This prompted Socci to ask: "And what are these exceptional cases for the Carmelites of Coimbra? Perhaps the finals of the world soccer championship?"[152]

By the date of the press conference informed members of the faithful were aware of a vast body of evidence, provided by direct witnesses to the content of the Secret. A full review of the evidence, presented fully in other sources,[153] is beyond the scope of this book. Suffice it to note that the evidence as of June 26, 2000 clearly pointed to the existence of a Secret involving the following elements:

- something so terrible that Sister Lucia could not commit it to paper without a direct order from her bishop in October 1943 and then a direct intervention of the Virgin Mary in January 1944;

- two parts, one of which contains the words of the Virgin that are the "logical continuation" of her statement "In Portugal, the dogma of the Faith will always be preserved etc." (source: Father Joseph Schweigl in 1952);

- a single page of some 25 lines of text (sources: Bishop Venancio [1959] and Cardinal Ottaviani [1967]);

- a text in the form of a letter to the Bishop of Leiria-Fatima in a sealed envelope (sources: Sister Lucia, Bishop da Silva, Father Jongen [1946]);

- a text that was lodged in the papal apartment during the pontificates of Pius XII, John XXIII and Paul VI (sources: Sister Pasqualina, Robert Serrou [1958], Father Caillon, Archbishop Capovilla [2006]);

---

[152] Socci, *The Fourth Secret of Fatima*, p. 34.

[153] For a detailed exposition of the evidence on this score cf. Christopher A. Ferrara, *The Secret Still Hidden* (New York: Good Counsel Publications, 2009), Chapters 2-3.

- a text that contains difficult expressions Pope John could not read without a written translation prepared in 1959, unlike the text he read in 1960, which he understood without need of translation (source: Archbishop Capovilla);

- a text whose prophecy would become clear in 1960, by which time Vatican II (which would have a disastrous aftermath) had been announced (source: Sister Lucia);

- a "divine warning" about "suicidal" alterations in the liturgy, theology and soul of the Church (source: the future Pius XII in 1931);

- a prediction that after 1960 "the devil will succeed in leaving the souls of the faithful abandoned by their leaders," by causing "religious and priests [to] fall away from their beautiful vocation... drag[ging] numerous souls to hell," and that "nations will disappear from the face of the earth" (source: Sister Lucia to Father Fuentes in 1957);

- contents "so delicate" that they cannot be allowed "for whatever reason, even fortuitous, to fall into alien hands" (source: Cardinal Ottaviani in 1967);

- a text "diplomatically" withheld because of the "seriousness of its contents" and which predicts, *after 1980*, "great trials" and "tribulation" for the Church which "it is no longer possible to avert" and the destruction of "whole areas of the earth" so that "from one moment to the next millions of people will perish" (source: John Paul II at Fulda, 1980);

- details that could be "badly interpreted" (source: John Paul II in 1982);

- a "religious prophecy" of "dangers threatening the faith and the life of the Christian and therefore of the world" (source: Cardinal Ratzinger in 1984);

- matters which would make for the "sensationalistic utilization of its contents" (source: Cardinal Ratzinger in 1985);

- a prediction of apostasy in the Church that "begins at the top" (source: Cardinal Ciappi in 1995);

- "details" that would cause "disequilibrium" in the Church (source: Cardinal Ratzinger in 1996);

- a warning of a material chastisement of the world which accompanies the great apostasy in the Church, like that predicted in the approved apparition of Our Lady of Akita in 1973, whose message is "essentially the same" as the message of Our Lady of Fatima (source: Cardinal Ratzinger to Howard Dee, as reported in 1998);

- a warning to avoid the "tail of the dragon" (the devil) referred to in the Book of the Apocalypse (12:3-4), which sweeps one-third of "the stars" (priests, bishops, cardinals and other consecrated souls) from Heaven and cast them into the earth (source: John Paul II in 2000).[154]

The vision published in 2000 involves *none* of these elements, but rather depicts a white-clad prelate, evidently a future Pope, being executed by a band of soldiers on a hill outside a half-ruined city filled with cadavers, followed by the execution of other prelates, priests, religious and laity—all without the least explanation from the Virgin of the meaning of the apocalyptic tableau. Besides the details provided by various witnesses and numerous other evidentiary facts indicating the existence of a companion text (see the table of 10 facts in *The Devil's Final Battle*, Chapter 13), the vision's ambiguity and the conspicuous lack of any explanation by the Virgin led Catholics around the world to conclude that there must be a missing companion text in which the Virgin would explain precisely what it signifies, and the "who, what, where and when" of the apocalyptic scenario.

By the end of the June 26 press conference at which the vision was published, however, it was clear that the Party Line would continue to advance with the assistance of three "false friends" who would pay tribute to the Fatima event even as they attempted to relegate it entirely to the past: Cardinal Sodano; then Archbishop (later Cardinal) Bertone, who would succeed Sodano as Secretary of State; and then Cardinal Ratzinger, the future Pope Benedict XVI, who would ultimately repudiate the Party Line and "reopen the file" on the Third Secret controversy. (See Chapter 11.)

Something is Missing

Some six weeks before the press conference, Cardinal Sodano had announced during the papal Mass for the beatification of Jacinta and Francisco at Fatima that the Secret would be published along with "an appropriate commentary."[155] The text of the purported Secret, spanning four pages and 62 lines, was photostatically reproduced as part of a booklet containing that commentary, entitled *The Message of*

---

[154] For a detailed exposition of the evidence on this score cf. Christopher A. Ferrara, *The Secret Still Hidden* (New York: Good Counsel Publications, 2009), Chapters 2-3.

[155] Vatican Information Service, May 13, 2000.

Fatima (*TMF*). Aside from the commentary, written by then Cardinal Ratzinger, serving at the time as Prefect of the Congregation for the Doctrine of the Faith (CDF), *TMF* included an Introduction by then Archbishop Bertone, serving at that time as Secretary for the CDF but soon to succeed Sodano as Secretary of State and enforcer of the Party Line on Fatima. According to *TMF*, the Third Secret that had been suppressed and kept "under absolute seal" since it arrived at the Vatican in 1957 is nothing more than the following:

J.M.J.

The third part of the secret revealed at the Cova da Iria-Fatima, on 13 July 1917.

I write in obedience to you, my God, who commands me to do so through his Excellency the Bishop of Leiria and through your Most Holy Mother and mine.

After the two parts which I have already explained, at the left of Our Lady and a little above, we saw an Angel with a flaming sword in his left hand; flashing, it gave out flames that looked as though they would set the world on fire; but they died out in contact with the splendour that Our Lady radiated towards him from her right hand: pointing to the earth with his right hand, the Angel cried out in a loud voice: "Penance, Penance, Penance!". And we saw in an immense light that is God; "something similar to how people appear in a mirror when they pass in front of it" a Bishop dressed in White "we had the impression that it was the Holy Father". Other Bishops, Priests, men and women Religious going up a steep mountain, at the top of which there was a big Cross of rough-hewn trunks as of a cork-tree with the bark; before reaching there the Holy Father passed through a big city half in ruins and half trembling with halting step, afflicted with pain and sorrow, he prayed for the souls of the corpses he met on his way; having reached the top of the mountain, on his knees at the foot of the big Cross he was killed by a group of soldiers who fired bullets and arrows at him, and in the same way there died one after another the other Bishops, Priests, men and women Religious, and various lay people of different ranks and positions. Beneath the two arms of the Cross there were two Angels each with a crystal aspersorium in his hand, in which they gathered up the blood of the Martyrs and with it sprinkled the souls that were making their way to God.

Tuy-3-1-1944.[156]

---

[156] Congregation for the Doctrine of the Faith, *The Message of Fatima* (*TMF*), (Vatican City: Libreria Editrice Vaticana, June 26, 2000) p. 21, http://www.vatican.va/

That this vision is *part* of the Third Secret can hardly be doubted. But the worldwide reaction of the Catholic faithful to its disclosure can be summed up with a single incredulous question: *"That's it?"* Yes, the vision is dramatic, but its meaning is far from clear: An angel with a flaming sword. Flames from the sword threatening to set the world afire, but repelled (temporarily?) by the Virgin. The angel thrice demanding penance from humanity. A "Bishop dressed in White," who seems to be the Pope, hobbling through a half-ruined city filled with corpses (what city? how ruined?). The execution of the Pope by a band of soldiers (who are they?) as he kneels before a rough-hewn cross on a hill outside the city (is it Rome?). And then the martyrdom of countless bishops, priests, religious and laity (who? when? where?), as two other angels gather up the blood of the martyrs to sprinkle on Heaven-bound souls.

What does it all mean? The vision as published does not contain a single word from the Virgin by way of explanation. Yet Our Lady had taken care to confirm for the seers the vision of hell they had clearly understood upon the very sight of it: "You have seen hell, where the souls of poor sinners go." *TMF* offered no explanation for the missing words of the Virgin, as if no one should be puzzled by this. But it defied belief that the Virgin had *nothing* to say about the dramatic but ambiguous content of the vision. Doubting questions immediately abounded:

- Where are the *words* of the Virgin which are the "logical continuation" of Her statement "In Portugal, the dogma of the Faith will always be preserved **etc**" as Father Schweigl revealed?

- What is so terrible about this ambiguous vision that Sister Lucia could not commit it to paper without a direct intervention of the Virgin Mary?

- Where is the letter to the Bishop of Fatima, comprising some 25 lines of text?

- Given that *TMF* stated that the text of the vision had been kept in the Holy Office archives,[157] where is the text that a living witness said was kept in the papal apartment under the Pope's personal custody during the reigns of Pius XII, John XXIII and Paul VI?

- Why is the vision devoid of any reference to a crisis of faith in the Church and dramatic consequences for the world,

roman_curia/congregations/cfaith/documents/rc_con_cfaith_doc_20000626_message-fatima_en.html

[157] *TMF*, p. 5.

alluded to by a train of witnesses who had either read the Secret or had indirect knowledge of it?

- Why is it 62 lines when Cardinal Ottaviani spoke of a text of only 25 lines?

- What of the testimony of various witnesses concerning the location, paper size, and date of delivery of the text to the Vatican, which did not at all correspond to the "official" account, thus indicating the existence of another text that accompanies and explains the vision?[158]

There was, on the face of it, no rational explanation for the Vatican's refusal to disclose the text of this vision in 1960, standing alone, or the rigorous suppression of it for forty years thereafter. Indeed, in his commentary on the Secret in *Message*, the same Cardinal Ratzinger who said in 1984 that the Secret is a "religious prophecy" concerning "dangers to the faith and the life of the Christian and therefore of the world", was now saying that in the Secret "No great mystery is revealed; nor is the future unveiled. We see the Church of the martyrs of the century which has just passed…"[159] If that were true, then why did Cardinal Ratzinger not simply *say so* back in 1984? As Portuguese bishop Januario Torgal declared: "If the Vatican knew it was not apocalyptic, why on earth did it make it public only now?"[160]

As even Mother Angelica of the Eternal Word Television Network declared on live television a year after the vision was published: "As for the Secret, well I happen to be one of those individuals who thinks we didn't get the whole thing…. Because I think it's scary."[161] She spoke for millions of skeptical Catholics around the world.

What about 1960?

Moreover, on its face the vision has absolutely nothing to do with 1960, the year the Secret was supposed to be revealed because it would be "more clear" then. Evidently in recognition of this problem, then Archbishop Bertone claims in *Message* that during an unrecorded "conversation" with Sister Lucia at Coimbra on April 27, 2000, weeks before the press conference, she allegedly told him that the Virgin *had never said anything* about 1960:

---

[158] Cf. *The Devil's Final Battle,* Chapter 13 for the pertinent facts.

[159] Ibid., p. 32.

[160] *The Washington Post*, "Third Secret Spurs More Questions; Fatima Interpretation Departs From Vision," July 1, 2000, quoted in Mark Fellows, *Sister Lucia: Apostle of the Immaculate Heart,* p. 190.

[161] "Mother Angelica Live," May 16, 2001.

Before giving the sealed envelope containing the third part of the "secret" to the then Bishop of Leiria-Fatima, Sister Lucia wrote on the outside envelope that it could be opened only after 1960, either by the Patriarch of Lisbon or the Bishop of Leiria. Archbishop Bertone therefore asked: "Why only after 1960? Was it Our Lady who fixed that date?" Sister Lucia replied: "*It was not Our Lady*. I fixed the date because I had the intuition that before 1960 it would not be understood, but that only later would it be understood...[162]

Tellingly, *TMF* failed to mention that on the envelope Sister Lucia had written: "*By express order of Our Lady,* this envelope can be opened only in 1960..." Nor does *TMF* include a copy of the envelope as part of its supporting documentation. During the famous telecast of May 31, 2007 (see Chapter 10). Bertone would finally reveal the envelope—or rather, *two* such envelopes bearing the same express order of the Virgin respecting 1960. But on June 26, 2000 Bertone had the temerity to claim that Lucia declared to him in private weeks earlier: "*It was not Our Lady*. I fixed the date!" We say temerity, because the future Secretary of State knew then that his representation was flatly contradicted by what Lucia had written on the envelopes he had chosen not to reveal.

One cannot overestimate the significance of what Bertone is claiming here. If the "express order of Our Lady" concerning revelation of the Secret in 1960 was purely Sister Lucia's invention— if she had misled Canon Barthas, Cardinal Ottaviani, the Bishop of Fatima, the Cardinal Patriarch of Portugal, the whole Church and the entire world—why should anyone believe anything she claimed to have heard from the Blessed Virgin? Why should anyone believe a single word of the Message of Fatima?

There are only two alternatives: Either Sister Lucia lied about this crucial matter throughout her life, which is inconceivable, or the words attributed to her by Bertone were not hers. In the latter case, Lucia's purported statement would be either an outright fabrication by Bertone, the product of undue influence upon the seer, or an utterance arising from a loss of mental capacity due to her advanced age. Here, in and of itself, is reason to doubt the entire "official" account of the Third Secret, as Socci does.[163] To quote

---

[162] *TMF*, p. 29.

[163] By "official account" I do not mean any teaching of the Holy Catholic Church regarding the Third Secret controversy, for there is no such teaching. As will become clear in the course of this discussion, the "official account" means nothing more than the representations of Cardinal Bertone and his collaborators in the Vatican apparatus, who have not been given any papal authority to bind the faithful to their version of the facts or their purported "interpretation" of the vision of the Third Secret. On the contrary, as we will see, the Pope has not intervened in this controversy, and the former Cardinal Ratzinger made it quite clear in 2000 that the commentary on the

Socci: "[B]ut Lucia would never have dared to establish herself a date to make it [the Secret] known to everybody: only the Madonna, who had imposed secrecy on the message, could do it."[164]

What about the Telltale "etc"?

And what of the famous "etc" in Sister Lucia's Fourth Memoir? To recall again Father Schweigl's testimony, the Third Secret includes the "logical continuation" of the Virgin's discourse following the phrase that ends with Sister Lucia's "etc"—"In Portugal, the dogma of the faith will always be preserved etc". In fact, the attention of Fatima scholars had always been focused on the "etc" as the key to the Third Secret, since it was obvious that the Virgin's words to the seers had not trailed off in the middle of a thought.

Yet, in a maneuver that has undermined all confidence in the official account, *TMF* evades any discussion of the "etc" by taking the text of the Message of Fatima from Sister Lucia's *Third* Memoir, where Our Lady's prophecy concerning Portugal does not appear, rather than the more complete Fourth Memoir. Like *TMF*'s attack on the credibility of the "express order of Our Lady" regarding 1960, this conspicuous avoidance of the Fourth Memoir could only engender suspicion. Why rely on the Third Memoir when the more complete Fourth Memoir was available? In his Introduction to *TMF* Bertone attempted to explain this curious behavior as follows: "For the account of the first two parts of the 'secret', which have already been published and are therefore known, we have chosen the text written by Sister Lucia in the Third Memoir of 31 August 1941; some *annotations* were added in the Fourth Memoir of 8 December 1941."[165] Significantly, Bertone's Introduction *does not specify* what is contained in these "annotations," which is none other than the very phrase of the Virgin he had to know was at the heart of the entire controversy.

According to *TMF*, then, the only difference between the Third and Fourth memoirs is "some annotations" by Sister Lucia, the suggestion being that no one should think it amiss that the drafters of *Message* had "chosen" the former document, which was not cluttered by these "annotations." The suggestion was less than honest, for the Virgin's words concerning the preservation of dogma in Portugal were manifestly not Lucia's "annotations" but *an integral part of the Fatima message*, immediately after which Our Lady Herself had said: "Tell this to no one. Yes, you may tell Francisco." Yet Bertone, having characterized the very words of the Virgin as "annotations", buries

---

Secret in *Message* has not been imposed upon the Church. Socci rightly recognizes that the faithful are at liberty to question the "official account."

[164] *The Fourth Secret of Fatima*, p. 38.

[165] *TMF*, p. 3.

the very words of the Mother of God in a footnote that *TMF* never mentions again.[166]

Socci calls attention to an evasive but extremely revealing comment by Bertone at the June 26th press conference. When asked about whether the "etc" is indeed the beginning of the Third Secret, Bertone stated to the press: "It is difficult to say if it [the "etc"] refers to the second or the third part of the secret [i.e., the Great Secret of July 13, 1917]... it seems to me that it pertains to the second."[167] The implications are astonishing: *Bertone does not deny that the "etc" could in fact be part of the Third Secret*, which would mean that the Third Secret includes the Virgin's *spoken words*. In a curious equivocation, Bertone stated that it "is difficult to say" whether this is so, and that it "seems" to him that the "etc" pertains to the second part of the Fatima message. It *seems* to him? Why would he not have determined the answer to this crucial question before the momentous Vatican presentation on June 26, given that he had a "conversation" with Sister Lucia concerning the content of the Third Secret only weeks before, on April 27, 2000, as his own Introduction to *TMF* reveals?[168]

Furthermore, even if it were the case that, as Bertone suggests, the "etc" pertains only to the Second Secret—i.e., the part of the Great Secret that predicts World War II, the spread of Russia's errors "throughout the world" and so forth—then it follows that the Vatican *has yet to reveal the Second Secret in its entirety*. Thus, no matter how it is viewed, Bertone's comment is a major blow to the credibility of the official account.

Socci poses the pertinent question: "How can one elude that explosive *incipit* [beginning] of the Virgin Mary as if it were a marginal 'annotation'?" There is, writes Socci, "a clear sense of a great embarrassment before a phrase of the Madonna that one cannot succeed in explaining and that one tries to remove silently."[169] Why the embarrassment? Because, as Socci and so many others have concluded, the "etc" is the gateway to the missing words of the Virgin that complete the Third Secret of Fatima. Hence the "etc" must be downplayed and ignored if the gateway is to remain closed.

A Telling Discrepancy

Bertone's Introduction to *TMF* contains another point that would prove to have decisive importance in the Third Secret controversy.

---

[166] *Message*, p. 15. The footnote reads: "In the 'Fourth Memoir' Sister Lucia adds: 'In Portugal, the dogma of the faith will always be preserved etc. ...'"

[167] *The Fourth Secret of Fatima*, p. 89; citing Aura Miguel, *Totus Tuus*, p. 141.

[168] *Message*, p. 8.

[169] *The Fourth Secret of Fatima*, pp. 75-76.

According to Bertone, John Paul II did not read the Third Secret until July 18, 1981, a full three years into his papacy, when the text of the Secret was taken from the Holy Office archives and brought to him at Gemelli Hospital, where the Pope was recovering from the assassination attempt.[170] But according to papal spokesman Joaquin Navarro-Valls, as reported by *The Washington Post*, John Paul II read the Third Secret *in 1978, within days of his election*.[171] There is no record, however, of any text of the Secret being brought to John Paul from the Holy Office archives in that year.

Thus, whatever text John Paul read in 1978 must have been located elsewhere—evidently in the papal apartment, as attested by the witnesses and photographs already cited (see Chapter 6). It is highly significant that *neither Navarro-Valls nor the Pope ever denied the report that the Pope had read the Secret in 1978*, even though (with explosive implications) that report flatly contradicted Bertone's own representations to the press.[172] But it could hardly be the case that John Paul II, the very Pope of Fatima, would have waited until three years after his election to read the Secret. This major discrepancy between the accounts of Bertone and Navarro-Valls in itself indicates the existence of two distinct but related texts of the Third Secret. (Cf. *The Devil's Final Battle*, Chapter 13, "The Third Secret Consists of Two Distinct Texts," for further explanation.)

Cardinal Sodano's "Preventative Interpretation"

The credulity of the faithful was strained past the breaking point by what Socci has called "the preventative interpretation" of the vision launched by Cardinal Sodano in May-June 2000—that is, an interpretation designed to prevent anyone from finding in the Third Secret what Sodano, Bertone and others did not wish them to find. Sodano, who had been busy covering up the Maciel scandal, journeyed to Fatima with the Pope in May 2000 to announce that the Secret would soon be published. Why did he, not the Pope, make the announcement, while the Pope sat behind him? Because Sodano was executing the Party Line, to which even the Pope had been induced to adhere. Sodano's announcement already suggested,

---

[170] *Message*, p. 5.

[171] Bill Broadway and Sarah Delancy, "3rd Secret Spurs More Questions; Fatima Interpretation Departs From Vision," *The Washington Post*, July 1, 2000: "On May 13, Vatican Spokesman Joaquin Navarro-Valls said the Pope first read the secret within days of assuming the papacy in 1978. On Monday, an aide to Cardinal Joseph Ratzinger [Bertone], Prefect of the Vatican's Congregation for the Doctrine of the Faith, said that the Pope first saw it in the hospital after his attack."

[172] The Associated Press, "Vatican: Fatima Is No Doomsday Prophecy," *The New York Times*, June 26, 2000: "'John Paul II read for the first time the text of the Third Secret of Fatima after the attack,' a top aide to Ratzinger, Monsignor Tarcisio Bertone, told journalists during a news conference to present the document."

in a "preventative" manner, that the Secret was nothing more than a prediction of events that had already come to pass, culminating in the 1981 attempt on the life of John Paul II. According to Sodano:

> The vision of Fatima concerns above all the war waged by atheist systems against the Church and Christians, and it describes the immense suffering endured by the witnesses to the faith *in the last century* of the second millennium. It is an interminable Way of the Cross led by the Popes of *the twentieth century.*
>
> According to the interpretation of the "little shepherds," which was also recently confirmed by Sister Lucia, the "bishop dressed in white" who prays for all the faithful is the Pope. As he makes his way with great effort towards the Cross amid the corpses of those who were martyred (bishops, priests, men and women religious and many lay persons), he too falls to the ground, *apparently* dead, under a burst of gunfire.
>
> After the assassination attempt of May 13, 1981, it appeared evident to His Holiness that it was "a motherly hand which guided the bullet's path," enabling the "dying Pope" to halt "at the threshold of death."…
>
> The successive events of 1989 led, both in the Soviet Union and in a number of countries of Eastern Europe, to the fall of the Communist regime which promoted atheism. For this too His Holiness offers heartfelt thanks to the Most Holy Virgin….
>
> *Even if the events to which the third part of the Secret of Fatima refers now seem part of the past,* Our Lady's call to conversion and penance, issued at the beginning of the twentieth century, remains timely and urgent today….[173]

In essence, Cardinal Sodano would reduce the Third Secret to the *Second* Secret—i.e., the second part of the Great Secret of July 13, 1917—which, as we saw in Chapter 1, predicted World War II, the spread of world Communism and the consequent persecution of the Church, the martyrdom of the faithful and the suffering of the Holy Father. But if the Third Secret merely predicts the very events Our Lady had already predicted in the Second Secret, what is the point of the Third Secret? Why would Sister Lucia have found it so difficult to commit the Third Secret to paper? Why would Our Lady have refrained from directing Sister Lucia to write down the Secret until 1944—*after* World War II and the spread of Communism were already well under way?

As for Sodano's claim that the Pope executed by soldiers outside a half-ruined city filled with bodies was John Paul II, it was manifest that Sodano had misled the public when he declared at Fatima

---

[173] Vatican Information Service, May 13, 2000.

the previous May that the Pope in the vision "falls to the ground, *apparently* dead, under a burst of gunfire." In truth, the Pope in the vision "*was killed* by a group of soldiers who fired bullets and arrows at him" outside the half-ruined city. John Paul II, on the other hand, was *not* killed by a lone assassin during the attempt that took place in a perfectly intact Saint Peter's Square.

Any attempt on the life of a Pope is a grave affair, and John Paul II had suffered greatly at the hands of his would-be assassin. Nevertheless, the Pope had completely recovered from his wounds and resumed an active life that included skiing and hiking in the Italian Alps and swimming in the built-in pool he had installed at Castelgandolfo shortly after his election. His physical condition after recovery was rightly described as "impressive."[174] The Pope's death *a quarter century* after the attempt resulted from the complications of Parkinson's disease, not the shot fired by Ali Agca in 1981. Moreover, why would Our Lady of Fatima give an "express order" (to recall Sister Lucia's writing on the envelope) that the Secret be revealed in 1960, when that year has no relation to the 1981 assassination attempt or to *any other particular* in the vision? In short, the suggestion that John Paul II is the Pope in the vision is not merely a "stretch," it is patently unbelievable. Sodano had blatantly twisted the content of the vision to suit his contrived interpretation.

It should go without saying that Catholics are not required to accept Sodano's "interpretation." As Cardinal Ratzinger stated during the June 26th press conference: "*It is not the intention of the Church to impose a single interpretation.*"[175] Ratzinger's own commentary in *TMF* would speak only of "attempting" an interpretation. And, ironically enough, *TMF*'s own supporting documentation demolishes Sodano's patently unsustainable construction. Bertone's Introduction cites a purported letter from Sister Lucia to John Paul II in 1982 regarding the contents of the Secret. Curiously, both the translation and the photo-reproduction of the original handwriting appended to *TMF* present only a fragment of the purported letter, without any address or salutation to the Pope or signature by Sister Lucia. The attempt on the Pope's life is not mentioned even glancingly in the fragmentary

---

[174] "He has been a terrific sportsman," said George Weigel, author of a biography of John Paul. Weigel said the Pope had a swimming pool built at his summer residence at Castelgandolfo during the first summer of his papacy. "The story goes that he justified it by saying it was cheaper than building a new conclave," he said. "The first 15 years of his pontificate [i.e., until 1993, 12 years after the assassination attempt] he took breaks to go skiing, and the miracle about that was the Italian paparazzi actually left him alone." Quoted in "Pontiff Was Sportsman as Well as Leader," Associated Press, March 4, 2005. After the assassination attempt the Pope "went on to a full recovery, and sported an impressive physical condition throughout the 1980s." *Pope John Paul*, Short Biography at wikipedia.com.

[175] "Vatican releases additional Fatima information," United Press International, June 27, 2000.

text, and there is nothing about the fragment to indicate that it was meant for the Pope as opposed to anyone else. But here, in pertinent part, is what the fragment says:

> Since we did not heed this appeal of the Message, we see that it has been fulfilled; Russia has invaded the world with her errors. And if *we have not yet seen the complete fulfillment of the final part of this prophecy*, we are going towards it little by little with great strides....[176]

That is, in *TMF*—the very document which argues that the vision of the bishop in white depicts the assassination attempt—Sister Lucia herself is quoted to the effect that, fully a year *after* the attempt, we have *not yet seen* the complete fulfillment of the Third Secret. Furthermore, Lucia makes *no reference whatsoever* to the attempt. As the fragment from the letter shows, the attempt was not even on Sister Lucia's "radar" in 1982, much less at the very center of her understanding of the Secret.

It must be noted that the Portuguese original of this strange epistolary fragment contains a phrase that negates any possibility it was addressed to John Paul II: "The third part of the secret, *that you are so anxious to know*, is a symbolic revelation..." It could not possibly be the case that in 1982 John Paul II was "so anxious to know" the Third Secret, because by all accounts he had already read it by then. The words "that you are so anxious to know" reveal beyond doubt that the addressee of the purported 1982 letter was someone other than the Pope. But, attention: The English and other translations of the fragment in *Message* all *omit the words* "that you are so anxious to know" so that the phrase reads simply: "The third part of the secret is a symbolic revelation" followed by the remainder of the sentence.[177] No ellipses are used to indicate the omission, as honesty would require. The systematic excision of the key phrase from translation after translation could only be a calculated deception. It would require a Portuguese reader, closely examining the photo-reproduced fragment, to discover the ruse.[178]

Ratzinger Follows Sodano—But Why?

Despite these enormous problems with Sodano's "preventative interpretation," Cardinal Ratzinger's theological commentary in *Message* adopts it uncritically, albeit while acknowledging that it is only an "attempt" at an interpretation:

---

[176] *TMF*, p. 9.

[177] Ibid., p. 8.

[178] From the English translation: "The third part of the secret [deleted: "that you are so anxious to know"] is a symbolic revelation..." The photo-reproduced fragment reads: "A terceira parte do Segredo, *que tanto ansiais por conhecer* [that you are so anxious to know], e uma revelacao simbolica ..." *Message*, p. 9.

Before attempting an interpretation, the main lines of which can be found in the statement read by *Cardinal Sodano* on 13 May of this year ...[179]

For this reason the figurative language of the vision is symbolic. In this regard *Cardinal Sodano* stated ...[180]

As is clear from the documentation presented here, the interpretation offered by *Cardinal Sodano*, in his statement on 13 May...[181]

First of all we must affirm *with Cardinal Sodano*...[182]

Cardinal Ratzinger's commentary follows Sodano in pronouncing the Third Secret a thing of the past:

A careful reading of the text of the so-called third 'secret' of Fatima, published here in its entirety long after the fact and by decision of the Holy Father, will probably prove disappointing or surprising after all the speculation it has stirred. No great mystery is revealed; nor is the future unveiled. We see the Church of the martyrs of the century which has just passed represented in a scene described in a language which is symbolic and not easy to decipher.

We must affirm with Cardinal Sodano that the events to which the third part of the 'secret' of Fatima refers now seem part of the past. Insofar as individual events are described, *they belong to the past.*[183]

These affirmations are plainly impossible to accept, for if the vision reveals "no great mystery" and concerns only 20th century events, there would have been no reason to keep it under lock and key at the Vatican since 1957, or to declare in 1960 that it would be kept "forever under absolute seal." Nor would there have been any reason for Cardinal Ratzinger to have declared in 1984 that the Secret speaks of "dangers threatening the faith and the life of the Christian and therefore of the world."

There is a mystery here: Cardinal Sodano's competence to "interpret" the Secret is never explained. The Vatican Secretary of State has no doctrinal authority over the Church, and Sodano did not receive any papal authority to undertake his "interpretation," which is presented as a mere "attempt" to explain the vision. Why, then, was Sodano even involved in the matter? We already know the answer: the ascendancy of the Vatican Secretary of State to the level of a veritable "prime minister" of the Church in keeping with the radical

---

[179] *TMF*, p. 32.
[180] Ibid., p. 38.
[181] Ibid., p. 39.
[182] Ibid., p. 42.
[183] Ibid., pp. 32, 42.

restructuring of the Roman Curia carried out by Cardinal Villot after Vatican II.[184] The Party Line on Fatima would now extend to the Third Secret. Just as the Secretary of State had declared—without authority—that the Consecration of Russia was over and done with, so had he arrogated to himself the "interpretation" of the vision. This is why even Cardinal Ratzinger, then head of the Congregation for the Doctrine of the Faith, deferred to Sodano as "prime minister" when he had no moral or doctrinal obligation to do so.

Did Our Lady Give Us a Cipher?

Sodano's "interpretation" of the Third Secret was said to be necessary because, as Cardinal Ratzinger states in his commentary, the vision is "not easy to decipher." But were the faithful really expected to believe that in 1917 the Blessed Virgin gave the visionaries a *cipher* that would have to be *de*ciphered by—of all people—the Vatican Secretary of State in 2000? That hardly seemed consistent with the clarity and detail of the Second Secret, which, as we have seen, predicted a whole train of clearly specified *future* events: the end of one war and the beginning of another "worse" war following an unknown light in the night sky; the very name of the Pope who would reign in the days leading up to that war; the very name of the nation that would spread its errors throughout the world; precise admonitions concerning war, famine, persecutions of the Church, the martyrdom of the good, the suffering of the Holy Father and the annihilation of various nations; and the ultimate conversion of Russia and the triumph of the Immaculate Heart.

The "not easy to decipher" vision would *not* require deciphering, however, if—as with the first two parts of the Great Secret of Fatima—there are *words* of the Virgin to explain it, as opposed to Vatican prelates "attempting an interpretation, the main lines of which can be found in the statement read by Cardinal Sodano on 13 May of this year ..."[185] The very claim that the Third Secret could not be understood without an "interpretation" suggested by Cardinal Sodano only demonstrated that there must be something more to the Secret than the vision standing alone.

Dispensing with the Consecration of Russia

Lest the Party Line concerning the Consecration of Russia be forgotten, Bertone's Introduction to *TMF* purports to enlist Sister Lucia for the proposition that Pope John Paul II's consecration of the world in 1984 sufficed for a consecration of Russia: "Sister

---

[184] For a detailed discussion of this development see *The Devil's Final Battle*, Chapter 8 (also at http://www.devilsfinalbattle.com/ch8.htm).

[185] *TMF*, p. 32.

Lucia personally confirmed that this solemn and universal act of consecration corresponded to what Our Lady wished.... Hence any further discussion or request [for the Consecration of Russia] is without basis."[186] But how could Sister Lucia "confirm" that the same sort of ceremony that did not suffice during the reigns of Pius XII and Paul VI—a consecration of the world with no mention of Russia and no participation by the world episcopate—was suddenly sufficient?[187]

Curiously, Bertone cites only one solitary piece of evidence in support of his claim: a purported letter from Sister Lucia, identified only as "Letter of 8 November 1989," in which Sister Lucia is alleged to have written: "'Yes it has been done just as Our Lady asked, on 25 March 1984" (*"Sim, està feita, tal como Nossa Senhora a pediu, desde o dia 25 de Março de 1984"*).[188] Even more curious: the addressee of the letter is not identified, nor is a copy of it provided as part of *Message*'s supporting documentation.

As already noted, the purported letter, generated by a computer at the dawn of the personal computer age, contained a blatant error: a statement by "Sister Lucia" that Paul VI consecrated the world to the Immaculate Heart during his visit to Fatima in 1967, when in truth he had consecrated nothing at all on that occasion. Sister Lucia, who was present throughout the Pope's visit, would hardly have made such a mistake. Nor was it credible that an elderly cloistered nun, who had written thousands of letters by hand over her lifetime, would suddenly switch to a word processor at age 80 to peck out a one-page note to a Mr. Noelker, especially when even many business offices in Portugal were without personal computers at that time.[189]

Still more curious: the dubious "letter of 8 November 1989" was the only evidence Bertone cited even though, as *TMF* states, Bertone had "conversed" with Sister Lucia on April 27, 2000, only two months earlier, and could have obtained her direct testimony on this question at that time—or indeed at any other time. The failure to cite *any* direct testimony by Lucia, when such testimony was readily

---

[186] *TMF*, p. 8.

[187] Concerning the consecration of the world by Pius XII and several bishops on October 31, 1942, Sister Lucia wrote: "The Good Lord has already shown me His contentment with the act performed by the Holy Father and several bishops, *although it was incomplete according to His desire*. In return He promises to end the war soon. The conversion of Russia is not for now." Letter to the Bishop of Gurza, February 28, 1943; quoted in *The Whole Truth About Fatima*, Vol. III, pp. 60-61.

[188] *TMF*, p. 8.

[189] Flatly contradicting himself, Bertone would admit seven years later that Sister Lucia "never worked with the computer." *See The Last Visionary of Fatima*, p. 101 ("Sister Lucia never worked with the computer, nor visited any website.") This is one of the many self-contradictions in which the Cardinal has embroiled himself, as Socci has noted.

obtainable, speaks volumes. And note well: During the April 2000 "conversation" Bertone *did not ask Sister Lucia to authenticate the "Letter of 8 November 1989"*, even though Bertone had to have known of the worldwide circulation of articles by Father Gruner's apostolate decisively debunking the letter.[190] The only reasonable inference is that Lucia was not asked to authenticate the letter because the letter was indeed a fake that could not be authenticated.

To knowledgeable Catholics, it was not surprising that Bertone had been forced to rely *entirely* on a non-authenticated and previously publicly debunked 11-year-old "letter" to an unidentified addressee. That purported letter was the only thing Bertone could pit against a lifetime of contrary testimony by Sister Lucia, which we have already surveyed.[191]

A Funeral for Fatima?

All in all, Sodano's "preventative interpretation" was patently designed to consign the Third Secret in particular and the Fatima message in general to the dustbin of history, evidently in the hope that all questions would cease after June 26, 2000. Following Sodano's lead, Bertone's Introduction goes so far as to declare:

> The decision of His Holiness Pope John Paul II to make public the third part of the 'secret' of Fatima brings to an end a period of history marked by tragic human lust for power and evil, yet pervaded by the merciful love of God and the watchful care of the Mother of Jesus and of the Church.

Not only is the Message of Fatima consigned to the past, but also the very lust for power and evil! But if the Pope had brought an end to the era of the lust for power and evil by publishing the vision of the "Bishop dressed in White" in the year 2000, why had he not ended that same tragic era by publishing the vision much sooner, indeed at the first opportunity? Bertone, however inadvertently, makes a mockery of the Vatican's suppression of the Third Secret for so many years.

Even worse than *TMF*'s defense of the "preventative interpretation" is its suggestion that Sister Lucia's entire witness might be suspect. The theological commentary cites one, and only one, "authority" on Fatima: the late Flemish theologian Edouard

---

[190] This letter was published and critiqued on pp. 10-11 of the May 1990 (No. 229) issue of *The Catholic Counter-Reformation* (CRC, English edition, published by Maison Saint-Joseph, F-10260 Saint-Parres-lès-Vaudes). This critique was explicitly referenced in *The Fatima Crusader*, No. 35 (Winter 1990-91), with a circulation of some 500,000 copies, in a story debunking the Noelker letter (on pp. 12ff, or at www.fatimacrusader.com/cr35/cr35pg12.asp).

[191] For a detailed presentation of Lucia's testimony from 1946-1987, see *The Devil's Final Battle*, Chapter 8 (also at http://www.devilsfinalbattle.com/ch8.htm).

Dhanis, S.J., whom the commentary identifies as an "eminent scholar" in the field of "private revelations." Cardinal Ratzinger knew, of course, that Dhanis, a modernist Jesuit, made a veritable career out of casting doubt on the Fatima apparitions. Dhanis proposed that everything in the Message of Fatima beyond a call for prayer and penance was cobbled together in the minds of the three children from things they had seen or heard in their own lives. Dhanis thus categorized as "Fatima II" all those things the "eminent scholar" arbitrarily rejected as fabrications—without ever once interviewing Sister Lucia or studying the official Fatima archives. Dhanis, in fact, flatly refused to speak to the seer or study the archives when invited to do so.[192] His intellectual honesty is non-existent when it comes to Fatima.

As Dhanis put it: "All things considered, it is not easy to state precisely what degree of credence is to be given to the accounts of Sister Lucia. Without questioning her sincerity, or the sound judgment she shows in daily life, one may judge it prudent to use her writings only with reservations. ... Let us observe also that a good person can be sincere and prove to have good judgment in everyday life, but have a *propensity for unconscious fabrication* in a certain area, or in any case, a tendency to relate old memories of twenty years ago with embellishments and considerable modifications."[193] In other words, according to Dhanis, Sister Lucia was a very sincere and pious fake.

Yet Dhanis, neo-modernist debunker of the Message of Fatima, is the one and only "eminent scholar" cited by *Message*'s theological commentary on the meaning of the Third Secret and the Fatima message as a whole. The commentary even follows Dhanis' methodology by suggesting that, after all, Sister Lucia may have concocted the vision from things she had seen as a child: "The concluding part of the 'secret' uses images which Lucia may have seen in devotional books and which draw their inspiration from long-standing intuitions of faith."[194] But if that were true of the images in the vision of the bishop in white, it could also be true of any and all aspects of the Fatima apparitions. With a single sentence inserted into the middle of things, the commentary, like Dhanis, undermines the credibility—at least in the minds of a gullible public—not only of the Third Secret proper, but the entirety of the Message of Fatima. No wonder the headline in the *Los Angeles Times* read: "The Vatican's Top Theologian Gently Debunks a Nun's Account of Her 1917 Vision

---

[192] See Frère Michel de la Sainte Trinité, "Part II: The Critical Study of Fatima," *The Whole Truth About Fatima,* Vol. I: *The Science and the Facts,* pp. 381-535.

[193] Dhanis' attack on the veracity of the Fatima message is explained and critiqued in more detail in *The Whole Truth About Fatima,* Vol. I, Part II, Chapter 1. All quotations of Dhanis are from this source.

[194] *TMF,* p. 42.

that Fueled Decades of Speculation."[195] Even the secular press could see what was going on: the attempt at a funeral for Fatima.

Bouquets of False Friendship

What was obvious to the secular press—that Sodano, Bertone and Ratzinger wished to be done with Fatima—was certainly obvious to Catholics who believed in the Message of Fatima and knew that its imperatives had been ignored on account of that same "blindness of the pastors" remarked by Antonio Socci.

And yet, in the usual style of those we call here the false friends of Fatima, *TMF* abounds in professions of respect for the Fatima event, while "remodeling" it to suit the Party Line. Hence Cardinal Sodano's announcement at Fatima on May 13, 2000, included in *TMF*, speaks of "Our Lady's call to conversion and penance... [which] remains timely and urgent today" and "[t]he insistent invitation of Mary Most Holy to penance" as "the manifestation of her maternal concern for the fate of the human family, in need of conversion and forgiveness..." Even as he was in the process of purging from the Fatima message the very prescriptions the Virgin had given for the protection of the Church and the world from calamity and the salvation of souls—the Consecration of Russia and the Third Secret—Sodano was exhorting his "brothers and sisters" to "thank Our Lady of Fatima for her protection. To her maternal intercession let us entrust the Church of the Third Millennium."

With a grand rhetorical flourish, Sodano even added some Latin, although the Roman liturgy had long since been ruthlessly stripped of that "dead" language in the name of Vatican II: "Sub tuum praesidium confugimus, Sancta Dei Genetrix! Intercede pro Ecclesia. Intercede pro Papa nostro Ioanne Paulo II. Amen." Translation: "We gather together under your care, Holy Mother of God. Intercede for the Church. Intercede for our Pope John Paul II"—the same Pope who had been induced by Sodano and his collaborators to eschew the intervention of the Mother of God by the consecration of Russia to Her Immaculate Heart.

In like manner, Archbishop Bertone, the man who would be Sodano's successor, offered pious sentiments concerning "The action of God, the Lord of history, and the co-responsibility of man in the drama of his creative freedom," adding that "Our Lady, who appeared at Fatima, recalls these forgotten values. She reminds us that man's future is in God, and that we are active and responsible partners in creating that future." Our Lady of Fatima was thus lowered to the level of a kind of high-powered "life coach," who came to Fatima to provide some generic advice on how we can better cooperate with

---

[195] *Los Angeles Times*, June 27, 2000.

God by recovering "values" that will help us to improve the human condition.

Finally, then Cardinal Ratzinger offered this strange rendering of the dogma of the Immaculate Conception of Mary and its relation to the Third Secret:

> I would like finally to mention another key expression of the "secret" which has become justly famous: "my Immaculate Heart will triumph". What does this mean? The Heart open to God, purified by contemplation of God, is stronger than guns and weapons of every kind. The fiat of Mary, the word of her heart, has changed the history of the world, because it brought the Saviour into the world—because, thanks to her Yes, God could become man in our world and remains so for all time.

The very core of the Message of Fatima—devotion to the Immaculate Heart—was thus facilely equated with prayer and contemplation of God by individual Catholics, whose personal purification of heart would be what overcomes the threat of war and destruction. There would be no need to worry about effecting a specific consecration of Russia to *Mary's* Immaculate Heart to avoid the annihilation of nations of which Our Lady of Fatima had warned. Nor would there by any need to worry about the content of the Fatima message that so alarmed the future Pius XII, when he foresaw in the light of Fatima the "suicide" of the Catholic Church by means of altering the Faith in the liturgy, theology and soul of the Church.

And so on June 26, 2000 the Message of Fatima was piously invoked by those who seemed to be its friends, even as it was stripped entirely of its prophetic content, its warnings to the Church and the world, and reduced to only a prescription for personal piety and holiness.

Exit Our Lady, Enter Gorbachev

The Third Secret having been "gently debunked" on June 26, "Prime Minister" Sodano immediately got down to what he considered the serious business of the Church. The very next day none other than Mikhail Gorbachev appeared at a Vatican press conference, seated as a guest of honor between Cardinals Sodano and Silvestrini, the Vatican diplomat who was instrumental in carrying out the policy of *Ostpolitik*—i.e., conciliating instead of confronting Communist regimes that oppress the Church. Gorbachev had come to the Vatican to help promote the posthumous publication of the memoirs of Cardinal Casaroli, the foremost architect of *Ostpolitik* and Cardinal Sodano's predecessor in office.[196] No questions from the press were permitted at this curious press conference—a press

---

[196] "Gorbachev Helps Introduce Casaroli Memoirs," *Catholic World News*, June 27, 2000.

conference without questions from the press! Evidently, Sodano wanted to be certain that no one inquired about the Third Secret, or why the Vatican was honoring the likes of Gorbachev, a man who admits he is still a Leninist and whose tax-free foundations are promoting the use of abortion and contraception to eliminate billions of people from the world's population.[197]

What can one conclude from all of this but that the Party Line of "prime minister" Sodano, soon to be carried forward by his successor, Cardinal Bertone, is radically inconsistent with the Message of Fatima, "that great sign of contradiction that makes evident a kind of blinding of the pastors"? And what Sodano and Bertone would impose from above would continue to be advanced by their allies below.

The Continuing Plot Against Our Lady of Fatima

Two False Friends of Fatima Meet
Cardinal Sodano (on right) and Carlos Evaristo (on left).

---

[197] In September 1995, Gorbachev held his "State of the World Forum" in San Francisco. Over 4000 of the world's "elite" paid $5,000 per person to attend the 5-day event. In a closing plenary session of the forum, a philosopher/author named Sam Keen provided a summary and concluding remarks on the conference. It reveals the forum's anti-life, anti-Christian ethos. To the conference participants, Keen said: "There was very strong agreement that religious institutions have to take the primary responsibility for the population explosion. We must speak far more clearly about sexuality, about contraception, about abortion, about the values that control the population, because the ecological crisis, in short, is the population crisis. *Cut the population by 90 percent and there aren't enough people left to do a great deal of ecological damage.*" *See* "World's Elite Gather to Talk Depopulation," John Henry Western, *The Interim*, April 1996.

Chapter 8

FATHER FOX'S MODERNIST MESSAGE OF FATIMA

After the famous press conference of June 26, 2000 with its attempted "funeral for Fatima," the Secretary of State's Party Line on Fatima underwent a development to incorporate the "official" version of the Third Secret, which (as we saw in the previous chapter) was not "official" at all but represented only an "attempt" at an "interpretation" by Cardinal Sodano, who had no authority in the matter in the first place. Now the Party Line was thus:

First, the Third Secret has been revealed entirely in the form of the enigmatic vision of the "Bishop dressed in White" as "interpreted" for us by none other than the Secretary of State, who opines that the vision relates only to events of the 20th century culminating in the failed attempt on the life of John Paul II in 1981 and that it contains no prophetic warnings for the Church or mankind.

Second, the consecration of Russia was accomplished in 1984 by means of a ceremony that made no mention of Russia but which, insists the Secretary of State, complies with Our Lady of Fatima's request for Russia's consecration.

Third, since the Secret has been revealed and the consecration done, the prophetic content of the Message of Fatima now belongs to the past and "what remains" is only "the summons to penance and conversion."[198] To recall Sodano's announcement at Fatima on May 13, 2000 concerning the impending publication of the vision on June 26, 2000: "Even if the events to which the third part of the 'secret' of Fatima refers now seem part of the past, Our Lady's call to conversion and penance, issued at the start of the twentieth century, remains timely and urgent today."[199]

In short, as of 2000 the Party Line in its totality could be summed up in one phrase: "Fatima is finished." At least so the Secretary of State would have it, applying pressure from above. And, true to form, members of the party of the innovators among the rank-and-file clergy and laity would adhere to the Party Line, applying pressure from below by dutifully attacking faithful Catholics who declined to go along with the Secretary of State's expedient human revision of

---

[198] *The Message of Fatima* (2000), "Theological Commentary," www.vatican.va/roman_curia/congregations/cfaith/documents/rc_con_cfaith_doc_20000626_message-fatima_en.html

[199] "Announcement by Cardinal Angelo Sodano, Secretary of State," in *The Message of Fatima (TMF).*

Our Lady's heavenly message.

No one among the rank and file clergy set himself more eagerly to the task of enforcing the Party Line than the late Father Robert J. Fox (1927-2009). It is fair to say that Father Fox's "Fatima Family Apostolate" became the exact antithesis of Father Gruner's Fatima Center. That is, it was dedicated to the work of obliterating the authentic Message of Fatima while preserving the appearance of a pious attachment to it. As early as 1989, when the first order came down from the Vatican (not the Pope) that no one must seek any longer the Consecration of Russia, Father Fox had been proclaiming Russia's non-existent conversion following the 1984 ceremony which made no mention of Russia. Father Gruner, of course, had done just the opposite: warning that Our Lady's request had yet to be heeded, as one can hardly consecrate a particular place while deliberately avoiding any mention of it, and that the Church and the world would suffer the consequences of fallible men playing games with the consecration the Mother of God had specified on God's authority.

Father Fox's defense of the Party Line necessarily placed him in direct conflict with Father Gruner. The conflict reached a fevered pitch in the April-June 2004 issue of Fox's *Immaculate Heart Messenger*. Citing the many letters he had received objecting to his position on Fatima, Father Fox devoted two articles and six pages to an attack on Father Gruner. As do all partisans of the Party Line, Fox avoided the merits of Father Gruner's eminently reasonable claim that a consecration of Russia requires *mention* of Russia. Instead, he descended to character assassination.

Fr. Fox's Argumentum Ad Hominem

"Father Gruner—A Suspended Catholic Priest," screamed the headline of one of the stories. Here we go again. We have already seen (*see* Chapter 3) that Father Gruner was not "suspended," but rather was the victim of a canonical ruse engineered by Secretary of State Sodano, which failed when Father Gruner achieved incardination in the Diocese of Hyderabad without objection by the Bishop of Avellino, who had no interest in Father Gruner's "return" to Italy after an approved absence of sixteen years. And, it must be stressed again, *the Vatican itself has never taken any disciplinary action against Father Gruner*. Rather, the Congregation for the Clergy has merely pointed to the Bishop of Avellino, who in turn has done nothing to contradict or countermand Father Gruner's valid incardination in Hyderabad.

That the "suspension" of Father Gruner is non-existent was clearly recognized by no less than the Pope's personal secretary for forty years, Archbishop Stanislaw Dziwisz. In 1996 Archbishop

Dziwisz, in a moment captured by a photographer for *L'Osservatore Romano*, was personally handed a copy of Father Gruner's canonical recourse to the Pope, detailing the Secretary of State's machinations. Thereafter, Archbishop Dziwisz sent Father Gruner personal notes of encouragement for his work on three different occasions. The last was a note of January 12, 2004 in which the Pope's secretary acknowledged Father Gruner's Christmas greeting by conveying "prayerful good wishes and blessing for the New Year to you *and the faithful entrusted to your care at The Fatima Center.*" Now the Pope's secretary receives many thousands of Christmas greetings at the Vatican, yet he responded to Father Gruner's greeting with a personal note, addressed to "*Father* Nicholas Gruner," referring to and encouraging his work at the Fatima Center. The Pope's secretary, who is well aware of Father Gruner's situation, would hardly send a *series* of such notes to a "suspended priest."

But even if we assume for the sake of argument that Father Gruner were "suspended," what would that have to do with whether the Consecration of Russia has been accomplished? Nothing, of course. As Fr. Fox well knew, he was engaging in an illegitimate *argumentum ad hominem*, attacking the man rather than addressing the merits of the man's arguments—the oldest and cheapest debating trick. It behooved Father Fox to address the merits of the Fatima controversy in a manly manner, instead of kicking his adversary in the shins and running away. To the end, however, he avoided any attempt to confront the overwhelming documentary and testimonial evidence against his position and in support of Father Gruner's position.

Who Wasted Millions of Dollars?

Rather, the shin-kicking continued with Fr. Fox's arch observation that "It would be interesting to see how many millions of dollars Father Gruner has collected over the years…" What did the amount of donations to Father Gruner's apostolate have to do with whether Russia has been consecrated to the Immaculate Heart of Mary? Nothing, of course. At any rate, Father Gruner has not "collected" one penny. The donations to his apostolate are made to a non-profit organization of which Father Gruner is president, and the amount of those donations is a matter of public record.

It must be said that Fr. Fox's question about millions of dollars in donations could fairly have been turned against him: How many millions did Fr. Fox raise to promote the delusion that a consecration of the world is just the same as a consecration of Russia? How much money did he and other similarly situated advocates of the Party Line spend trying to persuade Catholics that the current state of

Russia, the world and the Church represents the fulfillment of Our Lady's promises at Fatima? How much money has been squandered to support a misguided effort to *delay fulfillment of Our Lady's request* by promoting the fiction that Her request has already been honored? Why should any Catholic give money to a "Fatima apostolate" that *works against* the Triumph of the Immaculate Heart by impeding the Consecration of Russia that will bring it about?

A Simple Request Unheeded

If words have meaning, then the words of Our Lady of Fatima do not correspond to the Party Line, imposed from above, that Father Fox assiduously promoted from below. Aside from the lifelong testimony of Sister Lucy, already noted, that the Consecration of Russia must mention Russia, we note here that Sister Lucy explained that the object of the Consecration must be Russia, *specifically and distinctly*, because when that particular nation is converted following a ceremony consecrating only that nation to Mary, it will be obvious to everyone that Heaven has deigned to produce this miracle in honor of Her Immaculate Heart. As Sister Lucy revealed to her confessor on May 18, 1936: "Recently, I asked Our Lord why He would not convert Russia without the Pope making that consecration." Our Lord deigned to answer her, as Sister Lucy recorded in her letters: "Because I want My whole Church to recognize that consecration as a triumph of the Immaculate Heart of Mary in order that My Church will later on place devotion to the Immaculate Heart beside devotion to My Sacred Heart."

What is there about the Virgin's request that is difficult to understand? Nothing at all. Even a child can understand it, which is why it was delivered to three simple children who could not even read. For as Our Lord Himself said (with the contemptibly sophisticated Pharisees in view): "Suffer the little children, and forbid them not to come to Me: for the kingdom of heaven is for such... Verily I say unto you, Whosoever shall not receive the kingdom of God as a little child, he shall not enter therein." (Matt. 19:13, 10:16).

The Pope's advisors, however, seem to be under the impression that God sent His Mother to earth to ask for a gratuitous insult to the Russian Orthodox and a gesture that might provoke war— an absurdity we will address in Chapter 13. And so, instead of a Consecration of Russia, these papal advisors have given us substitute ceremonies from which any mention of Russia was deliberately omitted so that *no one would think Russia was being consecrated*. This, according to Fr. Fox and like-minded low-level defenders of the Party Line, is what Our Lady requested at Fatima.

The Neo-Modernist Deconstruction of Fatima

The failure to consecrate Russia to the Immaculate Heart of Mary for fear of offending the schismatic Russian Orthodox and the Moscow regime is only part and parcel of the disastrous liberalization of the human element of the Church carried forward by the party of the innovators whose program we have already sketched. We have noted thematically that the Consecration has been impeded by the novelties of "ecumenism" and "dialogue" which suddenly appeared in the Church during and after the Council. And we have seen that too late did Paul VI recognize that "the opening to the world has become a veritable invasion of the Church by worldly thinking." When all is said and done, it is worldly thinking—or, to be more precise, *Modernist* thinking—that has prevented the consecration of Russia since the Council's close.

Recall that a Modernist is one who practices the subtle art of undermining the Catholic Faith, not through blatant heresies that are easily identified, but rather ambiguities, studied omissions of truth, and "modern ways of speaking." By these means, the Modernist seeks to change the traditional meaning of Catholic terminology so that, in the end, the Faith is totally destroyed, just as a house is totally destroyed by the activity of termites, even though it still has the outward appearance of solidity.

Recall as well that in *Pascendi* (1907), discussed in Chapter 1, Pope St. Pius X succinctly defined Modernism—and the definition applies with equal force to today's neo-Modernists—as nothing less than "the synthesis of all heresies." As that sainted Pope declared: "Were one to attempt the task of collecting together all the errors that have been broached against the Faith and to concentrate the sap and substance of them all into one, he could not better succeed than the Modernists have done."

The basic technique of the Modernist is to pay lip service to Catholic verities—such as those enunciated in the Message of Fatima—while undermining them completely. The false appearance of orthodoxy is what makes Modernism so dangerous to the Faith. The heretics of old, such as Martin Luther, did not hesitate to proclaim their heresies openly and explicitly, thus subjecting themselves to exclusion from the commonwealth of the Church, once the Church had exposed and condemned their clear errors as heresy. The Modernist, however, is a far cleverer fellow. He endeavors to remain within the Church while attempting to bring her into line with his heretical views, passed off under the guise of seemingly Catholic terminology.

As St. Pius X warned in *Pascendi*, these ecclesial termites "are striving, by arts *entirely new and full of subtlety*, to destroy the vital energy of the Church, and, if they can, to overthrow utterly Christ's kingdom itself." Their principal technique, said Pius, is to appear to affirm Catholic truth at one moment, only to cast doubt upon it in the next by means of ambiguity or studied omission: "Hence in their books you find some things which might well be expressed by a Catholic, but on the next page you find other things which might have been dictated by a rationalist. When they write history they make no mention of the divinity of Christ, but when they are in the pulpit they profess it clearly; again, when they write history they pay no heed to the Fathers and the Councils, but when they catechise the people, they cite them respectfully."

St. Pius X noted how the Modernists, professing loyalty to the Magisterium, "express astonishment" at being exposed as enemies of the Faith. Nevertheless, they are "the most pernicious of all the adversaries of the Church. For as We have said, they put their designs for her ruin into operation not from without but from within; hence, the danger is present almost in the very veins and heart of the Church, whose injury is the more certain, the more intimate is their knowledge of her."

The key, then, to the great advance of Modernism in the post-conciliar period is that it is being carried forward by men who inhabit the very veins and heart of the Church, and who hold themselves out as exemplars of sound orthodoxy—and may even believe that they are!—even as they empty orthodoxy of its objective content. As Pius X made clear, Modernists can succeed in eating away at Catholic doctrine only to the extent they are able to cloak themselves in ecclesiastical legitimacy and respectability, thus persuading the faithful that they speak the mind of the Church and ought to be followed. That is why Pius called for the Oath Against Modernism to be taken by every Catholic priest and theologian, and for the exposure and removal of Modernists from every position of authority in the Church. After Vatican II, however, the Oath Against Modernism was abandoned by Paul VI, along with any systematic effort to eliminate Modernists from positions of authority. We have seen the results of this aspect of "the opening to the world." And we have seen the results with the Party Line concerning Fatima, which produces a Modernist version of the Fatima message.

The Modernist "Consecration of Russia"

Father Fox is no longer with us, and may God rest his soul. But in his time, he was emblematic of how, at the level of the rank-and-file clergy, the Modernist *modus operandi* produced an "interpretation" of the Fatima message that, like Ratzinger's theological commentary in *TMF*, is really an attempt to debunk it. Fr. Fox paid lip service to Fatima at the same time he eviscerated its prophetic content, leaving nothing that would offend the proponents of "ecumenism" and "dialogue"—Fr. Fox included. Let us see how Fr. Fox did what he did.

First there was Fr. Fox's Modernist "interpretation" of the Consecration of Russia. To "consecrate" means to set a place or thing apart for a sacred purpose. We have already mentioned the self-evident fact that in order to consecrate a place, one must *mention* the place being consecrated. It would be absurd for a bishop to insist that he could consecrate a new cathedral by consecrating his whole diocese without mentioning the cathedral, on the theory that the cathedral is part of the diocese. Yet Fr. Fox, following the Party Line, seriously proposed that the Pope could consecrate Russia by consecrating the world, *even if all mention of Russia is deliberately avoided* so as not to offend the Orthodox.

In support of his claim, Fr. Fox trotted out what he claimed was "a personal letter from Sister Lucia saying that the Collegial Consecration was accomplished" by the 1984 ceremony deliberately omitting any mention of Russia. This "personal letter" (from 1990) was one of five "personal letters" generated by a word processor and purportedly signed by Sister Lucia, who did not type letters on word processors but rather wrote her entire voluminous correspondence (not to mention hundreds of pages of memoirs) by hand. We have already noted that one of these "personal letters," to a Mr. Noelker in November of 1989 (*see* Chapter 3), states that during his visit to Fatima in 1967 Pope Paul VI consecrated the world to the Immaculate Heart—an event that never happened. Since Sister Lucy, who witnessed Pope Paul's visit, could not have made such a mistake, it could only have been made by the uninformed person who created the "personal letters" on a word processor. We have noted also that, oddly enough, the plainly discredited Noelker letter is *the one and only piece of evidence* cited in Cardinal Bertone's commentary to support the claim that the Consecration has been done (*see* Chapter 5). Recall how no effort was made to obtain Sister Lucy's personal testimony on the matter, even though she was readily available. *She was not even asked to authenticate the Noelker letter*—an omission that speaks volumes.

In any case, Fr. Fox never made the least effort to explain how the purported "personal letters" of 1989-90 could be squared with Sister Lucy's constant testimony, both before and *after* the 1984 ceremony, that Our Lady specified a consecration of Russia by name, not a consecration of the world (*see* Chapter 3). Again and again Fr. Fox was confronted with Sister Lucy's prior testimony by the publications of Father Gruner's appostolate; again and again he ducked the challenge to explain how his "personal letter from Sister Lucy" could be reconciled with that testimony. Instead, he signed on to the Modernist "ecumenical" version of the Consecration: a ceremony in which everything *but* Russia was mentioned. Hence, since 1984 we have seen not only a consecration of the world, but (on October 8, 2000) a consecration to Mary—called an "act of entrustment"—of a whole list of beneficiaries from which Russia was conspicuously omitted: "all people," "the babies yet unborn," "those born into poverty and suffering," "the young in search of meaning," "the unemployed," "those suffering hunger and disease," "all troubled families," "the elderly with no one to help them," and "all who are alone and without hope."

No one could argue that consecrating (or "entrusting") all these different groups to Mary is a bad thing. On the contrary, it is a good thing. But here we see another Modernist technique at work: emphasizing one good in order to obscure another—as, for example, when the Modernist speaks incessantly of God's mercy in order to obscure His justice, or the humanity of Christ in order to obscure His divinity. By consecrating everything and anything on the face of the earth but the one thing Our Lady asked to be consecrated, the purveyors of the Modernist version of Fatima endeavor to make us forget the reason Our Lady came to earth in the first place: to call for *Russia's* conversion as the harbinger of the Triumph of Her Immaculate Heart and peace in the world. Fr. Fox was instrumental in this Modernist obfuscation of the simple truth of Fatima.

The Modernist "Conversion of Russia"

Having promoted a Modernist "consecration of Russia," Fr. Fox and others in his camp likewise committed themselves to defending a Modernist version of Russia's supposed "conversion" since 1984. In the aforementioned article irrelevantly headlined "Father Gruner—a suspended Catholic priest," Fr. Fox himself conceded that "there are still wars, violence in the world and *Russia is far from converted.*" He then noted the objection no doubt posed to him by many of his own supporters: "If the Consecration is Accomplished, Why is Russia Not Converted?" Rather than answering the objection, Fr. Fox rhetorically sneered at those "who hold to a position that a paradise on earth, a Russia suddenly turning itself into a people of converted holiness and even as Roman Catholics must immediately follow a Collegial Consecration." That is, Father Fox sneered at the very miracle Our Lady of Fatima promised, caricaturing it as "paradise on earth," when what the Virgin promised, rather, was a period of peace for the world and the salvation of many souls.

In other words, Fr. Fox, driving a dagger through the heart of the Fatima message, maintains that Our Lady of Fatima did not promise the twin miracles of a period of world peace and the conversion of Russia to the Catholic Faith, and the consequent healing of a thousand-year-long schism. According to him, Our Lady promised nothing more than what we see today: no world peace, and no conversion of the Russian people. But if that were so, then what was the point of the Fatima apparitions? Did the Mother of God come to earth and call down the Miracle of the Sun only to announce that miracles would *not* happen upon the fulfillment of Her requests? What sort of nonsense is this? It is Modernist nonsense, which affirms and denies the Fatima event at one and the same time.

As Fr. Fox knew very well, however, Our Lady's intervention on earth did in fact produce the miraculous conversion of the entire nation of Mexico. Some nine million souls lost in the darkness of paganism were baptized and received into the Catholic Church over the short span of only nine years following the apparitions of Our Lady of Guadalupe in 1531. Yet *twenty* years after a "consecration of Russia" in which Russia was never mentioned—today, it is twenty-eight years after—Fr. Fox was still insisting that we could not expect Our Lady to produce a similar miracle in Russia or, indeed, to convert any considerable number of Russians to the Catholic Faith! And this, mind you, was the man who portrayed himself as a great champion of Our Lady of Fatima and the Triumph of Her Immaculate Heart.

When one thinks about it for a moment, one realizes that what Fr. Fox and those of like mind have argued is simply this: *God cannot bring about the miraculous conversion of Russia.* His vision clouded by the ecumenical fog that has bedeviled the Church since Vatican II, Fr. Fox implicitly denied divine omnipotence.

Compare Fr. Fox with the shining example of Fr. Leonid Feodorov (1879-1935), who journeyed to Rome when he was still a Russian Orthodox theology student and was united to the Catholic Church at the Gesu on July 31, 1902—fifteen years before Our Lady of Fatima came to ask all the Russian Orthodox to follow Feodorov's example. Feodorov was ordained a Catholic priest and elevated to head the Byzantine Rite Catholic Church in Russia as its Exarch, only to be sentenced to ten years in prison by the Bolsheviks in 1923 for the "crime" of promoting the reunion of the Orthodox with Rome. Concerning his sentence Fr. Feodorov declared: "It is all one to me whether I am shot or I am sentenced to ten years' imprisonment; yet I am no fanatic. Since the moment I gave myself to the Catholic Church my sole thought has been to bring my country to that Church, which I believe *is the only true Church*."

Our Lady of the Russian Orthodox?

In his attacks on Father Gruner in the magazine he dared to call *Immaculate Heart Messenger*, Fox made light of "horror stories about

Russia as evidence that no Consecration was accepted by God." Glossing over the "horror stories" (which he could not explain away) Fr. Fox cited, apparently in all seriousness, the view of Orthodox Patriarch Alexy II—a former KGB agent!—that he (Alexy) "believes" that the Russian Orthodox Church is undergoing a "rebirth." This is the same Alexy II who not long ago screamed that the Pope was "invading Russian territory" when His Holiness conducted *a closed-circuit* TV broadcast to a small group of Catholics in Moscow—closed-circuit because the TV stations controlled by Mr. Putin refused to broadcast images of the Pope to the Russian people at large.

So, Fr. Fox, a self-styled apostle of Fatima who loudly proclaimed his loyalty to the Pope, suggested that the Mother of God came to earth to bring about a "rebirth" of the Russian Orthodox Church— the same schismatic church that utterly rejects communion with the Pope and will not even allow him to visit Moscow unless the Catholic Church renounces any effort to make converts in Russia! But Our Lady did not come to Fatima to give aid to schismatic Russian Orthodoxy, but rather to reconcile the Russian people with the Catholic Church, as we see in the historic conversion of Fr. Feodorov.

Perhaps recognizing the absurdity of his own position, Fr. Fox attempted to claim papal authority for his Modernist "conversion of Russia" by claiming that John Paul II "speaks of the Orthodox as our sister Church." But Fr. Fox was wrong again, as are all the proponents of this falsehood of the party of the innovators. On June 9, 2000 the Congregation for the Doctrine of the Faith issued a doctrinal note, specifically approved by the Pope, which warns that

> *one cannot properly say that the Catholic Church is the sister of a particular church or group of churches...* Consequently, one should avoid, as a source of misunderstanding and theological confusion, the use of formulations such as our two churches which, if applied to the Catholic Church and the totality of Orthodox churches (or a single Orthodox church), imply a plurality not merely on the level of particular churches, but also on the level of the one, holy, catholic and apostolic church confessed in the creed, whose real existence is thus obscured.

Thus, in defending his neo-Modernist "conversion of Russia," Fr. Fox indulged in a bit of Modernist ecclesiology which even the relentlessly "ecumenical" Vatican apparatus was forced to condemn to avoid theological confusion—the same confusion caused by the ecumenical initiatives of certain Vatican bureaucrats. Such is the "diabolical disorientation of the Church" remarked by Sister Lucy.

In any case, what Fr. Fox presented as the "rebirth" of Russian Orthodoxy is a myth. It is well known that nearly all of those who designate themselves Russian Orthodox do not practice their religion. As *The Economist* noted in 2000: "Russia is suffering a crisis of faith… 94% of Russians aged 18-29 do not go to church."[200] Thus it is hardly surprising that the moral degeneration of Russian society continues to accelerate: two abortions for every live birth (an average of five to six abortions for each Russian woman), rampant alcoholism and violent crime which has lowered between 1991 and 2004 the life expectancy of the average Russian male from 68 years down to 60, a burgeoning AIDS epidemic following the legalization of homosexuality by Boris Yeltsin, a flourishing child pornography industry thanks to Russia's porn-friendly legal system (another way that Russia spreads its errors throughout the world), and so forth. (*See* Chapter 13.) The "rebirth" of Russian Orthodoxy, like Fr. Fox's entire attempt to revise the Message of Fatima along "ecumenical" lines, was a fraud.

And What of the Catholic Church in Russia?

Tellingly, Fr. Fox's attacks on Father Gruner avoided discussing the undeniable truth that there is no sign whatever of the conversion Our Lady actually prophesied: the conversion of the Russian people to the Catholic religion and their return to Rome. On the contrary, while Fr. Fox promoted his Modernist substitute for the conversion of Russia the persecution of the Catholic Church under the Putin regime worsened with each passing day.

Thanks to Russia's 1997 law on "freedom of conscience," the Church's very existence in Russia has been at the sufferance of "ex-communist" Russian bureaucrats who issue the annual permits for operation of Catholic parishes, while Russian Orthodoxy, Judaism, Islam and Buddhism are granted legal status without need of permits. Treated as foreign missionaries, Catholic clergy are required to renew their visitor's visas every three months in order to remain in the country. Key Catholic clerics have since been expelled following visa denials, including the very secretary of the Russian Catholic Bishops' Conference, Father Stanislaw Opiela, who was denied an entry visa three times without explanation: "I don't think I'll try again. It's just not worth it," he said. "Maybe there will be some kind of protest."[201] In April of 2002, Bishop Jerzy Masur, assigned by the Vatican to administer to the vast (but sparsely populated) region of Siberia, was also expelled from Russia, his entry visa confiscated without explanation. Bishop Masur learned that he had been added to a secret "list" of Catholic clergy who are considered "undesirables" and will no longer be allowed to enter Russian territory.

At the same time Father Fox was attacking Father Gruner—some

---

[200] Zenit news report, December 22, 2000.
[201] Catholic News Service Report, May 8, 2001.

twenty years after the "consecration" of 1984—the Catholic Church was keeping (and still keeps) such a low profile in Russia that the Moscow office from which Archbishop Kondrusiewicz conducted Church affairs was "tucked behind a military commandant's office and bears no signs saying it houses the Catholic Church's Russian leadership."[202] Catholics remain a tiny, benighted minority in the country; there are perhaps 500,000 nominal Catholics in a nation of 144 million people. The small percentage of Catholics who even go to Mass on Sunday (most of them in Siberia) is dependent almost entirely on non-Russian priests, whose visas can be revoked at will. In all of Russia, there are today only 200 Catholic priests of which only ten are Russian-born—vastly fewer than there were *before* the Bolshevik Revolution in October 1917.

All of these developments prompted Archbishop Kondrusiewicz to issue a formal protest on behalf of the Conference of Catholic Bishops of Russia, entitled "Religious Liberty in Russia Is in Serious Danger." The protest declares:

> Catholics in Russia ask themselves: What will happen next? Are the constitutional guarantees valid also for them, including liberty of conscience and of the right to have their own pastors, which comprises inviting them from abroad, not forgetting that for 81 years the Catholic Church was deprived of the right of forming and ordaining its own priests? Perhaps the State really considers Catholics second-class citizens? Are they (the State) returning to the times of persecution of the faith? ... The expulsion of a Catholic bishop who has not violated any law, surpasses all imaginable limits of civilized relations between the State and the Church. ... With grave worry, we express our decisive protest in respect to violation of the constitutional rights of Catholics.[203]

Even as he failed to produce any evidence of Russia's religious conversion besides the mythical "rebirth" of schismatic, anti-Roman Russian Orthodoxy, Fr. Fox was forced to admit that "Unfortunately, the Orthodox Church in Russia still has a mentality of confidence in the state for the furtherance of religious purposes." Confidence in the regime of Vladimir Putin, the pro-abortion former head of the KGB! What more needs to be said?

Just as Soloviev pointed out more than a hundred years ago, the Russian Orthodox Church, cut off from Rome and the universal Church, is little more than a creature of the state. Yet the non-existent "rebirth" of this state-controlled puppet Church, whose ex-KGB "patriarch" works hand-in-glove with Mr. Putin to persecute the

---

[202] AP report and photograph, February 28, 2002.
[203] *National Catholic Register* Online Web Edition, April 28 - May 5, 2002.

Catholic Church, is what Fr. Fox relentlessly attempted to pass off as the "conversion of Russia."

Here, too, Fr. Fox dutifully promoted the Party Line of Cardinal Sodano, according to which "conversion" as used in the Message of Fatima has been redefined to exclude any embrace of the Catholic religion. Likewise parroting the Party Line, no less than the Secretary General of the Conference of Roman Catholic Bishops of Russia, Igor Kovalesky, declared on May 6, 2004 that "There is no proselytism as a directive on the part of the Holy See, *nor is there any intention to convert Russia to Roman Catholicism.*"[204]

There we have it: the anti-Fatima elements of the Vatican bureaucracy, aided and abetted by Fr. Fox, are now *diametrically opposed* to God's own design for the conversion of Russia to the Catholic Faith. They openly declare that Russia shall *not* be Catholic. And yet these same characters, Fr. Fox included, present themselves as devotees and reliable interpreters of the Fatima message. Cardinal Sodano's own "interpretation" of the Third Secret, which pretends that the vision of the Pope being executed by a band of soldiers signifies John Paul II *not* being killed by a lone assassin in 1981, was cited no fewer than four times in Cardinal Ratzinger's commentary on the Third Secret. Sodano's "interpretation," like the rest of the neo-Modernist revision of Fatima, has one purpose only: to relegate Fatima to the past, and to oblivion.

No Conversion of Any Kind in Russia

Indeed, Fr. Fox was unable to demonstrate how Russia has converted in *any* sense, besides a certain liberalization of the consumer economy, which is hardly what Our Lady came to announce. Despite the "fall of Communism" in 1991, Russia today is an authoritarian state whose virtual dictator, Vladimir Putin, has seized control of the mass media, jailed or exiled all of his chief political opponents, banned the formation of grass roots opposition parties and prevented the emergence of an independent judiciary. As *The Washington Post* observed in late 2003, while Father Fox was still promoting his sham conversion of Russia: "We must now recognize that there has been a massive suppression of human rights and the imposition of a de facto Cold War-type administration in Moscow."[205] In a recent statement to Congress, Republican Congressman Christopher Cox told the truth that Fr. Fox never reports in his "don't worry, be happy" magazine: "Russia does not enjoy an open, competitive political system that protects freedom of expression and association and its government

---

[204] Itar-Tass news report, May 7, 2004.
[205] "The Failure of Putin's Russia," Bruce P. Jackson, *Washington Post*, October 28, 2003, p. A23.

does not uphold universal standards of human rights." Russian analyst Nikolai Zlobin of the Center for Defense Information put it most simply: "We're fighting a kind of new Cold War."[206]

Yet Fr. Fox belittles these developments as "horror stories," thus covering up the crimes of the Putin regime, much as leftist reporters in the West covered up the crimes of Lenin and Stalin, thus earning Lenin's appellation "useful idiots." Today, useful idiots in the Catholic Church cover up the true state of affairs in Russia in order to foist their "ecumenical" version of Fatima upon the faithful. To Fr. Fox one must say in all candor: You are complicit in the persecution of the Church in Russia, because you have abandoned the cause of Russia's conversion for the sake of a failed human program of "ecumenical dialogue." In fact, you use your "respectable" apostolate to *oppose* the consecration of Russia, as you dare to collect money from the faithful in the name of Our Lady of Fatima.

Russia Suffered, as Fr. Fox Boasted of His Russian Shrine

While the Russian people, Catholics especially, continued to suffer, Fr. Fox patted himself on the back for raising money to build a small Fatima shrine in St. Petersburg, Russia: "It was constructed with funds my apostolate gathered," he boasted. Fr. Fox noted that the shrine was dedicated by Archbishop Kondrusiewicz back in 1998—the same Archbishop Kondrusiewicz who was decrying the persecution of the Church in Russia at the same time Fr. Fox pretended it was not happening!

Having congratulated himself for collecting money to build the shrine, Fr. Fox sniffed that "Father Gruner continued his negative approaches." By "negative approaches" Fr. Fox meant remarking the obvious about the consequences of failing to honor Our Lady's request: that Russia will not convert, that Russia will suffer, that the Church will suffer, that the world will suffer. Fr. Fox apparently believed that the Putin regime's toleration of his little shrine represented some sort of triumph for the Church in Russia. A triumph it was not. Since the date Fr. Fox's shrine was dedicated, the persecution of Russian Catholics has only worsened, as demonstrated by the developments described above. Putin today, like Lenin and Stalin before him, makes a great show of allowing a few Catholic parishes to operate while persecution of the Church continues unabated. As Fr. Fox applauded himself, the tiny Catholic apparatus in Russia was enduring (and still endures) systematic state oppression. Irony of ironies, there are far fewer practicing Catholics in Russia today (2012) than there were in the time of Lenin and Stalin.

Perhaps Heaven expects a bit more from the Catholic hierarchy

---

[206] Fox News, May 6, 2004.

than Fr. Fox's Marian shrine in St. Petersburg. Perhaps Heaven expects what Our Lady of Fatima requested: *the consecration of Russia* to Her Immaculate Heart. But Fr. Fox insisted until the end that Our Lady of Fatima came to prophesy a consecration that is not a consecration, and a conversion that is not a conversion. In true Modernist fashion he "interpreted" the Message of Fatima into extinction.

The Scheme to Create an "Inter-religious" Fatima

The road Fr. Fox chose to follow does not end with the elimination of the consecration and conversion of Russia in their traditional Catholic sense. Having set off down the road toward a Modernist Fatima, Fr. Fox had to go the whole distance, or risk losing favor with the anti-Fatima ecclesial bureaucrats upon whom, ironically enough, his purported Fatima apostolate depends for its very existence. This meant that Fr. Fox had to be willing to defend the last stage in the Modernist transformation of Fatima: the creation of an "inter-religious" Fatima Shrine.

Hence, in the second of his articles attacking Father Gruner, "Fatima Will Retain Its Catholic Identity," Fr. Fox showed that he was willing and eager to do so. Notice, first of all, the curious phraseology of the article's title: Fatima will "retain" its "Catholic identity." Since Fatima is a Catholic place by definition, this is akin to saying that "St. Peter's Basilica will retain its Catholic identity." Clearly, something is going on at Fatima that required Fr. Fox to make this strange, and less than reassuring, affirmation.

Fr. Fox knew very well what was going on at the Fatima Shrine. In connection with an unprecedented "inter-religious congress" of Buddhists, Hindus, Muslims, Orthodox, Anglicans and Catholics held at the Shrine in October 2003, the Rector of the Shrine, Fr. Luciano Guerra, now retired, declared that:

> The future of Fatima, or the adoration of God and His Mother at this holy Shrine, *must pass through the creation of a shrine where different religions can mingle*. The inter-religious dialogue in Portugal, and in the Catholic Church, is still in an embryonic phase, but the Shrine of Fatima is not indifferent to this fact and is already open to being a universalistic place of vocation.

This remark, widely reported in the Catholic press (including the *Universe* and *Catholic Herald*), as well as the secular press in Portugal (*Noticias de Fatima* and *Portugal News*), provoked a storm of international protest by concerned Catholics. In response, Rector Guerra issued a series of equivocal statements, none of which actually denied that he had made the remark. On the contrary, the "denials" only *affirmed* that Guerra intended to promote "inter-religious" activities at the Shrine. For example, Guerra's "official" response on the Fatima Shrine's website declared:

> And, *when it seems to us to be opportune, after what is already happening in many other sacred places*, this new basilica *would be able to receive brothers from other faiths,* who may want, in a brotherly manner, to know how we pray.

Guerra was referring to the grotesque new "basilica," resembling a gigantic concrete banjo, that now disfigures the sacred ground of the Cova da Iria, near the original basilica of traditional Catholic design. As we can see, the "basilica" will be largely buried underground, thus serving as the perfect metaphor for what Guerra is trying to do with the Message of Fatima.

Guerra clearly had in mind for his new "basilica" something more than members of other religions observing how Catholics worship God at Fatima, for this they can do already in the existing basilica. Rather, Guerra expressly linked his plans to "what is already happening in many other sacred places," which he will evidently allow to happen at Fatima when, as he put it, "it seems to us to be opportune."

To show his inter-religious audience "what is already happening in many other sacred places," Guerra invited to address the conference one Fr. Arul Irudayam, Rector of the Catholic Marian Shrine Basilica in Vailankanni, India. This Shrine receives millions of pilgrims a year, including many Hindus, and Fr. Irudayam rejoiced to inform the audience that, as a further development of "inter-religious dialogue," *the Hindus now perform their religious rituals in the shrine at Vailankanni.* The audience, including Rector Guerra, applauded this sacrilege. The commandment "Thou shalt not have false gods before Me" was evidently lost on this crowd.

On January 9, 2004, nearly three months after his remark, Guerra finally admitted to a reporter from the English journal *Catholic Herald* that he had indeed stated that "the new shrine at Fatima, Portugal would be a place 'where different religions can mingle'," but claimed that his statement had been "taken out of context." The "context," however, was a gathering of Buddhists, Hindus, Muslims, Orthodox and Anglicans, addressed by an Indian priest who permits Hindu worship in a Catholic Marian shrine in India—to the applause of Msgr. Guerra.

Here it must be noted that Guerra's conference was also addressed by neo-Modernist "theologian," Fr. Jacques Dupuis. As eyewitness John Vennari reported, Dupuis's address contended that God has *positively willed* the existence of other religions as part of His plan for salvation, and that one should not even refer to other religions as non-Christian. *Noticias de Fatima* quotes Dupuis as follows: "The religion of the future will be a general convergence of all religions into one universal Christ which will satisfy everyone."

Dupuis descended into outright heresy when he pronounced as a "horrible text" the *infallible dogmatic definition* of the Council of Florence (1442), already mentioned, concerning no salvation outside the Church. To recall what the Council of Florence declared:

> The Holy Roman Church... believes firmly, professes and declares that none of those who are outside the Church, not only pagans, but also Jews or heretics and schismatics, can reach eternal life, but will go into the eternal fire 'prepared for the devil and his angels' [Matt. 25:41] unless before death they are united to it... *No one,* no matter how many alms he has given, even if he pours out his blood in the name of Christ, can be saved, if he does not remain in the bosom and unity of the *Catholic Church.*

As Vennari personally observed, Dupuis's address, including his dissent from this infallibly defined dogma, was applauded not only by Guerra, but also the Bishop of Leiria-Fatima, D. Serafim de Sousa Ferreira e Silva, and even the Papal Nuncio. Indeed, the next day, as Vennari reports, Archbishop Michael Fitzgerald stated to the conference: "Father Dupuis yesterday explained *the theological basis* of the establishment of relations with people of other religions."

To date, Guerra has not explicitly denied his apparent intention to allow inter-religious activities, including non-Catholic rituals, on the grounds of the Fatima Shrine. When asked to issue such denials in an email and fax sent by this writer, Guerra waited two months to issue a "reply" that completely avoids the issue.

Confronted with an international wave of outrage over Guerra's antics, the anti-Fatima elements of the Vatican bureaucracy, speaking through Archbishop Fitzgerald, later issued one of those "denials" so typical of the post-conciliar revolution: calculated to mollify the overly credulous, while providing cover for the launching of the revolution's latest trial balloon. According to the English Catholic journal *Universe,* Fitzgerald said that Guerra's motley inter-religious gathering "was merely 'part of an ongoing reflection' on the sanctuary's 'inter-religious dimension' in the Church and the modern world," but "'there were no practical conclusions."[207] This is rather like a married man who protests that in flirting with other women he is merely engaging in an "ongoing reflection" on adultery but hasn't yet decided how to commit it. But Fitzgerald conspicuously failed to deny that Msgr. Guerra had said, as the *Universe* reported: "The future of Fatima, or the adoration of God and His mother at this Holy Shrine, must pass through the creation of a shrine where different religions can mingle."

---

[207] *Catholic Times* online, November 18, 2003.

A Scheme Long in the Making

Guerra's pan-religious gathering in Fatima was but the latest point reached in a trajectory toward an "inter-religious Fatima" that he had established as early as 1992. In that year *The Fatima Crusader* reported that Guerra had invited to speak at a conference in Fatima Professor Robert Muller, Chancellor of the United Nations University for Peace. Muller dared to enlist the Pope himself in the cause of creating a one-world religion under the aegis of a one-world government: "Ecumenism is outmoded now," he declared to Guerra's congress. "We must now move to universal religiosity and spirituality under the aegis of one-world government, which will soon see the light of day, and under the impetus of John Paul II, who would be honored if he gave the Church this programme." Note the symmetry of remarks between Guerra's guest in 1992 and his guest in 2003, Fr. Dupuis, who, as noted earlier, declared that "The religion of the future will be a general convergence of all religions into one universal Christ which will satisfy everyone."

Who did Msgr. Guerra and Archbishop Fitzgerald think they were fooling? The Fatima revisionists floated a trial balloon; the trial balloon was shot down by outraged Catholics; and now, at least for the moment, they were trying to backpedal, but without actually shelving the plan to open the Fatima Shrine to "inter-religious" activity when "it seems to us to be opportune."

Two steps forward, one step back. The Fatima Shrine may not be an inter-religious Mecca today, but Fitzgerald implanted the suggestion that the shrine has "an inter-religious dimension" on which the unprecedented conference was part of "an ongoing reflection." Stay tuned for the "practical conclusions."

Hindus in the Capelinha

And the "practical conclusions" were soon revealed. Even as Fr. Guerra and Archbishop Fitzgerald hid behind equivocal "denials" that deny nothing, Guerra continued to move ahead with his scheme for an inter-religious Fatima Shrine.

In a stunning development that received no advance publicity, on May 5, 2004 Guerra allowed a busload of Hindus to conduct a pagan ritual in the Capelinha, or Little Chapel of the Apparitions, which stands on the very spot where Our Lady appeared in the Cova. A Hindu "priest," wearing Hindu robes and the mark of Shiva (a dot) on his forehead, took to the altar in the outdoor portion of the Capelinha and made an offering of food and flowers. One of the Hindu worshipers told a Catholic eyewitness that Hindus go to Fatima because they believe in many gods, and it is always better to approach the wife of a god (meaning Mary) than the god himself.[208]

No one is permitted to use the Capelinha without Guerra's permission. Moreover, during television coverage of the event by Portugal's SIC channel, Guerra provided approving comments on the Hindus' use of the Capelinha for their pagan idolatry. So, in the very midst of the explosive controversy his own remarks had caused, Guerra brazenly proceeded to do that which he "denied" having any intention to do. This is a man who clearly believes he has the full support of the Vatican apparatus and will be protected against any adverse consequences for allowing this sacrilege. And it is this man who was placed in charge of the holy ground of Fatima for some 30 years.

Fr. Fox Covers Up the Scheme

What did Fr. Fox have to say about Guerra's outrageous antics? As he did with the consecration and conversion of Russia, he engaged in a cover-up. He dismissed Father Gruner's public protest against Guerra's words and deeds as "slanted and sensational reporting," but never really disputed that Guerra said what he said and did what he did. While conceding that Guerra "was quoted as saying 'The future of Fatima, or the adoration of God and His Mother at this holy Shrine, must pass through the creation of a shrine where different religions can mingle'", Fr. Fox observed merely that "Msgr. Guerra, who is personally known to me, would never speak of 'adoration' with regard to Mary."

This is very curious. If Fr. Fox knew Msgr. Guerra personally, why did he not simply *ask Guerra* if he had made the statement attributed to him? The answer seems clear enough: Fr. Fox knew full well that Msgr. Guerra had made the statement, for, as noted above, Guerra *admitted* that he had made it, claiming only that it had been taken "out of context"—which is what every politician says when his own words come back to haunt him.

Fr. Fox only dug himself a deeper hole when, in keeping with his usual approach, he cloaked his position with the apparent authority of a Vatican bureaucrat who really had no authority at all. He quoted Archbishop Fitzgerald, who told Zenit news agency that "As far as I know, there are no plans that the building is designed *specifically* for inter-faith purposes. We recognize that Fatima is a place of pilgrimage for many religions [since when?]… [T]he shrine nonetheless retains its Catholic identity." Hence the title of Fr. Fox's article.

A Wall Street litigator could not have crafted a more lawyerly statement than Fitzgerald's loophole-riddled "denial": *as far as he*

---

[208] TV broadcast on Portuguese channel, SIC, May 5, 2004. See *Father's Fox's Modernist Assault on Fatima*, http://www.fatima.org/news/newsviews/062504frfox3.asp.

knows the new "basilica" is not designed *specifically* for inter-faith purposes, and the new structure will "retain" its "Catholic identity." That is hardly a denial of what Guerra actually said: that the new structure would be a place where the different religions can "mingle," even if its "Catholic identity" is "retained" in some manner.

Even worse, as Fr. Fox himself noted with evident approval, Fitzgerald endorsed Guerra's view, posted on the Fatima Shrine's website in defense of Guerra's "inter-religious congress," that "the Fatima apparitions were exhortations to ecumenical dialogue. Mary knew that her choice of the site in Portugal would one day be associated with the Islamic prophet Mohammed, whose daughter's name was Fatima."

Insanity! This is yet another Modernist subversion of the Fatima event, and Fr. Fox swallowed it whole. In truth, the village of Fatima was named after a Muslim princess who, following her *capture by Christian forces* during the Moorish occupation of Portugal, was betrothed to the Count of Ourem, converted to Catholicism, and was baptized before marrying the Count in 1158. Her baptismal name was Oureana, but her birth name had been Fatima, after Mohammed's daughter.[209] Thus, the naming of the village of Fatima is a testament, not to "ecumenism" or to the false prophet Mohammed, but to *the triumph of Christendom* over the Muslim occupiers of Portugal; it is a testament to precisely what Our Lady of Fatima came to proclaim: *the conversion of non-Catholics to the one true religion*, beginning with the Russian people. Contrary to Father Fox's counterfeit Message of Fatima, Our Lady did not come to Fatima to exhort us to engage in "ecumenical dialogue" or to give honor to the daughter of "the prophet" Mohammed. Mohammed was no "prophet" but an agent of the devil, whose false religion plagues the world to this day.

Wandering farther and farther down the Modernist road to oblivion for the Fatima event—the very thing he so ostentatiously professed to be promoting—Fr. Fox quoted with approval Msgr. Guerra's bizarre interpretation of the apparitions of the Angel of Peace at Fatima: "Communion under the species of bread is given to the oldest seer, while the two younger, Francisco and Jacinta, receive Holy Communion for the first time under the species of wine. Since the practice of receiving Holy Communion under both species has fallen out of wide use in the Latin-rite Catholic Church, but not in the Orthodox churches, the Message of the Angel of Peace is an exhortation to ecumenical dialogue with those Churches separated from Rome for a thousand years."

Nonsense. First of all, Our Lady of Fatima did not ask for

---

[209] There are many historical accounts of this event. See, for example, "Our Lady and Islam: Heaven's Peace Plan," by Fr. Ladis J. Cizik.

"ecumenical dialogue" with the Orthodox, but rather sought their outright, miraculous conversion through the consecration of Russia to Her Immaculate Heart—just as She miraculously converted the entire nation of Mexico. "Dialogue," ecumenical or otherwise, would not be necessary.

Furthermore, Communion under both kinds has always been administered in Eastern-rite Catholic Churches, so what the Angel of Peace did can hardly be viewed as a favorable reference to the schismatic Orthodox. Also, neither Eastern-rite Catholics nor the Orthodox receive the species separately, but rather by intinction, with the species of bread being dipped into the species of wine and placed directly on the tongue. If anything, the Angel's actions affirm the teaching of the Council of Trent, against the Protestants, that the Body, Blood, Soul and Divinity of Christ are received fully in the consecrated bread as well as the consecrated wine, and that *there is no need to receive both species* in order to receive the full grace of the Sacrament. The Angel also demonstrated that Heaven wishes us to receive *Communion on the tongue*, not in the hand, although Fr. Fox never voiced any objection to the latter.

Based on Msgr. Guerra's own words and deeds, it is plain that he does not harbor good intentions concerning the "Catholic identity" of Fatima. As he told *Noticias de Fatima*, his inter-religious congress was only "a first step. We are like the engineers in Portugal who begin by examining the structures of the bridges to see if we can trust them in the future." The Fatima Shrine's own December 28, 2003 Communiqué confirmed that Guerra told the inter-religious gathering arrayed before him: "[W]e rejoice in the brotherly presence of the representatives of the various spiritual schools and we are sure that their presence here *opened the way for a greater future openness of this Shrine*; a Shrine that seems already vocationed, thanks to divine providence, for contacts and for dialogue (...)."

Only a willing dupe would try to depict remarks such as these as anything but a direct threat to destroy the exclusively Catholic character of the Fatima Shrine. But Fr. Fox, it seems, was willing to play the dupe for Msgr. Guerra and his Modernist friends, both high and low. Such is the business of those we call the false friends of Fatima.

Try as he might, however, Fr. Fox was unable to conceal what Msgr. Guerra was saying and doing at Fatima. He could not explain away the mountain of evidence Father Gruner had presented concerning Guerra's heterodox agenda—including the public denial of defined dogma by a speaker he applauded. Knowing this, Fr. Fox descended once again to an underhanded *argumentum ad hominem*: "Father Gruner... has serious limitations as for years he has not been able to offer Mass at any of the official altars of the Fatima Sanctuary in Portugal…"

Indeed it is true that Msgr. Guerra, whose henchmen physically assaulted Father Gruner in the Fatima Sanctuary in 1992,[210] will not allow him to celebrate Mass there. Such is the penalty for a faithful priest who stands up to the Modernists who, incredibly enough, have been placed in charge of the very place where the three seers received the quintessentially anti-Modernist Message of Fatima. But what bearing does Father Gruner's lack of access to the altars of the Fatima Sanctuary have on Guerra's public statements and actions evidencing his designs for an "inter-religious dimension" at the Shrine? None, of course. Fr. Fox, finding himself without rational arguments, took another cheap shot and ran away.

Lending Support to an Attack on Dogma Itself

Fatima scholars have been unanimous in their conclusion that the Third Secret of Fatima begins with the telltale phrase: "In Portugal the dogma of the faith will always be preserved etc." From the context it is clear that the "etc", added by Sister Lucy to the words of the Virgin, is a place-holder for what She said immediately thereafter about the fate of dogma in *other* parts of the Church. Indeed, we have seen that Fr. Joseph Schweigl, who in 1952 was entrusted by Pope Pius XII with the secret mission of interrogating Sister Lucy about the Third Secret, said this to a colleague upon his return to Rome the very next day:

> I cannot reveal anything of what I learned at Fatima concerning the Third Secret, but I can say that it has two parts: one concerns the Pope; the other logically—although I must say nothing—would have to be the continuation of the words: "In Portugal, the dogma of the Faith will always be preserved."[211]

The only reasonable deduction—for otherwise the reference to dogma in Portugal would make no sense—is that the Third Secret foretells a catastrophic loss of faith and discipline elsewhere in the Church through an attack on dogma. In other words, the Third Secret predicts widespread apostasy in the Church. Cardinal Mario Luigi Ciappi, who was nothing less than Pope John Paul II's own personal papal theologian, and who had read the Third Secret, confirmed this unanimous view of Fatima scholars in a personal communication to a Professor Baumgartner in Salzburg, Austria: "In the Third Secret it is foretold, among other things, that the great apostasy in the

---

[210] Cf. article on the incident by J. Kaess, reprinted as an appendix in *Fatima Priest*, First Edition, (Good Counsel Publications, Pound Ridge, New York, 1997) pp. 360-364. See also Fourth Edition, pp. 154-155.

[211] *The Whole Truth About Fatima*, Vol. III, p. 710.

Church will begin *at the top*."[212] (This no doubt explains why, in his commentary on the Message of Fatima, Cardinal Ratzinger removed this key phrase from the Message, placed it in a footnote and declined to discuss it.)

By aligning himself with highly placed proponents of a Modernist revision of the Message of Fatima—men such as Msgr. Guerra, Archbishop Fitzgerald, Cardinal Kasper, Cardinal Sodano and, yes, even the former Cardinal Ratzinger—Fr. Fox aided and abetted the very attack on dogma foretold by Our Lady of Fatima. Guerra's pan-religious conference at Fatima was a direct attack on the dogma that is central to the Fatima message: that there is no salvation outside the Catholic Church—a dogma whose infallible definition by the Council of Florence Fr. Dupuis pronounced "horrible" during Guerra's congress.

But the Modernist attack on dogma is not confined to particular dogmas as such; the Modernist seeks to destroy the very notion of dogma as an unchanging, infallible definition of objective truth revealed by God to man through Christ and His Church. As St. Pius X warned the Church in *Pascendi*, the Modernist maintains that believers "may pass through different phases" in their belief as the welling up of a vague "religious sentiment" from within, rather than the proclamation of the Gospel as divinely revealed truth. "Consequently, the formulae too, which we call dogmas... are (according to the Modernists), therefore, liable to change. Thus the way is open to the intrinsic evolution of dogma. An immense collection of sophisms this [is], that ruins and destroys all religion."

An "evolution" of dogma that ends up destroying dogma is precisely what today's Modernist termites are promoting, even at the highest levels of the Church. For example, in an address to a group of Anglicans during the reign of John Paul II, Cardinal Kasper dared to call for "a re–evaluation of *Apostolicae curae* (1896) of Pope Leo XIII, who declared Anglican orders null and void, a decision which still stands between our Churches. Without doubt this decision, as Cardinal Willebrands had already affirmed, must be understood in our new ecumenical context in which our communion in faith and mission has considerably grown."[213]

In the same address Kasper also attacked the infallible definition of the First Vatican Council on papal infallibility: "As well, the historical conditionality of the dogma of the First Vatican Council (1869-70), which must be distinguished from its remaining obligatory content, has become clear. This historical development

---

[212] See Father Gerard Mura, "The Third Secret of Fatima: Has It Been Completely Revealed?", the periodical *Catholic*, (published by the Transalpine Redemptorists, Orkney Isles, Scotland, Great Britain) March 2002.

[213] "A Vision of Christian Unity for the Next Generation," *The Tablet*, May 24, 2003.

did not come to an end with the two Vatican Councils, but goes on, and so also in the future the Petrine ministry has to be exercised in line with the changing needs of the Church." That is, Kasper openly declared that Leo XIII's infallible papal declaration on the nullity of Anglican orders (and thus the lack of any true Anglican priesthood), and Vatican I's dogmatic definition of papal infallibility, are historically conditioned and can change in the "new ecumenical context." But if these infallible teachings can change, so can all the others. All dogmas are thereby destroyed, and the Faith itself is destroyed. This is the very essence of Modernism.

As this chapter has shown, Msgr. Guerra and his collaborators have brought the attack on dogma to the sacred ground of Fatima itself, as if to challenge the very prophecy of Our Lady that the dogma of the Faith will always be preserved in Portugal. Yet instead of opposing the assault on the Faith by these proponents of the "new" Fatima, Fr. Fox joined them and defended their heterodox pronouncements and gestures.

In *Pascendi*, St. Pius X spoke of the Modernist under various titles: the Modernist as believer, the Modernist as historian, the Modernist as theologian, the Modernist as reformer, and so forth, showing how the Modernist undermines belief, theology, history and everything else his way of thinking corrupts. Now we must add a new title to the many guises of the Modernist: the Modernist as professed devotee of Fatima. And Fr. Robert J. Fox was one of them. Like the Modernists described in *Pascendi*, Fr. Fox would no doubt have expressed "astonishment" at being declared an enemy of Catholic truth. But given the twisted version of Fatima he was prepared to defend to the hilt, no other conclusion was possible: unwittingly or not, Father Fox was no friend, but rather a determined foe of Our Lady of Fatima.

A New Fatima for the New Pharisees

This, then, is the counterfeit Message of Fatima Fr. Fox, false friend of Fatima, labored to pass off in place of the genuine article: a "consecration" of Russia with no mention of Russia; a "conversion" of Russia with no embrace of the Catholic Faith; "ecumenical dialogue" with no return of the dissidents to Rome. And this on the very ground of the Cova da Iria, where 70,000 souls gathered to witness an unprecedented public miracle invoked by the Mother of God to authenticate Her prophetic summons to achieve Russia's conversion through its consecration to Her.

Fr. Fox's Fatima was not the Fatima of the Catholic religion, but a new Fatima for the new Pharisees of the post-conciliar epoch— men who think themselves far too subtle to accept the notion that a simple public ceremony could convert a nation and bring peace to the world. As we have seen, Fr. Fox himself contemptuously dismissed the whole idea as "paradise on earth."

Like the Pharisees of old, the purveyors of the Modernist revision of the Message of Fatima exploit their prestige and positions of authority to promote falsehood and cow others into accepting it. The false argument from authority is what Fr. Fox deployed when he boasted of his Vatican connections and his good standing with the powers that be, while belittling Father Gruner as an outcast and a nobody. But who was speaking the truth, and who was promoting a lie?

As Our Lord admonished His disciples: "Take heed and beware of the leaven of the Pharisees and Sadducees." (Mt. 16:6) While at first they did not understand, soon our Lord's meaning dawned on them: "Then they understood that he had not said that they should beware of the leaven of bread, but of the *doctrine* of the Pharisees and Sadducees." (Mt. 16:12). In *The Devil's Final Battle*, the definitive work on the relation between the Message of Fatima and the crisis in the Church, there is a discussion of a classic commentary on this passage in Scripture by Archbishop Alban Goodier, S.J. As Archbishop Goodier explained, Our Lord was warning His disciples to be on their guard against the *subtleties* of the Pharisees and their professed obedience to authority, which only masked their insidious opposition to the truth:

> It was not so much their opposition that He feared for His own, it was their [the Pharisees'] *subtlety*. Before the Pharisees had blamed Him for His miracles and other good deeds; He knew that this would not take His friends away from Him. Now this morning they [the Pharisees] had come, with an affected simplicity, a show of desire to know the truth, an appeal to the *prophets, a zeal for tradition, a respect for law and order and obedience to the powers that be*; and all this, He knew, would be likely to affect His own *more than any open enmity.* Like leaven, unless they were careful, it would spread unconsciously among them.[214]

The Virgin of Fatima, like Our Lord Himself, spoke with utmost simplicity and directness. But the new Pharisees of the post-conciliar period, just like the Pharisees of old, seek to obscure the simple truth with subtle interpretations and demagogic appeals to authority and obedience. While professing devotion to the Message of Fatima, they are actually its most dangerous opponents, precisely because

---

[214] Father Paul Kramer, ed., *The Devil's Final Battle*, pp. 141-143. See also Archbishop Goodier, S.J., *The Public Life of Our Lord Jesus Christ*, Vol. I, (London, England: Burns, Oates & Washbourne Ltd., 1932) p. 462.

they enjoy positions of respect. Spreading the corrupting leaven of their Modernist views throughout the Church, they pose as staunch defenders of the Faith.

Like the Pharisees who willfully blinded themselves to the truth of the Gospel, Fr. Fox willfully blinded himself to the truth about Fatima. Whether or not he ever recognized it, Father Fox had ceased to serve Our Lady of Fatima and had become, instead, effectively an *opponent* of the Consecration of Russia the Virgin requested. And this Father Fox did under the guise of a *Fatima* apostolate, just as the Pharisees who connived against Our Lord acted under the guise of defenders of the Law. For all their prestige and respectability, the late Father Fox and his prominent successors in the campaign against the consecration and conversion of Russia—for that is what it is—play the role of blind guides who would lead us into a ditch were we to follow them. But we must not follow them. We must follow the Virgin along the path She indicated at the Cova da Iria, the one that leads to the Triumph of Her Immaculate Heart. We should not wish to be in the company of those who, following in Father Fox's footsteps, mock Heaven itself by attempting to persuade the faithful that the present state of Russia, the Church, and the world represent the fulfillment of Her most glorious promises and that we must expect nothing more from the Mother of God.

Chapter 9

THE WANDERER:
THE PRAVDA OF THE "NEW" FATIMA

Every Party Line needs its *Pravda*, the Soviet-era newspaper laughably named "Truth." The compliant journalist plays an indispensable role in persuading the mass of the people to accept uncritically what the authors of the Party Line have dictated for public consumption and in denouncing the hardy few that question it.

So it is with the weekly newspaper *The Wanderer* and the Party Line on Fatima. Under editor Alphonse Matt, *The Wanderer* has become nothing less than the "paper of record" for promoting the Modernist version of the Message of Fatima, which consigns the entire Fatima event to oblivion. Indeed, *The Wanderer* has been a reliable promoter of the entire program of the party of the innovators during the post-conciliar epoch, as sketched in Chapter 1. Like the Mensheviks during the Russian Revolution, *The Wanderer* deplores the worst excesses of the Bolsheviks while promoting the Revolution's general direction. Hence, in addition to "decommissioning" the Message of Fatima, *The Wanderer* has also doggedly defended the entire basic regime of unprecedented changes in the Church after the Council, from the New Mass to the new ecumenism, along with the New Fatima.

Declaring Father Gruner a Non-Person

In its role as the *Pravda* of the Party Line on Fatima, *The Wanderer* could be expected to declare a non-person the priest who has done more than any other to preserve the memory of the unreconstructed Fatima message in opposition to the Party Line: Father Nicholas Gruner. Hence, on October 25, 2001, *The Wanderer* published an attack piece by Farley Clinton entitled "The Strange Case of Father Gruner." Clinton's reportage was presented as "objective" coverage of a conference sponsored by Father Gruner's apostolate in Rome from October 7-13, 2001. But what Clinton delivered was a hatchet in Father Gruner's back, a rambling assortment of unproven accusations and snide remarks.

- *"There seems to be the suggestion* [in Father Gruner's literature] *that we may be seeing the last days described in the Apocalypse, at the time when a third of the stars of Heaven (the bishops, some commentators think) are dragged down by the tail of the dragon."*

There was indeed such a suggestion in Father Gruner's literature. It was found in his reprint of *the sermon by Pope John Paul II* at the beatification of Jacinta and Francisco in Fatima on May 13, 2000. As the Pope, not Father Gruner, declared on that occasion: "The Message of Fatima is a call to conversion, alerting humanity to have nothing to do with the 'dragon' whose 'tail swept down a third of the stars of heaven, and cast them to the earth'." (Apoc. 12:4)

Evidently, Clinton had not read Father Gruner's literature with a great deal of attention as to who was saying what. But then, as we shall see, Clinton's article really had nothing to do with Father Gruner's literature or, for that matter, the talks given by the many speakers at the conference in Rome which he purported to "cover." In fact, Clinton's article said nothing about the details of the conference. There is a reason for this: Clinton could find nothing wrong with it, as he admitted to this author over dinner in Rome during the conference. But the editor of *The Wanderer* was expecting a hatchet job, and Clinton delivered the goods.

- "*I spent three or four days with the inner circle of his pious associates.*"

Inner circle (read: cult) of his pious (read: phony) associates. It all sounded rather sinister, even though Clinton admitted there was nothing amiss with the conference as such. And it was rather curious that Clinton had no clear idea of how many days he had actually spent attending the conference: "three or four days" hardly bespeaks careful journalistic attention to the proceedings. But then, Clinton was not there as a journalist; he was there as a hatchet man.

- "*Father Gruner is a benign and kindly looking priest ... Superficially, he seemed exemplary from every point of view.*"

Superficially, yes! But underneath the appearance of good there must be something wrong, mustn't there? Clinton provided no evidence in support of the poisonous implication, yet he let it sit there, undermining the reputation of a priest who is indeed exemplary.

- "*I knew he is supposed to have an obsession with 'the visions of Fatima'.*"

A familiar tactic of Communist regimes: opponents of the Party Line must be mentally imbalanced.

- "*Someone said to me, 'Father Gruner claims to be the only expert on Fatima. On a scale of respectability, from 1 to 10, he is about a 2'.*"

Someone said this? Who? And on what grounds? Back in the

dark ages before the springtime of Vatican II, it would have been considered a mortal sin publicly to damage a priest's reputation by repeating the backbiting of an anonymous accuser. *The Wanderer's* brand of Catholic journalism dispensed with such quaint conventions.

- *"[Father Gruner's] recent letter to the Pope considerably undermined the impression of piety, sanity and good humor which I took away from the conference."*

In what way was Clinton's good impression undermined? What did Father Gruner *say* in his canonically justified complaint to the Pope that Clinton found objectionable? He offered no particulars. Instead, he launched the calumnious implication that Father Gruner is impious, insane, and without a sense of humor.

- *"The complaint [to the Pope] sets out a good deal of the history of Fr. Gruner's strange quarrels with the hierarchy and the Holy See."*

What was so "strange" about them? And why were they "quarrels" as opposed to legitimate grievances about the abuse of power by certain Vatican prelates, who had made a career out of hounding Father Gruner while doing little or nothing about clerical predators who molest children or preach heresy in nearly every diocese of North America? Once again, Clinton provided nothing but empty pejoratives.

- *"It [the complaint] does not inspire confidence."*

Why not? Clinton failed to say. Had he even read the document?

- *"What really disturbs me is that Fr. Gruner's writing seems to imply that the Pope ought to choose Fr. Gruner as his personal confessor, and if the Pope does not, he cannot fulfill his most essential duty.* **This is never said***, yet it is hard to draw any other conclusion." (Emphasis added)*

Amazingly enough, Farley Clinton accused Father Gruner of believing something he had never actually stated. But, Clinton claimed, it was "hard" not to conclude that Father Gruner believed what he had never said, because what Father Gruner did say "seems to imply it."

"Seems to imply" is a stock phrase of the shifty accuser, who hides behind ambiguity to evade the accusation that he is guilty of calumny. "Seems to imply" is calumny double-wrapped in ambiguity: as an implication *seems* to state something, but does not state it expressly, to say that someone *"seems* to imply" a given proposition is to say, in effect, that *it seems that he seems* to propose it. The accusation was utterly vaporous, but nonetheless had the desired effect: further damage to the victim's good name. And here we see again the tactic of Communist regimes: Father Gruner must be crazy, for only a priest who is crazy would think that he must serve as the Pope's confessor. Of course, Father Gruner had never actually *said* anything of the kind, but it *seemed* that he had implied it. Well, that was good enough for a front-page article in *The Wanderer*, wasn't it?

A small point for the reader to consider: Since Clinton was at the conference for "three or four days," why did he not simply *ask* Father Gruner whether, in fact, he believes what Clinton contends he "seems to imply"? I myself put the matter to Father Gruner after Clinton's hatchet job appeared on Uncle Al's front page. Father Gruner's reply to Clinton's accusation that he wishes to be the Pope's confessor was: "Are you kidding? Who would want *that* responsibility?"

This, then, is *The Wanderer's* notion of "Catholic" journalism: send a "reporter" to "cover" a conference featuring a certain priest; then have the reporter write about something the priest *never said*, on a matter concerning which the reporter asked the priest *not one single question*.

The Verdict of Self-Appointed Canonists

The Wanderer's campaign to declare Father Gruner a non-person continued with an article entitled "Yes, Virginia, Father Gruner Is Suspended," which appeared in its issue of June 6, 2003. The piece was written by a pair of young laymen, Pete Vere and Shawn McElhinney, who purported to address Father Gruner's canonical status as experts on Canon Law.

Vere and McElhinney based their entire presentation on a Vatican *press release* which advised that "the Congregation for the Clergy, upon a mandate from *a* higher authority [Vatican-speak for the Secretary of State], wishes to state that Rev. Nicholas Gruner is under an *a divinis* suspension, which has been confirmed by a definitive sentence of the Supreme Tribunal of the Apostolic Signatura." In other words, the anonymous author of a press release had stated that the anonymous "higher authority" had said that the Congregation should say that the Apostolic Signatura said that Father Gruner's "suspension" has been "confirmed."

Notice that nowhere in this chain of hearsay and buck-passing is there any indication of (a) *who* had "suspended" Father Gruner (note well: it is not the Vatican that has done so), (b) *when* he was "suspended" or (c) *why* he was suspended. There was a very good reason these particulars were missing from the press release: to reveal the particulars would be to reveal the lack of any grounds for Father Gruner's "suspension"—no offense against faith or morals, no violation of any law of the Church, nothing.

As we saw in Chapter 3, the essence of the canonical gambit to "suspend" Father Gruner deployed by Cardinal Sodano was to demand that Father Gruner be incardinated outside the Diocese of Avellino or else return there, prevent the incardination elsewhere, and then declare him "suspended" for "failing to return" to Avellino after "failing" to be incardinated in another diocese. We saw also that Father Gruner defeated the gambit by achieving incardination in the Archdiocese of Hyderabad, whose Archbishop refused to be cowed by Vatican bureaucrats into rescinding the incardination, declaring to Father Gruner: "Evil forces cannot destroy your work of love."

In essence, therefore, Father Gruner had been declared "suspended" on the basis of, quite literally, nothing at all. His alleged "offense" was to have failed to do precisely what his accusers had attempted to prevent him from doing: achieve incardination outside of the Diocese of Avellino, which in fact he had done despite Sodano's best efforts to prevent it. Man's God-given sense of justice tells him, first of all, that one cannot be punished for an offense unless one has *committed* an offense. If the five-year-old were spanked vigorously and consigned to his room all day for stealing cookies he had not in fact taken, his piteous cry of "That's not fair!" would melt the heart of anyone who knew the truth. Few cruelties of the human condition evoke more compassion than the knowledge that someone has been punished for nothing; and the more severe the unmerited punishment, the greater our compassion for its victim.

Likewise, even a child can understand the injustice of punishing someone for failing to do that which it was impossible for him to do. Let us suppose that our hypothetical five-year-old was spanked by his father and sent, weeping, to his room for not having put away his toys in his toy chest, when the father himself had padlocked the chest so that it could not be used. One could scarcely imagine a father who would treat his own child this way, and we would look with horror upon such stupefying cruelty.

The law of the Church, reflecting the justice and mercy of God, prohibits such cruel injustices by providing that no one may be punished unless he is actually guilty of an offense,[215] nor may anyone be punished for failing to do that which it was impossible or gravely inconvenient to do.[216] Thus, for example, if a bishop were to "suspend" one of his priests for failing to perform some arduous duty while the priest was in a hospital bed suffering from double

---

[215] The Code of Canon Law explicitly provides that no one can be punished for the commission of an external violation of a law or *precept* [i.e., particular command] unless it is *gravely imputable* by reason of malice or culpability. (Can. 1321§1)

[216] The law of the Church, in its mercy and its justice, also recognizes that no one may be punished for violating a precept if necessity or grave inconvenience prevents compliance. Code of Canon Law, Can. 1323, 2°, 4°, 7°.

pneumonia, the "suspension" would be null and void because it was impossible or at least gravely inconvenient for the priest to obey the bishop's unjust and unreasonable command.

What did Vere and McElhinney have to say about Father Gruner's point that, as Canon Law explicitly recognizes, a priest cannot be suspended when he has not committed any offense? The authors merely repeated that "Father Gruner's suspension was upheld by a sentence of the Apostolic Signatura." What suspension? Imposed by whom? And for what reason? Recognizing that they should make at least some effort to show what *offense* Father Gruner is supposed to have committed, Vere and McElhinney wrote:

> Father Gruner was ordered by his legitimate ecclesiastical superior to return to the diocese of his incardination [Avellino]...
> He was also warned that failure to return to his diocese of incardination would result in his suspension *a divinis* [and] subsequently his competent ecclesiastical superior followed through with the suspension.

But here the authors conveniently omitted every one of the crucial facts outlined above: that Father Gruner was ordered to return to Avellino *only if* he did not find another bishop; that his very accusers tried to prevent him from finding another bishop; that nevertheless he *did* find another bishop (the Archbishop of Hyderabad).

Thus, Vere and McElhinney's argument reduced to little more than the contention that Father Gruner had been "suspended" because a press release said that a "definitive sentence" of the Signatura "confirms" that he is "suspended"; and no one need care if the "suspension" had any legal, moral or factual basis. As the authors stated in reply to Father Gruner's objection that he has been suspended for no real reason: "Given the fact that Father Gruner's suspension was upheld by a sentence of the Apostolic Signatura, this [Father Gruner's objection] is simply amazing."

In other words, the authors essentially advocated the Orwellian notion that the sentence *is* the crime, whether or not any actual crime had been committed. For them, it was "amazing" that anyone would think to look behind a piece of paper to see if there were any basis for what the paper declares. Worse, the "suspension" the Signatura had supposedly upheld was not a suspension by anyone in authority at the Vatican, but only a purported suspension by the Bishop of Avellino. "The Vatican" itself had never even claimed to have imposed any discipline on Father Gruner, but merely pointed out what the Bishop of Avellino (under pressure from Sodano) was supposed to have done. But the Bishop of Avellino *had never actually done it*. Even Vere and McElhinney admit that the Bishop of Avellino merely "*warned* that failure to return to his diocese of incardination [within

30 days] would result in his suspension *a divinis*." But they misled the reader when they claimed that "subsequently his competent ecclesiastical superior followed through with the suspension." On the contrary, the Bishop of Avellino did not "follow through with the suspension." In fact, the only one who had followed through in this matter was Father Gruner, who notified the Bishop of Avellino of his incardination by the Archbishop of Hyderabad—who had insisted that his incardination of Father Gruner was valid—to which notice the Bishop of Avellino had offered no objection, nor indeed any response whatsoever.

Vere and McElhinney might have argued—although they did not do so—that Father Gruner's suspension took effect automatically, without any further decrees, after the 30-day period for his supposed "return" to Italy (after 16 years!) had elapsed. Church law describes such an "automatic" suspension as *latae sententiae*. But even if the bishop's threatened suspension were viewed as a *latae sententiae* penalty, the suspension could not operate against Father Gruner, because, as mentioned above, Church law forbids the imposition of penalties for actions that were taken out of necessity or to avoid grave inconvenience.[217]

To this, Vere and McElhinney could only reply that the provision of Church law exempting one from any penalty in cases of necessity or grave inconvenience does not apply to any act which is "intrinsically evil or tends to be harmful to souls." The authors then asked: "Is not disobedience to the lawful command of one's ecclesiastical superior harmful to souls?" But here the authors only beg the question. As just shown, however, the command to "return" to Italy was impossible to obey and no one is held to do the impossible. Nor was the command "lawful" since it amounted to a punishment for something Father Gruner had not in fact done—that is, he did not "fail" to find another bishop, and therefore he could not lawfully be ordered to "return" to Italy for a "failure" that had never occurred. The authors' position thus reduces to the absurdity that "failure" to obey an unfounded, unjust and impossible command is "harmful to souls" merely because the command has not been followed. What is truly harmful to souls, not to mention the very credibility of the Church, is the sort of ruthless abuse of power we see in Cardinal Sodano's overseeing of the persecution of Father Gruner.

Furthermore, Church law specifically provides that a bishop (or other legislator) may not threaten a *latae sententiae*—that is, an automatic—penalty except for a grave and malicious offense that cannot otherwise be corrected.[218] But Father Gruner had not

---

[217] Code of Canon Law, Can. 1323, 2°.

[218] The threat of "*latae sententiae*" (i.e. automatic penalty) by the Bishop of Avellino was

committed any offense at all, let alone a grave and malicious offense. He is accused only of "failing" to be incardinated when he *was* incardinated, and "failing" to return to a country whose immigration law *bars* his return. Father Gruner's "offense," therefore, rests on nothing but canonical thin air. This seemed to be of no concern to our authors, however, who take the position that no one may question a piece of paper stating that Father Gruner's "suspension" had been "confirmed."

A Pharisaical Notion of "Obedience"

The defense of the Vatican Secretary of State's Party Line on Fatima depends heavily upon the same false notion of obedience that has demanded passive acceptance of the entire program of the party of the innovators since Vatican II—none of it actually imposed by the Pope as a requirement of the Faith, but rather by Vatican functionaries who cloak themselves in papal authority they do not in fact possess.

Nevertheless, our two young authors, doing *The Wanderer*'s bidding, piously invoked the example of St. Gerard, an 18th century saint who remained silent in the face of a false accusation that he had engaged in fornication. They suggested that Father Gruner should likewise quietly endure his non-existent "suspension." But what does remaining silent in the face of a false *accusation* have to do with "obedience" to an unjust, unfounded and impossible *command* of a superior—especially when the superior in question can no longer rightly claim authority because the priest in question has been incardinated by another bishop? No one *commanded* St. Gerard to remain silent, and thus his case in no way involved the question whether Catholics ought to obey an unjust command and submit to an abuse of power by a superior. The authors' reference to the example of St. Gerard made no sense at all. Equally senseless was

---

null and void from the beginning. Canon 1318 does not allow the bishop to threaten a "*latae sententiae*" penalty unless ("*nisi*") perhaps for "certain particularly treacherous offenses (*singularia quaedam delicta dolosa*). For a crime to be "dolosum" it must be a "deliberate performance of an unlawful act ... involving trickery or deceit," and "bad faith." (Lewis & Short, *A Latin Dictionary*, p. 570)

No one can reasonably claim that Father Gruner acted "*dolose*", i.e. deliberately and in bad faith, when he refused to obey a precept to reside permanently as an illegal alien in Italy. Therefore, the threatened penalty is null and void.

Moreover, Father Gruner was not subject to "any penalty" (*nulli poenae*) because one is exempt from penalty if acting "out of grave fear, even if only relatively grave, or out of necessity or out of serious inconvenience." (Canon 1323, 4°) Now one who is subject to arrest by the Italian authorities, imprisonment and deportation can most reasonably claim to have not obeyed for reasons of grave fear, necessity and grave inconvenience. Even one, who without fault, thought that such condition existed, cannot be penalized (Canon 1323, 7°), and one who "erroneously and culpably thought" that such conditions of grave fear, necessity or grave inconvenience" (Canon 1324, 8°) existed is exempt from "*latae sententiae*" penalties. (Can. 1324§3)

the authors' reference to the Virgin Mary's consent to become the Mother of God. What did this have to do with the right of the faithful under Church law not to be punished for "failing" to "obey" unjust and impossible commands?

Equally unavailing was the authors' claim that Father Gruner should follow the example of Sister Lucy herself, who has lived her life "as a holy example of submission and obedience to legitimate authority." Father Gruner had the perfect right under Church law not to be punished if he had done nothing wrong, and Church law excuses one from any penalty if the act penalized was done out of necessity or to avoid grave inconvenience. Moreover, the authors failed to note that as the member of a religious order, Sister Lucy was required to take a vow of holy obedience which is more demanding than the promise of ordinary due obedience taken by diocesan (secular) priests like Father Gruner, who live and work in the world. A diocesan priest has many rights that priests and nuns in religious orders do not have, including freedom of association and the right to found and operate associations of the faithful, such as Father Gruner's Fatima apostolate.[219] The Code of Canon Law provides a whole host of protections against unjust commands for priests in Father Gruner's position, including the protections and excuses from operation of penalties I have discussed here. Is Church law of no account? Must a priest submit to any injustice imposed upon him, no matter what rights the law of the Church might guarantee? In that case, why have a Code of Canon Law at all? If "obedience" is the only law, why not repeal the Code and replace it with the dictum: "All commands of superiors, no matter how unjust, must be obeyed." That, essentially, is what the authors were advocating.

At any rate, as Father Gruner had pointed out many times, we are not dealing here with an injustice merely personal to him, as was the false accusation against St. Gerard. Father Gruner might well have preferred to suffer the personal injustice of "returning" to Avellino and living a quiet life with his books and superior Italian cuisine, rather than undergoing the constant stress of defending his apostolate and his good name against constant attacks from every Tom, Dick and Harry that would like to take a potshot at him, including our two young authors. But the injustice against Father Gruner personally extended beyond him to threaten the very existence of an apostolate that was (and is) inarguably the world's most effective promoter of the Message of Fatima, which is precisely why the Party Line requires its extinction. If the apostolate's position is correct—i.e., that the failure to consecrate Russia will lead to the worldwide calamity Our

---

[219] See, e.g. Canon 278, 298, 299: "Secular clerics have the right of association with others for the achievement of purposes befitting the clerical state."

Lady of Fatima described as the *annihilation* of various nations—then millions of lives and the eternal fate of millions of souls are bound up in fulfillment of the Message. That being the case, the destruction of the apostolate would have significant consequences for the Church's common good, to say the least.

The Right to Resist an Abuse of Power

Furthermore, to recall the words of the Archbishop of Hyderabad: "evil forces have conspired to destroy your work of love… bureaucratic forces cannot stifle God's work." Indeed, a true example of Catholic virtue in the face of injustice is the Archbishop himself, who had the courage to stand up to high and mighty bureaucrats of the sort that have plagued Rome throughout the Church's long history. The Archbishop's own actions reflect the *Catholic* teaching, rooted in the natural law, that the faithful have a God-given right to resist a prelate's abuse of power, even if that prelate is *the Pope himself*. The eminent 16th century Catholic theologian Francisco Suarez explained the same principle as follows:

> If [the Pope] gives an order contrary to right customs, he should not be obeyed; *if he attempts to do something manifestly opposed to justice and the common good, it will be lawful to resist him*; if he attacks by force, by force he can be repelled, with a moderation appropriate to a just defense.[220]

Likewise, St. Robert Bellarmine, a Doctor of the Church, taught that:

> Just as it is licit to resist the Pontiff that aggresses the body, it is also licit to resist the one who aggresses souls or who disturbs civil order, or, above all, who attempts to destroy the Church. I say that it is licit to resist him by not doing what he orders and by preventing his will from being executed; it is not licit, however, to judge, punish or depose him, since these acts are proper to a superior.[221]

Thus, for example, Polycrates of Ephesus and the synods of Asia Minor were within their rights in *refusing to obey* the command of Pope St. Victor I that they abandon the quartodeciman Easter. As the *Catholic Encyclopedia* notes: "The *resistance* of the Asiatic bishops involved no denial of the supremacy of Rome. It indicates solely that the bishops believed St. Victor to be abusing his power in bidding them renounce a custom for which they had Apostolic authority." If even a sainted Pope can be resisted when he abuses his power attempting to destroy an ancient custom in the Church, all the more

---

[220] *De Fide*, Disp. X, Sec. VI, N. 16.
[221] St. Robert Bellarmine, *De Romano Pontifice*, Book II, Chapter 29.

can Vatican bureaucrats be resisted when they abuse their power by attempting to orchestrate the bogus "suspension" of a faithful priest in order to further the illicit aim of burying any recollection of the Mother of God's prophetic warnings to the Church and the world at Fatima.

But Vere and McElhinney not only ignored the natural law principle that members of the faithful have the right to resist an abuse of power, they ignored the teaching of the Magisterium on the proper exercise of authority by a bishop over his priests. The relation between a bishop and his priests is like the relation between a father and son. As the Council of Trent teaches: "Bishops and all ordinaries must be pastors not persecutors. They must rule their subjects but not dominate them. They must love their subjects as brothers and sons..."[222] This means, obviously, that prelates, like natural fathers, have no right before God or man to punish their priests when no offense has been committed or to "suspend" them for "failing" to do the impossible.

In short, the notion of priestly "obedience" the authors advocated was more appropriate to Nazi Germany or Stalinist Russia than the Catholic Church. But is it not this very notion of a false and blind obedience to every command that has reduced the post-Conciliar Church to a shambles? Are we not today witnessing a situation in which faithful priests are routinely punished for "disobedience" while true enemies of the Church are ignored or even rewarded for their acts of ecclesiastical treason? Do we not see precisely that condition of injustice lamented by Saint Basil the Great at the height of the Arian heresy?: "Only one offense is now vigorously punished, an accurate observance of our fathers' traditions."

Despising the Fatima Prophecy

In the process of defending the Party Line on Fatima, it was only a matter of time before *The Wanderer* had to attack the very credibility of the Message of Fatima itself. For the Party Line's defenders have gotten themselves in a terrible bind. For decades they have maintained that Russia was consecrated to the Immaculate Heart of Mary in 1984 and that anyone who says otherwise is "disloyal to the Holy Father"—who himself has conspicuously refrained from pronouncing authoritatively on the matter. But, for decades, the evidence of Russia's ever worsening spiritual and material condition has been piling up. As the tension between reality and the Party Line becomes unsustainable, it finally becomes necessary to drop

---

[222] Council of Trent, quoted in Canon 2214 of the 1917 Code of Canon Law: *Meminerint Episcopi aliique Ordinarii se pastores non percussores esse, atque ita praeesse, sibi subditis oportere, ut non in eis dominentur, ses illos tamquam filios et fratres diligent.*

the pretense of respect for the Fatima event and openly declare that perhaps it was never really worthy of belief in the first place, which was precisely the innuendo of the "official" Vatican commentary on the Third Secret with its citation to Father Dhanis, a leading Fatima skeptic. Better that than to admit the Party Line is a fraud.

At *The Wanderer* that moment came in October 2001, just over a year after the Vatican's disclosure of the vision of the "Bishop dressed in White." In the aforementioned article by Farley Clinton, *The Wanderer* revealed that it was to be numbered among Our Lady of Fatima's false friends. Wrote Clinton:

> Father Edouard Dhanis suggested, not implausibly, in the early 1940s that *the Blessed Virgin could not have asked for the consecration of Russia by the Pope and the bishops—for it is morally impossible. God does not demand impossibilities.* Sixty years ago, the Church looked much less infested by imposters than now, the bishops less likely to be recalcitrant. But Dhanis saw great practical difficulties even then from the fact that Russia was a Marxist nation, of Orthodox tradition.

There it was, right on the pages of *The Wanderer*. Siding with a Modernist Jesuit who contributed heavily to the infamously heretical Dutch Catechism,[223] a leading neo-Catholic organ now openly repudiated the Message of Fatima, daring to suggest that the Blessed Virgin never asked for the Consecration of Russia and that Sister Lucy simply made the whole thing up. In other words, *The Wanderer* was now willing to say that perhaps *Sister Lucy was a liar*—a very pious liar, to be sure, who sincerely believed her lies, but a liar nonetheless, who had misled the entire Catholic Church for the better part of a century until her death in 2005.

As Dhanis himself had put it: "All things considered, it is not easy to state precisely what degree of credence is to be given to the accounts of Sister Lucy. Without questioning her sincerity, or the sound judgment she shows in daily life, one may judge it prudent to use her writings only with reservations. Let us observe also that a good person can be sincere and prove to have good judgment in everyday life, but have a *propensity for unconscious fabrication* in a certain area, or in any case, a tendency to relate old memories of twenty years ago with embellishments and considerable modifications."[224] That Sister Lucy's testimony was authenticated by an unprecedented public miracle witnessed by 70,000 people did not impress Dhanis.

---

[223] See, *The Devil's Final Battle*, edited and compiled by Father Paul Kramer (Terryville, Connecticut: The Missionary Association, 2002), Chapters 5-9, "Appendix: A Chronology of the Fatima Cover-up"; Francis Alban and Christopher A. Ferrara, *Fatima Priest*, Fourth Edition, Chapters 9-13, 18-20.

[224] Dhanis' entire thesis against Fatima is explained and critiqued in Frère Michel, *The Whole Truth About Fatima*, Vol. I, Part II, Chapter 1. All quotations concerning the writings of Dhanis are taken from this chapter of Frère Michel's work.

No, according to him, God worked a miracle in order to vouch for His choice of *an unreliable witness*. This borderline blasphemy was now being advanced by *The Wanderer*.

In Chapter 5 we saw how, in the Vatican's commentary on the Third Secret, Cardinal Ratzinger called Dhanis an "eminent scholar" on Marian apparitions, including the apparitions at Fatima. But this "eminent scholar" refused to examine the official Fatima archives which are the very basis of Fatima scholarship. Then, relying on his willful ignorance of the facts, Dhanis cast doubt on every aspect of the apparitions that did not accord with his Modernist theology: the prayer taught by the angel he called "inexact"; the vision of hell he called an "exaggeratedly medieval representation"; the prophecy of "a night illumined by an unknown light" heralding the advent of World War II he described as "grounds for suspicion". And as for the consecration of Russia, Dhanis flatly declared that: "Russia could not be consecrated by the Pope, without this act taking on the air of a challenge, both in regard to the separated hierarchy, as well as the Union of Soviet Socialist Republics. *This would make the consecration practically unrealizable.*" Thus, Dhanis declared that the consecration of Russia would be "morally impossible by reason of the reactions it would normally provoke." Says who? Says Dhanis, who evidently considered himself more prudent than the Mother of God.

Dhanis' deconstruction of the Message of Fatima is a typical example of how Modernists undermine truth based upon premises they themselves invent. Since the consecration of Russia is morally impossible—a premise Dhanis assumed without proof—how could Our Lady of Fatima have requested it? Having thus stacked the deck against Sister Lucy, Dhanis stated the "inevitable" conclusion: "But could the Most Holy Virgin have requested a consecration which, taken according to the rigor of the terms, would be practically unrealizable? This question indeed seems to call for a *'negative response'*. Thus, it hardly seems probable that Our Lady asked for the consecration of Russia."[225] Based entirely on his own premise he had not bothered to demonstrate, Dhanis pronounced Sister Lucy's testimony a fake. The entire process of "refutation" occurred in Dhanis' head, with no examination by this "eminent scholar" of the crucial documents contained in the Fatima archives.

But there was one premise Dhanis—and *The Wanderer*—forgot, a premise that Catholics are bound to accept: With God, all things are possible. On the other hand, the omnipotence of God has never figured very prominently in the thinking of "eminent scholars" like the Modernist Dhanis. Nor, it would seem, is divine omnipotence of any account in the editorial policy of "establishment" newspapers

---

[225] *Ibid.*

like *The Wanderer* respecting the Fatima event. Rather, their faith would appear to lie in the dictates of Vatican bureaucrats who have no authority over the matter in the first place.

Why?

There have been at least a dozen *Wanderer* articles attacking Father Gruner on one pretext or another, although not even *The Wanderer* can deny his orthodoxy and commitment to the sacred priesthood. This is a priest who has traveled the world spreading authentic Roman Catholicism, including devotion to the Blessed Virgin; a priest whose sound preaching and distribution of millions of Brown and Green Scapulars have helped to obtain innumerable conversions; a priest whose apostolate supports an orphanage in one of the most impoverished regions of the world.

Another example of this bizarre anti-Gruner editorial campaign was an article condemning Father Gruner's opposition to Communion in the hand and women attending Mass with uncovered heads.[226] Generally, however, *The Wanderer* assails Father Gruner for his objection to the effort by members of the Vatican apparatus to revise the Message of Fatima to suit the Secretary of State's Party Line—including a 1984 "consecration" of Russia that deliberately avoided any mention of Russia so that the Russian Orthodox would not be offended.

The Wanderer's obsession with discrediting Father Gruner is a very curious editorial priority, given the widespread moral and doctrinal corruption in the priesthood today. But what is to account for it? The answer would appear to be that *The Wanderer*'s editorial policy is in keeping with its general line of enabling the post-Conciliar revolution in the Church by helpfully denouncing anyone who opposes the "reforms" of the revolution. *The Wanderer* is not merely a servitor of the Party Line on Fatima, but also the entire program of the party of the innovators, whose disastrous handiwork was foreseen by the future Pius XII in light of the Fatima revelations.

Be it the ruinous imposition of the New Mass, Communion in the hand, altar girls, or even papal prayer meetings with witchdoctors, *The Wanderer* has been there to defend the innovation and to condemn any significant opposition to it by tradition-minded Catholics. Hence the famous family split between Al Matt, editor of *The Wanderer*, and Walter Matt, his cousin, who left *The Wanderer* to found *The Remnant* newspaper in 1967 in order to offer loyal opposition to the changes already being imposed on the Church by Vatican bureaucrats, including Bugnini, with disastrous effect.

---

[226] That attack on Father Gruner was responded to at length in the article "Defending the Revolution," in the March 2003 issue of *Catholic Family News*.

As the human element of the Church descended ever deeper into chaos and apostasy, *The Wanderer* became ever more obstinate in its defense of destructive novelties the great pre-Conciliar popes would undoubtedly have viewed with utter horror. Just imagine St. Pius X's reaction to what *The Wanderer* would defend as "reverent" Novus Ordo Mass, complete with altar table, Communion in the hand, lay ministers—*The Wanderer*'s editor is himself a lay "lector"—and banal music.

Only a perverse determination to defend indefensible changes in the Church—the very changes foreseen with dread by Pius XII—could explain *The Wanderer*'s preoccupation with Father Gruner. Since Father Gruner is clearly the world's foremost exponent of the "old"—that is to say, the authentic—Message of Fatima, *The Wanderer*'s ongoing defense of the post-Conciliar "reform" of the Church in general would logically impel it to condemn the most prominent opponent of the "reform" of Fatima. Just as *The Wanderer* defends the scandalous novelties of Communion in the hand and altar girls (while perhaps "preferring" more traditional practices), so it now defends a Fatima message scandalously innovated according to the dictates of the Vatican Secretary of State and his collaborators.

Chapter 10

CARDINAL BERTONE AND
THE COLLAPSE OF THE PARTY LINE

On February 13, 2005, Sister Lucia passed on to her eternal reward at the age of 97, to be followed by Pope John Paul II on April 2. By the closing months of 2006 the former Archbishop Bertone, Secretary of the CDF, had become Cardinal Bertone, successor to Cardinal Sodano as Vatican Secretary of State under Pope Benedict XVI. In a manner befitting the ecclesiastical politician he is, Sodano "hunkered down in the apartment and offices he occupied as former Secretary of State and [defied] the Pope to remove him," threatening "that any attempt to remove him will be met by Sodano's revelation of 'where the bodies are hidden' from the last ten years of John Paul II's pontificate—meaning the many things that went terribly wrong on account of the Pope's declining capacity during that period."[227]

As Bertone assumed his new office—forced to reside temporarily in Saint John's Tower on account of Sodano's refusal to relocate—the controversy over the Third Secret had not only failed to abate, it had reached a higher intensity than ever before. Antonio Socci's *Fourth Secret* (published in November 2006) had shifted to the Vatican a heavy new burden of proof.

A Remarkable Change of Mind

When he set out to write his book on the Third Secret affair, Socci was at first determined to demolish the claims of the so-called "Fatimists" that the Vatican is holding something back. He had once viewed such claims as mere "dietrologies," an Italian idiom for conspiracy theories that look behind (*dietro*) events for hidden plots. He was convinced that the vision of the bishop in white was all there was to the Third Secret, and that in *The Message of Fatima*, the Vatican-published commentary on the vision and the Fatima message in general, Ratzinger and Bertone had laid all questions to rest.

As Socci first believed, "Fatimist" literature casting doubt on the completeness of the Vatican's disclosure originated "from the burning disappointment of a Third Secret that controverted all of their apocalyptic predictions." The "Fatimists" had to be refuted, he thought, because the "polemical arms" in their arsenal were "at the disposal of whoever wanted to launch a heavy attack against the

---

[227] Christopher A. Ferrara, "World Waits for Indult to Come and Sodano to Go," *The Remnant*, March 5, 2007, http://www.remnantnewspaper.com/Archives/archive-2007-0215-news_from_rome.htm.

Vatican."[228] But then Socci encountered unexpected strength in the "Fatimist" case, which he had never studied closely. At the same time, his own suspicions were aroused when Cardinal Bertone declined to grant him an interview, despite their friendly relations and Socci's intention to defend Bertone's position. That refusal opened Socci's eyes to the possibility "that there are embarrassing questions and that there is above all something (of gravity) to hide."[229]

As Socci explains: "In the end, I had to surrender.... Here I recount my voyage into the greatest mystery of the 20th century and set forth the result I honestly reached. A result that sincerely contradicts my initial convictions..."[230] As Socci flatly declares, in agreement with vast numbers of skeptical Catholics, something must be missing: "[T]hat there is a part of the Secret not revealed and considered unspeakable *is certain*. And today—having decided to deny its existence—the Vatican runs the risk of exposing itself to very heavy pressure and blackmail."[231] What completely changed Socci's mind and made him "surrender" is simply this: overwhelming evidence, which will be surveyed here. The evidence convinced Socci that the "dietrologies" of the "Fatimists"—i.e., loyal Catholics who have reasonable doubts about the official account—were actually correct: there must be a separate but related text of the Secret, not yet revealed, containing "the words of the Madonna [which] preannounce an apocalyptic crisis of the faith in the Church starting from the top." This second text is probably "also an explanation of the vision (revealed on June 26, 2000) where there appear the Pope, the bishops and martyred faithful, after having traversed a city in ruins."[232] That explanation, writes Socci, would involve "the preannounced assassination of a Pope [the white-clad bishop in the vision] in the context of an immense martyrdom of Christians and of a devastation of the world."[233] Only such an explanation would make sense of the otherwise inexplicable vision.

A Devastating Eyewitness

Socci gave wide publicity in particular to the testimony of Archbishop Loris F. Capovilla, the still-living personal secretary of John XXIII. As Socci recounts, in July of 2006 Capovilla was interviewed by the Fatima scholar Solideo Paolini concerning the existence of the posited second text. During that interview Paolini

---

[228] Antonio Socci, *Il Quarto Segreto di Fatima* ["The Fourth Secret of Fatima"], (Milano: Rai and Eri Rizzoli, 2007) English ed., p. 3; popular ed., p. 10; Italian ed., pp. 12, 13.

[229] Ibid., English ed., p. 4; popular ed., p. 11; Italian ed., p. 14.

[230] Ibid.

[231] Ibid., English ed., p. 162; popular ed., p. 111; Italian ed., p. 173.

[232] Ibid., English ed., p. 74; popular ed., p. 55; Italian ed., p. 82.

[233] Ibid., English ed., p. 55; popular ed., p. 43; Italian ed., pp. 63-64.

asked the Archbishop whether there was an unpublished text of the Secret, and the Archbishop replied evasively: "I know nothing. (*Nulla so!*)" Note well: he did not answer simply "No!" That answer puzzled Paolini, who expected that the Archbishop, "among the few who know the Secret, would have been able to respond to me that this is a completely impracticable idea and that everything had already been revealed in 2000. Instead he answered: 'I know nothing.' An expression that I imagined he wished ironically to evoke a certain *omertá* [code of silence]."[234] Paolini's impression was confirmed by subsequent events.

After the interview, Paolini received from Capovilla in the mail a package of papers from his files, along with a perplexing cover letter advising him to obtain a copy of *TMF*, which Capovilla must have known that Paolini, a student of Fatima, would already possess. Was this not, thought Paolini, "an invitation to read something in particular in that publication in relation to the documents sent by the same Archbishop?" That intuition was correct. Among the documents Capovilla had sent was one stamped "confidential note" by him, dated May 17, 1967, in which he had recorded the circumstances of a reading of the Third Secret by Pope Paul VI on June 27, 1963, only six days after his election to the papacy and before he had even been seated officially at the coronation Mass (which took place on June 29). But according to *TMF* and the "official account" in general, Paul VI did not read the Secret until nearly two years later: "Paul VI read the contents with the Substitute, Archbishop Angelo Dell'Acqua, on 27 March 1965, and returned the envelope to the Archives of the Holy Office, deciding not to publish the text."[235]

The huge discrepancy between the date recorded by Capovilla and that set forth in *TMF* prompted Paolini to telephone Capovilla, at precisely 7:45 p.m. on the same day he received the documents, to ask the Archbishop to explain the discrepancy. Capovilla protested: "Ah, but I spoke the truth. Look I am still lucid!" When Paolini politely insisted that, still, there was an unexplained discrepancy, Capovilla offered explanations that suggested "eventual lapse of memory, interpretations of what he had intended to say," whereupon Paolini reminded him that he had recorded the date of the reading by Paul VI in a stamped, official document. Capovilla then gave this reply: "But I am right, because perhaps *the Bertone envelope is not the same as the Capovilla envelope.*"

Stunned, Paolini then asked the decisive question: "Therefore, both dates are true, because there are two texts of the Third Secret?"

---

[234] Ibid., English ed., p. 131; popular ed., p. 91; Italian ed., p. 140.

[235] Ibid., English ed., p. 131; popular ed., p. 91; Italian ed., p. 141; and citing *TMF*, p. 15 (English print edition).

After a brief pause, the Archbishop gave the explosive answer that confirmed the existence of a missing envelope and text of the Third Secret of Fatima: "Exactly so! (*Per l'appunto!*)."[236]

The "confidential note" completely corroborated Capovilla's testimony.[237] According to the note, on the date Pope Paul read the Secret (again, June 27, 1963), Monsignor Angelo Dell'Acqua—the same "Substitute" referred to in *TMF*—telephoned Capovilla to ask: "I am looking for the Fatima envelope. Do you know where it is kept?"[238] The note records that Capovilla replied: "It is in the right hand drawer of the writing desk called Barbarigo, *in the bedroom*." That is, the envelope was in the former bedroom of John XXIII, which was now the bedroom of Paul VI; it was *not* in the Holy Office archives, where the text of the vision was lodged. The existence of two different texts comprising the entirety of the Third Secret of Fatima—the text of the vision and the text in the papal writing desk—now stood confirmed beyond any reasonable doubt.

A Feeble Reply

In May of 2007, Rizzoli, the same publisher that had published *Fourth Secret*, rushed into print a book by Cardinal Bertone entitled *L'Ultima Veggente di Fatima* ["The Last Visionary of Fatima"] (*Last Visionary*).[239] *Last Visionary*, which appeared in bookstores a mere six months after *Fourth Secret*, is essentially a 100-page interview of the Cardinal concerning various subjects, followed by another 50 pages of appendices. This mass of verbiage surrounded a mere nine pages of comment in response to the claims of Socci and the "Fatimists" (including Father Gruner, whose name was also mentioned by the Cardinal). The interviewer was a layman, Giuseppe De Carli, a *vaticanista* (reporter on the Vatican beat) and ardent admirer of the Cardinal, whose fawning questions not only posed no real challenge to the Cardinal, but actually attempted to assist him in promoting what Socci had called "the official reconstruction" of the Third Secret. But *Last Visionary* failed utterly to address the substance of Socci's book, and in particular the testimony of Archbishop Capovilla, which was simply ignored—a telling omission in a book that was supposed to have been an answer to Socci.

---

[236] Ibid., English ed., p. 132; popular ed., p. 92; Italian ed., p. 142.

[237] The Italian original and English translation of the stamped "confidential note," dated May 17, 1967, are reproduced in Appendix I of *The Secret Still Hidden*.

[238] Notice Dell'Acqua evidently presumed that the envelope was somewhere in the papal apartment, not in the Holy Office archive, of which Capovilla was not the custodian. Otherwise, Dell'Acqua would have asked the custodian of the archive, Cardinal Ottaviani, where the "Fatima envelope" was, rather than Capovilla, Pope John's former personal secretary.

[239] Bertone, Cardinal Tarcisio, *The Last Visionary of Fatima* (Milano: Rai and Eri Rizzoli, 2007). All English translations are mine.

On May 12, 2007, Socci published in his widely read Internet column this astonishing challenge to Bertone: "Dear Cardinal Bertone: Who—between you and me—is deliberately lying?"[240] Socci was responding to the Cardinal's suggestion in *Last Visionary* that Socci had misled the Catholic faithful in *Fourth Secret*. The significance of this public challenge to the credibility of the Vatican Secretary of State by one of Italy's most prominent laymen could not be overestimated; nor could Bertone afford to ignore it.

A Mountain of Evidence

By the time Socci's book was published, Cardinal Bertone, the new custodian of the Party Line, was facing a public relations crisis provoked by the same growing mountain of evidence that had changed Socci's mind and caused him to publish his breakthrough book affirming the existence of a text of the Third Secret that the Vatican was withholding. We note here some of the key points developed by the sources Socci had studied and by Socci's own work on the subject, some of which have been mentioned in Chapter 5:

- Sister Lucia revealed that a text of the Secret is in the form of a letter to the Bishop of Fatima, but the text describing the vision is not a letter.

- Our Lady clearly had more to say following the momentous "etc," which clearly begins another, and thus the third, part of the Great Secret, but the vision contains not a word from Her.

- Our Lady explains everything in the vision contained in the first part of the Great Secret, but we are asked to believe that there is absolutely no explanation from Her concerning the vision in the third part—i.e., the Third Secret.

- Father Schweigl revealed that the Third Secret has two parts: one concerning the Pope, and the other "a logical continuation of the words 'In Portugal the dogma of the faith will always be preserved etc,'" but the vision does not contain that logical continuation of the Virgin's words.

- The Vatican-initiated press release from 1960, announcing suppression of the Secret, describes the suppressed text as *"the letter"* that "will never be opened," containing *"the words* which Our Lady confided as a secret to the three little

---

[240] Article of May 12, 2007 in archive at http://www.antoniosocci.it/Socci/index.cfm; see English translation at http://www.fatima.org/news/newsviews/052907socci. asp.

shepherds…", but the vision is not a letter and contains no words confided by the Virgin as a secret.

- Cardinal Ottaviani, who read and had custody of the Secret, revealed that it involved a "sheet of paper" bearing 25 lines of text recording "what Our Lady *told her* [Lucia] to tell the Holy Father…", but the vision spans 62 lines, and in it the Virgin does not tell Sister Lucy anything at all.

- A text of the Secret was kept in the papal apartment during the pontificates of Pius XII, John XXIII and Paul VI, and at least at the beginning of the pontificate of John Paul II, even though Bertone's "official account" speaks only of a text in the Holy Office archives.

- John XXIII read a text of the Secret that was so difficult it required an Italian translation of the Portuguese, but he also read another text, the following year, that he could understand perfectly without a translation.

- The text of the vision contains no particularly difficult Portuguese expressions.

- There are two different Italian translations of the Secret: the one prepared for John XXIII, and the one prepared in 1967, neither of which we have been allowed to see.

- Three different Popes (John XXIII, Paul VI, John Paul II) read texts of the Secret on two different dates—years apart— during their respective pontificates, but all three of these second readings are mysteriously omitted from the "official account."

- Those who have read the Secret have revealed that it speaks of a coming state of apostasy in the Church as well as a planetary crisis, but the vision standing alone says nothing of apostasy in the Church.

- Cardinal Ratzinger revealed that the Third Secret refers to "dangers threatening the faith and the life of the Christian, and therefore of the world," and further revealed a correspondence between the Message of Fatima and the Message of Akita, in which Our Lady, *in Her own words*, warns of a coming crisis in the Church accompanied by a fiery chastisement of the world. The vision standing alone, however, contains no such warning from Our Lady.

- When pressed to explain in 2000 what text of the Secret John Paul II reportedly read in 1978, given that Bertone claimed John Paul did not read the Secret until 1981, Bertone was evasive and finally said merely that "in my opinion" John Paul did not read a text in 1978, when it would have been a simple matter to ascertain this from innumerable sources at his disposal, including the Pope himself—an omission clearly suggesting that Bertone knew the report was true.

- Archbishop Capovilla, personal secretary to John XXIII, confirmed to Solideo Paolini the existence of two texts and two envelopes relating to the Third Secret, one of which, bearing his (Capovilla's) handwriting and kept in the papal apartment, had never been produced.

- Capovilla had never retracted his testimony to Paolini, even though he had had every opportunity to do so.

- Bertone, in the process of producing *Last Visionary*, had evidently not even asked Capovilla to retract what he had revealed to Paolini, or had sought a retraction but was refused.

- Bertone had failed and refused to produce the reopened and resealed Capovilla envelope.

- The Vatican had issued no official denial of the allegations in Socci's book, even though Socci had literally accused Bertone of covering up the very words of the Mother of God.

- On the contrary, Pope Benedict XVI had sent Socci a note "concerning my book, thanking me for 'the sentiments which have suggested it,'" without the slightest indication that the book is in error.

A Televised Disaster

Having failed to quell mounting skepticism over the "official version" with his publication of *Last Visionary*, which had only conceded Socci's entire case for a cover-up, Bertone next undertook the extraordinary initiative of appearing as a guest on the Italian talk show *Porta a Porta* ["Door to Door"] on May 31, 2007 in a further bid to refute Socci. Incredibly, while the show was entitled "The Fourth Secret of Fatima Does Not Exist," a clear reference to the title of Socci's book, Socci was not invited to defend himself. The field was left open for Bertone to kick a goal into an undefended net, yet he fumbled the setup completely, not only failing to refute Socci but providing further devastating admissions and revelations.

But this was the risk Bertone was forced to incur by making such an extraordinary televised appearance: If he said nothing in response to Socci's book, he would have conceded the existence of a cover-up and his own involvement in it. But if he made the appearance, there was the potential for further slip-ups and inadvertent revelations. And that is exactly what happened. The details of this televised disaster for the Party Line are set forth elsewhere.[241] Here, an adumbration of key points will have to suffice:

- During the telecast Bertone, under mounting public pressure, finally revealed on camera that there are actually *two* identical sealed envelopes of Lucia's, bearing the "express order of Our Lady" that the contents were not to be revealed until 1960, even though he had been representing for seven years that there is only one envelope, falsely claiming that Lucia "confessed" she had never received any order from the Virgin linking the Secret to 1960 and forbidding its disclosure until then.

- That is, Bertone had been caught in two demonstrable falsehoods: that there was only one envelope pertaining to the Third Secret, and that the Blessed Virgin had never connected the Secret to the year 1960. Both were exposed as falsehoods by the very evidence Bertone himself displayed on camera, acting as if he did not appreciate the significance of his own revelation.

- Bertone further revealed a *third* envelope of Lucia's, unsealed and addressed to Bishop da Silva, which, together with the Bishop's outer envelope, would make a total of *four* envelopes we are supposed to believe were all created for only one text of the Secret.

- Yet, when he held up Bishop da Silva's outer envelope to a bright light, auxiliary Bishop Venâncio saw only *one* envelope inside, and took exact measurements of both the envelope and the single sheet of paper within it, which contained 20-25 lines of text, just as Cardinal Ottaviani testified.

- The measurements of the envelope and the sheet of paper taken by Bishop Venâncio are entirely different from the measurements of the envelope and the sheet of paper revealed by Bertone on *Porta a Porta*.

---

[241] Cf. *The Secret Still Hidden*, Chapter 8.

- Bertone himself revealed, only weeks before his appearance on *Porta a Porta*, in his book *Last Visionary of Fatima*, that in April 2000 Sister Lucia "authenticated" *sheets* of paper pertaining to the Secret, even though on *Porta a Porta* Bertone revealed only one sheet, folded to make four sides, that contained the text of the vision.

- In *Last Visionary* Bertone also revealed that there was also an outer envelope, not Lucia's, bearing the note "Third Part of the Secret," which likewise has never been produced.

- During the telecast Bertone admitted that Cardinal Ottaviani had indeed testified "categorically" ("*categoricamente*") to the existence of a text of the Secret spanning only one page and 25 lines, whereas the text of the vision displayed on camera spans four pages—four sides of a folded-over sheet of paper—and 62 lines. After a commercial break, Bertone offered the lame explanation that Ottaviani had somehow miscounted the 62 lines of the vision to arrive at 25 lines.

- Confronted with mounting evidence of a cover-up, Bertone adopted on *Porta a Porta* the new line of referring repeatedly to an "authentic" text of the Secret, an "authentic" envelope, and the "only folio that exists in the Holy Office archives," when he knew full well that there was a text and envelope in the papal apartment, thus suggesting, as Socci would note,[242] that he deems a second text of the Secret "inauthentic."

- Regarding this new notion of an "authentic' text, Bertone referred during the telecast to a document that "actually existed in the archives," insisting that "there was only this folio in the archive of the Holy Office in 1957, when by order of Our Lady and the Bishop of Leiria, Sister Lucia accepted that the Secret be brought to Rome from the archives of the Patriarch of Lisbon...." Yet the document in question *was never in the archives of the Patriarch of Lisbon*. It is an undeniable historical fact that in 1957 copies of all Lucia's writings and the envelope containing the Secret were personally delivered by auxiliary Bishop Venâncio directly from the chancery in Leiria to the Papal Nuncio in Lisbon, Msgr. Cento, who took the documents directly to Rome.[243]

---

[242] *See* "Bertone nel 'vespaio' delle polemiche" ["Bertone in the 'Wasp's Nest' of the Polemics"], June 2, 2007, http://www.antoniosocci.com/2007/06/bertone-nel-%e2%80%9cvespaio%e2%80%9d-delle-polemiche/.

[243] Cf. *The Whole Truth About Fatima*, Vol. III, pp. 480-481.

As Socci concluded in his reply to the telecast from which he had so suspiciously been excluded, despite the absence of any real challenge to Bertone's version of the facts the Cardinal had only succeeded in demonstrating that the doubt Pope John professed to have concerning the supernatural origin of the Third Secret

> could not refer to the text of the vision revealed in 2000, that does not contain anything "delicate." But only to that "fourth secret" that—as Cardinals Ottaviani and Ciappi revealed—spoke of apostasy and the betrayal by the upper ecclesiastical hierarchy. That "fourth secret" of which John Paul II, in 1982, said that it "had not been published because it could be badly interpreted." That "fourth secret" of which Cardinal Ratzinger, in 1996, said that at the moment certain "details" could be harmful to the faith...[244]

Bertone's every effort to answer Socci had only dug a deeper pit for him and the other defenders of the Party Line. As Socci had said in defense of himself, Bertone had "offered the proof that I am right," that there is indeed a missing text of the Secret. This disaster prompted yet another unprecedented initiative by the Cardinal Secretary of State.

The Cardinal Bertone Show

On September 21, 2007, with the "official account" crumbling around him, Cardinal Bertone staged his own personal television show in an auditorium at the Pontifical Urbaniana University in Rome near the Vatican. The pretext was the "introduction" of *Last Visionary*, which had been published and introduced at a press conference months before. Like the appearance on *Porta a Porta*, this spectacle only confirmed the existence of the very thing Bertone was attempting to conceal. Here, too, a summary of the key elements of this latest debacle will have to suffice:[245]

- During the telecast Bertone continued his mysterious failure to address a single question that would penetrate to the heart of any of these matters, which he knows to be in controversy, and in particular has avoided like the plague any questions about the "etc.," the text in the papal apartment, the testimony of Solideo Paolini concerning the admissions by Archbishop Capovilla, the never-produced Capovilla envelope, and the mysterious sudden appearance of multiple envelopes never mentioned before.

---

[244] Antonio Socci, "Bertone nel 'vespaio' delle polemiche" ["Bertone in the 'Wasp's Nest' of the Polemics"], loc. cit.

[245] For a more complete explanation, see Christopher Ferrara, *The Secret Still Hidden*, Ch. 10, pp. 167-197.

- Called as a witness by Bertone, Bishop Seraphim of Fatima, who purportedly witnessed Lucia's authentication of the text of the vision in April 2000, employed the even more nuanced declaration by declaring on camera that "the Secret of Fatima has been revealed in an *authentic* and integral way," declining to affirm simply that the Third Secret of Fatima had been revealed entirely and that nothing had been withheld.

- Unable to avoid any longer the subject of Archbishop Capovilla's explosive testimony, Bertone broadcast a heavily edited video interview of Capovilla conducted, not by an official Vatican representative, but by Giuseppe De Carli, the journalist who had collaborated with Bertone on *Last Visionary*. The interview *never once addressed Capovilla's admissions to Solideo Paolini*, and Capovilla was never asked by De Carli to retract them.

- Quite the contrary, during the interview *Capovilla fully confirmed the existence of the never-produced Capovilla envelope* and the reading of its contents by John XXIII and Paul VI on dates different from those provided in the "official account" for the reading of the text of the vision published in 2000.

- Despite this devastating revelation, De Carli—but *not* Capovilla—declared on camera that the "Capovilla envelope" which the Vatican has never produced, and the "Bertone envelope" containing the text of the vision, are one and the same envelope—a manifest absurdity from which De Carli would retreat during his later appearance at a Fatima conference sponsored by Father Gruner's Fatima apostolate in Rome.

- Socci and Paolini, who waited outside the auditorium in the hope of confronting Cardinal Bertone with a key question about the Secret, relating to the famous "etc," were ejected from the premises by security guards.

- Before they were ejected, however, they were able to play for the other journalists present an audiotape of a subsequent meeting between Paolini and Archbishop Capovilla during which the Archbishop states that: "Besides the four pages [of the vision of the bishop in white] there was also something else, an attachment, yes." As the reporter from the prominent Italian newspaper *Il Giornale* concluded, Capovilla's statement "would confirm the thesis of the existence of a second sheet with the interpretation of the Secret. The mystery, and above all the polemics, will continue."[246]

- Bertone has never denied the existence of this "attachment," even though *Il Giornale* had declared that it "would confirm the thesis of the existence of a second sheet with the interpretation of the Secret."

The final speaker on "The Cardinal Bertone Show" was Bertone himself. This is the Cardinal's moment to answer the many concerns raised by Socci and Catholics the world over concerning his version of events. But, as he had done for the past seven years, he continued to duck every issue. But even in the act of doing so, he made another serious misstep with the following statement: "On the famous Third Secret, on the truth of the Third Secret, I will not return. Certainly, if there had been some further element, of commentary, of integration, it would have appeared in her [Lucia's] letters, in her thousands of letters—something that isn't there."

It seems that every time he opens his mouth to speak on the subject, the Cardinal cannot help but raise further doubts about the veracity of his account. Why would he say that *if* there were a missing part of the Third Secret it would have appeared in Sister Lucia's correspondence with various people around the world, rather than in a text she wrote specifically at the direction of the Virgin? Why would Lucia reveal an element of the Third Secret in her letters to third parties when, as we know, the Secret was transmitted in two envelopes which state they "can only be opened in 1960 by the Cardinal Patriarch of Lisbon or the Bishop of Leiria"? Did the Cardinal mean to direct our attention away from those two envelopes, or the never-produced "Capovilla envelope" bearing the dictation of John XXIII? And on what basis did he assert that there was nothing pertaining to the Secret in Lucia's thousands of letters? Had he read and studied them all?

Cardinal Bertone's every effort to salvage the credibility of his account since becoming Secretary of State had only called his credibility further into question. Even the Wikipedia entry for "Tarcisio Bertone" now contains this entry:

> After Bertone's book [*Last Visionary*] was published, Italian journalist Antonio Socci published an article entitled, "Dear Cardinal Bertone: Who—between you and me—is Deliberately Lying?" Catholic attorney Christopher Ferrara wrote an entire book called *The Secret Still Hidden* (content available online) aimed at exposing and debunking the claims of Cardinal Bertone

---

[246] "The Fourth Secret of Fatima does not exist," *Il Giornale*, September 22, 2007.

with respect to Fatima. The book contains an appendix entitled, *101 Grounds for Doubting Cardinal Bertone's Account*.[247]

And, soon enough, the Pope himself would reject Bertone's "official account" and "reopen the file" on the Third Secret of Fatima, clearly suggesting that there is much more to the Secret than has been revealed, as Antonio Socci would be happy to note. At the same time, however, as if the Pope had never spoken, various false friends of Fatima down low would rush to save the Party Line dictated by Bertone and his collaborators from on high.

---

[247] "Tarcisio Bertone," http://en.wikipedia.org/wiki/Tarcisio_Bertone.

Chapter 11

A FALSE FRIEND BECOMES A TRUE FRIEND

From May 3-7, 2010, the famous Ergife Hotel in Rome was the venue for a conference entitled "The Fatima Challenge," sponsored by Father Gruner's Fatima Center. The event would prove to be perhaps the most productive in the apostolate's history—what Americans call a "game-changer," although the matter involved is hardly a game. A major reason for this outcome was the appearance of none other than Giuseppe De Carli as a speaker on the second day of the conference. What he said in the course of his remarks underscored dramatically the reasons for worldwide skepticism concerning Bertone's version of events. Indeed, immediately after the conference the mainstream Italian media, following the lead of the Pope himself in another May development, would declare that the case of the Third Secret had been "reopened."

A Remarkable Appearance at a Remarkable Conference

To his everlasting credit, by appearing at the conference De Carli did something no one in the Vatican party had ever done before during all the years of the Third Secret controversy: engage face-to-face with the "Fatimists" and respond to some of their objections to the "official" version of events. De Carli had agreed to appear for the stated purpose of introducing a second edition of *The Last Visionary of Fatima* [*L'Ultima Veggente di Fatima*] bearing the new title *The Last Secret of Fatima* [*L'Ultimo Segreto di Fatima*], a copy of which he held in his hand (the book had just come off the press that morning). By the time his appearance was over, however, it had become something far more significant than the introduction of essentially the same book he and Bertone had already published once.

After De Carli's prepared remarks and the showing of an inconsequential film on Sister Lucia and her life in the convent at Coimbra, something quite unexpected happened. De Carli remained at the podium to take questions from the audience, despite his earlier indications outside the conference hall that he would have no time for Q & A after his presentation. For more than an hour, De Carli would field questions (in Italian) from this author, Father Gruner and the Catholic attorney and apologist John Salza, all of whom were speakers at the conference. The results of this encounter (along with the conference as a whole) were most fruitful, as the Italian media would immediately recognize.

De Carli's three questioners knew this face-to-face encounter with Bertone's close collaborator in promoting the "official" account was an opportunity that probably would never present itself again. Given the limited window of opportunity, the questioning focused primarily on facts that were undeniable and which De Carli would have no choice but to admit. For one, there was the existence of the yet-to-be-seen Capovilla envelope and the text it contained, lodged in the papal apartment rather than the Holy Office archive, where the text of the vision was kept. Bertone's failure to produce that envelope and its contents were unanswerable evidence of a cover-up.

The Capovilla Envelope

Accordingly, this author repeatedly pressed De Carli (in Italian) to explain why the Capovilla envelope had never been produced. In response, De Carli repeatedly suggested, contrary to all the evidence, that the Capovilla envelope and the "Bertone envelope" displayed on *Porta a Porta*—namely the Bishop of Fatima's outer envelope—were one and the same. The first question and answer were as follows:

> **Ferrara**: Hello, Mr. De Carli, I am constrained by the limits of my Italian, but it seems that there are some obvious problems with your presentation. One problem is this: It is established as a fact that there is a so-called "Capovilla envelope" on which, outside of which, was written the name of Archbishop Capovilla, the heads of the Vatican departments, the judgment of John XXIII—to not *give* a judgment. And this critical envelope was in the papal apartment. So, a simple question: Where is this envelope?

> **De Carli**: The Bertone envelope *is* the Capovilla envelope; there is *no difference*. The Capovilla one is the one that ended up in the papal apartment. If you read the [Capovilla] interview in detail [i.e., the transcript presented during the "Cardinal Bertone Show" in 2007]… it explains how the envelope ended up in the hands of Paul VI, who was very interested—but a few days after his election, not months later—he wanted to read the text immediately. *Then the envelope remains there.* This is recounted by Msgr. Capovilla, who is a credible witness, the only living one. If you wish, you can give credit to what has been published by others, who are no longer with us. I give credit instead to a living person who, before me, recorded his testimony.

De Carli's answer was flatly contradicted by the very evidence he himself had presented during the "Cardinal Bertone Show": the envelope in the papal apartment is simply not the envelope produced on *Porta a Porta*, since the Capovilla envelope bears the Archbishop's handwritten list of the names of those who had read the contents and the dictation of John XXIII concerning his decision not to render any judgment on the text. Furthermore, all the envelopes Bertone *did* produce on camera—including the Bishop of Fatima's outer envelope, inside of which were the three envelopes prepared by Lucia—came from the archives of the Holy Office, now called the Congregation for the Doctrine of the Faith, not the papal apartment.

Pressed again on this point, De Carli made a stunning observation:

Ferrara: I understand, but *living people* said that there is an envelope [the Capovilla envelope] there [in the papal apartment]—

De Carli [interrupting]: It doesn't appear that way to me—

Ferrara:—But *we never saw the envelope.*

De Carli: *I saw the envelope, and I said that what's reproduced in here* [*Last Secret*, formerly *Last Visionary*] *is exactly what I had photographed by my own photographer*, and not by the one for the Holy See, because **I did not trust them completely**. I asked Bertone: "Seeing that we are here, would you let me go look at the Capovilla envelope?"… It is the same envelope. The Bertone envelope corresponds with the Capovilla envelope.

De Carli's distrust of the Vatican's photographer was understandable, but his personally commissioned photograph of what he claimed was the Capovilla envelope does not appear in *Last Secret*. Under repeated questioning on how he could maintain that the never-produced Capovilla envelope was the same as the Bertone envelope, De Carli finally conceded defeat:

Ferrara: The document of Archbishop Capovilla[248] said clearly that there is an envelope on the outside of which is found my [Capovilla's] writing. On *Porta a Porta, Cardinal Bertone did not show this envelope. It is a fact. Therefore, there are two envelopes. With all due respect, you haven't answered my question.*

De Carli: *Yes, these are useful precisions.* However, do not fasten yourselves on these things, which are important but not critical. I personally went to see the writing on the envelope there. When Cardinal Bertone showed it on *Porta a Porta* it is not like he didn't want us to see it. *He took the envelope in his hands, which was simply turned to the other side.* And if you go back to listen to the recording, *Cardinal Bertone at one point read the sentences that Pope John XXIII dictated to Msgr. Capovilla to write on the envelope, but he did not turn it around to the camera so that*

---

[248] His "confidential note" of 1967. *See, The Secret Still Hidden*, Chapters 6 and 10, and reproduction of original typewritten text (English and Italian) at Appendix I, pp. 217-221.

we could see it. But these are small things. The envelope is the same, it is the same. Then again, **they could have tricked me,** showing me something different. But my clear *impression* was that the envelope is the same: the Capovilla envelope is equal to the Bertone envelope.

Having retreated to the position that it was his "clear *impression*" that the two envelopes were the same, while admitting "they could have tricked me," De Carli here made a devastating slip, attributable (one must assume in charity) to the pressure of the moment as opposed to any preconceived intent to deceive. For, in fact, on the *Porta a Porta* video, it is clear that Bertone *had* turned the envelope he displayed "around to the camera" to reveal that there was *no seal or writing on the other side.* Clearly, at this point De Carli was reeling in confusion in his attempt to deny the undeniable: that the Capovilla envelope is not the Bertone envelope, and thus contents of the Capovilla envelope remain well hidden in the Vatican.

The Virgin's "express order" concerning 1960

De Carli was also asked to address another element of incontrovertible proof of cover-up: that Bertone has misled the Church and the world concerning the Virgin's "express order" regarding revelation of the Third Secret in 1960 as indicated on *both* of the sealed envelopes Bertone had revealed on *Porta a Porta*. Here John Salza took the lead with a question that produced another staggering misstep:

Salza: According to Cardinal Bertone, Sister Lucy never received any indication from the Virgin Mary that the Secret should have been revealed in 1960. Yet Cardinal Bertone said that Sister Lucy had confessed to him that she chose that date, without direction by the Virgin. However, on *Porta a Porta,* Cardinal Bertone showed the two envelopes of Sister Lucy to the cameras, evidencing that it was a fact that it was by explicit order of the Virgin that the Secret should not be disclosed before 1960. And so how can we reconcile this testimony? Is it possible that the account of Cardinal Bertone is not true?

De Carli: No. This 1960 question is one that *I have also posed to myself many times,* because Sister Lucy wrote on the envelope that "you must open it in 1960." But I think the answer by Cardinal Bertone is a convincing answer. [!] Please note that we are dealing with a Sister *who could neither read nor write. She began to read and write when she was about 30, 35 years old—so 15 years, if not 20, after the apparitions.* She began to understand the value of words, but she never had a good understanding of time.

So, De Carli's attempt at an explanation was that Sister Lucia did not know how to write when she *wrote* on both of her sealed envelopes: "By express order of Our Lady, this envelope can only be opened in 1960 by the Cardinal Patriarch of Lisbon or the Bishop of Leiria." To this nonsensical proposition, De Carli had added the demonstrably false assertion that Lucia did not learn to read or write until she was thirty or thirty-five years old, when in fact she had learned when she was still a teenager—also by "express order" of the Virgin during the second Fatima apparition, on June 13, 1917, *precisely so that she could make the Message of Fatima known to the world in writing.* It is a documented historical fact that Lucia was writing to her bishop as early as 1922, when she was only fifteen years old.[249]

This notion of an ignorant and illiterate peasant girl who had no idea what she was doing when she wrote the Virgin's express order on the two envelopes is part of what Father Gruner called "fables told by those who do not believe in Fatima. The Fatima documentation is very well done, and it negates the theory according to which Sister Lucy did not know what she wrote. This is a fabrication," he told De Carli.

When Father Gruner pressed him further on this issue, De Carli had to admit that he had no real explanation for why Bertone had claimed the Virgin never said anything to Lucia about the Secret being linked to 1960—and thus the opening of the Second Vatican Council and the crisis that followed—when the two envelopes confirm exactly the opposite:

> **De Carli:** *I do not know what to say.* That mystery of 1960 remains. There's an explanation that, in my opinion, is plausible and I think could be accepted, which is that, in my opinion, Lucy saw that date of 1960 as very far from her, so it was like saying: "Open this in the next century." She imagined that in 1960—remember that she wrote it in 1944, so 1960 is sixteen years after that date—she would probably no longer be.

> **Father Gruner:** Yes, but she said "according to *the explicit order*

---

[249] Lucia wrote a letter on June 21, 1921 to her mother only several days after she had left Fatima on June 16, 1921. Contrary to what De Carli affirmed, she had learned to read and write when she was only 14 years old or less. Lucia wrote additional letters to her mother on July 4, July 17, October 2, October 23 and December 18 of 1921, followed by letters to her mother and others on January 2, February 2, April 16 and June 4 of 1922. She was only 15 years old at this time and wrote quite well. Frère Michel de la Sainte Trinité quotes excerpts of some of these letters in *The Whole Truth About Fatima*, Vol. II, pp. 217-221. Lucia wrote her first account of the apparitions in a letter to her confessor on January 5, 1922 (before she was 15). See Father António Maria Martins, S.J., *Cartas da Irmã Lúcia*, (printed by Fraternidade Missionária de Cristo-Jovem, Samerio-Braga, 1978) pp. 80-84. This 4 1/2-page handwritten letter is photographically reproduced on pp. 468-476 of *Documentos de Fatima* (Porto, 1976).

of Our Lady." In this writing she denies that it was her idea and says that it was the order of the Madonna. *Why did Bertone say that Lucy confessed to him that it was just her idea?*

De Carli: I collected only what Cardinal Bertone told me. I cannot invent things. I write what I hear, what I see, what I think, and what I record. You can think whatever you wish....

The discrepancy of the envelopes

On the question of the revelation by Bertone on *Porta a Porta* of not one, but *two* envelopes, bearing Our Lady's "express order" concerning 1960, Father Gruner asked De Carli to explain why, in *Last Visionary* (now *Last Secret*), Bertone recounts having had Lucia authenticate only *one* such envelope. Perhaps not realizing that he was treading in a minefield planted by Bertone himself, De Carli provided an explosive answer:

De Carli: I don't recall this detail, sorry, I just don't have recollection of that, that part of the book has not been changed. I myself saw that document. I took my photographer with me, who photographed it for me. *And there is an envelope which has written on it: "For delivery to the Bishop of Fatima," and a second envelope on which had been written: "to be opened after 1960."*

That is, De Carli himself was shown only *a* second envelope— only one—bearing the Virgin's order concerning 1960 when his photographer took a photograph of the document (the vision) published in 2000. Yet, on *Porta a Porta* a *second* such envelope suddenly "jumped out of the top hat," to employ a phrase of Socci's. Thus it seems that De Carli himself was deceived in this matter, just as he had, apparently, been sold a bill of goods about Sister Lucia's ignorance and illiteracy. The truth of his own words—"They could have tricked me"—and his repeated expressions of distrust in Vatican photographers here seem to be confirmed. And, given his evident lack of knowledge of the Fatima documentation and the historical details of the Third Secret controversy and the life of the seer, De Carli would have been particularly susceptible to being misled by those who wished to use him for their purposes.

The Secret "belongs to the past" canard

Still another patently indefensible element of the "official" position is that the Third Secret "belongs to the past," according to Cardinal Bertone, following Cardinal Sodano. De Carli's answer to the pertinent question was clearly at variance with the "official" version, as De Carli himself seemed eager to note:

Father Gruner: ... I do not understand why Cardinal Bertone told us that the age of lust for power and evil is over now—that is, on June 26, 2000, with the decision to reveal the Third Secret. We're seeing that this time of evil and lust of power for mankind *is not over yet!*

De Carli: *This is certain.* By reading the Third Secret, we understand that the Third Secret is also valid today. It is not just relegated to the past. *I tried to show this in the book with a reflection by Cardinal Bertone, who then arrives at my thesis.* Read it carefully. The Third Secret is not something that concerns only an event of the past, but is something that concerns us today, as well. It has, therefore, a power that goes far beyond a mere historical memory.

While De Carli, at least, now admitted that the Third Secret does *not* belong to the past, a review of *Last Secret* does not reveal any such change of position by Bertone himself, but only his "reflection" (in a newly added chapter) that "it is good, therefore, that they [the events of Fatima] are consigned to the collective memory, leaving behind traces not deprived of meaning."[250] What is that nebulous remark supposed to mean? And notice that De Carli indicated that Bertone had supposedly "arrived" at *his* (De Carli's) "thesis," not that Bertone had actually admitted to an error of fact about the portent of the Secret.

Archbishop Capovilla's "Confidential Note"

Yet another piece of incontrovertible evidence brought to De Carli's attention was the "confidential note" by Archbishop Capovilla, in which he recorded that on June 27, 1963 Paul VI had read a text of the Third Secret retrieved from the Barbarigo writing desk in the papal bedchamber of John XXIII—a fact radically at odds with the "official" account, which asserts that Paul VI read the Secret for the first and only time on March 27, 1965. (*See* Chapter 6.) We have already seen (in Chapter 10) that during the "Cardinal Bertone Show" in September 2007, De Carli attempted to explain away this devastating discrepancy by leading Capovilla to suggest during his interview of the Archbishop that Pope Paul read the same text twice—in 1963 and 1965—even though Capovilla himself demolished that contention *in the same interview* by stating that after the reading in 1963 "the envelope was resealed [*richiude* in Italian; 'resealed' or 'reclosed'] and *it was not spoken of further.*"

That is, according to Capovilla himself, *the envelope was not spoken of again* after the reading of its contents and its resealing

---

[250] *The Last Secret of Fatima*, p. 40.

in 1963. Capovilla's own testimony, far from supporting Bertone's contrivance, rules out a second reading in 1965, which would have required reopening the resealed (or "reclosed") envelope. What did De Carli have to say about this, now that he could be questioned directly? Curiously, his earlier reliance on Capovilla as the only reliable living witness was suddenly replaced by skepticism about the Archbishop's testimony:

> **Father Gruner:** Just one other point: Socci, referring to the interview by Solideo Paolini on this subject, said, "How come there are two dates: that of June '63 and the other one of March '65?"

> **De Carli:** This, too, is in my book. Because I wondered why there were two dates, but only one recorded officially. The fact is that *we are not sure about the second date, the only one who gave us two dates is Mons. Capovilla*. Now, he is a precise man and has marked that date in his diary, but it doesn't appear in the official archives. I don't have the certainty arising from the record of audiences of what was done by Paul VI, which in this case does not correspond to the archives of the Secretary of State and the Congregation for the Doctrine of the Faith. And if this is coming only from one man, even if it's his [John XXIII's] secretary, then I do not think it can be considered official. It has to be included in the interview [shown on the "Cardinal Bertone Show"], but we still consider the official date June 26 or 27, 1963 [sic]. I'm a little confused myself, too, with the dates.

Notice, first of all, De Carli's admitted confusion about the dates: he gave June 26 or 27, 1963 as the "official" date for the reading of the Secret by Paul VI, rather than March 27, 1965 (according to *TMF*, the "official" Vatican booklet published in June 2000). Clearly, he lacked a command of the most basic facts concerning the controversy, even though Bertone had used him to produce a book on it. As for the claim that Capovilla's note does not "correspond to the archives of the Secretary of State and the Congregation for the Doctrine of the Faith," it should have been obvious to De Carli that there is more to the story than what is contained in those archives, for Capovilla categorically places a text of the Secret in the papal apartment.

Here De Carli effectively conceded that he had no answer to this evidence other than *to cast doubt on the testimony of the very witness he had pronounced most reliable only moments before.* Worse, De Carli had pronounced utterly reliable Capovilla's memory that the text Pope John read in 1959 "corresponded" to the vision published in June 2000—which, once again, is not at issue—while casting doubt on *a written record* of what the Archbishop witnessed and confirms today concerning the reading of the Third Secret by Paul VI in 1963.

Here it must be noted that *Last Secret*, in a dramatic departure from *Last Visionary*, "adjusts" the "official" account to claim that Paul VI "read it [the Secret] two times, according to what has been reported by Monsignor Capovilla. Certainly on March 27, 1965, and he opted for its non-publication."[251] But we have seen that the claim of two readings of the *same* text in the *same* envelope is flatly contradicted by Capovilla himself, who testified that the envelope opened in 1963 by Paul VI was resealed and that, so far as he knows, it was not spoken of after that. And why would Paul VI open yet again the same envelope he had *resealed* in 1963? Clearly, the envelope he read in 1965 was other than the one he had read two years earlier; from which it follows, as all other evidence shows, that there are two companion texts pertaining to the Third Secret of Fatima.

Capovilla's testimony to Paolini

We have seen that at no time was Archbishop Capovilla asked by Bertone, De Carli or anyone else to deny specifically his admission to Solideo Paolini—"Exactly so!"—in response to the question whether there were two different envelopes and two different texts pertaining to the Third Secret. Confronted on this telling point, De Carli not only declared that Paolini was a liar who invented his conversation with Archbishop Capovilla, but also claimed to have in his possession yet another secret document the Vatican is not allowing anyone to see:

> **Father Gruner**: ... Why did he [Capovilla] not deny what Paolini said?

> **De Carli:** No, easy now, no. Let us speak of how that interview was obtained. It was a meeting, this Solideo Paolini, who went to Mons. Capovilla. It was a simple chat, and then he pulled from it an interview that truly and properly did not exist, *and much of that interview was invented wholesale.*

> **Ferrara:** Why did no one ask Archbishop Capovilla "yes or no" regarding the fact that he answered Paolini "Precisely so!" as an answer to his question if "There are two texts of the Third Secret of Fatima?" Why has no one asked him this?

> **De Carli:** Look, I have in hand [*i.e.*, available to him] a letter by Mons. Capovilla sent to the Secretary of State and to the Holy Father in which he denies he ever responded in such way to Solideo Paolini. He denies it. So either this Solideo Paolini is a liar, and has profited from it, or Mons. Capovilla is a liar. *I believe Solideo Paolini is a liar.*

---

[251] *The Last Secret of Fatima*, p. 70.

Ferrara: May I have a copy [of the letter]?...

Salza: Why have you not published this letter from Capovilla, if it could answer all the questions?

De Carli: Because it's private correspondence, I can't; I'm sorry.

So, De Carli publicly accused Paolini of being a liar and then refused to publish his evidence for the charge—a purported letter from Capovilla to the Pope and the Secretary of State—claiming it was "private"! Yet he had been given a copy of that same "private" letter, and was now dangling its alleged existence before the entire world while refusing to produce it. Nor had the Vatican seen fit to publish Capovilla's denial, if such it was. It is telling indeed that *Last Secret* makes no mention of this secret but not-so-secret letter, even though De Carli, the co-author of *Last Secret*, had freely revealed its existence in connection with his promotion of that very book at *The Fatima Challenge* conference.

What about the "etc"?

The "official" account had always been fatally compromised by its glaring failure to ask Sister Lucia a single question about the very heart of the Third Secret controversy: that fateful "etc" which Sister Lucia had placed at the end of the recorded Great Secret in her Fourth Memoir to indicate the beginning of its third and final part, which clearly related in some way to a crisis (among the faithful) regarding Catholic dogma outside of Portugal. Pressed on this patent evidence of a cover-up, De Carli pleaded a lack of memory:

> **De Carli:** *I do not remember this.* When I'm not sure I do not answer. With regards to that "etc"—following the phrase "Portugal will not lose the Catholic faith and Catholic nations etc" [sic], what's in that "etc"?—I said to Bertone: "Look, many have imagined that behind that 'etc' is another text which doesn't exist." And he answered—*I don't recall any longer what he answered to me. I am sorry, on this point I do not have a precise recollection.*

Asked once again to comment on the "etc" controversy, De Carli conceded that it did indeed represent the beginning of the Third Secret of Fatima:

> **De Carli:** The "etc" was by Sister Lucy. She had suspended that etcetera *because she had yet to write the last part of the Secret.* That etcetera said: "leave it for me." But that etcetera gathered a lot of attention by the bishops, by her confessors—not to mention journalists, "doomsayers" and apocalypse-sayers. And when Sister Lucia was finally pressed, put on the ropes, *she filled*

in the etcetera with the Third Secret.

Now, if the "etc" represents something that Lucia later "filled in... with the Third Secret"—which indeed it was—then it is obvious that what Lucia "filled in" could only have been the *words of the Virgin Mary* following her reference to the preservation of dogma in Portugal, because the "etc" interrupts a sentence in which the Virgin was speaking. And yet De Carli claimed a lack of memory about what Bertone told him concerning this utterly crucial point.

What can one say? More than ten years after the controversy over the completeness of the Vatican's disclosure of the Third Secret began, we still have no answer from the Vatican party to the one question that would reveal the truth of the matter: What were the *words* of Our Lady which conclude the Great Secret of Fatima by completing its third and final part? It seems that the plan is to keep those words from the faithful forever, if it were possible.

The testimony of Cardinal Ottaviani

Confronted with the testimony of the late Cardinal Ottaviani that the text of the Third Secret he had in view was 25 lines in length, not the 62 lines of the vision, De Carli joined Bertone in affirming that *this was indeed Ottaviani's testimony*, but offered the "thesis" (as had Bertone) that Ottaviani had somehow mistaken a 62-line text for one with 25-lines:

> **Father Gruner:** On television, on the *Porta a Porta* [telecast] of May 31, 2007, there was a Vaticanist who asked: "But Cardinal Ottaviani said that the text consists of 25 lines, why then has this text 62 lines?" And Cardinal Bertone affirmed that Cardinal Ottaviani had said this, trying to explain how he had erred. I do not know—in your book is there an answer to this question?

> **De Carli:** Yes, this is also in my book. The thesis—since I cannot interview him because he is in the embrace of God—the thesis is that Ottaviani was wrong to say 25 lines, he was wrong.

Pressed further on the point, De Carli admitted that he had no real answer to the glaring discrepancy between what was published in 2000 and what Cardinal Ottaviani described:

> **Father Gruner:** But this explanation by Cardinal Bertone, who said that perhaps Ottaviani had not looked at the other side, and the fact that even adding these two sides the sum is... 31-32... not 25 lines—how could he be so wrong? And how is it that the Bishop of Fatima [who] looked up to the light—one can only say that there are [according to him] two envelopes [not four]—and said that there were 25 lines, how come this

text has 62 lines instead? Bishop Venâncio put everything in writing. It's in the archives of Fatima.

De Carli: *I cannot answer this,* and when I cannot answer I do not answer. I have the notes of the meeting between the Cardinal and Sister Lucy. Bertone showed to Lucy the 64 lines of text, which she then turned, turned again, examined; and the precise question is: "Sister Lucy, is this the text that you wrote in 1944, which was then placed in the envelope?" "Yes, it is my text." "And this is your envelope?" "Yes, this is my envelope."

De Carli's reference to Lucia's authentication of a *single* envelope, when Bertone had displayed *three* envelopes of Lucia's on *Porta a Porta*, prompted the next series of questions, with answers that highlighted dramatically the untrustworthiness of the "official" account.

One sheet or multiple sheets: a convenient "correction"

When Sister Lucia authenticated the text of the Third Secret in April of 2000, she told Bertone: "Yes, these are my *sheets* of paper (*fogli*) and the envelope is mine; they are the *sheets* (*fogli*) that I used and this is my writing. This is my envelope, this is my writing, this is my text."[252] Recall once again that on *Porta a Porta*, on May 31, 2007, Bertone displayed a *sheet* of paper and three *envelopes* prepared by Lucia (her unsealed outer envelope and the two sealed envelopes bearing the Virgin's express order concerning 1960). Yet, according to Bertone's/De Carli's *Last Visionary*, published on May 10, 2007, several weeks earlier, Lucia had authenticated *sheets* of paper (*fogli*) and only *one* envelope—*exactly the opposite* of the document ensemble Bertone displayed weeks later on camera.

This enormous and never-explained discrepancy prompted questions that revealed another "adjustment" of the words Bertone attributed to Sister Lucia, as allegedly recorded in Bertone's remarkably adaptable "notes":

Salza: But in your book with Cardinal Bertone, he said that Sister Lucy said: "Yes, these are my *sheets* [*fogli*]"—using the plural form. But what was shown on *Porta a Porta* was only one sheet. Where are the other sheets?

De Carli: This *is better explained* here [in *Last Secret*] because *we went back to check at the Archives,* which is one of the reasons why we did a second edition. There are two sides. The book reports it exactly because I repeat it several times: 4 pages on 2 sheets—two on one side and the other two on the other

---

[252] *The Last Visionary of Fatima*, p. 37; *see also, The Secret Still Hidden*, Chapter 8, pp. 128, 136.

side. Because in the Cardinal's notes—keep in mind that when I wrote that book [*Last Visionary*] we were in 2006, Cardinal Bertone was moving to Rome, he had shelves full of books and had these diaries, at least 50 pages of his diary notes, we read them a bit faster. So back then we relied on the 64 lines count, but now it is clear that there are two sheets (*fogli*) [!] of four pages.

Father Gruner: My Italian is not perfect, but in English we speak about a "sheet" like this [holding up one sheet of paper]. You can fold this sheet, but it is only one sheet. When Sister Lucy said that these are my sheets, she said that there was another piece of paper besides this.

De Carli: *You are right to point out this thing.* I should find the text. I cannot find it now [in the copy of *Last Secret* he is holding]. But the book specifies, in almost a maniacal manner, this thing about the sheets that Sister Lucy had in her hand. *It is no longer multiple sheets, but a single sheet,* divided into 4 sides, a single sheet exactly like he showed her—in half, 2 sides and 2 sides. It is repeated twice.

Salza: So you were wrong when you said that there are two sheets, and now you're saying that there is only one? We must be exact, here, because you have already said [here] that there are two sheets, and so the question is: Is there just one sheet or two?

De Carli: I'm looking at the text [of my book], because I can't remember all these details. Here is what is in the book: We talked about a large envelope, stamped with the seal of the Congregation for the Doctrine of the Faith. On the envelope [written in 1944] is the writing about 1960, and which contained another envelope, with a single sheet with lines, folded in two, and four sides handwritten by Sister Lucia.

Ferrara: The first book talks about sheets!

Salza: This is a change!

De Carli: We did a second edition of the book just to clarify better, also from an Italian point of view with regards to different language translations. And what we *wanted* to say is that it is a *single* lined sheet, folded in two, and four sides.

Salza: Therefore you made a mistake when you said that it was "sheets," in plural, right?

De Carli: I was wrong. Can't I make mistakes? Aren't we human?

Salza: But [today] you said this, two or three times, specifically.

De Carli: One can make a mistake. In fact, I wanted to check again the text [of the book] because it was important to clarify this point: a lined sheet, folded in two, written on four sides. But Fatima—it is not just a lined sheet written on four sides. Fatima is the marvelous secret of Mary who appears to the three shepherds! This is what really counts.

De Carli's statements were fraught with disaster for the "official" account. For one thing, even in the midst of attempting to explain that the Secret involved only one sheet of paper, he referred to *two* sheets, evidencing his confusion on the matter. Further, the "mistake" about the number of sheets involved—one rather than two or more—could not have been *his* mistake because, according to Bertone in *Last Visionary*, it was *Sister Lucia* who had referred to *sheets* of paper (*fogli*) and Bertone had provided, as noted above, a purported *verbatim quotation of the seer* to that effect. But, as has happened so often in the annals of the "official account," the words of "Sister Lucy" were altered to meet current exigencies. So, whereas in *Last Visionary* she is quoted as having said "these are my *sheets* of paper (*fogli*) ... they are the *sheets* (*fogli*) that I used," in *Last Secret* "Sister Lucy" now says "Yes, yes, this is my *paper.*" As De Carli had put it: "it is *no longer* multiple sheets, but a single sheet..." In other words, when it is necessary to change the "official account" to meet serious objections, what Sister Lucy said before is "no longer" what "she" says now, when she is conveniently dead! Simple!

Yet not so simple. For in his non-committal letter of introduction to *Last Visionary*, reproduced without change in *Last Secret*, none other than Pope Benedict XVI relates that in preparing the "theological commentary" on the Secret when he was Cardinal Ratzinger (see Chapter 4) he had "prayed and meditated deeply on the *authentic* words of the third part of the Secret of Fatima, contained in the *sheets* [*fogli!*] written by Sister Lucia." Or, in the original Italian: "le parole autentiche della terza parte del segreto di Fatima contenute nei *fogli* scritti da Suor Lucia."[253] So, *the Pope himself* reveals that the Third Secret involves *multiple* sheets of paper, whereas Sister Lucy, who once said this as well, "no longer" says it—according to Bertone and De Carli, now that the visionary is no longer alive to contradict them. But not even Bertone would dare to claim that *the Pope* was mistaken when he wrote *fogli* instead of *foglio*! Nor was Bertone in any position to "correct" the papal letter of introduction. He was stuck with it, and with the glaring discrepancy it causes—the umpteenth—in his ever-changing story.

---

[253] *The Last Secret of Fatima*, p. 10.

And notice the Pope's telltale reference to "the *authentic* words of the third part of the Secret" in said *fogli*, indicating yet again what Socci (as we saw in Chapter 8) has called a "road to the truth" opened up by the Pope's suggestion that "there exist words of the secret held '*not* authentic.'"[254] That is, the Pope is hinting that there is indeed another text containing what someone has conveniently adjudged to be "inauthentic" words of the Virgin, and that he read this text as one of the *fogli* (sheets) to which he refers in his letter of introduction, although it is not considered part of what Bertone and Sodano have deemed the "authentic words" of the Secret. But, as Socci says: "Courage, then: publish everything. 'The truth will make you free.'"[255]

Why did he appear?

After having submitted to questioning that only demonstrated, yet again, why the "official account" had been deprived of all credibility, De Carli excused himself and left the conference. The net impression one had of his appearance was that of a decent man who, years earlier, had entered into a battle for which he was poorly equipped, as he himself admitted, had raised his flag for the wrong side, and now, perhaps, had begun to entertain some serious doubts about the version of the facts he was expected to defend. "They could have tricked me" is a phrase that could not be more revealing of a man having second thoughts.

In tribute to De Carli we must agree with the commentator who wrote of his appearance: "As his case collapsed in one exchange after another, Mr. De Carli never displayed any sign of irritation or animosity, as usually occurs when a person's claims are radically challenged. He patiently listened and tried to reply to all questions, and gave the impression of an honest man, now rather confused, who had perhaps been drawn into an orchestrated deception of which he was unaware at the time. When he departed the conference, Father Gruner offered to shake his hand; instead, Mr. De Carli embraced Father Gruner and thanked him for the work he was doing."[256]

All in all, De Carli's honesty had led him to become, however unexpectedly, a true rather than a false friend of Fatima. For his appearance at the conference had contributed to making the conference as a whole a tipping point for handling of the Third Secret affair within the Vatican. The Pope himself would soon make this dramatically apparent during his trip to Fatima from May 11-14, 2010.

---

[254] Antonio Socci, "Bertone in the 'Wasp's Nest' of the Polemics," *Libero*, June 2, 2007.
[255] Ibid.
[256] Edwin Faust, "The Latest Chapter in the Story of Fatima," http://www.fatima.org/exclusives/pdf/epilogue_summary.pdf

Chapter 12

POPE BENEDICT REFUTES THE PARTY LINE

On May 11, 2010, a week after De Carli's appearance at *The Fatima Challenge* conference, and only four days after the conference ended, Pope Benedict was on his way to Portugal for a pilgrimage to the Fatima shrine at the Cova da Iria on May 13, 2010, the anniversary of Our Lady's first apparition at the Cova. The Fatima Center's technical team had detected monitoring of the conference proceedings from an IP (Internet Provider) address within the Vatican. Surely, Cardinal Bertone had watched some or all of the proceedings, including De Carli's appearance on his behalf. And it is probable that the Pope himself had seen or been informed of the proceedings—a conclusion well supported by what the Pope said on the papal plane en route to Portugal.

Speaking calmly and deliberately to reporters on the plane, the Pope reopened the entire Third Secret controversy by expressly rejecting—at last!—the universally disbelieved Sodano/Bertone "interpretation" of the vision as nothing more than a tableau of 20th century events, including the 1981 assassination attempt, which "belong to the past." Rather, said the Pope, the Third Secret prophesies what is happening in the Church today, is not at all limited to "the past," and predicts *future* events in the Church *which are still developing day by day.* Here is the question and the pertinent parts of the Pope's answer, which he gave as Cardinal Bertone literally hovered behind him on camera:

> **Lombardi:** Holiness, what significance do the apparitions of Fatima have for us today? And when you presented the text of the Third Secret, in the Vatican Press Office, in June 2000, *it was asked of you whether the Message could be extended, beyond the attack on John Paul II,* also to the other sufferings of the Pope. Is it possible, according to you, to frame also in that vision the sufferings of the Church of today for the sins of the sexual abuse of minors?

> **Pope Benedict:** Beyond this great vision of the suffering of the Pope, which we can in substance refer to John Paul II, *are indicated future realities of the Church which are little by little developing and revealing themselves.* Thus, it is true that beyond the moment indicated in the vision, it is *spoken,* it is seen, the necessity of *a passion of the Church that naturally is reflected in the person of the Pope; but the Pope is in the Church, and therefore the sufferings of the Church are what is announced....*

As for the novelty that we can discover today in this message, it is that **attacks on the Pope and the Church do not come only from outside, but the sufferings of the Church come precisely from within the Church**, from sins that exist in the Church. This has always been known, but today we see it **in a really terrifying way**: that the greatest persecution of the Church **does not come from enemies outside, but arises from sin in the Church.**[257]

First of all, it is critical to note that the Pope's explosive remarks were not some off-the-cuff statement. They came in answer to a question read to him by papal spokesman Fr. Federico Lombardi, one of three questions selected as a "synthesis" of the questions to which the press pool had sought answers. As the *National Catholic Reporter* observed, the Pope "was hardly caught off-guard. The Vatican asks reporters traveling with the Pope to submit questions for the plane several days in advance, so Benedict has plenty of time to ponder what he wants to say. If he takes a question on the plane, *it's because he wants to talk about it, and he's chosen his words carefully*."[258]

The significance of the Pope's carefully chosen words cannot be overstated. The Pope went out of his way to bring up the Third Secret of Fatima, ten years after the subject was supposedly laid to rest by Sodano and Bertone; and he did so because *he wished to speak of the Secret* and its relation to the current and *future* state of the Church: "*future realities* of the Church which are *little by little developing and revealing themselves*." **Note well:** *Future* realities, developing *little by little* and revealing themselves *today*, not merely "in the past." And here the Pope spoke of something *not seen in the vision* of the bishop in white: "attacks on the Pope and the Church... *from within the*

---

[257] "Oltre questa grande visione della sofferenza del Papa, che possiamo in sostanza riferire a Giovanni Paolo II sono indicate realtà del futuro della chiesa che man mano si sviluppano e si mostrano. Cioè è vero che oltre il momento indicato nella visione, *si parla*, si vede la necessità di una passione della chiesa, che naturalmente si riflette nella persona del Papa, ma il Papa sta nella chiesa e quindi sono sofferenze della chiesa che si annunciano. Il Signore ci ha detto che la chiesa sarà per sempre sofferente, in modi diversi fino alla fine de mondo. L'importante è che il messaggio, la risposta di Fatima, sostanzialmente non va a situazioni particolari, ma la risposta fondamentale cioè conversione permanente, penitenza, preghiera, e le virtù cardinali, fede, speranza carità. Così vediamo qui la vera e fondamentale risposta che la chiesa deve dare, che noi ogni singolo dobbiamo dare in questa situazione. Quanto alle novità che possiamo oggi scoprire in questo messaggio è anche che non solo da fuori vengono attacchi al Papa e alla chiesa, ma le sofferenze della chiesa vengono proprio dall'interno della chiesa, dal peccato che esiste nella chiesa. Anche questo lo vediamo sempre ma oggi lo vediamo in modo realmente terrificante che la più grande persecuzione alla chiesa non viene dai nemici di fuori, ma nasce dal peccato nella chiesa." Transcript by Paolo Rodari, www.corriere.it/esteri/10_maggio_11/ vecchi-parole-papa_fa994a90-5ce9-11df-97c2-00144f02aabe.shtml, confirmed by this author, who watched the video of the Pope's remarks.

[258] "On the crisis, Benedict XVI changes the tone," *National Catholic Reporter*, May 11, 2010.

Church" which show in "*a really terrifying way*" that "the greatest persecution… arises from sin *in the Church.*" This went well beyond even the pedophilia scandal to a generalized assessment of the state of the Church in light of the Secret; it was a frontal attack on Bertone's and Sodano's "official" position, which in fact had never been anything but their already widely rejected opinion in the matter.

Now, the vision of the Third Secret (published in June 26, 2000) says nothing at all about a crisis involving attacks upon the Church and persecution of the Church *from within her* on account of the sins of her own members. On the contrary, the vision seems to depict an external persecution of the Church in the midst of a post-apocalyptic scenario where a future Pope is executed outside a half-ruined city by soldiers who are not internal enemies. There is only one way to reconcile the Pope's remarks with what the vision depicts, and it is the same way both the "Fatimists" and Socci have proposed, and as this book itself proposes: a missing text related to the vision in which the Virgin explains in Her own words how an internal crisis of faith and discipline in the Church is accompanied by a chastisement of the whole world, including the bishops, priests and laity who are killed, "one after another," by the same soldiers who have already executed the Pope.

The Pope himself appeared to confirm the existence of precisely such a text when he said that "*beyond the moment* indicated in the vision, **it is spoken**, it is seen [*si parla, si vede*] the necessity of a passion of the Church, which naturally is reflected in the person of the Pope, but the Pope is in the Church and therefore what is announced are the sufferings of the Church."

> **Note well: The Pope refers to a prophecy *beyond the moment indicated in the vision*, involving both *spoken words and images* relating to sufferings in the Church caused, not by the soldiers seen in the vision, but rather by the Church's *internal persecution* on account of the sins *of her own members*.**

The Vaticanist Paolo Rodari was quick to recognize the significance of the Pope's words, asking the question: "Was Socci right?" Wrote Rodari:

> It is true that the Pope did not speak of a fourth secret explicitly. But to read the response he gave today to the journalists, one cannot but think of Socci, who has always linked the contents of a hypothetical fourth secret to the corruption of the Church and to the sin which is born within the Church and is presently operative. Reading what the Pope said today, it seems that for him Fatima *is not reducible only to the past and*

thus only to the text of 2000.[259]

If there were any doubt of this, the Pope all but extinguished it two days later on May 13 when, during his homily at the Mass to commemorate the anniversary of the first Fatima apparition, the Pope declared: "One would be deceiving himself who thinks that the prophetic mission of Fatima is concluded." ["*Si illuderebbe chi pensasse che la missione profetica di Fatima sia conclusa.*"] Another direct attack on the "official" version and indeed on Bertone and Sodano themselves for having promoted it as the Party Line: "*he* would be deceiving himself" meant particular individuals, and it was clear that both of these individuals had promoted assiduously and precisely the fiction that the prophetic mission of Fatima had been concluded or "fulfilled" with the failed assassination attempt, and that publication of the Third Secret, as Bertone had so absurdly contended, "brings to an end a period of history marked by tragic human lust for power and evil."

That the Pope has made this declaration on the most solemn possible occasion—his homily during the Mass at the Fatima Shrine—gave it the force of a teaching of the Church's universal pastor. *Some 500,000 souls in the Cova alone—not counting the millions who followed him on live television—heard the Roman Pontiff say that whoever thinks the prophetic mission of Fatima is concluded has deceived himself.*

It is only typical of Vatican bureaucratic maneuvering, however, that the English translation of the Italian homily neuters the Pope's words to read: "We would be mistaken to think that the prophetic mission of Fatima is concluded." No! It is not "we" would be "mistaken." The Pope said that *he* who thinks **the prophetic mission** (the foretelling of future events) of Fatima is finished (that there is not still more to unfold) would be *engaged in self-deception*, not merely "mistaken". There was no doubt who the Pope meant by "he," nor any doubt about who was deceived—and leading others into his state of deception.

In short, with a few well-chosen words the Pope had utterly destroyed the Sodano-Bertone "interpretation" of the vision as belonging "to the past" and with it the Party Line on Fatima. The Secretary of State's purported dictates on the meaning of the Fatima

---

[259] Paolo Rodari, "Fatima. Aveva Ragione Socci?" ["Fatima. Was Socci Right?"], http://www.ilfoglio.it/palazzoapostolico/2675. As Rodari wrote in the original Italian: "E' vero il Papa non ha parlato del quarto segreto esplicitamente. Ma a leggere la risposta che ha dato oggi ai giornalisti non si può non pensare ad Antonio Socci il quale ha sempre legato il contenuto di un ipotetico quarto segreto alla corruzione della chiesa e al peccato che nasce all'interno della chiesa ed agisce nel presente. Leggendo oggi il Papa sembra che anche per lui Fatima non sia riconducibile al solo passato e dunque soltanto al testo del 2000."

event now join other pseudo-official pronouncements in the discard bin of the post-Vatican II era in the Church. Even more dramatically, the Pope had not only repudiated Bertone's and De Carli's suggestion that *Last Visionary*—and now *Last Secret*—was the "official position" of the Church, but also *his own adherence to the "party line" dictated by the Secretary of State*, which he had followed as the former Cardinal Ratzinger, whose theological commentary on the vision declared that "we must affirm with Cardinal Sodano: '... the events to which the third part of the 'secret' of Fatima refers now seem part of the past'."[260]

Socci on Pope Benedict's "Operation Truth"

The Pope's momentous declarations during his pilgrimage to Fatima prompted a rapid-fire series of articles from Antonio Socci on the theme of the patent vindication of the "Fatimist" cause, which had become his cause once he considered the evidence.

Writing in *Il Libero* on May 12, 2010, in an article entitled "So there was a Fourth Secret after all...", Socci exclaimed that the Pope's statements "bring back again into the mainstream news the whole dossier on the Third Secret. His words upset the 'official version' given in 2000, *which was never considered official*—neither by Ratzinger nor by Pope John Paul II." Referring to *Fourth Secret* and the "cheap shots" he had had to endure for writing it, Socci noted that Pope Benedict "reopens the discussion in the direction that I tried to investigate and that the documents themselves suggest." By declaring that the Third Secret concerns "realities of the *future* of the Church, which unfold and reveal themselves day by day" and which we "now see in a really terrifying way," the Pope, Socci continued, "reinforces the belief" that what he said about filth and corruption in the Church during his Way of the Cross meditations as Cardinal Ratzinger on March 25, 2005 was "perhaps, indeed, the revelation (even if not declared as such) of *the part of the Third Secret that was not revealed in 2000*. The part which contains *the words of Our Lady Herself*, as a comment on the vision."

On May 13, also in *Il Libero*, Socci published a searing commentary on the Pope's obvious demolition of Bertone's/Sodano's entire position. It is now a matter of black and white, Socci wrote, that "*The 'fourth secret' (that is, a part of the Third Secret which has not been published yet) exists*, and the words of the Pope on the pedophilia scandal are the proof." The Pope, he continued, is "performing a great truth-telling work, even if this means *contradicting the interpretation given by the Vatican Secretaries of State*." Sodano's contention that the events depicted in the vision

---

[260] *The Message of Fatima*, p. 43.

"seem to" belong to the past—from which Bertone had removed the words "seem to," converting Sodano's opinion into a pseudo-dogma—had been rejected by Pope Benedict, "who explains to us *the complete opposite, which is that the Third Secret regards events which came after* the assassination attempt of 1981... and even events which are still in our future." In fact, he added, "the assassination attempt of 1981 *is nowhere to be found in Benedict's words*, therefore it is not pointed out as 'the' fulfillment of the Third Secret."

Socci went on to mention that telltale letter of Lucia's from 1982, purportedly addressed to the Pope, in which—making no mention of the assassination attempt—she declared that "we have not yet seen the complete fulfillment of the final part of this prophecy [i.e., the Third Secret]." Bertone, Socci reminded us, had "struck out an explosive phrase, which contradicted his version" from that letter, a fraudulent tampering with the documentary evidence, as we have seen, designed to conceal the fact that this letter, only a fragment of which was published, could not have been addressed to the Pope.[261] Socci pronounced this "only one of so many anomalies in this fifty-year-old story that, unfortunately, is filled with *lies* and silences, twisted interpretations and omissions."

But now, wrote Socci, the Pope has "reopened the Fatima file in such a precise and obvious way that everyone who, in these past years, rushed to give his praise to the Curial version is now caught in a panic when confronted with the Pope's words..." Even Vittorio Messori expressed embarrassment that "Now, in the vast party of the 'Fatimites' [vast!] there will be excitement, to demonstrate that Pope Benedict XVI has betrayed himself..." But, wrote Socci in a conclusion aimed directly at Bertone and his collaborators, the Pope:

> wants us to understand... that we must never be afraid of the truth, even when it is embarrassing or painful. *Because we do not serve God with lies.* When we lie with pretense that we are doing it for God, we are actually doing it for ourselves. God *does not need our lies to defend and build His Church.* It is better to do a *mea culpa*, because God is stronger and bigger than any of our sins. Obviously, *this behavior is not understood in the Curia*, not even by the 'Ratzinger fans.'

In a postscript to the article, Socci noted a remarkable about-face by Vittorio Messori, "who, three years ago, had rushed to praise Bertone's version," but on an episode of *Porta a Porta* broadcast on May 12, 2010 had "without even batting an eyelash... said the complete opposite of what he has said so far." As summarized by Socci, Messori freely admitted that, quite contrary to Bertone, Pope Benedict "does not see the fulfillment of the Third Secret in

---

[261] Cf. *The Secret Still Hidden*, Chapter 4 and Appendix IV.

the assassination attempt of 1981" and "does not consider it part of the past, but sees it projected into the future, because he is now considering a new fact—the pedophilia scandal—as part of the Secret (and it is obvious that the Pope cannot make all this up: *he must have taken this from the complete text of the Secret...*)." Yet Messori "did not show even the least sign of recognizing that he had been mistaken all these years, nor did he treat the consequences of what he himself had said. Same for the confident Bertone."

As Socci put it: "Either Bertone is right (and the prophecy was fulfilled in 1981 and was concluded in the past) or Benedict XVI is right (and therefore the text of the Secret is wider, the prophecy still open and the martyrdom of a Pope and of the Church are still in our future). You cannot pretend that both versions can coexist; it would not be logical. It would be desirable that love for truth would prevail, as well as a loyal recognition of our own mistakes... The call of the Pope for repentance, self-critical examination, and penance should be taken much more seriously." Almost overnight, Bertone now found himself an *opponent* of the papal view of the Secret, and rightly subject to public rebuke from the very man (Socci) he had tried to portray as a knave for disputing his patently incredible version of the facts! So much for the "official version" Bertone had labored for so long to impose upon the Church.

In yet a third article on these developments, published on his blog on May 15, Socci focused precisely on the *mea culpa* that Bertone owes the Church. The article, entitled "Advice to Bertone: *mea culpa* and penance," focuses on the Pope's homily before the universal Church at Fatima, and the Pontiff's resounding declaration to the whole Church that "He would be deceiving himself who thinks that the prophetic mission of Fatima is concluded." In light of the papal homily, even *Il Corriere della Sera* had announced in a headline: "The Fatima prophecy is not accomplished; there will be wars and terrors."

The Pope's words at Fatima, said Socci, "contain a warning to whoever does not wish to hear and does not wish to understand. Words of Benedict XVI that... are *the exact antithesis of the lies that, sadly, Cardinal Bertone has been spreading about for years* (caught above all by me). Here in fact is what he [Bertone] has said: 'The prophecy is not open to the future; it is realized in the past.' Thus he wrote on page 79 of his book [*Last Visionary*], repeating it a thousand times in those pages and also in interviews with journalists and on TV, where he has not hesitated to insult the one who simply spoke the truth and called for love of the truth and of the Holy Virgin, Mother of God."

"Now," Socci added, "finally the Pope has spoken and everyone can understand. That Bertone, in the face of the evidence (and the bad impression he gives of himself), has precipitously reached out to the Vaticanists to attempt a tragicomic reverse march (without a *mea culpa*), only adds to the sadness. Writes Tornielli in *Giornale*: 'now Bertone has *adapted his words*, stating that the prophecy can also be extended to the 21st century.' In a little while he will say that he has always said this... Any comment is useless."

And then this withering assessment of Bertone's tenure: "Except to note the many problems the current Secretary of State has caused the Pope, who deserves to have alongside him collaborators worthy of the task at this historical moment. Collaborators (I speak also of bishops) who will aid him in his mission. Collaborators humble and competent like him, not arrogant and inadequate. Collaborators he evidently has not found. This speaks to the drama of the situation of the Church and the solitude of the Pope."

Bertone, he concluded, could profit from reaching the age of retirement by "dedicating himself to prayer and meditation on the warnings and maternal solicitudes of the Queen of Heaven. In fact, the things of this world soon pass, and forever (including power and, above all, lies). Only the truth remains, which is Jesus Christ. That is, the Truth made flesh. And Who has said: 'There is nothing hidden that will not be revealed. Nothing secret that will not be brought into the light.'"

From the Vatican, there was only silence on the part of Cardinal Tarcisio Bertone. There was nothing he could say against Socci's well-deserved rebukes. For Socci was right to declare that the Pope has "reopened the file" on the Third Secret and that His Holiness is "trying to prepare the Church for this immense trial... entrusting everyone to the hands of the Madonna of Fatima. These are extraordinary hours." Indeed they are.

The Media Awaken

If it is reasonable to think that *The Fatima Challenge* conference and De Carli's appearance there had contributed to the Pope's inauguration of what Socci calls "Operation Truth" concerning the Third Secret, there is no question that what happened at the conference had prompted the Italian media to begin an Operation Truth of their own. On June 23, 2010 several major figures in the Italian press, including no less than Andrea Tornielli, appeared on the "Top Secret" television show on Rete 4, a channel operated by Mediaset, the largest commercial broadcasting company in Italy. The show discussed recent developments in the Third Secret controversy under the title "Fatima: An Unfinished Business"—*the very title of one of the talks delivered at The Fatima Challenge conference*.

As the show opened, the narrator declared that "the mystery

about the Third Secret does not end with the publication of the Secret. Forty years of silence and reticence have led many people to believe that the Message contains something shocking. There are many questions which still remain open. If the prophecy refers to the failed attempt in 1981, why keep it hidden for 20 years? Those who cast doubts about the interpretation given... think that the message of Our Lady is actually pointing to the future and would describe apocalyptic scenarios related to the crisis of the faith and the end of the Church."

The narrator went on to recount (as noted here) that "Father Fuentes, a Mexican priest and postulator of the beatification of Jacinta and Francisco, published a summary of an interview he had with the religious, whose content was disturbing. Sister Lucy stated that the Virgin was disappointed by the souls of priests and pastors and that the punishment of Heaven would be imminent." Further, the narrator continued:

> There is also the testimony of Father Alonso, the official archivist of Fatima, who met several times with Sister Lucy. In his work of more than 5000 pages, the religious claims that probably the Third Secret makes concrete references to the crisis of the faith within the Church.... But there is more: ... [a] version of the Third Secret of Fatima, published by *Neues Europa* [the so-called diplomatic version], which described an apocalyptic scenario of death and destruction. *This text has never been officially denied by the Vatican.* Why then is there no trace of these words in the published message? Is it credible that this text was part of a secret, which has been kept hidden because it was too frightening?

Shortly into the broadcast, there occurred this extraordinary exchange between Tornielli and Claudio Brachino, a Mediaset journalist:

Brachino: There are interesting elements in what John Paul II said during various interviews and declarations. In Fatima he spoke about the apostasy—we should tell the public what apostasy is.

Tornielli: Yes, it's the "expulsion from the faith," the loss of faith, the ultimate and most terrible thing, because it means that we no longer believe. It should be noted that in his document *Ecclesia in Europa* John Paul II spoke about the apostasy in Europe, a term that indicates *the precise and heavy secularization of the Church, and the fall of any relationship with the absolute.*

Brachino: We will discuss this and the apocalyptic vision, but I must insist on this important element: Even among the Catholics, all over the world, *there is suspicion about the official revelation; we're not talking about the secular world or protesters who want to challenge or dispute the Church's policy. We're talking about the so-called Fatimites and other parts of the world's clergy, who do not believe the official version.*

And so the tone was set: Disbelief in the "official version" and the conviction that the whole and entire Third Secret relates to apostasy in the Church can no longer be considered unacceptable for Catholics. This was followed by no fewer than three film clips of Father Gruner providing grounds to doubt the "official version," with the narrator making the obligatory reference to "Fatimites," but then observing as follows: "However, one can not help but notice some inconsistencies in the text, with regards to the 1981 event of Saint Peter's Square. In the vision of the Third Secret, the 'Bishop dressed in White' falls, killed by a group of soldiers, and after him other men die. Pope Wojtyla, instead, was shot by a single killer, and survived. Is it possible, then, that the official interpretation of the Fatima text is wrong?"

After some typically sceptical comments by the Vaticanist Giovanni Ercole about "extremists," the narrator returned to the prevailing theme of reasonable doubt of the "official" version: "But there is another testimony that makes Fatima an unfinished business: Father [Don] Luigi Bianchi, the priest of Gera Lario, in the province of Como, who was a friend of Sister Lucy and met her many times, when she was still alive." In a video clip Bianchi reveals that "The most important thing that I asked Sister Lucy was what she thought we had to expect from this new world, considering that humanity today seems to be so hostile. She said: 'The world is in serious danger.'" When asked by the narrator what precisely Lucia had told him about the Secret, Father Bianchi replied, "Sister Lucy told me that the Secret of Fatima is something *that is still in God's plan.*" And that, as we have just seen, is precisely what the Pope said on the plane and during his homily at the Cova da Iria.

The narrator restated yet again the theme of a newly acceptable reasonable doubt: "So is it not yet possible to write the final word on the Fatima Secrets? The debate about the Third Secret of Fatima, which affected almost the entire 20th century, *seems not to be closed,* not even with the death of two of its greatest protagonists, John Paul II and Sister Lucy." And with that introduction, Brachino and Tornielli conducted a discussion which *presumed the existence of two distinct but related texts* of the Third Secret, one of which, kept in the papal apartment, has never been revealed (precisely as Socci and the

"Fatimists" contend), and has been deemed "inauthentic" by Bertone and company:

> **Brachino:** [A]re there two texts of the Third Secret of Fatima? Or are there multiple interpretations of the revealed text? So, are there two—implying that the Church has only revealed one text or just one part of it?

> **Tornielli:** *Well, certainly there are inconsistencies, there is evidence that shows the existence of two manuscripts. One that was kept in the apartment of the Pope and another one at the Holy See archives.* I don't think that we can call them two different texts of the Secret, because the Secret is what has been revealed, that is the vision; *it is possible, however, given what Sister Lucy has sent to the Vatican during the years, that there might be an attachment, or an explanation to it...* [I]t is clear that John XXIII and his successors *didn't consider it as being fully part of the Third Secret, but just as an interpretation given by Sister Lucy* rather than being part of Our Lady's apparition. In this sense it was declassified to a mere, personal interpretation.

Brachino, stating that "I have to push on this point," noted that the famous "etc" indicated that something was missing, to which Tornielli frankly replied: "Well, it *certainly gives you the idea of something that continues.* Indeed, in the same booklet published officially by the Vatican *there is no explanation to that sentence*, it remains suspended, and it seems to be referring to something else that *the published version of the Third Secret actually doesn't contain.*" At this point in the proceedings Brachino introduced the "story told by Socci's book on Fatima: Archbishop Capovilla *admitted to Solideo Paolini in 2006 the existence of two different but complementary texts of the Third Secret.* One was kept at the Holy Office archives, the other one in the apartment of the Pope..."

After showing the same video interview of Capovilla by De Carli, broadcast during "The Cardinal Bertone Show," which we examined in Chapter 8, Tornielli simply dismissed it as unpersuasive. And, in a massive setback for Bertone and his "official" version, he declared that the existence of a second text of some sort pertaining to the Third Secret is now *well established*:

> **Tornielli:** Yes, we have just seen the interview of Capovilla, in which he said that there is no fourth secret. *But we must remember one fact: Capovilla has repeatedly said that a text of the Secret, an "attachment," has always been kept inside the desk of the Pope, and has stated that it was he who revealed to Pope Paul VI, just a few days after his election, the place where the Secret was located: he told him that the text was kept inside John XXIII's desk called "Barbarigo".* When John XXIII read the Secret in

1959, he decided not to publish it, and Capovilla wrote a note on the envelope (this is confirmed not only by Capovilla, but also by Paul VI, who found that note on Capovilla's envelope). *Now, when it was shown on television in 2007 [on* Porta a Porta*], [Cardinal Bertone] showed the envelopes to the cameras, and there was no handwriting by Capovilla on it....* Not all the time when there is an evidence does it have to confirm a certain theory... *But the existence of two texts in two different places seems to me now a well established fact.*

At this point the discussion was joined by Alessandro Banfi, a prominent Vaticanist, who praised "the reasoning that inspired Socci, with courage and great skill," to question the official version, and then asked and answered his own question, with devastating impact to the credibility of Bertone's position: "This is the matter which I think we should talk about: Is the successor of Peter in possession of a more complete version of the vision, with deeper and confidential information? *In my opinion it is quite credible.* But it was also more than possible a few weeks ago that this controversy could have never been solved. And now the Pope, as always, *has reopened the discussion about it*!" To which Brachino replied: "And he did indeed, as I said at the beginning of the transmission, in a very sensational way. Probably it was a decision that is part of Ratzinger's overall project, his new 'Operation Truth' for a different attitude within the Church, even with regards to herself."

These publicly administered hammer-blows to the Vatican Secretary of State's position were followed by discussion of "the dramatic problem of the apostasy" (Banfi), "the abandoning of the faith, but by the members of the Church themselves" (Brachino), "the abandoning of the faith inside the Church. Exactly." (Banfi). Then, following a video segment on Ali Agca and the 1981 assassination attempt, Brachino, Tornielli and Banfi took aim at the Sodano/ Bertone "interpretation" that events contained in the Third Secret "need to be interpreted as if they were referring to the past, and precisely to the assassination attempt against John Paul II on May 13, 1981, in St. Peter's Square." What Socci calls the "preventative interpretation" was essentially deemed no longer operative, particularly in view of the Pope's statement on the papal plane:

> **Brachino:** I want to ask Andrea Tornielli the following question: Between what is shown in the vision and what happened in St. Peter's Square, I don't think the two events coincide: in the vision the Pope died, but in 1981 he survived!

> **Tornielli:** The big difference is that Pope John Paul II didn't die, he fell "as if dead", to use the same expression used by Cardinal

Sodano in 2000. But we must also say, as Ratzinger himself said in the presentation of the official Secret, that these prophecies are not a "film about the future"... *but that inconsistency is there.*

Brachino: About this interpretation, Mr. Banfi, there are many things *that are actually leading us away from the true interpretation of the Third Secret that is being given now* [by Pope Benedict]. If not everything has to happen afterwards, *certainly not everything has happened already!*

Banfi: True, the plot that leads to the attack against John Paul II has not been clarified yet: Okay, Ali Agca was caught and imprisoned, but it is hard to understand any connection, any link between that event and Providence, its secret designs, as Sodano tried to imply in his interpretation of the Secret. *So there's more than one contradiction that leaves us perplexed.* Moreover, the vision speaks of arrows and shots, so not just a single gunshot, but a collective attack. *The vision suggests a Vatican which seems to have been bombed and is now just a heap of rubble; the remaining faithful would climb the hill towards the cross, and those soldiers would attack them, and the Pope, with arrows and bullets, killing them all.*

In sum, Brachino concluded, echoing Socci: "The Pope reopens the case, although he doesn't say the old interpretation is totally wrong, he said it still refers to the suffering of John Paul II and probably of the Popes and *of the Catholic world.*" To this Tornielli added an observation concerning Jacinta's famous vision of a future Pope under attack: "I remember that one of the seers, Jacinta, speaking once with Sister Lucy, told her of a vision in which she saw the Pope as if he were kneeling before an altar, and people from outside were throwing stones at him... it is a stoning or a moral attack like the one we're seeing now." Continuing in the same vein, Brachino alluded to "the words of John Paul II said at Fatima on May 13, 1982 concerning the danger of the apostasy from God, the fight against God and all that is sacred and divine. Are we near the time predicted by St. Paul, the time of the Antichrist, who rises against God and against any sort of religion? It is a time, however, in which the Holy Spirit mobilizes the whole Church, through the Blessed Virgin." Here Brachino, just before playing a video of Pope Benedict's stunning remarks on the plane to Portugal, quoted above, returned to the theme sounded by Socci, declaring: "On May 13, 2010, another Pope, Benedict XVI, made some remarkable statements *which reopened the case.* On May 13th, *a date that will remain forever in the history of Catholicism.*"

Brachino punctuated the video with a comment that indicated that the Italian media, joining Catholics all over the world, now recognized that a new chapter had been opened in the Third Secret controversy in a book that would not be closed until the whole story unfolds, a chapter in which the Secret as a prophecy of apostasy in the Church is foretold: "Here Benedict XVI brings to mind the speeches of Paul VI about the '*smoke of Satan within the Church*,' and it seems also to echo the great writings of Charles Hodge, who spoke about Christianity after Christ and without Christ. What comes to our minds is the dramatic question, in the form of poetry, posed by T.S. Eliot: 'Is it the Church that has abandoned humanity, or is it humanity that has abandoned the Church?'"

Ten years after the Vatican Secretary of State had ventured to put an end to the Third Secret of Fatima and the Message of Fatima as a whole, the Mediaset broadcast demonstrated a growing awareness among the faithful that the prophecies and warnings of the Virgin Mother of God to Lucia, Jacinta and Francisco were more alive, and more urgent, than ever.

An Untimely Passing

Less than three weeks after the critical dissection of the "official version" on Mediaset, Giuseppe De Carli passed away unexpectedly at the Gemelli Polyclinic in Rome at the age of 58, reportedly while undergoing radiotherapy for a suddenly discovered inoperable throat cancer. Gemelli was the same hospital in which John Paul II had called for the text of the vision in 1981 while recovering from the nearly fatal wounds Ali Agca had inflicted on him.

Did De Carli know about his terminal illness when he appeared at *The Fatima Challenge* conference, stepping from behind the Vatican's stone wall of silence and evasion to encounter his fellow Catholics on the revealing ground of a free and open discussion in search of the truth? Or did he discover his illness after his appearance at the Ergife Hotel? We do not know. But we do know that, along with the conference as a whole, De Carli's decision to appear and attempt a defense of Bertone's indefensible position must have contributed to the impetus for Pope Benedict's "Operation Truth," an operation that, one must hope and pray, will lead at last to a full disclosure of the Virgin of Fatima's message-warning to the Church and all humanity, while there is still time to avert the worst of what it foretells.

Giuseppe De Carli died on July 13, 2010, the very anniversary of the day on which the Mother of God revealed the Third Secret in its entirety to the seers of Fatima. It is impossible to dismiss the connection as a mere coincidence. May the perpetual light shine upon him.

Chapter 13

FATHER APOSTOLI'S *FATIMA FOR TODAY:*
PROPPING UP THE PARTY LINE

Although the Pope himself had publicly negated the Party Line on Fatima during his Fatima pilgrimage of May 2010, the Secretary of State was sticking to his story; and there were still apologists willing to ignore all the evidence and defend his discredited version of events. One of these was Father Andrew Apostoli, a founding member of the "Franciscan Friars of the Renewal" (what renewal?) and a celebrity of the Eternal Word Television Network, whose mixed bag of appalling novelty, modernist theology, crass pop culture, and elements of traditional Catholic piety has been the subject of a book-length exposé.[262]

In October 2010, four months after the Pope's explosive remarks during the Fatima pilgrimage, Apostoli published a book entitled *Fatima for Today* (*FFT*), as if to address in a great hurry what the Pope had said. *FFT* is a perfect example of the *modus operandi* of "Operation False Friends" regarding Fatima, which is to remove from the apparitions all prophetic content at odds with the program of the party of the innovators, while avoiding any disturbance of the faithful by a direct attack on the Fatima event. *FFT* is the same sort of work as Bertone's *Last Visionary*, retitled and rehashed as *Last Secret*. Like Bertone's efforts, Apostoli's book is a seeming tribute to the Message of Fatima, filled with pious statements about prayer and penance and the life and writings of Sister Lucia. But this material thinly conceals an overriding polemical intent revealed in key passages: to advance the Party Line that the Fatima prophecies belong to the past and all that remains of Fatima for the faithful is a summons to say their prayers and do penance. The Consecration of Russia and the Third Secret are to be forgotten forever. As a prophecy, Fatima is finished.

But Why?

Why would Fr. Apostoli publish a book that perpetuates the Vatican Secretary of State's clearly discredited campaign to bury Fatima when no one has any obligation to heed his opinion and the Pope himself had rejected it months before? What is going on here? Only one answer seems reasonable: the Secretary of State is behind the publication *Fatima for Today*. Like Bertone's books, Fr. Apostoli's

---

[262] Cf. Christopher A. Ferrara, *EWTN: A Network Gone Wrong* (Pound Ridge, NY: Good Counsel Publications, Inc., 2006). For a full-length treatment on this subject, read Christopher A. Ferrara, "*Fatima For Today:* A Response", on the web at http://www. fatima.org/news/newsviews/fatima-for-today-a-response.pdf.

book is yet another exercise in "damage control" by Cardinal Bertone.

That conclusion is supported by the enlistment of a high-ranking Vatican prelate to give *FFT* the false appearance of authority: a preface by Cardinal Raymond Burke, Prefect of the Apostolic Signatura, the Vatican's canonical high court. Like the Secretariat of State, however, the Signatura has nothing to do with Marian apparitions and has no more competence in this matter than the Secretary of State does. Yet Cardinal Burke had lent his name to what was clearly yet another effort by Fatima's false friends in the Vatican bureaucracy to strip the Message of Fatima of its prophetic content. The strategy at work in the production of *FFT* seems obvious enough: Since Bertone had lost all credibility concerning Fatima, perhaps the faithful would believe Cardinal Burke if he uttered the same incredible things.

Continuing Bertone's cavalcade of the incredible, Cardinal Burke, citing one Fr. C.C. Martindale, S.J., who died about 50 years ago and had no knowledge of recent Fatima research, asserts in his preface that there is nothing new in the Third Secret because, after all, "the first two parts of the secret contain nothing new" inasmuch as hell is not a novel doctrine and thus the vision of hell contains "no novel or startling *information* [emphasis in original]..." (p. xv). But it seems the Cardinal has overlooked a few pieces of "novel or startling information" in the first two parts of the Great Secret: (1) the imminent end of World War I; (2) the commencement of World War II after the appearance of a strange light in the night sky during the pontificate of Pius XI (identified by name); (3) the spread of Russia's errors throughout the world; (4) the loss of souls, further wars and persecutions of the Church, the martyrdom of the faithful, the suffering of the Pope, and the annihilation of nations; and (5) the express connection of these future events to an ultimatum: they will all take place unless Our Lady of Fatima's specific requests are granted, including the Consecration of Russia to the Immaculate Heart and the Communions of Reparation on the Five First Saturdays.

According to Cardinal Burke, however, the Consecration of Russia and the Third Secret are mere "controversies" that have "distracted from Our Lady's maternal instruction and have hindered others from attending to it." (p. xiv). But the Consecration of Russia is at the very heart of Our Lady's "maternal instruction," while the Third Secret undoubtedly foretells the consequences of failing to heed that instruction, including "various nations will be annihilated." It is, therefore, the Party Line, not "controversies" among the faithful, that has hindered obedience to the instructions our Mother gave us at Fatima.

Yet promoting the Party Line is really what this book is all about. Hence, in his preface Cardinal Burke also expresses the opinion— of course binding on no one—that "Pope Benedict concludes that the Secret is, in the end... 'the exhortation to prayer'... and, likewise, 'the summons to penance and conversion.'" (p. xv) In other words, the Cardinal states the Party Line: The Message of Fatima no longer concerns future events. Catholics must now think only of prayer and penance when they think of Fatima. No other thoughts are permitted, as these are mere "distracting controversies."

With all due respect, the Cardinal's reference to the Pope is misleading. He is not quoting Pope Benedict, who had rejected the Party Line months before, but rather the former Cardinal Ratzinger, writing eleven years ago in his theological commentary on the Secret in *The Message of Fatima* (*TMF*), the booklet the Vatican published together with the vision. For some reason never explained, *TMF* parroted the Party Line even though the Secretary of State manifestly had no competence or authority to dictate it to the Church: "First of all," wrote the former Cardinal Ratzinger in *TMF*, "*we must affirm with Cardinal Sodano*: '... the events to which the third part of the 'secret' of Fatima refers now seem part of the past.'" We must affirm with Cardinal Sodano? But why must we affirm with Cardinal Sodano? No reason has ever been given, because none exists. Quite to the contrary, as already noted, during the very press conference at which the vision and *TMF* were published the same Cardinal Ratzinger was at pains to note: "It is not the intention of the Church to impose a single interpretation."[263]

During his pilgrimage to Fatima, Pope Benedict declared that the Secret relates to "*future realities of the Church* which are little by little developing and showing themselves." In view of that papal affirmation, one would think the Party Line would be discarded once and for all, even by those who had defended it until now. Yet the author of *FFT* presses ahead with the latest propaganda on behalf of the Secretary of State, assisted by another Vatican cardinal with no competence in the matter, who—quite contrary to everything the Pope had said only four months earlier—would have us believe that there is nothing new or startling in the Message of Fatima.

The Promotion of a Demonstrable Falsehood

FFT's arguments in favor of the Party Line—the standard litany of long-since-refuted contentions—begins with its unquestioning adoption of the claim by Cardinal Bertone, already mentioned, that

---

[263] *See* "Vatican Issues Text of Third Secret of Fatima," *New York Times*, June 27, 2000, at http://www.nytimes.com/2000/06/27/world/vatican-issues-text-of-third-secret-of-fatima.html.

radically undermined Bertone's credibility and rendered his entire version of events unworthy of belief. Echoing Bertone, *FFT* asserts that "Because *Sister Lucia had chosen the year 1960* as the time to reveal the Third Secret... curiosity and even dread about what the message might contain had heightened significantly over the years..." (p. 211). According to Bertone—in three conflicting versions of his story given between 2000 and 2007[264]—Sister Lucia "confessed" to him during conveniently unrecorded interviews that she, not Our Lady, had fixed the year 1960 for disclosure of the Secret and that Our Lady had never said anything to her about this.

Recall that for seven years Bertone maintained that Our Lady had never told Lucia that revelation of the Secret was connected to the year 1960, which happens to be the year following John XXIII's announcement of the Second Vatican Council. Then, during the *Porta a Porta* telecast of May 31, 2007, the Cardinal blithely revealed to the world not one, but two, sealed envelopes recording in Lucia's own handwriting that *"By express order of Our Lady, this envelope can only be opened in 1960* by the Cardinal Patriarch of Lisbon or the Bishop of Leiria."[265] Only one conclusion is possible: Bertone's claim that Lucia "confessed" that Our Lady had never said anything to her about 1960 is simply a lie. For it is impossible that the visionary would have taken it upon herself to decide when the Secret would be revealed, invented an "express order of Our Lady" justifying her arbitrary choice, recorded that express order on the outside of the two envelopes, and then allowed the Church and the world to believe for decades that, as she told Cardinal Ottaviani in 1955, the Virgin did not wish the Secret to be revealed before 1960 "because then it will be clearer *(mais claro)*." Or, as she told the Bishop of Leiria-Fatima, "because the Blessed Virgin wishes it so." Or, as she told Canon Barthas: "Our Lady wills that it can be published beginning in 1960."[266]

Either Sister Lucia, the visionary chosen by Heaven itself, was a serial liar on a fundamental point or it is Bertone who has misled us. No argument is needed to establish which is the case. The envelopes speak for themselves. Yet *FFT* uncritically accepts and promotes Bertone's demonstrable falsehood—a falsehood clearly intended to negate the Virgin's linkage of the Secret to 1960 so as to support Bertone's "interpretation" of the vision as culminating with the 1981

---

[264] *See The Secret Still Hidden*, p. 145 for a comparative chart of the conflicting versions, complete with ever-changing "quotations" respecting Lucia's alleged "confession."

[265] *See The Secret Still Hidden*, pp. 124-148 for a discussion of Bertone's changing story concerning Lucia's "confession" and the photographs of the envelopes negating Bertone's claim.

[266] Cf. *The Devil's Final Battle* (2010 edition), Ch. 4, pp. 30-31 (one-volume version), pp. 21-22 (two-volume version).

assassination attempt. Even more important for the Party Line,[267] however, is that any connection between the Secret and 1960 would raise questions about the completeness of the Vatican's disclosure in 2000, as there is nothing about the vision *standing alone* that would be clearer *("mais claro")* in that year. Hence Sister Lucy had to "confess" that there was never any such connection and that she had simply made the whole thing up. The claim is an insult—both to the seer and to the intelligence of the faithful.

FFT's adoption of Bertone's blatant misrepresentation undermines the credibility of Apostoli's book as much as it does Bertone's account itself, concerning which there are 101 reasons for doubt, of which this is but one.[268]

The Alleged "Silence" of Our Lady Regarding the Vision

FFT begins its defense of the Sodano/Bertone Party Line with a discussion of the apparition of July 13, 1917, during which Our Lady of Fatima confided the three parts of the Great Secret. Fr. Apostoli writes: "In the first two parts of the July apparition, Our Lady spoke. In the third part [i.e., the Third Secret] *she did not speak at all*, rather the children saw a series of images that unfolded before them." (*FFT*, p. 81).

Without even examining the massive contrary evidence, this affirmation is dubious on its face. Why would Our Lady narrate the first two parts of the Secret, carefully explaining even something as obvious as the vision of hell, only to fall silent during the enigmatic third part? Why would She leave us with the vision of a "Bishop dressed in White" being executed by soldiers outside a devastated city littered with bodies, but no indication of how, why, where and when the catastrophic events depicted occur? Why would She leave it to Cardinal Sodano, of all people, to provide more than eighty years after the fact a "symbolic interpretation" that blatantly fails to correspond to what the vision depicts?

The answer is that Our Lady did not do so. Quite the contrary, Lucia's Fourth Memoir, her most complete written record of the Fatima apparitions, records that *after* the Blessed Virgin had revealed the first two parts of the Secret, She *continued to speak*:

> "In Portugal the dogma of the faith will always be preserved etc. Tell this to no one. Yes you may *tell it* to Francisco."

Lucia added "etc" to indicate the Virgin's continuing discourse, which quite clearly begins another part of the Secret: the third and the final part, which is the Third Secret of Fatima. This is clear because

---

[267] For an explanation of what a Party Line is, see pp. 41-42.
[268] *See, The Secret Still Hidden*, Appendix II, pages 233-235.

the reference to Portugal and dogma has no evident connection to the first two parts of the Great Secret, and yet it clearly *is* part of the Secret as a whole. Thus the Virgin's continuing discourse, marked by Lucia's "etc", must logically connect the third part—the Third Secret—to the first two parts so that all three comprise a unified whole. The Mother of God did not appear on earth to utter stray irrelevancies.

Note that *after* revealing the entire Great Secret, including the portion of the third part indicated by the "etc", Our Lady grants Lucia permission to *tell* all of it to Francisco. That permission was necessary because, as we know, Francisco could not hear what was *said* during the apparitions, although he could see their visional aspect—that is, the vision of hell and the vision of the "Bishop dressed in White." Now, if the vision of the white-clad bishop were all there was to the Third Secret, Our Lady would not have said: "You may *tell* it to Francisco," for he had already *seen* the vision. Therefore, what Lucia was given permission to tell Francisco could only have been *the words he had not heard*, including the Virgin's reference to Portugal and Catholic dogma and what follows, as indicated by the telltale "etc".

In the face of these inescapable inferences, the Vatican commentary in *TMF* very conspicuously avoids the Fourth Memoir, suggesting that the "etc" merely involves some unimportant "annotations" by Lucia:

> For the account of the first two parts of the "secret", which have already been published and are therefore known, we have chosen the text written by Sister Lucia in the Third Memoir of 31 August 1941; some *annotations* were added in the Fourth Memoir of 8 December 1941.[269]

But why "choose" the Third Memoir when *TMF* itself admits that Lucia, under orders from her bishop, wrote the Fourth Memoir *for the sake of completeness*? As *TMF* states:

> In the 'Fourth Memoir' of 8 December 1941 Sister Lucia writes: "I shall begin then my new task, and thus fulfill the commands received from Your Excellency as well as the desires of Dr. Galamba. With the exception of that part of the Secret which I am not permitted to reveal at present, *I shall say everything*. I shall not knowingly omit *anything*, though I suppose I may forget just a few small details of minor importance."[270]

Given the Vatican's own acknowledgment that Lucia wrote the Fourth Memoir in order to "say everything" she was permitted to say about the apparitions, there is only one reasonable explanation for this curious avoidance of the more complete record: Cardinal Sodano

---

[269] *TMF*, pp. 3-4.
[270] *TMF*, footnote 6, p. 15.

and his collaborators in *TMF* wanted to avoid having to discuss the "etc" and what it so clearly indicates: further words of the Virgin.

But *why* would they wish to avoid this subject? There can be only one reasonable explanation: there is something to hide. For if there were nothing to hide, why not simply address what Our Lady said to the seers in the place held by the "etc"? Why not simply explain the relationship between the mysterious dangling phrase concerning Portugal and the Message of Fatima as a whole? Why not simply ask Lucia to provide that explanation and then convey it to the public in order to lay all speculation to rest?

Instead, however, *TMF* characterizes the Virgin's very words as having originated with Lucia: "In the 'Fourth Memoir' Sister Lucia adds: 'In Portugal, the dogma of the faith will always be preserved, etc. ...'"[271] That representation is both misleading and an implicit slur on the visionary. Lucia did not *add* anything to what the Mother of God had revealed to her; she merely recorded what she saw and heard during the apparitions, including "everything" Mary *said* to her with permission to *tell* Francisco. And in 1944—also under orders from her bishop—Lucia would write down everything the Virgin had *told* her, including the rest of the words She had confided to the seer and given her permission to *tell* Francisco concerning the Third Secret of Fatima.

Fr. Apostoli and all those who deny that something has been hidden, something embraced within the mysterious "etc", must confront these questions:

- If there is nothing to hide, why does the Vatican commentary avoid the Fourth Memoir, which it admits is the more complete record of the Message of Fatima?

- If there is nothing to hide, why does *TMF* mischaracterize as "annotations" by Lucia, or something she "added," what is patently a direct quotation of the very words of the Mother of God?

- If there is nothing to hide, why have Sodano and Bertone steadfastly refused to answer any questions concerning the "etc"?

- If there is nothing to hide, why did both Sodano and Bertone fail and refuse to put to Sister Lucia a single question regarding the "etc", even though they were both well aware that it stands at the very heart of the Third Secret controversy and they had unrestricted access to the seer until her death in 2005?

---

[271] *TMF*, footnote 7, p. 16.

Indeed, Fr. Apostoli's very reliance upon Sodano's "interpretation" of the vision is a proof that something is missing from the Vatican's disclosure in 2000. For it can hardly be the case that the Mother of God envisioned a future Vatican functionary— much less Cardinal Angelo Sodano, the aider and abettor of scandal—as the authentic interpreter of Her message. Nor can it be the case that Our Lady would have permitted Her message to become the subject of *eight different interpretations* that contradict each other, as I have noted elsewhere.[272] Therefore, the Virgin's own explanation of the vision must exist and must have been withheld for some reason. The words of the Mother of God for which we seek can only be those which follow the "etc" that both Sodano and Bertone have avoided like the plague in a maneuver that would otherwise be inexplicable.

What Sort of Oracles Are These?

Having been deprived of the Virgin's own explanation of what the vision revealed in the year 1917 means, we are asked to rely on Cardinal Sodano's "interpretation" in the year 2000—an objectively ludicrous proposition given the immense magnitude of the Message of Fatima as an urgent prophecy conveyed to the whole world by the very Mother of God. Recall that this is the same Cardinal Sodano who was instrumental in covering up the Father Maciel scandal for decades. The very idea that this ecclesiastical politician and "fixer" has some special authority to tell us the meaning of the Fatima event is a mockery of the Mother of God and Her divine Son.

Yet, Fr. Apostoli writes: "Cardinal Sodano said that the children saw a 'prophetic vision,' which must be understood as symbolic..." (p. 81). Cardinal Sodano said? *Must*? But Cardinal Sodano has no authority at all in the matter, much less authority to tell us how we "must" understand the vision. *FFT* takes no notice of this fact. Instead, this privately published book, marketed on Amazon.com by an American publisher, labors to create the false impression that it is presenting official Church teaching on the meaning of the vision. But why is Fr. Apostoli not sounding the alarm that something must be gravely amiss because as of 2011 *we have no authoritative interpretation of the vision*, nearly a century after the Virgin conveyed it to the seers? Does anyone, even the author of *FFT*, really believe the Mother of God left us in this perilous situation?

Continuing to quote the former Secretary of State as if he were a Fatima oracle, *FFT* cites his mere opinion that the vision "does not

---

[272] *See* "Is There a Missing Text of the Third Secret?", http://www.fatimachallenge. com/index.php?Itemid=15&catid=25&id=67:is-there-a-missing-text-of-the-third-secret&option=com_content&view=article" (video presentation).

describe photographically the details of future events" and "must be interpreted in a symbolic key." (p. 82). According to this "symbolic key," says Fr. Apostoli—quoting the former Cardinal Ratzinger's non-binding theological commentary, which in turn follows Cardinal Sodano's non-binding "interpretation"—the vision depicts only the threat of nuclear war, and the Angel with the flaming sword is only a symbol for nuclear weapons: "man himself, with his inventions, has forged the flaming sword." (p. 83).

So, despite what the vision clearly depicts, we are asked to believe that: (a) there is no Angel with a flaming sword, (b) there is no future execution of a Pope, bishops, priests and laity by soldiers on a hill, and (c) there is no half-ruined city filled with corpses from which a hobbling Pope escapes before he is executed. Instead there is only a symbolically depicted threat of nuclear war. The Church and the world are supposed to rely with complete tranquility on the Secretary of State's assurances that the vision does not foretell a divine chastisement, but only man's inhumanity to man. Yes, as Fr. Apostoli would have it, *Sodano and his successor Bertone are literally the oracles we must consult on the fate of the world in light of Fatima*! Does anyone, even Fr. Apostoli, take that claim seriously?

Continuing to explain away what the vision plainly depicts, Fr. Apostoli—faithfully hewing to the Party Line—asserts that when Mary is seen repelling the destructive flames emanating toward the world from the Angel's flaming sword, this means only that "Our Lady's intervention is powerful enough to stop the chastisement of war." (p. 83). Well, of course Our Lady *is* powerful enough to stop the chastisement of war, but the problem for Fr. Apostoli and the Party Line he defends is that in the vision we see that the chastisement depicted *has not been averted*. On the contrary, the city *is* in ruins and filled with bodies; the Pope *is* killed by a band of soldiers on the hill outside the ruined city; bishops, priests, religious and lay people *are* killed by the same band of soldiers.

Further, while we see that the flames emanating from the sword of the avenging Angel "died out in contact with the splendour that Our Lady radiated towards him from her right hand," this happens in the context of the devastation, death, and martyrdom that do take place in the same vision. It would thus appear that the vision shows either that Our Lady obtains a stay of a divine chastisement that is nonetheless ultimately inflicted, or that She mitigates it in order to spare the rest of the world from destruction. But we cannot be certain of this because, in the absence of the missing explanatory text that must exist, we have only the opinions of two Vatican prelates with absolutely no competence in the matter. Once again: the claim that the Mother of God left us in this situation of depending upon Sodano and Bertone for an understanding of this vision is a complete absurdity.

Based on the oracular Sodano/Bertone "interpretation", we are also expected to consider "part of the past" Our Lady's dire warning, in the second part of the Great Secret, that if the Consecration of Russia is not accomplished "The good will be martyred; the Holy Father will have much to suffer; *various nations will be annihilated.*" In fact, a scenario suggesting a future annihilation of nations *is exactly what we see in the vision*, as well as the Message of Akita that Cardinal Ratzinger described as "essentially the same." But we must ignore the grim future the vision appears to depict and trust in Cardinal Sodano and Cardinal Bertone, says Fr. Apostoli—*even though the Pope himself says we have no such obligation.* Truly astonishing.

Concerning the execution of "a Bishop dressed in White" by a band of soldiers outside the city in ruins, Fr. Apostoli, aping the Party Line, reduces this event to John Paul II *not* being executed by a band of soldiers and *escaping* death at the hands of a lone assassin in the perfectly intact city of Rome. After all, he argues, the Pope "lost six pints of blood" and (quoting Bertone) "It was *as if* he had died, and then been snatched back from the jaws of death." (p. 90). Close enough for government work! That is, the government of the Vatican city-state as exercised by Sodano and his successor Bertone, who had to wait patiently for Sodano the Fatima oracle to vacate his luxurious apartments after being replaced as Secretary of State.

To be serious, Cardinal Sodano patently falsified what the vision depicts when he first advanced this "interpretation" back in 2000. According to him, the Pope in the vision "makes his way with great difficulty towards the Cross amid the corpses of those who were martyred (bishops, priests, men and women Religious and many lay people), he too falls to the ground, *apparently* dead, under a hail of gunfire."[273] But this was plainly a deception. The Pope does not fall to the ground "apparently" dead. Rather, he "*was killed* by a group of soldiers who fired bullets and arrows at him…" Moreover, the Pope is not killed "amid the corpses of those who were martyred," but rather the martyrdom of bishops, priests, religious and lay people occurs *after* he is killed and at the hands of *the same band of soldiers who kill the Pope.* As the text of the vision states: "and in *the same way* there died one after another the other Bishops, Priests, men and women Religious, and various lay people of different ranks and positions."

On the other hand, the victims the Pope encounters as he hobbles through the half-ruined city are not martyrs, as Sodano falsely

---

[273] Ibid.

suggests. Rather, they have all died *before* the martyrs on the hill *outside* the city, including the Pope, are slain by the soldiers: "before reaching there [the steep hill] the Holy Father passed through a big city half in ruins and half trembling with halting step, afflicted with pain and sorrow, he *prayed for the souls of the corpses* he met on his way." Further, it is highly implausible that all the dead in the ruined city are martyrs. But even if the vision depicted a city full of dead martyrs, versus the martyrs on the hill that Sodano glosses over, they would not need the Pope's prayers, for they would have entered immediately into the Beatific Vision.

In short, Sodano twisted the vision to suit his polemical aim of consigning the Message of Fatima to the past. To put it mildly, his "interpretation" has been met with widespread incredulity among the Catholic faithful. To put it bluntly, the interpretation is a joke. But Fr. Apostoli insists that we take it seriously and indeed that we literally *bet our lives and even our souls on it.*

Here it seems no absurdity is large enough to arouse Fr. Apostoli's skepticism concerning Sodano's twisted interpretation. Addressing the insurmountable objection that "John Paul II could not have been the Pope of the Third Secret because he did not die," he asserts (without evidence) that John Paul "recognized himself as the Pope who was slain in the vision..." (p. 212). A *living* Pope recognizes himself as a *slain* Pope? Fr. Apostoli further asserts that John Paul "knew about this objection, which is the reason he said he came to the very threshold of death and should have died, but Our Lady prevented him from doing so." (p. 212) But he fails to quote any statement by John Paul that the vision depicts the failed assassination attempt and that he is thus the Pope in the vision. That is because no such statement exists.

Fr. Apostoli adds his own gloss to the Sodano/Bertone "interpretation" with even more absurd results. Having contended only a few lines earlier that the Pope who is killed in the vision is John Paul II, who was *not* killed, he attempts to explain the subsequent mass execution of martyrs seen in the vision: "Just as the Holy Father was killed [?] in the vision, so were all those who followed *after him*. These were the men and women who died as martyrs because of their love for the Church. We have already seen the tremendous number of martyrs in Russia. There were countless others who sacrificed their lives as well." (p. 81). So, the author of *FFT* seriously proposes that the 20th century martyrs in the Soviet Union, who died *before* the assassination attempt in 1981, somehow died *after* John Paul II "died" but did not die. And while the deaths of the 20th century martyrs are to be taken literally, the "death" of John

Paul is to be taken figuratively—in one and the same vision!

It seems Sodano's "symbolic key" is an amazingly rubbery device, bending in any direction in which one wishes to twist it. But here Fr. Apostoli contradicts Sodano/Bertone, who would have us believe that the martyrs in the vision die *before* the Pope, not after. Well, which is it? Does the Pope in the vision "die" figuratively before or after the martyrs die literally? Either or both, apparently. Self-contradictions do not matter so long as the Party Line is maintained. The vision "means" whatever it needs to mean in order to relegate the Fatima prophecies to the 20th century and their culmination to the year 1981 according to the preconceived intention of the Secretary of State, who has somehow usurped control over the Message of Fatima.

Clearly, the Church and the world are most urgently in need of the Virgin's remedy for this utter nonsense: Her own words explaining the events in the vision and their historical context, just as She explained to the children a vision of hell far less ambiguous than the vision of the "Bishop dressed in White." Fr. Apostoli's own contortions demonstrate that the Virgin's precious explanation is, as Socci says, "well hidden" somewhere in the Vatican.

Obscuring Pope Benedict's Revelations

Since *FFT* was published four months after Benedict's explosive statements during his pilgrimage to Fatima, during which he repudiated the Party Line, Fr. Apostoli had to confront that development. The approach *FFT* takes is to pretend the Party Line remains intact despite Benedict's clear rejection of it, which *FFT* studiously avoids mentioning, although Socci has proclaimed it to the world. Worse, *FFT*'s discussion of the Pope's remarks deliberately obscures their import. For one thing, *FFT*'s quotation of the Vatican's English translation of the Pope's remarks during the flight to Fatima departs from the Vatican text and is suspiciously cropped as shown by the italics:

<u>Vatican Translation</u>

As for the new things which we can find in this message today, there is also the fact that attacks on the Pope and the Church come not only from without, but the sufferings of the Church come precisely from within the Church, from the sin existing within the Church.[274]

---

[274] "Interview of the Holy Father Benedict XVI with the Journalists During the Flight to Portugal," May 11, 2010, at www.vatican.va/holy_father/benedict_xvi/ speeches/2010/may/documents/hf_ben-xvi_spe_20100511_portogallo-interview_ en.html. In the original Italian remarks: "*Quanto alle novità che possiamo oggi scoprire in questo messaggio è anche che* non solo da fuori vengono attacchi al Papa e alla

Translation in *FFT*

Attacks on the Pope and the Church do not come only from the outside, but the sufferings of the Church come precisely from within the Church, from the sin existing within the Church. (p. 215)

Notice that the key phrase "As for *the new things* which we can find *in this message* [the Third Secret] today, there is also the fact that..." is removed and the sentence is made to begin with the word "Attacks". This neatly eliminates the Pope's explicit linkage of "new things which we can find in this message" to attacks on the Pope and the Church by *internal* enemies, not the band of soldiers seen in the vision—a clear indication that there is more to the Secret than the vision alone.

That internal enemies of the Church are involved in the events foretold by the Secret must be why Benedict chose the words: "*beyond the moment indicated in the vision*, it is *spoken*, it is seen, the necessity of a passion of the Church..." ["oltre il momento indicato nella visione, si parla, si vede la necessità di una passione della chiesa..."]. If the Secret involves something *spoken* beyond the moment indicated in the vision, it could only be in a text that accompanies the vision since the vision does not *speak* about attacks on the Church by enemies within nor make *any reference at all, even symbolically*, to such attacks. In fact, there are no spoken words in the vision save the thrice-repeated admonition of the avenging Angel: "Penance, Penance, Penance." As for what the vision depicts wordlessly, it is exactly the contrary of an internal attack upon the Church: an external attack by a band of soldiers. The conclusion is inescapable: the Pope must have learned of the Fatima prophecy concerning internal subversion of the Church from another source related to the Secret, a source not yet revealed: i.e., the Secret Still Hidden.

FFT does concede that the Pope "linked the suffering caused by these accusations [of sexual abuse] and the terrible sins committed by some priests *with that seen in the vision*." (p. 215). But Fr. Apostoli avers that the Pope has merely "further interpreted the Third Secret..."—meaning the vision standing alone. (Ibid.) Once again we encounter the notion that the vision is something to be "interpreted" without guidance from Our Lady, including such "further" interpretation as might emerge at any given moment. Thus the Third Secret, reduced to the vision alone, becomes an endless work-in-progress whose current meaning depends upon the eye of

---

chiesa, ma le sofferenze della chiesa vengono proprio dall'interno della chiesa, dal peccato che esiste nella chiesa."

the beholder, like some piece of modern art in a museum. This is surely not what the Mother of God conveyed to the seers.

So, what does the suffering depicted in the vision, wherein soldiers execute a future Pope and then bishops, priests and laity after him, have to do with the suffering due to sexual abuse committed by priests? There is no apparent connection. Hence, as Socci has noted, the Pope's linkage of the vision to the priestly sexual scandals erupting in recent years must point to what we already know: that there is a text wherein the Virgin provides the missing connection. This text most probably foretells how a future Pope meets a violent end at the hands of soldiers outside a ruined city filled with corpses in the midst of a post-apocalyptic scenario related to an internal crisis in the Church, leading to a chastisement of both the Church and the world.

Here we must consider once again that the Message of Akita, which the former Cardinal Ratzinger has described as "essentially the same"[275] as the Message of Fatima, predicts just such a twin chastisement on account of sin in the Church. Read carefully Our Lady's warning to Sister Sasagawa in an apparition approved as authentic after a diocesan investigation by Bishop John Shojiro Ito, the local ordinary:

> As I told you, if men do not repent and better themselves, the Father will inflict a terrible punishment on all humanity. It will be punishment greater than the deluge, such as one will never have seen before. *Fire will fall from the sky and will wipe out a great part of humanity, the good as well as the bad, sparing neither priests nor faithful.* The survivors will find themselves so desolate that they will envy the dead. The only arms that will remain for you will be the Rosary and Sign left by My Son. Each day recite the prayers of the Rosary. With the Rosary, pray for the pope, the bishops, and the priests.
>
> *The work of the devil will infiltrate even the Church* in such a way that one will see cardinals opposing cardinals, bishops against other bishops. The priests who venerate Me will be scorned and opposed by their confreres...churches and altars sacked, *the Church will be full of those who accept compromise and the demon will press many priests and consecrated souls to leave the service of the Lord.* The demon will be especially implacable

---

[275] Howard Dee, former Philippine ambassador to the Vatican, revealed in a 1998 interview with *Inside the Vatican* magazine that "Bishop Ito was certain Akita was an extension of Fatima, and Cardinal Ratzinger personally confirmed to me that these two messages, of Fatima and Akita, are essentially the same." *Catholic World News*, October 11, 2001, www.cwnews.com/news/viewstory.cfm?recnum=20583. The Message has apparently since been disparaged by the Japanese bishops' conference, although the local ordinary, Bishop Ito, investigated the apparitions and found them worthy of belief.

against souls consecrated to God. The thought of the loss of so many souls is the cause of My sadness. If sins increase in number and gravity, there will be no longer pardon for them.

Given the recent geological and nuclear catastrophe in Japan, centered on the very diocese in which Our Lady of Akita appeared (the Diocese of Sendai), we ought to be alarmed by the connection between Akita and Fatima, between the words quoted above and what must be contained in the text of the Secret that predicts an attack on the Church by her own members sinning against her—*the one thing we do not see in the vision standing alone.*

Finally, *FFT* simply ignores the Pope's statement at the Fatima Shrine that "One deceives himself if he thinks that the prophetic mission of Fatima is concluded." There can be only one reason *FFT* so conspicuously fails to mention the Pope's dramatic admission: it refutes the lie that the Fatima prophecies "belong to the past" and that all that remains of the Fatima message is prayer and penance. But then nothing could be clearer than that *FFT* was written to defend the Party Line, no matter how untenable it has become. That is, it was written to promote precisely what the Pope called a deception "that the prophetic mission of Fatima is concluded." Thus, the Pope himself indicts the undertaking.

A Non-Answer to Objections

In a scant seven pages, an appendix to *FFT* (pp. 263-269) purports to answer all objections to the claim that the vision of the "Bishop dressed in White" is the entirety of the Third Secret of Fatima. Here we give the appendix the passing treatment it deserves. For rather than answering objections the appendix avoids them, addressing only four of a multitude, and those four only weakly:

Objection #1: "The original Third Secret was written on one sheet of paper." That is not a fair statement of the objection. Fairly stated, the objection is that *a* text pertaining to the Third Secret was written on a single sheet of paper, as the Auxiliary Bishop of Fatima could discern when he held the envelope containing it up to the light before it was transmitted to the Vatican. That sheet contains 25 lines of text—not the 62 lines of the vision. Cardinal Ottaviani attested "categorically" to a text of 25 lines, as Cardinal Bertone himself admitted on camera during his appearance on *Porta a Porta* while claiming (absurdly) that Ottaviani mistook the 62 lines for 25 lines. Evidently, we are dealing with two different texts, just as Archbishop Capovilla confirmed in his testimony, which *FFT* (like Bertone and Sodano) ignores.

FFT quotes *TMF* for the proposition that when Lucia was asked to authenticate the Secret during a purported meeting with Bertone on April 27, 2000 she stated: "This is my letter," and "this is my writing." In the first place, the text of the vision is not a letter. *FFT* simply ignores that discrepancy. And here *FFT* commits the same fatal misstep as Bertone in *Last Visionary*, stating that during the purported authentication meeting in 2000 Bertone "presented two envelopes to Sister Lucia. The first or outer envelope contained the second envelope, which held the Third Secret." (p. 264). As we know from the *Porta a Porta* telecast, however, Bertone produced *four* envelopes, *three* of which were prepared by Lucia: the Bishop of Fatima's sealed outer envelope, Sister Lucia's unsealed outer envelope, and the *two* sealed envelopes on which Lucia had recorded the "express order of Our Lady"—which Bertone concealed for seven years—that the contents of these *two* envelopes were not to be opened before 1960. Yet Bertone produced only *one* text pertaining to the Third Secret, that of the vision, but not the text of 25 lines. Moreover, he failed to produce the Capovilla envelope kept in the papal apartment, even though its existence is now admitted. *FFT* ignores these enormous and telling discrepancies as well.

FFT repeats uncritically the claim in Bertone's second edition of *Last Visionary of Fatima* (2007), now entitled *Last Secret of Fatima* (2010), that Lucia supposedly told him the text she authenticated in April 2000 "is the Third Secret, and I never wrote any other." But this purported statement of the visionary was never mentioned in *Last Visionary* or anywhere else in Bertone's account over the previous ten years, including *TMF* in 2000. It suddenly "jumped out of the top hat" (to borrow Socci's phrase) after Lucia was conveniently dead and could no longer contradict the words attributed to her for the first time in 2010. Like the claim that Lucia "confessed" that she invented the connection between the Secret and 1960—a demonstrable lie—this *post mortem* surprise revelation is unworthy of belief.

On this point it must be mentioned that while *Last Visionary* reveals that during the April 2000 authentication meeting Lucia purportedly stated "Yes, these are my *sheets* of paper [*fogli*]... they are the *sheets* of paper [*fogli*] that I used" in writing down the Secret, on *Porta a Porta* Bertone produced only *one* sheet of paper from a notebook on which Lucia had written the text of the vision. Hence at least one sheet of paper pertaining to the Secret is missing. Recall that when faced with this damning inadvertent admission, Bertone simply altered Sister Lucia's statement in the later-published *Last Secret*. Now it reads: "this is my paper" instead of "these are my *sheets* of paper... these are the *sheets* I used." Like Bertone's other constantly morphing "quotations" of the visionary—none of which are verifiably recorded in audio or video format—this one lacks all credibility.[276]

Objection #2: *FFT* purports to address the objection that "The text of the Secret contains no words attributed to the Blessed Virgin Mary." The "answer" to this objection is the naked assertion that "the Third Secret was not conveyed in words by Our Lady, but in the various visions the children saw." But that is no answer. Like Bertone and Sodano, *FFT* ignores the telltale "etc" at the end of Our Lady's momentous reference to the dogmas of the Faith and their preservation in Portugal. Like Bertone and Sodano, *FFT* pretends that the "etc" does not exist and that Our Lady had nothing to say about the meaning of an enigmatic vision for which Sodano/Bertone have provided the "interpretation", whose absurdities I have already examined. Like Bertone and Sodano, *FFT* asks no questions about what follows the "etc"—evidently because *FFT*'s author, like Bertone and Sodano, does not wish to explore the implications for the credibility of the Party Line.

Objection #3: "The Vatican's copy of the Third Secret contains no information about a nuclear holocaust, a great apostasy, or the satanic infiltration of the Church." In purporting to address this objection, *FFT*'s author ignores his own earlier argument that the vision depicts the threat of a nuclear holocaust. More important, he ignores Pope Benedict's linkage of the Third Secret to events "*beyond the moment indicated in the vision*" which indicate precisely "satanic infiltration of the Church" by internal enemies whose attacks on the Pope and the Church are manifesting themselves in a "really terrifying way."

FFT ignores as well the testimony of witness after witness who read the Third Secret in its entirety and revealed that it pertains to apostasy in the Church accompanied by a chastisement of the world at large.[277] As no less than Cardinal Ratzinger revealed in 1984, for example, the Secret concerns "dangers *threatening the faith* and the life of the Christian, and therefore of *the world*" and reveals "things which correspond to what has been *announced* in Scripture and *said* again and again in many other Marian apparitions..."[278] But the vision standing alone does not *announce* anything in Sacred Scripture, nor does it *say* anything that has been *said* in numerous other Marian apparitions—such as the one at Akita, in which Our

---

[276] See *The Secret Still Hidden*, pp. 130 and 144-152 for comparative charts of Bertone's ever-changing account of what Lucia is supposed to have said to him concerning the connection of the Secret to 1960, the envelopes and texts involved in the Secret, the Sodano/Bertone "interpretation" of the Secret, and the Consecration of Russia.

[277] See *The Secret Still Hidden*, Chapter 3 for a chronological account of these testimonies.

[278] "Here is Why the Faith Is in Crisis," *Jesus* magazine, November 11, 1984, p. 79.

Lady *speaks* of a great part of the world being destroyed by heavenly fire if "men do not repent and better themselves." Yet the same Cardinal Ratzinger has revealed that the Message of Fatima and the Message of Akita are essentially the same. If the two messages are essentially the same, something is missing from the essence of the Third Secret: the *words* of Our Lady of Fatima, which would comport with Our Lady of Akita's *spoken prediction* of a coming apocalypse, as seen (but without explanation) in the vision of the white-clad bishop being executed outside a devastated city.

Only a missing text containing the words of the Virgin on the vision's meaning would explain events occurring "beyond the moment indicated in the vision" of which Pope Benedict speaks, and "dangers threatening the faith and the life of the Christian, and therefore of the world" of which the former Cardinal Ratzinger spoke. And it is that very text whose existence Father Joseph Schweigl, sent by Pius XII to interrogate Sister Lucia in her convent at Tuy, confirmed long ago: "I may not reveal anything with regard to the Third Secret, but I am able to say that it has two parts: One part concerns the Pope. The other part is the logical continuation—though I may not say anything—of the words: 'In Portugal, the dogma of the Faith will always be preserved etc.'"[279]

On this point *FFT* cites what it claims is a "clear and definitive statement" by Archbishop Capovilla, quoted in a news story, that there is no such missing text: "There are not two truths from Fatima, nor is there any fourth secret. The text which I read in 1959 is the same distributed by the Vatican..." (*FFT*, p. 267) But this "clear and definitive statement" is, on close reading, a carefully worded evasion of the real issue. No one denies that the text the Archbishop read in 1959 is an authentic part of the Secret. Nor does anyone claim that there is literally a "fourth secret" of Fatima. The issue, rather, is the existence of a text that *accompanies* the wordless vision in which Our Lady explains its meaning so that we do not have to rely on such people as a scandal-plagued Vatican Secretary of State to provide absurd and self-contradictory "interpretations" the better part of a century later.

Here *FFT* conveniently fails to mention what really is a "clear and definitive" statement by Capovilla: "Exactly so! [*Per l'appunto*]" in answer to the question whether there are two different envelopes and two different texts comprising the Secret in its totality. Nor does *FFT* mention Capovilla's "clear and definitive statement"—captured on audiotape and published in the Italian press—that there was an "attachment" to the text of the vision that has never been revealed

---

[279] *The Whole Truth About Fatima*, Vol. III, p. 710.

or even mentioned by Bertone/Sodano. Archbishop Capovilla *has never denied either statement*, yet *FFT* pretends these statements were never given.[280]

Further, *FFT* fails to mention that when asked during the video interview—an interview Bertone himself arranged—whether the vision of the white-clad bishop was the text he read in 1959, Capovilla hedged, stating: "I have said it, and I repeat it gladly now: that is the text. I don't recall it word for word, but the *central nucleus* is the same."[281] The central *nucleus*? What is that supposed to mean? Is it the same text he read or not? This was easy enough to confirm, as the text of the vision had been published to the world and Capovilla need only have examined it to refresh his recollection. Yet the Archbishop claimed a lack of memory regarding the exact contents of *a text at his very fingertips*. Small wonder: he had already confirmed the existence of the companion text in statements he has never denied and cannot deny because he knows the companion text exists and has himself revealed that there was an "attachment" to the text of the vision. Hence, the ambiguous reference to a "nucleus," suggesting that something surrounding this "nucleus" has yet to be revealed.

Objection #4: The last objection *FFT* purports to address is that "The text released by the Vatican is not written in the form of a letter." Here *FFT* descends to outright silliness. The author concedes that "some of the clerics who lived at the time the Third Secret was written mentioned it in terms of a letter," yet he argues that "this was not an emphatic point they were making." (p. 267) So the testimony of all the clerics who attested that the Secret involves a letter from Lucia[282] should be disregarded because they did not exclaim when so attesting: "This is an emphatic point!" Here, once again, Fr. Apostoli appears to forget what he himself had written in the earlier pages of his own book. In Chapter 16 of *FFT* he quotes the personal diary of John XXIII concerning the day the commissary of the Holy Office brought him a text of the Secret: "[he] brought me *the letter* containing the Third Part of the Secrets of Fatima. I intend

---

[280] Recall that at *The Fatima Challenge* Conference at the Ergife Hotel in Rome in May 2010, the late Giuseppe De Carli, co-author with Bertone of both *The Last Visionary of Fatima* and *The Last Secret of Fatima*, claimed to be in possession of a letter in which Capovilla denies his testimony to Paolini about the existence of two envelopes and two texts comprising the Secret *in toto* (*"Per l'appunto!"*). But De Carli refused to provide a copy or even to quote from the letter, stating that it was "private correspondence." An alleged secret denial of testimony never denied publicly is typical of the manner in which the Party Line is defended by its partisans. But every defense only adds to the grounds for suspicion.

[281] *The Secret Still Hidden*, p. 182.

[282] Cf. *The Secret Still Hidden*, pp. 17-18.

to read it with my confessor." (p. 211) But as *FFT* would have it, we are not to make anything of this papal notation of a text of the Secret in epistolary form because John XXIII did not add: "and I note this emphatically."

As it does with so many other key facts, *FFT* fails to mention Sister Lucia's own testimony to Father Hubert Jongen: "I communicated the third part [i.e. the Third Secret] in *a letter* to the Bishop of Leiria..."[283] In his evident determination to explain away all evidence contrary to the Party Line, Fr. Apostoli would no doubt argue that we should disregard even the visionary's own statement that the Secret involves a letter because she did not state this with sufficient *emphasis*. Also conveniently overlooked is the revelation in the famous Vatican-initiated press release of 1960 that "most likely *the letter* will never be opened in which Sister Lucia wrote down *the words* which Our Lady confided as a secret to the three little shepherds" because (among other specious reasons) "the Vatican already knows the contents of *the letter*."[284]

Quoting Bertone, *FFT* assures us that "the point about the document being written in the form of a letter is not very important. He [Bertone] said of some of his critics that 'they look at everything through the magnifying glass of their own biases. They latch on to the most unbelievable things.'" (p. 268) Yes, what could be more "unbelievable" than a string of clerics, the Pope, the Vatican in 1960 and Sister Lucia herself attesting that the Secret involves a text in the form of a letter—a letter we have never seen. No, instead of turning our "magnifying glass" on such trivia as a missing letter from the last surviving Fatima visionary recording the words of the Mother of God, we should put on the blinders Fr. Apostoli prescribes for the faithful and place all of our trust in the Vatican Secretary of State.

According to EWTN—the veritable network of "Operation False Friends"—quoting the *National Catholic Register*, which EWTN now owns, *FFT* "answers every possible objection so thoroughly and so clearly with no detail or fact ignored or unexplained."[285] As we can see, however, *FFT* does not "answer" objections, but simply ignores them or covers them up. And the claim that "no fact or detail has been overlooked" is simply laughable. But at least we have here another admission of what *FFT* is really all about: not a tribute to the Message of Fatima, but rather another attempt to obfuscate the fatal infirmities in the Party Line by "answering objections" without answering them. *FFT* as a whole is typical of what has been called

---

[283] Ibid., p. 18 and n. 43.

[284] Ibid., p. 26, quoting ANI press release.

[285] See http://www.wafusa.org/the_message.html.

"Bertone's Method."[286] Like Bertone, Fr. Apostoli makes a great show of responding to objections, but produces instead only evasions, inadvertent admissions and telling silences.

Defending the Consecration that Wasn't

Unswervingly loyal to the Party Line, *FFT* also dutifully advances its claim that the consecration of Russia was accomplished by ceremonies from which any mention of Russia was *deliberately omitted* so that the Russian Orthodox would not be offended.[287] We are expected to believe that the current condition of Russia under the Putin dictatorship represents its miraculous "conversion" and, even more improbably, that the current state of the world represents the Triumph of the Immaculate Heart that Our Lady promised if the Consecration of Russia were carried out in accordance with Her request. Recall here the keynotes of Sister Lucia's decades of testimony that the Consecration of Russia needs to make mention of Russia specifically—as if this were a debatable proposition! (See Chapter 3.)

Like Sodano and Bertone, Fr. Apostoli does not deny that Sister Lucia gave the testimony set forth above. Rather, hewing to the Party Line, *FFT* argues that she changed her mind for some unknown reason. The book cites the usual "evidence" for this sudden about-face: computer-generated letters from "Lucia" that first began to appear in 1989. (*FFT*, p. 197) We are asked to believe that a cloistered nun switched to a word processor at the age of 82—but only when writing about the Consecration of Russia, while continuing to handwrite her other correspondence. These computerized "letters from Lucia" have long since been debunked as patent fakes.

FFT cites one such purported letter, from March of 1989, wherein "Sister Lucia" inadvertently makes the fatal concession that the 1984 consecration ceremony, which failed to mention Russia, involved only "those bishops who wished to associate themselves with His Holiness." (p. 197) Thus *FFT* presents us with a collegial Consecration of Russia—called for by the very Mother of God—in which the bishops could participate if they felt inclined to "associate" themselves with the Roman Pontiff. Or perhaps they had more pressing business to attend to that day than obtaining world peace, the Triumph of the Immaculate Heart and the salvation of many souls. Ridiculous.

---

[286] Cf. *The Secret Still Hidden*, Ch. 11.

[287] Recall that Cardinal Tomko revealed to *Inside the Vatican* that "Rome [i.e. certain of the Pope's advisors] fears the Russian Orthodox might regard it as an 'offense' if Rome were to make specific mention of Russia in such a prayer, as if Russia especially is in need of help when the whole world, including the post-Christian West, faces profound problems ...".

The purported letter concludes with this manifestly dubious affirmation by "Lucia": "Afterward people asked me if it [the Consecration] was made, and I replied: 'Yes.' From that time, it is made." Really? But why would "Lucia" suddenly declare in 1989 that "it was made" when she had said over and over again before 1989 that it was *not* made—in either 1984 or 1982—because of the failure to mention Russia or to obtain the participation of the world's Catholic bishops? No explanation is given. Like Sodano and Bertone, Fr. Apostoli simply asserts that Sister Lucia reversed herself—and doesn't ask why.

In yet another inadvertent admission, Fr. Apostoli surmises: "John Paul II chose to follow Pius XII's formula for consecrating Russia *not by name*, but by a *veiled reference.*" (p. 195) Evidently, he is referring to Pius XII's consecrations of the world on October 31 and December 8 of 1942, following which Sister Lucia revealed that while these acts had not fulfilled Our Lady's request, nevertheless Our Lord had promised her during Lent of 1943 that "the present distress [World War II] would be shortened," which indeed it was. As Winston Churchill observed regarding the history of the war, in early 1943—that is, almost immediately after the consecration of the world in December 1942—"the hinges of fate turned in favor of the Allies," who won every major battle thereafter. As already noted in Chapter 3, however, in July of 1946 Lucia told Professor William Thomas Walsh that: "What Our Lady wants is that the Pope and all the bishops of the world shall consecrate *Russia* to Her Immaculate Heart on one special day."

Lucia's insistence on a public consecration of Russia *by name* in a ceremony involving the Pope and the world's bishops, acting jointly, was in keeping with what Our Lord Himself had revealed to her in 1936. In response to her question why He would not convert Russia without an explicit consecration of that nation to the Immaculate Heart, Our Lord replied: "Because I want My whole Church to acknowledge that consecration as a triumph of the Immaculate Heart of Mary so that it may extend its cult later on and put the devotion of the Immaculate Heart beside the devotion to My Sacred Heart."

It seems Fr. Apostoli has failed to consider the implications of his own argument that a "veiled reference" to Russia by John Paul II sufficed: Given that Pius XII's "veiled reference" manifestly failed to produce the promised conversion of Russia, the end of the persecution of Catholics and world peace, what sense did it make for John Paul to *repeat the same inadequate formula* some 42 years later?

In this connection Fr. Apostoli has overlooked a major historical fact: On July 7, 1952 Pius XII, acting in response to petitions from the still-persecuted Catholics of Russia that he "consecrate the entire people of Russia, in the anxieties of the present moment, to the Immaculate Heart," pronounced such a consecration in his apostolic letter *Sacro Vergente Anno*: "just as, a few years ago, we consecrated the whole world to the Immaculate Heart of the Virgin Mother of God, so today, in a very special way, we consecrate all the peoples of Russia to the same Immaculate Heart..."[288] There was also a private consecration ceremony in the Vatican in which only Pope Pius participated.

Yet not even this explicit mention of Russia by Pius XII produced the miracle promised by Our Lady because the participation of the bishops in a great public act of the whole Church was lacking. Unfortunately, it seems Pius XII was not made aware of what Lucia had insisted upon repeatedly and would continue to insist upon for decades following 1952: that what Our Lady had prescribed was that "the Pope and all the bishops of the world shall consecrate Russia to Her Immaculate Heart on one special day."

In an appendix on this subject, *FFT* argues in favor of a "Consecration of Russia" that avoids mentioning Russia by contending that after the 1942 "veiled reference" ceremony by Pius XII, Lucia "never raised an objection..." (p. 251) Nonsense. We have already noted Lucia's repeated testimony to numerous witnesses that the only consecration of Russia that would suffice is one that specifically identifies Russia as its object. Moreover, as just shown, Our Lord Himself warned Lucia that what Our Lady promised at Fatima would not be obtained without a public and explicit consecration of that nation, not a "veiled reference." And history bears this out: Russia has not converted and the world does not have peace.

Fr. Apostoli concludes his argument for the consecration-that-wasn't by quoting a purported statement by Lucia to Cardinal Bertone concerning whether Russia was properly consecrated in 1984: "I've already said [when? where?] that the consecration Our Lady wished for was performed in 1984, and that it was accepted by Heaven." (p. 198) But the words attributed to Lucia are part of Bertone's two-hour "interview" of the seer on November 17, 2001, as to which we have no transcript or audio or video recording, but only a communiqué from Bertone providing a scant 463 words from the seer out of two hours of alleged conversation with her, including exactly *nine* words concerning the very matter about which she was

---

[288] *Sacro Vergente Anno* (1952), n. 9 (".... come pochi anni fa abbiamo consacrato tutto il mondo al Cuore immacolato della vergine Madre di Dio, così ora, in modo specialissimo, consacriamo tutti i popoli della Russia al medesimo Cuore immacolato...").

supposedly interrogated at length: the Third Secret of Fatima.[289]
I agree with Socci's assessment of this so-called interview: "The
few words attributed to her... are such as not to have objective
credibility."[290]

Bear in mind that the source of Lucia's purported statement is
the same Cardinal Bertone who claimed for seven years that she
"confessed" to him that Our Lady had never linked disclosure of the
Secret to the year 1960, only to reveal on camera in 2007 the two
sealed envelopes on which Sister Lucia had written down precisely
the "express order of Our Lady" that the envelopes were not to be
opened before 1960. This is the same Cardinal Bertone who claims
to have had a total of some sixteen hours of conversations with Lucia
of which not a single word was recorded in any objectively verifiable
manner. This is the same Bertone whose "quotations" of Lucia on key
issues change every time he repeats them.[291] And this is the same
Bertone whose account is so full of holes that there are literally 101
reasons to doubt its veracity.[292]

But let us suppose for argument's sake that Lucia was finally
induced to repudiate her own prior testimony on the necessity of
Russia's explicit consecration to the Immaculate Heart by the Pope
and the bishops acting together. When a steady and reliable witness
suddenly reverses her lifelong testimony without explanation, a
reasonable observer can only conclude that the witness has been
tampered with. Only this would explain why defenders of the Party
Line have never offered any explanation for Lucia's abrupt about-face
on a matter so fundamental to the Message of Fatima. There is no
need to decide the question, however, for no matter what Sister Lucia
is alleged to have said toward the end of her life, the fact remains
that Russia could not have been consecrated in ceremonies that
deliberately avoided any mention of Russia for the specious reasons
offered by the proponents of the "substitute" or "compromise"
ceremonies. The "consecration of Russia" without mention of Russia
is just more utter nonsense in defense of the Party Line.

Now, if our own experience confirms beyond doubt that
we cannot obtain the promises of Our Lady of Fatima without a
Consecration of Russia that fulfills two conditions—explicit mention
of Russia *and* the participation the world's bishops—why persist in
doing the wrong thing in 1982 and 1984? We have heard it attributed

---

[289] For a complete exposition of the details that render the "interview" completely
incredible, see *The Secret Still Hidden*, Chapter 5.

[290] Socci, *The Fourth Secret of Fatima*, p. 179.

[291] Cf. *The Secret Still Hidden*, pp. 130 and 144-152.

[292] Cf. Ferrara, *The Secret Still Hidden*, Appendix II; accessible online at http://www.
secretstillhidden.com/pdf/appendix2.pdf.

to various famous personages, from Ben Franklin to Albert Einstein, that the definition of insanity is doing the same thing over and over again and expecting different results. It is not going too far to say that these repeated attempts to "consecrate Russia" without mentioning Russia are an insane approach to the simple task Our Lady of Fatima has set before the leadership of the Church.

But what is to account for this insane approach? We know the answer: John Paul II's advisors talked him out of a true and proper Consecration of Russia because, in their manifestly fallible judgment, it would offend the Russian Orthodox (see Chapter 3). Tellingly, *FFT* cites the following purported statement by Lucia to Father Kondor (vice-postulator for the causes of canonization for Francisco and Jacinta), shortly before the 1984 consecration ceremony: "The reply she gave me was that now the Holy Father will do all that is in his power." (p. 196) Regarding Father Kondor's claim, *FFT* asserts—without providing the least evidence—that "The Pope was happy with this reply [to Father Kondor]. After all, if the Pope did all he could and it was not enough, then the consecration could not be made by him or any other Pope."

The Pope did "all that is in his power"? Was the mention of Russia by name beyond the power of the Supreme Pontiff? The Pope need only have opened his mouth to utter a single word. And yet he did not do so. He did not do so because his advisors—no doubt including the Secretary of State—were of the opinion that "the Russian Orthodox might regard it as an 'offense' if Rome were to make specific mention of Russia in such a prayer, as if Russia especially is in need of help when the whole world, including the post-Christian West, faces profound problems..." After all, what did the Mother of God know about diplomacy and ecumenical relations when She appeared at Fatima to ask for Russia's consecration? She had not even bothered to consult the Secretary of State in such a delicate matter! As for the participation of the world's bishops, how could a mere Pope be expected to command the bishops to do anything in the age of "collegiality" inaugurated by Vatican II?

A Most Revealing Statement

In the aforementioned appendix *FFT* quotes Bishop Paul Josef Cordes to devastating effect—devastating, that is, to the Party Line:

> I recall that [Pope John Paul II] thought, some time before [the Consecration], of mentioning Russia in the prayer of benediction. *But at the suggestion of his collaborators he abandoned the idea.* He could not risk such a direct provocation of the Soviet leader. The Pope also decided not to mention

Russia directly *out of sensitivity to the Orthodox bishops* he had invited to join in the consecration prayer. So for good reasons, he followed the discreet approach of Pope Pius XII and of the bishops at the Second Vatican Council, where he himself was very prominent. (p. 251)

One could write a short book on the implications of this statement alone. Here a few salient remarks will have to suffice. First of all, the foremost of John Paul's "collaborators" concerning the Consecration of Russia was no less than the Virgin Mary, Mother of God. It was Her advice that should have been followed, not the advice of assorted ecclesiastical bureaucrats presiding over a Church in crisis in a world in crisis. To do exactly what Our Lady had requested was all the more incumbent on John Paul given that, as he himself acknowledged, She had saved his life during the 1981 assassination attempt.

The idea that consecrating Russia by name would be "a direct provocation of the Soviet leader" represents worldly wisdom at its worst. Consider that the second part of the Great Secret, known to the world long before 1984 and published by the Vatican itself in 2000 as part of the commentary in *TMF*, plainly declares: "If My requests are heeded, Russia will be converted, and there will be peace; if not, *she will spread her errors throughout the world*, causing wars and persecutions of the Church..." If publication of this heavenly indictment of Russia's role in the worldwide spread of error, war and persecution of the Church was not a "direct provocation of the Soviet leader," why would the consecration of Russia to the Immaculate Heart "provoke" him? If anything, "the Russian leader" in 1984 (Konstantin Chernenko) would probably have found the ceremony amusing. The idea that, as *FFT* suggests, an explicit consecration of Russia would have caused "reprisals by the president of the Soviet Union" who would "send Russian tanks and troops into Poland" is ludicrous.

Furthermore, as already noted, in 1952 Pope Pius XII explicitly consecrated Russia by name in an apostolic letter published to the world, albeit without the necessary participation of the bishops in a public ceremony. Yet this mention of Russia did not "provoke the Soviet leader" at the time, the diabolical maniac Josef Stalin (who died in 1953). This fact alone dispels the fantasy of Soviet retaliation for any mention of Russia in the Consecration of Russia.

Putting aside the lack of any evidence for this preposterous theory, are we to believe that the Queen of Heaven would prescribe a ceremony that would provoke war with Russia instead of preventing it? Consider what *FFT* is arguing here: that what the Mother of God, *Virgo Prudentissima*, requested at Fatima was dangerous to the world unless amended by Vatican diplomats! But since the very effect of the Consecration was to be Russia's conversion, how could it possibly have been the cause of war with Russia? Would the Mother of God and Her divine Son be powerless to restrain "the Soviet leader" if he were "provoked" by Russia's explicit consecration? Evidently there is no limit to the size of the whoppers the faithful are expected to swallow for the sake of the Party Line.

As for Bishop Cordes's claim that John Paul decided not to mention Russia "out of sensitivity to the Orthodox bishops" he had invited to participate in the 1984 ceremony—the first time we have heard of this invitation—this was not some social event at which one wishes to avoid offending the guests. This was supposed to be a dramatic public appeal to Heaven for nothing less than the conversion of those same Orthodox bishops and their reunification with Rome, the conversion of Russia as a whole, peace in the world, and the Triumph of the Immaculate Heart. It was to be, in sum, a miraculous manifestation of the immense spiritual power that God Almighty has deigned to place at the disposal of the Vicar of Christ. But, as *FFT* would have it, the paramount concern on this utterly momentous occasion was "sensitivity" to the feelings of some Orthodox bishops. Their feelings would be hurt! This argument would be a joke were its consequences not so serious for the Church and the world.

By the way, just what did the Orthodox bishops allegedly invited to participate in the 1984 ceremony think they were doing? If, as the defenders of the Party Line maintain, a "veiled reference" to Russia was quite sufficient to indicate Russia, why were the Orthodox bishops not offended by the "veiled reference"? Moreover, if they knew that the Pope "really" intended to consecrate Russia while avoiding any explicit reference to Russia, why would they have agreed to participate (if they did participate) in this disguised "offense" to their spiritual leadership?

Further, if "everyone knew" that Russia was being consecrated, why not simply say so openly? What sort of silly game was this? Or were the invited Orthodox bishops positively assured that Russia was *not* the object of the 1984 ceremony, only to learn afterwards that, according to the Party Line, Russia was the "veiled" object all along? But that would mean the Orthodox bishops were the victims of a cynical bait-and-switch—hardly the kind of trickery the sinless and Immaculate Mother of God would countenance.

At any rate, what evidence is there in the first place that the Orthodox would be "offended" if their nation were singled out for Mary's special favor and intervention? Exactly none. Indeed, common sense indicates the contrary conclusion. As the Catholic scholar Cathy Pearson observed in her seminal article on the

Consecration in *Inside the Vatican*:

> A consecration of a country, after all, is not an anathema or an exorcism. It is an invocation of a special blessing and protection. That Mary should single out a particular nation for such a request is a sign of Her special maternal affection.... One might expect that any nation that honors the Blessed Mother would consider it an enviable privilege to be uniquely selected for such a dignity by Holy Mary Herself... The Russian Orthodox do honor Mary, and while they may not accept the Fatima miracle and message as such, unlike some branches of Christianity they do believe that She can and does intervene personally in human history...[293]

On this point Fr. Apostoli demolishes his own position by reporting the putative remark of some unnamed Orthodox priests to an unnamed Catholic priest following the 1984 ceremony: "It was Our Lady of Fatima who saved our country." (*FFT*, p. 259) So much for the fable that the Orthodox would be gravely offended by a true and proper consecration of their nation to Mary's Immaculate Heart. Once this is really done, Russia will indeed be saved, the whole world will receive the divine benefits of that miracle, and the Orthodox, reunited with Rome, will be among the first to acknowledge it with gratitude.

Finally, we have Bishop Cordes's reference to "the discreet approach of... the bishops at the Second Vatican Council." This is perhaps the most damning admission in the bishop's revealing statement. For here he is clearly referring to the Vatican-Moscow Agreement, rightly described as an act of "religious treason" by Jean Madiran. As we saw in Chapter 2, under this shameful accord, negotiated between the Orthodox Metropolitan Nikodim and Cardinal Tisserant in Metz, France just before the Council, the Council would observe a "discreet" silence concerning the scourge of Soviet Communism to avoid offense to the Russian Orthodox observers in attendance at the Council, who were themselves tools of the Kremlin. As Paul Joseph Schmitt, the Bishop of Metz, later revealed: "It was in our region that the 'secret' meeting of Cardinal Tisserant with Archbishop Nikodim occurred. The exact place was the residence of Fr. Lagarde, chaplain for the Little Sisters of the Poor in Borny.... After this meeting, the conditions for the presence of the Russian church's observers were established by Cardinal Willebrands, an assistant of Cardinal Bea."[294]

---

[293] Cathy Pearson, "Now is the Time: Consecrating Russia Will Help, Not Hurt, Catholic-Orthodox Dialogue," *Inside the Vatican*, August-September 2008, p. 32.

[294] "Mystery of the Rome-Moscow Pact," *30 Dias*, October 1989, pp. 55-56, quoting a February 9, 1963 interview with the journal *Republicain Lorrain. See also* "The

In a letter on the subject, Msgr. Georges Roche, the biographer of Cardinal Tisserant, confirmed: "That accord was negotiated between the Kremlin and the Vatican at the highest level.... Cardinal Tisserant received formal orders to negotiate the accord and to make sure that it would be observed during the Council."[295] And so it was. All entreaties from Council Fathers to condemn Communism were kept from the Council hall, including an intervention by the Coetus Internationalis Patrum group involving 450 bishops. As noted in *The Devil's Final Battle*, this major written intervention "was mysteriously 'lost' after being delivered to the Secretariat of the Council, and Council Fathers who stood up to denounce Communism were politely told to sit down and be quiet."[296]

Thus the Council that declared it was reading "the signs of the times" would "discreetly" avoid offending Russia by failing even to mention, much less condemn, the most alarming sign of the times on display before its very eyes: the genocide and brutal persecution of Catholics in the very nation whose conversion Our Lady had appeared at Fatima to obtain. Madiran's phrase "religious treason" is not too strong a description of this craven act of ecclesiastical "diplomacy."

Can we not see how the Vatican-Moscow Agreement has been perpetuated to this very day by the Party Line of the Vatican Secretary of State, with its pathological determination to bury the Message of Fatima and prevent at all costs the "offensive" consecration of Russia? The parallel between the Council's "discreet" failure to mention Russian totalitarianism and the "discreet" refusal to mention Russia in any consecration ceremony is too striking to be a mere coincidence. The two things represent the same policy in action, the *Ostpolitik* ("politics of the East") we discussed in Chapter 2.

In fact, Cardinal Joseph Zen Ze-kiun has condemned the campaign by Vatican bureaucrats, led by Cardinal Bertone, to encourage the persecuted Catholics of the "underground" Church in China to abandon their opposition to the Red Chinese regime and join its pseudo-church, the Catholic Patriotic Association, which has consecrated more than a hundred captive bishops in defiance of Rome. In a letter to Chinese Catholics "Cardinal Bertone argues for careful efforts to cooperate with the 'official' Church," while

---

Vatican Silenced by Moscow" (pp. 4ff), "The Catholic Church Betrayed" (pp. 7ff), and "Why the Vatican-Moscow Agreement Must be Repudiated" (pp. 11ff) in *The Fatima Crusader*, Issue 17, Feb.-April 1985, http://www.fatimacrusader.com/cr17/toc17.asp).

[295] Ibid., p. 57.

[296] Cf. *The Devil's Final Battle*, Ch. 6, "The Motive Takes Hold," citing Father Ralph Wiltgen, *The Rhine flows into the Tiber*, (New York: Hawthorne, 1967; TAN, 1985) pp. 272-278.

Cardinal Joseph Zen's letter, "released a week later... argues that faithful Catholicism in China still requires heroic resistance against the encroachments of the government—including the Patriotic Association."[297]

Quite recently Cardinal Zen declared publicly that Vatican bureaucrats in the Congregation for Evangelization (no doubt under Bertone's oversight as Secretary of State) are undermining the Pope's 2007 instruction concerning the Church in China by pursuing "the *old 'Ostpolitik'*... This policy of *Ostpolitik*—which is compromise at any cost, to please the government always, to always avoid confrontation—led to the present situation..."[298]

The Cardinal was referring to November of 2010, when "the Chinese government ordained a bishop without the approval of the Holy See, at a ceremony in which several bishops loyal to Rome were reportedly forced to participate. In December, police officers rounded up a large number of bishops and escorted them to a state-sponsored meeting of an unauthorized 'bishops conference.'" This, said the Cardinal, "is completely against the doctrine of the Church. It was like a slap in the face of the Holy Father.... But unfortunately, these people in the Congregation for Evangelization... still believe that they must carry on the policy of compromise." The Cardinal concluded with the scathing assessment that underground Catholic opposition to the Beijing regime "will be very difficult, because now the difficulty is not only to face a government, *but to face our own people, who are already more on the side of the government than on the side of the Church*. That's the very sad reality."[299]

Indeed it is, for the pernicious policy born in Metz with the Vatican-Moscow Agreement still operates, not only to neutralize the Church's opposition to Communist regimes, but also to turn Vatican prelates into *collaborators* with those regimes. And the regimes with which they collaborate have arisen precisely from the spread of Russia's errors throughout the world on account of the Vatican bureaucracy's unwillingness to "offend" Russia by consecrating it to the Immaculate Heart.

What Conversion?

Of course the consequence of failing to consecrate Russia is that Russia has not converted. Here, too, *FFT* parrots the Party Line: the fall of the Berlin Wall, *glasnost, perestroika*, and the dissolution of the Soviet Union are cited as evidence of the "conversion of Russia."

---

[297] "Vatican journalist sees key cardinals at odds on China policy," Catholicculture.org, December 4, 2009.

[298] "Cardinal Zen: Vatican officials have blocked Pope's plan for Chinese Church," EWTN News, April 12, 2011.

[299] Ibid.

(pp. 255-258) So, as Fr. Apostoli would have it, Our Lady appeared at Fatima and produced the Miracle of the Sun in order to prophesy a mere regime change in Moscow.

Never mind that this regime change has given way to authoritarian rule under Vladimir Putin—recently reelected as effectively "president for life" in an election stage-managed from the Kremlin, which controls the mass media. In the Russian Federation today national elections are a sham, governors of the Russian regions are appointed by Moscow without local elections, a free and independent press and mass media have all but ceased to exist, anti-government journalists have been murdered one after another, and key political opponents have all been arrested, jailed on trumped-up charges or targeted for assassination, as in the case of Alexander Litvinenko, former head of the KGB (renamed the FSB under Putin), who was fatally poisoned with Polonium-210 slipped into his tea, and Viktor Andriyovych Yushchenko, the Ukrainian opponent of the Putin regime who barely survived an attempt to poison him with Dioxin.

Never mind that, in sum, "political rights and civil liberties have become so restricted in Russia that the country has been downgraded to 'Not Free,'" as reported by the respected human rights organization Freedom House, which noted that "Russia was the only country to register a negative category change in 2004, moving from Partly Free to Not Free."[300]

Never mind that Russia continues to lead the world in the per capita rate of abortions, has become the international hub of the child pornography industry that exploits Moscow's 1 million street children,[301] and that its population, decimated by mass murder in the womb, alcoholism and premature death, is dwindling at the rate of 700,000 per year.

Never mind that Russia today is dominated by a corrupt plutocracy that has amassed billions upon billions in ill-gotten wealth in league with Putin while the great masses of common people suffer under Third World conditions.

Never mind that the Catholic Church clings to a minuscule and precarious existence in Russia under a 1997 law on "freedom of conscience" that has been used to expel numerous key Catholic

---

[300] "Russia Downgraded to 'Not Free,'" Freedom House press release, http://www.freedomhouse.org/template.cfm?page=70&release=242.

[301] Cf. Irina Sandul, "Russia's Trade in Child Pornography," *Inside Russia Journal*, No. 146, February 2002 ("Some 20-30 percent of Moscow's street children are involved in prostitution or child pornography, according to a study conducted in 2001 by the International Program on the Elimination of Child Labor [IPEC] under the aegis of the WTO. Russia's Deputy Minister of Labor Galina Karelova said in an interview that the number of children on the street in Moscow is at least 1 million.")

clerics from the country and that requires the foreign-born priests (in Russia) who make up almost the entire priesthood in that nation to depart every 90 days in order to renew their visas, so that it has become impossible for the Church to develop a true and proper parish and diocesan system on Russian soil.

Never mind that today—irony of ironies—there are fewer Catholics, Catholic priests and Catholic parishes in Russia than at the time of the October Revolution in 1917.

Never mind that there has been no dimunition in Russia's preparations for war since the non-consecration of 1984. Quite the contrary, the situation in that regard has only grown more perilous. On May 3, 2012, for example, Russia's top military officer, Chief of General Staff Nikolai Makarov, warned that "Moscow would strike NATO missile-defense sites in Eastern Europe before they are ready for action, if the U.S. pushes ahead with deployment." Makarov declared publicly that "A decision to use destructive force pre-emptively *will be taken* if the situation worsens." As one commentator rightly observed: "That Makarov would make this kind of threat in a public forum is chilling."[302]

What sort of "conversion of Russia" is this? It is no conversion at all, obviously. Undeterred by reality, however, *FFT* assures us that Russia is undergoing a "conversion process" involving "gradual changes." (p. 254) So, according to Fr. Apostoli, Our Lady of Fatima promised the world a miracle that would proceed at the pace of a glacier, moving so slowly that no one can detect it. Today, some 28 years after the-consecration-that-wasn't, there is not the least sign of any true religious conversion in "that poor nation," as Sister Lucia called it. On the contrary, Putin's Russia is sinking ever deeper into spiritual, moral, political and economic corruption, while allying itself militarily with Red China, producing a new and unprecedented threat to world peace.

Unable to deal convincingly with the evidence that makes a mockery of his glacial "conversion process," Fr. Apostoli finally plays the trump card of all defenders of the Party Line: John Paul II was (so they claim) convinced that he had consecrated Russia—while deliberately avoiding any mention of Russia—so let that be the end of it. Fr. Apostoli writes: "Now if the Pope believed in his heart that he had made the consecration properly, what are these people who still deny the consecration thinking?" (p. 260)

In other words, we should ignore the evidence of our senses and mindlessly maintain that Russia has been consecrated simply because the late Pope is *alleged* to have been convinced of it. Yet the

---

302 Shaun Waterman, "Russia Threatens to Strike NATO missile defense sites," *Washington Times*, May 3, 2012.

fact is that John Paul never made any official papal declaration that the Consecration had been effected. Quite contrary, as many sources have noted, during and after the 1984 ceremony the Pope stated before thousands of witnesses that Our Lady was *still awaiting* the explicit consecration of Russia to the Immaculate Heart, referring pointedly to "those peoples for whom You Yourself *await* our act of consecration and of entrustment." Hours after the ceremony, speaking to a vast crowd in Saint Peter's Basilica, the Pope clearly alluded to the inadequacy of what he had done earlier that day: "We have been able to do all this according to *our poor human possibilities* and the measure of human *weakness*, but with immense confidence in Your maternal love and immense confidence in Your maternal solicitude."[303]

Telling words indeed. They recall Fr. Apostoli's own phrase: "the Pope did all he could." That is, he did all he could *within the illicit restrictions imposed upon him* by his worldly-wise human advisors— restrictions Fr. Apostoli himself readily confirms as if they were helpful to his position, when in fact they are the very proof that the Consecration of Russia has been thwarted deliberately by the contrary plans of mere men.

In the end, there is no rational basis for the perverse refusal to mention Russia in the Consecration of Russia the very Mother of God requested. Not even those who so obstinately defend the Party Line can seriously propose that the Church and the world would suffer harm if the Pope were to utter the word "Russia" during the act of consecration. At the very least, there is nothing to lose. What, then, is to account for the bizarre decades-long campaign to prevent at all costs the utterance of that single word? Only one logical explanation presents itself: Those who have prevented Russia's consecration by name *know or at least suspect that it would actually bring about Russia's conversion*, and this they do not wish to see.

Let us be clear about what is suggested here: the longstanding refusal to consecrate Russia by name is ultimately diabolical in origin. This is not—repeat: *not*—to say that those involved in the refusal are conscious agents of the devil. The point, rather, is that whatever their subjective intentions may be, they are lending themselves to what is objectively an evil end. The sheer irrationality of those who contrive specious arguments in defense of a "Consecration of Russia" that refuses to mention Russia is evidence of "diabolical disorientation" in the matter, to borrow Sister Lucia's famous phrase concerning the crisis in the Church. For nonsense is always a sign of the Father of Lies at work in the minds of men, even those who might be convinced they are defending truth and justice.

---

[303] *Avvenire*, March 27, 1984; cf. *The Devil's Final Battle*, Chapter 8.

A Fatima for Yesterday

What has Fr. Apsotoli given us with *Fatima for Today*? He has given us, in short, what the Vatican Secretary of State would give us: a Fatima for yesterday. A Fatima that is over and done with. A Fatima that will not alter the disastrous ecclesial status quo over which the Vatican bureaucracy, controlled by the Secretary of State, has presided since Vatican II. A status quo Pope Benedict described with a single scathing word only days before he became the Vicar of Christ: "filth." That filth was covered up in large part by none other than Cardinal Angelo Sodano, who protected the sexual predator Father Maciel. Yet it is Sodano's preposterous "interpretation" of the Third Secret that is now urged upon the faithful by Fr. Apostoli, a false friend of Fatima.

In sum, Fr. Apostoli presents "an urgent Marian message of hope" that holds no urgency nor any hope for a restoration of the Church, peace in the world or the Triumph of the Immaculate Heart in our time because, as he and the Secretary of State would have it, the Consecration of Russia was accomplished 28 years ago, and what we see is what we get. "One deceives himself who thinks that the prophetic mission of Fatima is concluded." So said Pope Benedict XVI a few months before *FFT* made its appearance. How telling it is that Fr. Apostoli's pious tribute to the Fatima event fails to mention the Pope's momentous declaration. But then Father Apostoli, and those who think like him, do not wish us to link the Fatima message to what the Pope called "*future realities of the Church* which are little by little developing and revealing themselves... *in a really terrifying way...*" The mission of the false friends of Fatima is the opposite of Marc Antony's: to bury what they come to praise.[304]

---

[304] For a complete refutation of the Fatima revisionist contentions in Fr. Apostoli's *Fatima for Today*, see Christopher A. Ferrara, "*Fatima For Today*: A Response," at http://www.fatima.org/news/newsviews/fatima-for-today-a-response.pdf; or see his article at http://www.fatimacrusader.com/cr99/cr99pg43.pdf for a less complete version.

Chapter 14

THE WORLD APOSTOLATE OF FATIMA: MERCHANTS OF "FATIMA LITE"

In 2006 the Blue Army, now renamed "World Apostolate of Fatima" (WAF) in keeping with the general "demilitarization" of the Church Militant since Vatican II, was granted the status of an "international association of the faithful" by the Pontifical Council for the Laity. The former Blue Army claimed that this constituted explicit "papal approval" of its activities, although the council is not an organ of the papal magisterium but merely a Vatican department whose decrees are issued by its President and Secretary, not the Vicar of Christ.

Worse, WAF immediately began boasting that it is "the only Fatima organization that speaks with ecclesiastical authority on the message of Fatima."[305] The claim borders on false advertising. WAF has not been endowed with any more "ecclesiastical authority" to speak for the Church regarding Fatima than is possessed by any knowledgeable member of the laity. WAF, whose U.S. branch is headquartered in Asbury Park, New Jersey, has no teaching authority in the Church, and as a mere "association of the faithful" it can bind no one to its opinions on Fatima, which are manifestly dubious to say the least, as we shall see. The Pontifical Council's decree merely accorded a formal recognition of WAF's existence *not required* for the existence of an association of the faithful in the first place. With or without an official stamp of approval, Church law specifically recognizes the God-given right of Catholics to associate for the advancement of their own faith: "by means of a private agreement made among themselves, the Christian faithful are *free to establish* associations to pursue the purposes mentioned in can. 298, §1," including those in which "clerics and lay persons together, strive in a common endeavor to foster a more perfect life, to promote public worship or Christian doctrine, or to exercise other works of the apostolate, such as initiatives of evangelization, works of piety or charity, and those which animate the temporal order with a Christian spirit."[306]

With good reason had Father Gruner's Fatima apostolate never sought the formality of Vatican approval as an association of the faithful or any other form of "ecclesiastical approval," for it comes at the price of fatal compromise: adherence to the Party Line on Fatima dictated by the Secretary of State. The Pontifical Council's decree "erecting" WAF as an association of the faithful was clearly a

---

[305] http://www.wafusa.org/press.html.
[306] 1983 Code of Canon Law, 298, § 1 and 299, § 1.

reward for its willingness to proclaim that the Consecration has been done, the Third Secret has been revealed, and all that remains of the Fatima message is prayer and penance on the part of the faithful. In short, WAF is willing to purvey "Fatima Lite" instead of the real thing, with its politically incorrect, all-too-Catholic elements.

Driving Home the Party Line

The WAF is a case study of how, at the level of the lay apostolate, the moving parts of "Operation False Friends" all work together to keep alive the Party Line the Pope himself had discredited during his journey to Fatima. Father Apostoli, the EWTN celebrity whose Party Line-friendly *Fatima for Today* we have just examined, serves as "spiritual advisor" to WAF, which EWTN in turn presents to the faithful as the "official" Fatima apostolate for the Church today.

In keeping with its function in the false friends operation, WAF's promotion of "Fatima Lite" among the faithful is as relentless as it is heavy-handed. A prime example is an hour-long video on the WAF website entitled simply "The Message of Fatima," which EWTN broadcast on August 22, 2010 as an episode of its "Sunday Night Live" series.[307] The show was hosted by Fr. Apostoli, whose guest was Michael La Corte, Executive Director of the United States branch of WAF. Their on-camera chat revolved around the requisite Party Line theme: Fatima means prayer and penance, and nothing more. Repeat as often as necessary: Fatima means prayer and penance.

La Corte began with a discussion of Pope Benedict's pilgrimage to Fatima, but without mentioning any of the Pope's explosive statements regarding the contents of the Third Secret.[308] Like Apostoli's book, the show steered clear of the subject entirely, including even the vision published in 2000. La Corte did allude to (but without quoting) the Pope's declaration that "one would deceive himself who thinks that the prophetic mission of Fatima is concluded," on which La Corte commented: "don't believe it's fulfilled...it's still so important today. There's still much that needs to be done, that we need to do..."[309] Yes, so much! But, lest viewers get the wrong impression, Apostoli immediately interjected: "that doesn't mean that the Holy Father—he has done the Consecration, that part has been fulfilled." La Corte, taking his cue, responded: "Yes, yes."[310]

---

[307] *See* "The Message of Fatima," http://www.youtube.com/watch?feature=player_embedded&v= S2X_9JGFR00

[308] http://www.youtube.com/watch?feature=player_embedded&v=S2X_9JGFR00#t=495s.

[309] http://www.youtube.com/watch?feature=player_embedded&v=S2X_9JGFR00#t=554s.

[310] http://www.youtube.com/watch?feature=player_embedded&v=S2X_9JGFR00#t=546s.

And then Apostoli sounded the mandatory theme: "we have to follow through with prayer, sacrifice, offering of even our sufferings—a good Christian life..."[311] So, obeying the Message of Fatima is now simply and only a matter of praying, doing penance, and being a good Christian. He went on to say that "There's so many ways to put the message of Fatima," only to insist a moment later that there are really only two ways permitted: prayer and penance. Citing the former rector of the Fatima Shrine, Monsignor Guerra, author of the scandal of Hindus in the *Capelinha* which we noted in Chapter 6, Apostoli drove home the prayer-and-penance theme once again: "The Message of Fatima can be put in two words: prayer and sacrifice."[312] In a manner typical of the false friends of Fatima, Apostoli piously adverted to John Paul II's declaration at Fatima (in 1982) to the effect that "Fatima is more important now than it was in 1917."[313] Yes, so much more important! But in what respect? Is it the Consecration of Russia to bring about Russia's conversion to the Faith and return to union with Rome? Is it revelation of the entire Third Secret and its precious warnings for the safety of the Church and the world? Hardly. What was more important than ever was—what else?—prayer and penance: "the importance of Mary's message," said Apostoli to La Corte, is "seen, as you summed it up so well there, with the words: prayer and sacrifice."[314]

True to the *quid pro quo* for its Vatican department stamp of approval, WAF reminds the faithful—again and again and again— that the Consecration of Russia and revelation of the Third Secret as requested by the Virgin must no longer concern us, but only Her requests for *prayer and penance*. Our Lady of Fatima, said Apostoli,

> kept asking for *prayers and for sacrifice* for the conversion of sinners. That's *the key*, I think. She said, if people heed My message... many souls will be converted and an era of peace will be given to the world.... We have to do our part. The Pope has done his part. So if we keep focusing on the Pope and worrying about what he is doing and not doing, we're mistaken. We need to be able to look at our part: are we living those good Christian lives. Are we, you know, offending God....[315]

---

[311] http://www.youtube.com/watch?feature=player_embedded&v=S2X_9JGFR00#t=578s.

[312] http://www.youtube.com/watch?feature=player_embedded&v=S2X_9JGFR00#t=596s.

[313] http://www.youtube.com/watch?feature=player_detailpage&v=S2X_9JGFR00#t=867s.

[314] http://www.youtube.com/watch?feature=player_embedded&v=S2X_9JGFR00#t=991s.

[315] http://www.youtube.com/watch?feature=player_detailpage&v=S2X_9JGFR00#t=2816s.

Translation: Stop pestering the Pope for a consecration of Russia that actually consecrates Russia. Stop seeking full disclosure of the Secret that *not even EWTN's own Mother Angelica* believes has been fully disclosed. Instead, trust Cardinal Sodano and Cardinal Bertone, whose bureaucratic apparatus has approved the World Apostolate of Fatima. Rather than being concerned about those terrible "future realities of the Church" the Pope himself had linked to the Secret only weeks before Apostoli and La Corte appeared on EWTN, the faithful should simply say their prayers, make some sacrifices, live good lives, and hope for the best. This is "Fatima Lite" in its essence, and "Fatima Lite" is what WAF had been given Vatican approval to promote. WAF can be seen as a kind of Authorized Dealer in the Fatima Lite franchise system. Should WAF begin to question the Party Line, however, there is little doubt its franchise would be revoked.

Now, of course, Our Lady of Fatima did call for prayer and sacrifices for sinners. Prayer and penance are necessary and indeed indispensable in the economy of salvation, with or without the Message of Fatima. But the party of the innovators is very clever, and one of its cleverest tactics is to harp on one truth in order to hide another—the classic ploy of the Modernist. By harping on prayer and penance, WAF hides the truth that Our Lady also called for the Consecration of Russia *by name* so that its conversion to the Faith would be seen clearly as a miracle resulting from the maternal intercession of the Mother of God, and thus the means to "establish in the world devotion to My Immaculate Heart" and the triumph of the Immaculate Heart.

That is, the Virgin proclaimed a specifically and gloriously *Catholic* outcome for the Fatima event, which the world has obviously not seen since the "consecration" of 1984. And Our Lady also directed Lucia in 1944 to have the contents of the Third Secret disclosed in 1960 so that the Church and the world could benefit from the warnings embraced within *Her words* following Her momentous declaration that "In Portugal the dogma of the Faith will always be preserved etc." We have never seen these words of the Blessed Virgin—a fact WAF is on a mission to obliterate from the memory of the faithful, just as required by Cardinal Bertone and his collaborators.

The New "Inter-Religious" Fatima Event

"Fatima Lite" does not involve only the reduction of the Fatima message to prayer and penance, however. The very notion of prayer is subjected to a radical reductionism that strips it of a Catholic orientation. In WAF's "Fatima Lite" propaganda, Our Lady of Fatima becomes Our Lady of Inter-religious Harmony, much as Monsignor

Guerra's tenure as rector of the Fatima Shrine produced the sacrilege of Hindus in the *Capelinha*.

Waxing to the theme of Fatima as an inter-religious rather than a "merely" Catholic prophecy, La Corte spoke of his trip to the Russian city of Kazan and his conversation with a Russian named Dimitri. WAF, said La Corte, is working for "one world praying for life and peace... I said to Dimitri we would love it if we could film the Muslims praying, along with the Orthodox, and the Catholics, and everybody else in Kazan—all the religions—praying with us for life and peace and then air it on EWTN...."[316] Yes, *all* the religions! And the more religions the better! As required by the post-Vatican II "updating" of the Church by the party of the innovators, Fatima Lite dispenses with the idea that non-Catholics have any positive duty or real need to belong to the Catholic Church. "Inter-religious dialogue" and "ecumenism" require a revision of the Fatima event to suit these innovations, and WAF is eager to oblige.

Recounting a celebration of the return of the Icon of Kazan to that city during the pontificate of John Paul II, La Corte was pleased to note that "Half the people that attended that celebration were Orthodox and the other half were Muslim...." and that he spent part of his time in Kazan "going to these beautiful mosques...."[317] So, it appears the donations of the faithful to the "World Apostolate of Fatima" have financed La Corte's tour of the Russian mosques in Kazan. La Corte noted, however, that the city was building a new Catholic church (which only replaces the one the Soviet authorities stole after the Russian Revolution and which the city has refused to return since the "fall of Communism"). This new church, notes one news article, "is the latest addition to the city's mosaic of mosques, Orthodox cathedrals and synagogues. Home to Tatars and Russians, Kazan is known as a model of ethnic and religious tolerance." In this wonderful spirit of religious pluralism, a local sculptor in Kazan "is building what he calls a Temple of All Faiths. He sees it as a cultural centre of the future and a unique meeting point for people of all beliefs."[318]

The "mosaic" of religions in Kazan meets with WAF's hearty approval. As La Corte exclaimed to Apostoli during his appearance on EWTN: "It is amazing how Mary... goes above the differences. You know, the Catholics, the Orthodox, being Christians, and then the Muslims. She can bring us together. There's no fighting, no

---

[316] http://www.youtube.com/watch?feature=player_embedded&v=S2X_9JGFR00#t=1269s.

[317] http://www.youtube.com/watch?feature=player_embedded&v=S2X_9JGFR00#t=1372s.

[318] "Kazan Catholics Blessed with New Church," September 6, 2008, http://rt.com/news/prime-time/kazan-catholics-blessed-with-new-church/.

enmity. What struck me as we venerated that image [of Kazan] is the Moslem women that came and prayed before that image.... Mary's there. She's a bond. She's bringing together these people."[319] There is no need for any actual conversion to the Catholic religion, of course. It suffices that Mary unites everyone in good feelings in spite of their religious "differences," which the Mother of God is "above."

Accordingly, WAF is now promoting something it calls the "Worldwide Inter-Religious Prayer Campaign."[320] Catholics involved in this initiative "would be encouraged to pray the Rosary as requested by the Virgin Mary in Fatima," whereas "[e]veryone would be encouraged to pray the universal Fatima intentions *according to their faith* and to build up to at least 15 minutes of meditative prayer." And what are these "universal Fatima intentions"? They are something WAF has invented to convert the Message of Fatima, which could not be more explicitly Catholic, into a pan-religious phenomenon. Thus a statement on WAF's website asserts that the prayer the Angel of Peace taught the children at Fatima is "appropriate for people of all faiths..."[321] To recall the prayer: "My God, I believe, I adore, I hope and I love You. I beg pardon for those who do not believe, do not adore, do not hope and do not love You." WAF is promoting the idea that the nature of the God to which the prayer refers is a matter of indifference, so long as people pray to whatever deity they choose to worship "according to their faith."

In a WAF video in which both La Corte and Apostoli participate, La Corte announces the creation of international "prayer cells" that will pray for the "universal Fatima intentions," which exclude the specifically Catholic intentions of the conversion of Russia, the Triumph of the Immaculate Heart, and the establishment of devotion to the Immaculate Heart throughout the world. As La Corte explains:

> And anybody can do this, *no matter what your faith is.* Because we all align with these intentions. The intentions are: To pray to bring God back into our lives and back into our cultures. For peace. And for the salvation of souls. And the purpose is because we know that when we don't open the door to God in prayer, our lives become more self-centered and material-oriented, leaving little if any room for God. And our world suffers the consequences. We see the consequences of our failure to pray all around us today. And that's because the world is not asking for God's help and the graces are not flowing. So I ask all of you to consider joining this program. The concept is to get as many people as we can throughout the

---

[319] http://www.youtube.com/watch?feature=player_embedded&v=S2X_9JGFR00#t=1486s.

[320] http://www.wafusa.org/prayer_announcement.html.

[321] http://www.wafusa.org/the_message.html.

world to pray these intentions so that God's graces can flow, so that they will have the insight necessary to make decisions that are God-based decisions rather than self-based decisions. [322]

While La Corte is speaking, we see an image of what appears to be Shintoists praying in their temple. Taking up the inter-religious theme, Father Apostoli is next seen at the podium, declaring: "Many of the saints said that prayer is like the key that unlocks the heart of God."[323] At this point in the video we see an image of Muslim children "unlocking" God's heart with their prayers to Allah. "If you want to get to the heart of God, pray, because God will listen to you," Apostoli continues. As he speaks we see the image of a vast crowd of Muslim men prostrating themselves in the direction of Mecca; or perhaps they are actually at Mecca.[324] This is followed by an image of Buddhists at prayer.[325] Catholics in prayer are included in the inter-religious video montage.

Notice what is going on here: *the specifically Catholic Message of Fatima has been converted into "universal Fatima intentions" that no longer pertain to the Catholic Faith*. It is suggested that "God's graces can flow" in response to the prayers of any and all religions, and that people will make "God-based decisions" if—no matter what their religion—they pray for the "universal Fatima intentions" without the guidance of the Church or the grace of her sacraments. The conversion of Russia and the Triumph of the Immaculate Heart are replaced by "bring God back into our lives and into our cultures"— whatever that means. But which God? Apparently, it doesn't matter; any sort of deity will do, including the semi-divinized Buddha.

The peace of which Our Lady of Fatima speaks, "the peace of Christ, which is the only true peace,"[326] as Pius XI insisted in *Quas Primas,* is not-so-subtly replaced by a pan-religious "peace" attainable without the Social Kingship of Christ that *Quas Primas* defends as indispensable for true peace among men. As for the "salvation of souls," how is this to be obtained without the Catholic Church of which Mary is the Mother? There is not the least indication in WAF's "Worldwide Inter-Religious Prayer Campaign" that souls are in danger of eternal damnation without the helps that only the Church can provide, which is precisely why the Mother of God came

---

[322] http://www.youtube.com/watch?feature=player_embedded&v=W7RP5PU109A#t=38s.

[323] http://www.youtube.com/watch?feature=player_embedded&v=W7RP5PU109A#t=116s.

[324] http://www.youtube.com/watch?feature=player_embedded&v=W7RP5PU109A#t=125s.

[325] http://www.youtube.com/watch?feature=player_embedded&v=W7RP5PU109A#t=129s.

[326] Pius XI, *Ubi Arcano Dei* (1922), n. 37.

to Fatima. As She said to the terrified seers:

> "You have seen hell, where the souls of poor sinners go. *To save them*, God wishes to establish in the world devotion to My Immaculate Heart."

But WAF's version of the Message of Fatima dispenses with this embarrassing "pre-Vatican II" connection of salvation to membership in the Catholic Church—outside of which, as the Church has thrice declared infallibly, no one is saved.[327] As WAF would have it, Muslims, Shintoists, Buddhists—the members of any religion, in fact—are in fine spiritual condition so long as they pray for the "universal Fatima intentions" WAF has extracted from the Fatima message.

WAF even offers "a free 'starter kit' for people *of any faith* to help them benefit from the power of prayer and to pray for the intentions of Our Lady of Fatima"[328]—that is, the "universal Fatima intentions," not the Catholic intentions the Mother of God actually specified. But what does WAF mean by the "power of prayer"? Any prayer? The prayer of Buddhists to Buddha? The prayers of Hindus to Vishnu or Krishna? The prayer of Animists to the Great Thumb? What of Saint Paul's teaching that "the things which the heathens sacrifice, they sacrifice to devils, and not to God. And I would not that you should be made partakers with devils."[329] Evidently, the teaching of Saint Paul has been annulled by "the spirit of Vatican II" and the Blue Army and WAF.

As for the Muslims, one wonders whether it occurred to La Corte during his tour of Kazan's "beautiful mosques" that "Muslims in Europe are increasingly converting empty Christian churches into mosques" and that "the proliferation of mosques housed in former churches reflects the rise of Islam as the fastest growing religion in post-Christian Europe."[330] The very village of Fatima is named after a Muslim princess who, following her capture by Christian forces during the Moorish occupation of Portugal, was smitten by the Count of Ourem, *converted to Catholicism*, and was *baptized* before marrying the Count in 1158. But the "World Apostolate" of Fatima apparently has no problem with the development "there are now

---

[327] The three *ex cathedra* pronouncements are: Pope Innocent III, Fourth Lateran Council, 1215; Pope Boniface VIII, Bull *Unam Sanctam*, 1302; Pope Eugene IV, Bull *Cantate Domino*, 1442. Only God knows how non-Catholics become incorporated into the Mystical Body of Christ in those exceptional cases where, through no fault of their own, they do not attain formal membership in the Church. There are no "exceptions" to the dogma itself, however. All souls in Heaven have attained beatitude as members of the Church Triumphant. There are no non-Catholics in Heaven.

[328] http://www.wafusa.org/prayer_announcement.html.

[329] 1 Corinthians 10:20.

[330] Soeren Kern, "Muslims Converting Empty European Churches into Mosques," January 16, 2012, Gatestone Institute, International Policy Council, http://www.gatestoneinstitute.org/2761/converting-churches-into-mosques.

more practicing Muslims than practicing Christians in many parts of Europe, not only in large urban centers, but also in smaller towns and cities across the continent."[331] Perhaps WAF views the rising Muslim population of a once-Catholic Europe as prime territory for its "Worldwide Inter-Religious Prayer Campaign." All the Muslims in Europe can contribute their Muslim prayers to WAF's new version of the "Triumph of the Immaculate Heart," which would seem to involve the triumph of Islam in formerly Catholic nations. But, no doubt, there will be many more "beautiful mosques" that La Corte can visit at the expense of the Catholic faithful.

Thanks to WAF the members of all religions can "obey" the "Message of Fatima" without becoming members of the Catholic Church. All they need is a WAF starter kit to be on their way to world peace and eternal felicity. In WAF's revisionist propaganda, the Message of Fatima becomes a New Age plan for the "brotherhood of man" that not even a Freemason would find objectionable. In fact, if a Freemason had set out to rewrite the Message of Fatima according to Masonic requirements, he could not have done a better job than WAF's "Worldwide Inter-Religious Prayer Campaign."

But here the WAF is only doing what the Vatican bureaucracy of newly invented "pontifical councils" expects it to do in furtherance of a new, post Vatican II program of "inter-religious dialogue" that could not be further from the Triumph of the Immaculate Heart of Mary in a converted Russia. Typical of these bureaucrats is Cardinal Jean-Louis Tauran, the Vatican's head of the "Pontifical Council for Inter-religious Dialogue," which, despite its name, is not an arm of the papal Magisterium or teaching office but a mere Vatican department whose documents and initiatives bind no one as matters of faith. In April of 2012, Tauran "praised Buddhism for instilling the values of wisdom, compassion and non-violence in young people in a message to mark the Buddhist feast day of Vesak." Hailing a "religion" devoted to a semi-divinized human being, Tauran declared: "As Buddhists you pass on to young people the wisdom regarding the need to refrain from harming others and to live lives of generosity and compassion." Buddhist education, he said, is "a precious gift to society," and he noted with approval that "Today, in more and more classrooms all over the world, students belonging to various religions and beliefs sit side-by-side."[332] This is the brave new world promoted by the forward-thinking prelates of the party of the innovators: the Masonic brotherhood of religions, with religion reduced to a means

---

[331] Ibid.

[332] "Vatican Cardinal Hails Buddhist Wisdom," *Daily Star*, April 3, 2012; at: http://www.dailystar.com.lb/News/International/2012/Apr-03/169076-vatican-cardinal-hails-buddhist-wisdom.ashx#ixzz1r61fsMBW.

of promoting toleration, non-violence, and generally being nice to others.

Tauran called upon young people to "put pressure on us to destroy all the walls which unfortunately still separate us" and he condemned "the 'ignorance' in relations between Christians and Muslims, criticizing in particular rising Islamophobia in Europe." Even as Islam threatens to overwhelm and destroy what little remains of Christian civilization—alarming even the authorities of a secular French state[333]—Tauran urges us to welcome the rise of Islam in former Christendom with open arms. While Vatican bureaucrats cheer them on, the Muslims will accomplish without firing a shot what Our Lady prevented them from doing at the Battle of Lepanto, when the Rosary produced the miraculous defeat of the invading Muslim armada through Her intercession on October 7, 1571, as Pope Saint Pius V recognized in establishing the Feast of Our Lady of the Rosary on that October 7.

Tauran the innovator is a perfect example of why Paul VI was forced to decry the "auto-demolition" of the Church after Vatican II. And the "World Apostolate of Fatima," whose executive director delights in all the "beautiful mosques" in Kazan, is only too happy to assist in the auto-demolition.

In sum, WAF is helping to promote throughout the world the very error condemned by Pius XI in his encyclical *Mortalium Animos*, only 34 years before Vatican II and three years before Pius XII foresaw disaster for the Church at the hands of the "innovators" he saw all around him in light of the Fatima message. That error, wrote Pius, is the

> false opinion which considers all religions to be more or less good and praiseworthy, since they all in different ways manifest and signify that sense which is inborn in us all, and by which we are led to God and to the obedient acknowledgment of His rule. Not only are those who hold this opinion in error and deceived, but also in distorting the idea of true religion they reject it, and little by little, turn aside to naturalism and atheism, as it is called; from which it clearly follows that one who supports those who hold these theories and attempt to realize them, *is altogether abandoning the divinely revealed religion.*

WAF would undoubtedly protest vehemently that it promotes a specifically Catholic Message of Fatima among Catholics, including "a spiritual pledge to the Blessed Mother promising daily sacrifices, to pray the Rosary, wear the Brown Scapular, meditate on Mary, go

---

[333] "France to Deport Five Muslims Amid Intensified Crackdown," http://abna.ir/data.asp?lang=3&id =306489.

to confession and Communion, and to attend five consecutive first Saturday devotions."[334] But that is precisely the point: WAF purports to divide the Fatima prophecies into two parts: Catholic Fatima and Non-Catholic Fatima, when no such division exists. On the contrary, the Message of Fatima is integrally and indivisibly Catholic. The Catholic intentions enunciated by the Virgin *are* the "universal Fatima intentions," because the Catholic Church is the one and only *universal* Church, to which the salvation of all souls is ordered by the divine decree of the Second Person of the Holy Trinity: "Go forth and make disciples of *all nations*, baptizing them in the name of the Father, and of the Son, and of the Holy Ghost, teaching them to observe all things whatsoever I have commanded thee."[335] "He that believes and is baptized, shall be saved: but he that believes not shall be condemned."[336] Indeed, the very name "Catholic" is derived from the Greek καθολικός (katholikos) meaning universal. Therefore, the true "universal Fatima intentions" to be promoted for the good of *all* men, not just Catholics, are these:

- the consecration and consequent miraculous *conversion* of Russia to the Catholic Faith and Russia's reunion with Rome;

- the Triumph of Mary's Immaculate Heart;

- devotion to the Immaculate Heart as the means of saving souls from hell and bringing true peace—the peace of Christ, not "inter-religious harmony"—to the world;

- the Five First Saturdays and the Communions of Reparation;

- the praying of the Rosary every day for the *conversion* of sinners and the salvation of souls, not merely peace;

- *and* the offering of sacrifices for sinners *by Catholics*.

The problem with the Message of Fatima thus understood is that it is *too Catholic* for the Party Line, and thus too Catholic for organizations that seek "official approval" by the same Vatican bureaucracy whose worldly-wise officials have been trying to "sanitize" Fatima since the Second Vatican Council. Thus, WAF has created one Fatima for Catholics—reduced to personal prayer and devotions—and another "universal" Fatima, suitable for "all faiths," that eliminates anything non-Catholics might find offensive. In the process, like the Catholic proto-ecumenists of the 1920s whose activities Pius XI reprobated, WAF is "little by little, turn[ing] aside

---

[334] http://www.wafusa.org/press.html.
[335] Matthew 28:19-20.
[336] Mark 16:16.

to naturalism" and implicitly "abandoning the divinely revealed religion" in favor of a pan-religious substitute. WAF is promoting exactly the vision of Monsignor Guerra, whose stated intent we noted in Chapter 6: "The future of Fatima, or the adoration of God and His mother at this Holy Shrine, *must* pass through the creation of a shrine where different religions can mingle."

As WAF assures us, however, it is "the only Fatima organization that speaks with ecclesiastical authority on the message of Fatima." Who, then, would dare to question its new "inter-religious" version of Fatima with its new "universal Fatima intentions" for people of "all faiths"? Here we see yet again how the appearance of authority, where none actually exists, is employed to cloak error with respectability. And so it has gone with all the ruinous ecclesial innovations imposed by the party of the innovators since Vatican II, which have left the once Christian West in a state that John Paul II was forced to describe as nothing less than "silent apostasy." At the same time, a resurgent Islam is filling the void, while Mr. La Corte visits "beautiful mosques" in Kazan.

What Conversion?

Since Fatima Lite is no longer an intrinsically Catholic message, predicated on membership in the Catholic Church for salvation, it follows that the purveyors of Fatima Lite at WAF, like all the others we have encountered, must revise the very concept of conversion in order to address the problem of Our Lady's prophecy that Russia "will be converted..." Here WAF advances the same modernist Message of Fatima advanced by the late Father Fox, who, as we saw in Chapter 6, sneered at those "who hold to a position that a paradise on earth, a Russia suddenly turning itself into a people of converted holiness and even as Roman Catholics must immediately follow a Collegial Consecration."

Because it is conformed completely to the Party Line laid down by the party of the innovators, Fatima Lite rejects the very idea that the intercession of the Mother of God can obtain such a miraculous world *metanoia*, which Socci describes as "an extraordinary change of the world, an overthrow of the mentality dominating modernity, probably following dramatic events for humanity." For the purveyors of Fatima Lite it is equally inconceivable that the Triumph of the Immaculate Heart could mean a reversal of the disastrous innovations of the Church Pius XII predicted with the Fatima prophecies in view, a reversal also described by Socci:

> a clear 'conversion' to doctrinal orthodoxy after the frightening deviations following the Council [and] a return also to adoration, therefore also a return to the bimillennial liturgy of the Church... [A] different face from the Church of today: more

adoring than worldly, more mendicant of the grace of salvation from God, than occupied by its own plans and projects... A Church that expects everything from Christ, not from political ability, from activism and from the mania of aggiornamento...[337]

As far as WAF is concerned—and it is the same with all the false friends of Fatima, including those we have encountered on these pages—the "conversion of Russia" is nothing more than the current religious and geopolitical status quo. What we see is what we get. It's a miracle! Thus, during his aforementioned appearance on EWTN, which has become the Official Network of Fatima Lite, La Corte enthused about "phenomenal changes" in Russia. By this he did not mean Russia's conversion to the Faith and her return to communion with Rome—of course not!—but rather that "The Russian Orthodox Church... is thriving now... the Faith seems to be reviving."[338] Apostoli agreed: "faith is rising up again" in Russia, by which he meant Russian Orthodoxy.

So, as La Corte, Apostoli, WAF, EWTN, and the entire Fatima Lite establishment would have it, the Mother of God came to Fatima to prophesy the "conversion" of Russia to Russian Orthodoxy, part of a thousand-year-old schism whose hierarchy was, and remains today, a tool of the Kremlin. But even this supposed "thriving" of the Russian Orthodox Church is a fiction. A U.S. State Department report on the state of religion in Russia as of 2010 notes that while "[a]pproximately 100 million citizens identify themselves as Russian Orthodox... only 5 percent of Russians call themselves observant." As for members of the religion the Mother of God had in view at Fatima, in all of United Russia there are only "600,000 Catholics, *most of whom are not ethnic Russians.*"[339] The Muslim population of Russia is between "10 million and 23 million," there are "one million Buddhists" and "Protestants make up the second largest group of Christian believers, with 3,500 registered organizations and more than two million adherents." That is, even Buddhists outnumber Catholics in "converted" Russia.

Neither La Corte nor Apostoli had anything to say about the continued standing of the Catholic Church in Russia as a tiny minority hemmed in by government restrictions at every level. Russia has manifestly failed to embrace the Catholic Faith since 1984—the only reasonable meaning of the word "conversion." On the contrary, in the years that have passed since 1984 we have witnessed a steady

---

[337] Socci, *The Fourth Secret of Fatima*, p. 127.

[338] http://www.youtube.com/watch?feature=player_embedded&v=S2X_9JGFR00#t =1786s.

[339] "Russia, Bureau of Democracy, Human Rights, and Labor, International Religious Freedom Report 2010, November 17, 2010," accessed at http://www.state.gov/j/ drl/rls/irf/2010/148977.htm.

decline of the Church's position, to the point where today the Church is undergoing *outright persecution* under the Putin regime. Consider these facts:

- In 1997 Russia enacted a new law on "freedom of conscience" which gave privileged status to Russian Orthodoxy, Islam, Judaism and Buddhism as Russia's "traditional religions," while forbidding Catholic "proselytism" and requiring Catholic parishes to obtain approval from local bureaucrats for their very existence.

- The small percentage of Catholics who even go to Mass on Sunday (most of them in Siberia) is dependent almost entirely on a total of 165 Catholic priests, nearly all of whom are foreign-born clerics not allowed into Russia without visitor's visas that require a departure from the country every three months to seek renewal, which can be denied at any time and for any reason, often for no reason at all.

- In 2002 Russian authorities began expelling non-Russian Catholic clergy from the country. As of November 2002 five priests, including the bishop for Siberia, Bishop Jerzy Mazur, had been expelled and their visas confiscated without explanation. Bishop Mazur learned that he had been added to a secret "list" of Catholic clergy who are considered "undesirables" and will no longer be allowed to enter Russian territory. After ignoring even the Pope's request for an explanation of the expulsions, Vladimir Putin sent a perfunctory letter stating nothing more than that the expulsions were in accordance with Russian law.[340]

- The Russian Orthodox hierarchy exploded in outrage when the Vatican announced in February 2002 that its "apostolic administrations" in Russia would be designated as dioceses. These would not even be dioceses in the traditional Catholic sense. There would, for example, be only an "Archdiocese of the Mother of God *at* Moscow"; and the Archbishop in charge of this structure will not be called the Archbishop of Moscow, lest the Vatican give offense to the Russian Orthodox Partriarch of Moscow, the ex-KGB agent, Alexy II.

- On March 2, 2002, Pope John Paul II conducted a Saturday prayer service that was broadcast from the Vatican by satellite into Russia. The broadcast was totally blacked

---

[340] "Rebuff for the Pope: Vatican Fears New Persecution," *The Catholic World Report*, October 2002, p. 9.

out by the same Russian television networks now under Vladimir Putin's thumb. Only by shipping special equipment into the country (that was held up at customs until the last possible moment) could a few thousand Catholics see the Pope on television screens set up at Assumption Cathedral in Moscow. The BBC reported that "Patriarch Alexy of the Russian Orthodox Church said it (the satellite broadcast) was an 'invasion of Russia' and referred to the Polish occupation of Moscow in the early 17th Century. John-Paul is of Polish origin."[341] Hence, after 40 years of *Ostpolitik* and "ecumenical dialogue", the Orthodox hierarchy will not even tolerate a video image of the Pope in even one single Catholic church in Moscow.

- Trying to put a happy face on the debacle in Russia, Archbishop Tadeusz Kondrusiewicz, the then head of the "Archdiocese of the Mother of God *at* Moscow", claimed that "It's all a misunderstanding," referring to Orthodox charges that the Catholic Church is "proselytizing" in Russia.

- An Associated Press story on Kondrusiewicz's reaction to Orthodox hostility noted that "Parishioners have come to Kondrusiewicz in tears recently, complaining that the indignant rhetoric by Orthodox leaders on national newscasts since February 11 has made them afraid to practice their faith."[342]

- Archbishop Kondrusiewicz has issued a formal protest on behalf of the Conference of Catholic Bishops of Russia, entitled "Religious Liberty in Russia is in Serious Danger." The protest declares:

> Catholics in Russia ask themselves: What will happen next? Are the constitutional guarantees valid also for them, including liberty of conscience and of the right to have their own pastors, which comprises inviting them from abroad, not forgetting that for 81 years the Catholic Church was deprived of the right of forming and ordaining its own priests? Perhaps the State really considers Catholics second-class citizens? Are they (the State) returning to the times of persecution of the faith? ... The expulsion of a Catholic bishop who has not violated any law, surpasses all imaginable limits of civilized relations between the

---

[341] *BBC Online*, March 2, 2002.
[342] AP News, March 1, 2002.

State and the Church. ... With grave worry, we express our decisive protest in respect to violation of the constitutional rights of Catholics.[343]

- By October 2002 Pope John Paul II's own spokesman, Joaquin Navarro-Valls, had declared that the actions against the Catholic Church by Russian authorities had reached the level of "a true persecution."[344]

The situation has not improved materially since 2002. In at least one way it has gotten worse. As the U.S. State Department reported in its 2008 International Religious Freedom Report, in 2007 "the Russian government introduced new visa rules that allow foreigners (including religious workers) with business or humanitarian visas to spend only 90 of every 180 days in the country."[345] The State Department's report for 2010, quoted above, confirms that "[t]he effect of these rules has been to *restrict severely* religious groups that rely upon foreign religious workers. *The Catholic Church, which relies almost exclusively on priests from outside the country... [has] been particularly hard hit by this provision*." The new visa rules create a preposterous situation for the Church in Russia: *nearly every Catholic priest in the country is obliged to leave Russia for what amounts to six months out of every year*, to remain in Russia for no more than 90 days at a time, and to reapply at least twice a year for readmission at the discretion of bureaucrats. The aim of the 2007 law is clear: to prevent the Catholic Church from sinking any roots in Russian soil, while giving the false appearance of "religious freedom" to a marginalized and bureaucratically hounded tiny minority of priests and faithful, struggling to survive.

Even at the level of basic morality, Russia today is a sinkhole of degradation; there has been no religious conversion of any kind. **Quite the contrary, since 1984 Russia has undergone a rapid moral decline, as if to make a mockery of this revisionist claim. Consider these facts:**

- Today, Russia has *the highest abortion rate in the world* at 53.7 per 1,000 women between the ages of 15 and 44—a rate even higher than that in China (which has more total abortions).[346]

- Fr. Daniel Maurer, C.J.D., who spent eight years in Russia, says that statistically, the average Russian woman will have

---

[343] *National Catholic Register* Online Web Edition, April 28 - May 5, 2002.

[344] *The Catholic World Report*, October 2002, p. 10.

[345] U.S. Department of State, "International Religious Freedom Report 2008", at http://www.state.gov/g/drl/rls/irf/2008/108468.htm.

[346] CBC News, July 30, 2009, "13 million abortions a year reported in China," at http://www.cbc.ca/health/story/2009/07/30/abortions-china.html.

eight abortions during her childbearing years—though Fr. Maurer believes the actual number averaged out to be about 12 abortions per woman. He has spoken to women who have had as many as 25 abortions. A major reason for these dreadful figures is that other contraception methods (which are immoral anyway) have not been introduced in Russia, nor are they trusted. This leaves abortion as the "cheapest way to limit the family size."[347]

- *In Russia, abortions are free, but childbirth is not.*[348]

- The Russian birth rate is plummeting and Russia's population is dropping at the rate of 700,000 people each year—an unprecedented event in a civilized nation during "peacetime."[349]

- Russia has the highest per capita rate of alcohol consumption in the world.[350]

- Homosexuality is rampant in Moscow and throughout the country. In fact, in April 1993, nine years after the 1984 "consecration", Boris Yeltsin allowed homosexuality to be de-criminalized. Homosexuality is now "legal" in Russia.[351]

- Russia is a leading world center for the distribution of child pornography. The *Associated Press* reported on a Moscow-

---

[347] Father Maurer's remarks appeared in an interview in *Catholic World Report*, February 2001. A synopsis and commentary on this interview was published in "The Myth of a Converted Russia Exposed", Marian Horvat, Ph.D., *Catholic Family News*, March 2001.

[348] Ibid.

[349] See Mark Fellows, "This Present Darkness", Part III, *Catholic Family News*, October 2000.

[350] Regarding alcohol in Russia, researchers concluded: "Russia's rate of alcohol consumption, traditionally among the highest in the world, and rising significantly in the 1990s, is a major contributor to the country's health crisis ... alcoholism has reached epidemic proportions, particularly among males ... A 1995 Russian study found that regular drunkenness affected between 25 and 60 percent of blue-collar workers ... In 1994 some 53,000 people died of alcohol poisoning, an increase of about 36,000 since 1991." In the ten years since the alleged consecration of Russia, there has also been a sharp increase in illegal drug use: "In 1995 an estimated 2 million Russians used narcotics, more than twenty times the total recorded ten years earlier in the entire Soviet Union, with the number of users increasing 50 percent every year in the mid-1990s." From Mark Fellows, "This Present Darkness", Part II, *Catholic Family News*, September 2000.

[351] "Russia Legalizes Homosexuality", *United Press International*, May 28, 1993. To quote the beginning of the article: "Russia's homosexual activists Friday celebrated a major victory for gay rights in post-Soviet Russia following the repeal of Article 121 of the Soviet criminal code, which outlawed consensual sex between men. 'This is great news for gays and lesbians in Russia,' said Vladislav Ortanov, editor of the Moscow gay magazine *Risk*."

based child pornography ring linked to another child pornography ring in Texas. To quote AP: "Russian law does not distinguish between child pornography and pornography involving adults, and treats the production and distribution of either as a minor crime, said Dmitry Chepchugov, head of the Russian Interior Ministry's department for high technology crimes. Russian police often complain about the legal chaos that has turned Russia into an international center of child pornography production. *'Unfortunately, Russia has turned into a world trash bin of child pornography,'* Chepchugov told reporters in Moscow."[352]

- Russians are addicted to grossly immoral "reality-based" TV. On the vilest of the "reality-based" shows, cameras film the intimate personal lives of Russian "couples," including their activity breaking the 6th Commandment. Despite grumbles of disapproval from old hard-line Communists, Russian viewers "cannot get enough" of this pornography. The program "boasts an audience share of more than 50% and thousands of Russians have endured sub-zero temperatures and stood in line for more than an hour to catch a glimpse of it through a window of the apartment. Millions have logged on to the website, which has crashed frequently under the weight of the heavy traffic."[353]

Here, however, we have a recent positive, albeit inadvertent, development. The Kremlin, recognizing that the Russian population is exterminating itself in abortion mills, has enacted legislation to make it more difficult to obtain abortions. The new laws include a waiting period and the elimination of all "social grounds" for abortion between 12 and 22 weeks of pregnancy, although before then, up to the fourth month of pregnancy, abortion on demand is still available, essentially on demand. Despite these desperate measures, the countries of the former Soviet Union maintain the highest rate of abortions in the world. And in Russia proper, there were 1.32 million live births, but 1.8 million abortions in 2001.[354]

To speak of a "conversion of Russia" in the face of these facts is ludicrous. But then the Party Line itself is ludicrous, and WAF is nothing if not an organization whose *raison d'être* is to promote the Party Line unswervingly no matter how untenable it becomes.

---

[352] "Activist Says Child Porn Prosecutions Will be Difficult in Indonesia, Russia", Christine Brummitt, *Associated Press*, August 9, 2001 (emphasis added).

[353] "Big Brotherski goes too far for Staid Russians", Mark Franchetti, *Sunday Times* (London), November 25, 2001.

[354] "Abortion in Russia," http://en.wikipedia.org/wiki/Abortion_in_Russia#cite_note-8.

A New Twist on Russia's "Conversion"

Apparently without recognizing the disastrous implications for the Party Line, Apostoli admitted during the EWTN telecast that since the "consecration of Russia" in 1984, "There's a religious indifference that seems to be spreading. In formerly Christian countries, people have just fallen away from their faith... People have just fallen away from their faith. There's a progressive secularism—even here in America—intruding into our life..."[355] He further admitted that before he ordered its return to the Russian Orthodox, John Paul II had prayed before the Icon of Kazan that "the Orthodox Church would come back home again—he called it the two lungs of the Church—so that they would be breathing in harmony again."[356] Thus, even WAF's spiritual director concedes that, since the "consecration" in 1984, apostasy has been spreading throughout the Western world and John Paul II's hopes for an end to the Orthodox schism were dashed. Where, then, is the promised "conversion of Russia" and the Triumph of the Immaculate Heart?

Undaunted by reality, WAF has added a new and even more ludicrous twist to the "Russia has converted" canard. During the EWTN broadcast, La Corte went so far as to assert that there is a "spiritual resurgence that is taking place in Russia, as we watch the spiritual decay that's taking place throughout the rest of the world...." To this Apsotoli added that *Russia is going to help reconvert the rest of the world...* It's funny, isn't it? They sent out the evil of atheism and secularism, now they're regaining the faith and we have the evil of secularism and atheism..."[357] Regaining the faith? What faith? Certainly not the Catholic Faith; and not even the Orthodox faith, as only 5% of Russia's nominal Orthodox are actually observant. Yet WAF's head and its spiritual advisor both solemnly assured EWTN's trusting audience that Russia—a secular state ruled by an autocrat, in which abortions exceed live births—will now convert the rest of the world to "the faith." Apparently, for the purveyors of Fatima Lite no lie is too big to ask the faithful to swallow.

What Peace?

During the EWTN telecast, one caller, named "John," managed to get by the call screener and pose the obvious question: "If the Consecration of Russia had already taken place, why is there not an end to wars?... I thought peace should have taken place..." Apostoli

---

[355] http://www.youtube.com/watch?feature=player_detailpage&v=S2X_9JGFR00#t=809s.

[356] http://www.youtube.com/watch?feature=player_detailpage&v=S2X_9JGFR00#t=1188s.

[357] http://www.youtubecom/watch?feature=player_embedded&v=S2X_9JGFR00#t=2593s.

quickly administered the cure for this insurrection against the Party Line, observing that "Gorbachev took down the Soviet flag... on Christmas of 1991," as if Our Lady of Fatima had promised the world nothing more than a regime change in Moscow.

Even Apostoli, however, noted the objection "what about our abortions, what about our euthanasia, our destruction of human life?..." How could this mass slaughter of innocents, all over the world, be consistent with the period of peace Our Lady of Fatima promised if Her request for the Consecration were obeyed? Referring to the supposed "conversion" of Russia since 1984, Apostoli could only say that "many places of the world that's [sic] gotta have conversion also or there can never be that full peace. But it's coming." Some 26 years after the Consecration-that-wasn't, Apostoli seriously proposed to his Catholic audience that the world would have "full peace" and turn away from the holocaust of abortion when the world had "converted" like Russia, *which has the world's highest per capita abortion rate*. Yes, according to Father Apostoli, "full peace" will be attained once the rest of the world becomes like Russia! One might ask: Is this for real? Indeed it is. And it comes from the "spiritual advisor" of the "World Apostolate" of Fatima. The phrase "blind guides" somehow seems inadequate.

La Corte took a different tack, offering the alternative standard Party Line "explanation" that the "period of peace" Our Lady of Fatima promised is nothing other than the geopolitical status quo we have been experiencing since 1984. That is, wars, genocides, and the endless holocaust of the unborn in Russia and throughout the "civilized" world—not even the primitive tribes of the "undeveloped" world practice abortion on demand—are what the intercession of Our Lady has obtained, thanks to the "Consecration of Russia" in 1984. Here La Corte cited as his "authority" none other than Monsignor Guerra, whose name, ironically enough, means *war* in both Portuguese and Italian: "Monsignor Guerra, the rector *emeritus* of the shrine in Fatima, Portugal, his perspective is that we *are* in the era of peace." [358]

Well, that settles that. Monsignor Guerra has spoken! According to La Corte and the "World Apostolate" of Fatima Lite, the world is now in the midst of the Triumph of the Immaculate Heart. Behold the miracle! But that preposterous assertion is rather difficult to reconcile with the pronouncements of the Pope to whom La Corte and his organization profess to be so loyal. In his homily at the Fatima Shrine on May 13, 2010, Pope Benedict XVI made a mockery of La Corte's shameless propaganda by intimating that the world is on the

---

[358] http://www.youtube.com/watch?feature=player_embedded&v=S2X_9JGFR00#t=2706s.

verge of a divine chastisement precisely because the Triumph of the Immaculate Heart has *not* taken place:

> *One would deceive himself* who thinks that Fatima's prophetic mission is concluded. Here there takes on new life the plan of God which asks humanity from the beginning: "Where is your brother Abel [...] *Your brother's blood is crying out to me from the ground!*" (Gen. 4:9). Mankind has succeeded in unleashing a cycle of death and terror, but *failed in bringing it to an end...* In sacred Scripture we often find that God seeks righteous men and women in order to save the city of man and he does the same here, in Fatima, when Our Lady asks: "Do you want to offer yourselves to God, to endure all the sufferings which he will send you, in an act of reparation for the sins by which he is offended and of supplication for the conversion of sinners?" (*Memoirs of Sister Lúcia*, I, 162)... May the seven years which separate us from the centenary of the apparitions *hasten the fulfilment of the prophecy of the triumph of the Immaculate Heart of Mary*, to the glory of the Most Holy Trinity.[359]

Seeing a world steeped in violence and unprecedented evil— the same world the Pope sees—La Corte, being a fairly clever propagandist, proposed the theory that his imaginary Triumph of the Immaculate Heart consists in the avoidance of World War III, which surely would have happened had John Paul II not "consecrated Russia" in 1984: "Our Lady was foreseeing World War III, which was going to be this huge devastating war, with nuclear arms that weren't even foresawn [sic] in 1917.... But She was talking about the annihilation of nations at that time.... And that didn't happen after the Consecration, after the millions and millions of Rosaries. So, the world war was averted."[360] Notice that La Corte's argument is conveniently non-falsifiable: the supposed Triumph of the Immaculate Heart involves a world war that did *not* happen. How is

---

[359] "Homily at Holy Mass, Esplanade of the Fatima Shrine," May 13, 2010, http://www.vatican.va/holy_father/benedict_xvi/homilies/2010/documents/hf_ben-xvi_hom_20100513_fatima_en.html. We have corrected the Vatican's erroneous English translation, which deletes the key phrase in the original, "one would deceive himself" and replaces it with "we are mistaken." The intent was clearly to hide the fact that the Pope speaks here of a *self-deception*, not merely a "mistake." As the Pope said in the original Portuguese homily: "*Iludir-se-ia* quem pensasse [one would deceive himself who thinks] que a missão profética de Fátima esteja concluída." And in the Italian: "Si illuderebbe chi pensasse [one would deceive himself who thinks] che la missione profetica di Fatima sia conclusa." The Portuguese verb for "to deceive" is *iludir-se*, and the Italian verb is *illudere*. This mistranslation, unfortunately, is typical of the unreliability of the Vatican apparatus on matters pertaining to Fatima. Indeed, the Vatican approved defective vernacular translations of the Mass itself that went uncorrected for forty years, including the mistranslation of "for many" [*pro multis*] as "for all" [*pro omnes*].

[360] http://www.youtube.com/watch?feature=player_embedded&v=S2X_9JGFR00#t=2706s.

one to disprove that contention?

But then, what about the "cycle of death and terror" which, as the Pope himself declared at Fatima, is crying out to Heaven for divine retribution? In perfect harmony with the Party Line, La Corte opined that "this concept of there would be no war or strife in the world" pertains to "the Second Coming of Jesus, a thousand years— but I don't know that Our Lady was talking about every little war and skirmish..." After all, what are a few little wars and skirmishes compared to the Third World War we escaped? Besides, said La Corte, the fault for all these little wars and skirmishes lies with the simple faithful, who have fallen down on the job, not with the Pope and the bishops for having failed to perform the Consecration of Russia: "we haven't followed the Message of Fatima. We haven't done our part. We can't expect the bishops just to do their part, and run around and ignore the rest of the message..."[361]

Come again? Only a few moments earlier La Corte had declared that World War III was averted "after the Consecration, *after the millions and millions of Rosaries*" offered by the same faithful he had just accused of failing to do their part in heeding the Fatima message. How is it that these millions of Rosaries averted World War III, but not "every little war and skirmish"—meaning the "cycle of death and terror" that has convulsed the globe since the "consecration" of 1984?

Continuing his double-talk, the head of the "World Apostolate" of Fatima Lite made sure to cover his bases by suggesting that if the cycle of death and terror that has unfolded since 1984 *does* result in a world war (which may be what is depicted in the vision published in 2000) then this must mean that the Triumph of the Immaculate Heart is already behind us and that once again we face the "annihilation of nations," which will be the fault of the faithful, not the utterly blameless hierarchy: "We're not doing our part, so we're slipping back again, and we can fall right into that problem we had in the past, and *nations are again on the precipice of perhaps being annihilated* if we don't wake up."[362] Laughably, La Corte pronounced these words with a satisfied smile on his face, as if to say: "See, that explains everything in case the world explodes. We can blame it all on the lazy laity, not the failure to consecrate Russia."

Doing what was expected of "the only Fatima organization that speaks with ecclesiastical authority," La Corte had provided what he seemed to think was the perfect cover for the Vatican Secretary of State's decades-long campaign to prevent the Consecration. At

---

[361] http://www.youtube.com/watch?feature=player_embedded&v=S2X_9JGFR00#t =2706s.

[362] http://www.youtube.com/watch?feature=player_detailpage&v=S2X_9JGFR00#t =2877s.

one and the same time he was arguing that the 1984 "consecration" had succeeded in bringing peace to the world, but that the world was *still* on the verge of the "annihilation of nations" because the faithful are spiritual slackers. If the world is divinely chastised by a terrible conflagration, it's all the fault of the simple faithful, who squandered the Triumph of the Immaculate Heart by not doing their part. And doing their part would naturally include donations to "the only Fatima organization that speaks with ecclesiastical authority" so that the Muslims, Buddhists, Hindus, and other religionists can obtain WAF's "starter kits" and join the "Worldwide Inter-Religious Prayer Campaign"—while there is still time! But absolutely nothing further is required from the Vatican bureaucrats who have given WAF a stamp of approval for the dissemination of this nonsense, nor from the bishops, and certainly not from the Pope. The laity, and only the laity, will be to blame for the annihilation of nations.

La Corte concluded his EWTN performance by concocting an entire conversation between Sister Lucia and John Paul II in which she assures the Pope that he most certainly had consecrated Russia without ever mentioning Russia:

> And who do you turn to find out if the Consecration has taken place? Normally, you would turn to the Pope, the highest authority in the Church. But the Pope turned to Sister Lucia and said: "Sister Lucia, has it been done?" And the first two times the consecration took place Sister Lucia said "No, Holy Father, it hasn't been done." But when Pope John Paul did it on March 25, she said "Yes, Holy Father, it has been done."

Of course, no such conversation ever took place, except in La Corte's imagination. And, as we saw in Chapter 3, Sister Lucia declared no fewer than three times that the 1984 ceremony did not fulfill Our Lady's request: on March 22, 1984, just before the ceremony; in 1985 in *Sol de Fatima* magazine; and on July 27, 1987 (to journalist Enrique Romero). Try as he might, Cardinal Bertone never could induce Sister Lucia to recant an entire lifetime of testimony that the Consecration of Russia requires that Russia be identified as the object of the consecration—as if this were a seriously debatable proposition. Bertone has given five different versions of Lucia's supposed about-face; but his claim here was no more credible than his patently false representation that Lucia told him Our Lady never linked disclosure of the Third Secret to the year 1960, when the very envelopes in his possession show conclusively that that is exactly what She did.[363]

Notice, however, that even La Corte's imaginary conversation between Lucia and the Pope has Lucia saying "No, Holy Father, it

---

[363] Cf. Chapter 5; *see also, The Secret Still Hidden*, pp. 148-152.

hasn't been done" after the "first two times the consecration took place." But the 1984 consecration suffered from *the same defects as the two previous attempts*, so why should the outcome of the third defective ceremony have been any different? In the real world, it's "three strikes and you're out." But in the world of Fatima Lite, a strike-out is a home run.

A Shot over Father Gruner's Bow

Near the end of the EWTN episode we have been examining as typical of WAF's Fatima revisionist propaganda, a caller complained about a Fatima apostolate that was presenting a "gloom and doom thing" and is headed by a priest who "didn't obey his bishop"—the usual canard concerning Father Gruner, already refuted in Chapter 3. "I don't think Fatima is gloom and doom," the caller added.[364] The Mother of God, who speaks of hell, wars, persecution, suffering, martyrdom, and the annihilation of nations in the Message of Fatima, could be expected to disagree, even if the Message does embrace the hope of deliverance from these evils if only foolish men will cease interfering with the execution of Her requests.

Without mentioning Father Gruner by name, La Corte replied: "The only thing I'd like to say is that the World Apostolate of Fatima is the only pontifical organization.... which means it's officially part of the Church under Canon Law.... You can look to this apostolate for the correct information on Fatima...." WAF is no more "officially part of the Church" than any Catholic in good standing. The suggestion that it has some sort of teaching office akin to that of the Pope, the bishops and the priests who are part of the *divine constitution* of the Church is misleading at best. At any rate, as we have seen, WAF is the *last* place to which one can look for correct information on Fatima. Its function is precisely to disseminate *dis*-information on Fatima as widely as possible.

The example of WAF demonstrates that the application of a rubber stamp by a Vatican department under the control of the Secretary of State is no guarantee of an organization's orthodoxy or reliability. On the contrary, in these times of diabolical confusion in the Church, a Vatican department's approval is more often than not a grounds for extreme caution respecting an organization's claims, especially where Fatima is concerned. Have we not seen enough of the damage caused by "Vatican-approved" innovations and initiatives over the past fifty years? Here we must stress that by "the Vatican" we do not mean the papal magisterium exercised in an authentic manner by the Pope, intending to bind the universal Church. The magisterium

---

[364] http://www.youtube.com/watch?feature=player_embedded&v=S2X_9JGFR00#t=2403s.

has not imposed any obligation to believe anything WAF says about the Message of Fatima that does not correspond to the objective facts or right reason.

A Hard Truth

However hard this truth may sound, the sheer absurdity of WAF's Fatima revisionist propaganda leaves one with the net impression that custody of the Fatima prophecies has fallen into the hands of bumbling incompetents who have received Vatican approval precisely *because* they are bumbling incompetents. What better way to neutralize the Message of Fatima in its authentic Catholic meaning than to confer the appearance of special authority upon zealous merchants of Fatima Lite, who, in return for the empty honor of an "official franchise" that is not required anyway, would be willing to say whatever they need to say—no matter how false, how implausible—to sell their product to the faithful and accomplish the sales goal of the Vatican "franchisor": the consignment of the Fatima prophecies to the oblivion of the past.

Like the "useful idiots" of the West who assisted the rise of the Bolsheviks to power after Our Lady warned of their coming ascendancy, the "useful incompetents" who promote Fatima Lite are fervent cheerleaders for the very program that would destroy them, and us, should it be accomplished. In the divine plan, however, all the efforts of the false friends of Fatima will ultimately come to naught, no matter how hard they labor to bury what they profess to praise.

Chapter 15

The Party Line in Retreat

In Chapters 11 and 12 we saw how in the immediate aftermath of the "Fatima Challenge" Conference staged by Father Gruner's apostolate in May 2010, which featured the momentous participation of Giuseppe De Carli, the Pope went to Fatima and made the explosive declarations that negated the Vatican Secretary of State's entire "official account" of the Third Secret and the Fatima prophecies in general. The Party Line would suffer further reversals just before and just after the apostolate's 2011 conference in Rome under the title "Consecration Now!" (an allusion to the demand for "Sainthood Now" respecting John Paul II), held from May 9 to May 13. That conference would include important interventions by two of Italy's most prominent Vaticanists: Andrea Tornielli and Paolo Rodari. Their very appearance at the conference signaled a tectonic shift in public opinion on Fatima by which the "Fatimist" position, based on unanswerable evidence, had found acceptance in the Vatican press corps, much to the consternation of the false friends of Fatima, who were accustomed to exclusive possession of the mantle of respectability.

Papal Doubts About the Consecration

On Good Friday 2011, April 22, Pope Benedict made an unprecedented appearance on Italian television, not to deliver an address, but to answer selected questions from the faithful—something no Pope has ever done, even in the age of television, much less on Good Friday. Note well: these questions were selected by the Pope; he did not have to address them at all. But the Supreme Pontiff chose to address *this* question, which represents the concern that has animated the writing of this book and the entire movement for the accomplishment of what the false friends of Fatima have labored so hard to prevent: "And, on the subject of entrusting, do you intend to renew a consecration to the Virgin at the beginning of this new millennium?" The Pope's answer reveals significant doubt—if not indeed a conviction he feels unable to state explicitly—that Russia has never been consecrated to the Immaculate Heart of Mary. Consider very carefully the emphasized words:

> And so we arrive at the meaning of entrusting ourselves: the Popes—whether it was Pius XII, or Paul VI, or John Paul II—have made a great act of entrusting the world to the Madonna and *it seems to me*, as a gesture before humankind,

before Mary herself, that it was a very important gesture.... I *think* that the great, public act has been made. *Perhaps* one day it will be necessary to *repeat* it again, but at the moment it *seems* more important to me to live it, to make it real, to enter into this entrusting so that it might truly be our own.... For example, at Fatima I saw how the thousands of persons present truly entered into this entrustment. In themselves, for themselves they entrusted themselves to her; they made this trust real within them. It thus becomes a reality in the living Church and thus also the Church grows. The common entrustment to Mary, letting ourselves be penetrated by this presence, creating and entering into communion with Mary makes the Church, makes us together with Mary, truly the Bride of Christ. Thus, *at the moment*, I do not intend to make *a new act of public entrustment*...[365]

Notice how the Pope carefully avoided any definitive statement that the Consecration of *Russia* as such has been effected. Rather, he referred indifferently to the ceremonies by Pius XII, Paul VI (who consecrated the world to the Immaculate Heart during Vatican II) and John Paul II, not declaring that any of them was a Consecration of Russia or that any was more in accord with what Our Lady of Fatima requested. The Pope opined only that "it seems to me" that all three ceremonies were "a very important gesture"—that is, a consecration of the world. But Pope Benedict *never relates any of these papal ceremonies to the Virgin's request for Russia's consecration.* The Pope merely *thinks*, but does not declare, that the "great, public act has been made," but never states or even implies that the act in question was a consecration of Russia. In fact, as we have seen, *no Pope* has ever declared that the Consecration of Russia has been accomplished, despite the contrary intimations of the false friends of Fatima, hewing obediently to a Party Line that does not come from the Pope in the first place, and which the Pope himself had fatally undermined the previous year.

Further, why would the Pope say that "*perhaps* one day it will be necessary to *repeat* it [the "entrustment" to Mary] again" if the prior consecrations or "entrustments" definitively fulfilled Our Lady of Fatima's request? And why say "*at the moment*, I do not intend to make a new act of public entrustment" unless the Pope was suggesting that it may well be necessary to try again. And why would the Pope go out of his way to broach the suggestion in response to a question he did not even have to address in the first place, unless he knows or at least suspects that something is lacking in the ceremonies John Paul II

---

[365] "Pope Benedict Answers Questions on Special Television Broadcast," April 22, 2011, http://www.radiovaticana.org/en1/Articolo.asp?c=480959.

performed after—as Bishop Cordes admitted—he "abandoned" the idea of Russia's consecration "at the suggestion of his collaborators"? (See Chapter 3.)

Bertone's Further Retreat

On April 30, 2011, eight days after the Pope's remarks had introduced the specter of doubt concerning the adequacy of prior consecration ceremonies, Cardinal Bertone retreated from his long-maintained position that the Third Secret of Fatima and the Fatima prophecies in general depict only events that "belong to the past," culminating in the failed attempt on the life of John Paul II in 1981. Appearing on Italy's Radio 1 station, Bertone stated: "The third mystery of Fatima is fulfilled *in part* in the description that was given by Sister Lucia [the vision published in 2000]. But, as then Cardinal Ratzinger has said, the triumph of the Immaculate Heart *will* happen. It is necessary to cultivate hope and not be catastrophists."[366]

Now, if the Third Secret has been fulfilled only "in part" in the vision Sister Lucia recorded, where would one find mention of the remainder to be fulfilled? Quite suddenly, and clearly in response to the turning point of the Pope's linkage of the Secret to "future realities" in the Church a year earlier during the papal pilgrimage to Fatima, Bertone had quietly abandoned the very core of his own Party Line. Andrea Tornielli was quick to note the significance of the development:

> Words fully in harmony with what was affirmed by Benedict XVI on the flight that brought him to Portugal, a year ago, as well as in a passage of the homily for the Mass celebrated at Fatima. Concerning 2000, when there was offered a reading of the vision of Fatima turned solely toward the past, there is therefore *a major caution* ("is fulfilled in part"), and thus is left open the possibility that not all of the prophecy—understood in a Biblical sense and not as a film that describes the future—is yet accomplished.[367]

---

[366] http://www.grr.rai.it/dl/grr/notizie/ContentItem-af44bb70-17aa-4c04-8cfb-077d28ffab92.html: "Il terzo mistero di Fatima è compiuto in parte nella descrizione che è stata fatta da suor Lucia, ma come ha detto (l'allora) cardinale Ratzinger il cuore immacolato di Maria trionferà. Bisogna coltivare la speranza e non essere catastrofici."

[367] "The Third Secret is Not Fulfilled," http://2.andreatornielli.it/?p=1562. ("Parole in piena sintonia con quanto affermato da Benedetto XVI sul volo che lo portava in Portogallo, un anno fa, come pure in un passaggio dell'omelia della messa celebrata a Fatima. Rispetto al 2000, quando della visione di Fatima venne offerta una lettura rivolta soltanto al passato, c'è dunque maggiore cautela ('è compiuto in parte') e dunque si lascia aperta la possibilità che non tutta la profezia – da interndersi in senso biblico e non come un film che descrive il futuro – sia ancora compiuta.").

Another Fateful Conference

At the *Consecration Now!* conference, the addresses by both Rodari and Tornielli at the Ergife Hotel signaled a whole new climate surrounding the Third Secret affair. What was once considered an unseemly conspiracy theory was now accepted as a real possibility by some of Italy's most prominent Catholic voices.

Paolo Rodari took to the podium and reviewed the evidence of Archbishop Capovilla's admission of the existence of two texts and two envelopes pertaining to the Third Secret as if it were now a commonplace beyond serious dispute. He then observed, as the previous chapters suggest, that "2010 is a turning point with respect to all the questions that are still outstanding"—meaning the Pope's pilgrimage to Fatima. "And I think it's significant," he continued, referring to the radio interview just mentioned, that "just a few days ago Cardinal Bertone... said that the Third mystery of Fatima has been partly fulfilled... *This makes quite a difference*, because it wasn't said in 2000. So here also we find *a contradiction*. So perhaps here there's a will, *a will to say something*."

The Pope's revelations that the Secret pertains to "future events" that "progressively unfold" in the Church and that "the greatest persecution does not come from the external enemies but arises from the sin that springs from within the Church," Rodari called "quite surprising, and unprecedented, unexpected." And, in a clear reference to the machinations of the Secretary of State, Rodari remarked that "some authorities within the Roman Curia, the Holy See, try to avoid or downplay—water down—these explicit statements made by the Pope *so that they may not be understood in their full scope.* But the scandal of pedophilia has brought to the fore this great lesson of the Pope: *never fear the truth*, even when the truth is painful, and even when it's shameful for the Church."

"Is there such a thing as a Fourth Secret," Rodari queried? While the vision has been "automatically linked to the attack of 1981," he concluded, "many questions remain unanswered." One cannot overestimate the importance of these remarks coming from a Vaticanist of the first rank.

Tornielli's brief address was no less portentous of bad times for the Party Line and its defenders. Referring to the remarks of Cardinal Ratzinger at the press conference back in 2000, when the vision of the "Bishop dressed in White" was published, Tornielli stressed that "These words are very important: *there's no official interpretation of the vision of Fatima*—Ratzinger said this, *there is no such thing.*" Note well: *no* official interpretation—no such thing. And this from perhaps the most renowned Vaticanist in the world.

Tornielli noted that Monsignor Rino Fisichella, who had served as a consultor to the Congregation for the Doctrine of the Faith, had written a commentary on the vision published in 2000 which stated "at one point that 'we might think that the Fatima prophecy has not been fulfilled.'...." In a telling reference to the impact the efforts of the so-called Fatimists had had on the Third Secret controversy since 2000, Tornielli commented that "It is interesting to note that ten years after the release of the text of the Secret, *the Pope and even Cardinal Bertone are saying the same: basically the prophecy cannot be considered fulfilled entirely*."

Tornielli then spoke of a revelation by Archbishop Pasquale Macchi, personal secretary of Paul VI, that "When Paul VI spoke about 'Satan's smoke,' he was actually referring to the priests who challenge the Church, who are not faithful, who are not true to their identity, who are not true and faithful to their celibacy. And he refers to disobedience toward the Magisterium of the Church. *The Pope connects these phenomena to the Secret of Fatima*." Paul VI, Macchi further revealed, had wept over the mountain of requests for dispensation from the clerical state presented for his signature, calling it "my Calvary...." It is very interesting what Macchi wrote, "*that the Pope associated these phenomena, that so many priests wanted to leave the Church, with the Secret of Fatima...*" The implications were devastating for the Party Line: not only Benedict XVI, but also Paul VI, had linked the Third Secret to mass defections and rebellion among the Catholic clergy, *when nothing of the kind is depicted in the vision standing alone.* Where did this come from if not another text pertaining to the Secret—the one Paul had read in 1963 as opposed to the one he had read in 1965, the year given in the "official account"?

In fact, what Monsignor Macchi revealed concerning Paul VI was quite in line with the Message of Akita, already noted (see Chapter 7). Tornielli made that very point, quoting from the text of the Akita apparitions: "the work of the devil will infiltrate the Church in such a way that cardinals shall be pitted against other cardinals, bishops against other bishops. And the priests who venerate Me shall be despised and rejected by their own brothers. Altars shall be sacked, churches shall be teeming with people who accept compromises." Noting that then Cardinal Ratzinger had recognized the authenticity of the Message of Akita as head of the Congregation for the Doctrine of the Faith, Tornielli cited the testimony of the former Philippine Ambassador to the Holy See, Howard Dee, that Ratzinger had revealed to him that the Message of Akita and the Message of Fatima are "basically one and the same." (See Chapter 13.)

And, in a major surprise, Tornielli revealed that it was his own question on the Third Secret that had prompted Pope Benedict's explosive comments during the flight to Portugal concerning the

Secret's revelation of "future realities in the Church" involving an attack upon her by enemies within—again, not what is seen in the vision published in 2000 standing alone. Here Tornielli cited Pope Benedict's exhortation during the Mass inaugurating his pontificate: "Pray for me, that I do not flee for fear of the wolves."[368] Thus it was not a "Fatimist" but the world's foremost Vaticanist who had prompted the Pope to "reopen the file" (as Socci had put it) on the Third Secret of Fatima.

Pope Benedict Consecrates Italy

There is no doubt the Pope was fully aware of the *Consecration Now!* proceedings, especially given the participation of Rodari and Tornielli. And the Pontiff was probably also aware, if only second-hand, of the giant sign positioned above the central escalator bank at Porta di Roma, the largest shopping center in the City of Rome, from April 15 to May 13, 2011—seen by half a million pedestrians a week—and the seventy other massive signs placed throughout the city, all saying the same thing: *"Solo il Papa può salvare Roma, con una preghiera speciale di 5 minuti."*—"Only the Pope can save Rome, with a special five-minute prayer." And, while this publicity was having its effect, the apostolate's Rome branch commenced 24/7 television programming on April 15 on a new Roman channel: Fatima TV.

Romans concerned about the state of Italy and its teetering economy must have been bombarding Vatican offices with telephone calls concerning this "special prayer" and suggesting that it be done as soon as possible. On May 3, 2011, reversing his own declaration of April 22, 2011, noted above, that he did not contemplate any further ceremonies of "entrustment" to Mary, the Pope caused it to be announced that he would consecrate/entrust the nation of Italy to the Immaculate Heart of Mary. And so he did, along with the entire Italian episcopate, in a ceremony conducted at Saint Mary Major Basilica on May 26, 2011—less than two weeks after the *Consecration Now!* conference had ended.[369]

Commenting on the apparent success of this campaign, Father Gruner remarked: "I was once struck by the logic of an article arguing that only if the medical profession were forced by public pressure to accept the health benefits of a certain natural 'panacea' would they begin to include it in their medical practice. Why should the faithful not exercise their God-given right to petition the Pope

---

[368] "MASS, IMPOSITION OF THE PALLIUM AND CONFERRAL OF THE FISHERMAN'S RING FOR THE BEGINNING OF THE PETRINE MINISTRY OF THE BISHOP OF ROME," http://www.vatican.va/holy_father/benedict_xvi/homilies/2005 /documents/hf_ben-xvi_hom_20050424_iniziopontificato_en.html.

[369] Cf. text of proceeding at http://magisterobenedettoxvi.blogspot.com/2011/05/ affidamento-del-popolo-italiano-alla.html.

by the only means available, given his isolation in the Vatican—publicity—for resort to the 'panacea' of consecration to Mary? And so we did. But we limited our petition to something Roman citizens could understand and support themselves: their own local problems and the crises threatening the very existence of the Italian nation today, which have their common root in the problems afflicting the world at large: apostasy from God and His Holy Church."[370]

Thus did the year 2012 signal new hope for the cause of Our Lady of Fatima, despite the best efforts of Her false friends to impede accomplishment of the mission She launched at the Cova da Iria in 1917. "May the seven years which separate us from the centenary of the apparitions *hasten the fulfilment of the prophecy of the triumph of the Immaculate Heart of Mary*," said the Vicar of Christ at Fatima on May 13, 2010 during the apostolate's Rome conference of that year. The Pope, like the true friends of Fatima everywhere, was looking to the year 2017 as an obvious historical landmark respecting the Fatima prophecies. The question is: What will the Church and the world be witnessing when that landmark is reached? Will it be triumph or disaster?

---

[370] Telephonic interview with author, Holy Saturday 2012.

CONCLUSION

It has been nearly a century—ninety-five years—since Our Lady first appeared at Fatima. She came because Pope Benedict XV on May 5, in an anguished cry for help on behalf of mankind, asked ever so humbly but insistently for Our Lady to show him and mankind the way to peace. World War I was raging and it was obvious to Pope Benedict XV that there were no mere human efforts that could stop the insane war.

In response to Benedict XV's plea, on May 13, 1917, eight days later, Our Lady came to the Cova da Iria to announce *Heaven's* plan for peace in the world. The Consecration of Russia to the Immaculate Heart of Mary is no mere option, but rather a plan that must be followed. As Our Lady said to Sister Lucia, there is no other way: "Make it known to the Holy Father that I am still awaiting the Consecration of Russia to My Immaculate Heart. Without this Consecration, Russia cannot be converted, *nor can the world have peace*."[371]

At the very essence of the Message of Fatima stands the proposition so despised by the party of the innovators: that the Pope—the monarchical ruler of a monarchical Church in a world made "safe for democracy"—would be Our Lady's and Our Lord's instrument to shame all worldly powers by producing miraculously what their grand schemes had never produced, and never could produce.

But Heaven's peace plan has been ignored by the leaders of the Church, just as Pope Benedict XV's peace plan was ignored by all the worldly powers involved in World War I, except still-Catholic Austria-Hungary, which was crushed under President Woodrow Wilson's tank treads. Since 1917 and the Great Miracle of the Sun on October 13 of that year—an unprecedented sign of God's direct intervention in the history of nations—the world has descended into an orgy of violence without parallel in its history:

- The Russian Civil War (1917-23) between the Red Army and the anti-Bolshevik White Army, assisted by the Allied Forces, with a death toll of 4 million, both military and civilian, from battlefield casualties, disease and starvation.

- The Bolshevik genocides perpetrated by Trotsky and Lenin, who had been smuggled from Switzerland into Russia by the German High Command during World War

---

[371] Frère Michel de la Sainte Trinité, *The Whole Truth About Fatima*, Vol. III: *The Third Secret*, p. 327. Cf. *Il pellegrinaggio delle meraviglie*, (Rome, 1960) p. 440. Published under the auspices of the Italian Bishops Conference.

I in a successful bid to destabilize the Entente Powers and provoke Russia's withdrawal from World War I: 7 million dead, including the murdered Czar, his wife and five children.[372]

- The mass murder of *56 million* people by Josef Stalin from 1924 until his death in 1953—a holocaust for which he was personally responsible, perpetrated in order to maintain and expand his tyranny over Russia and Eastern Europe.[373] (This does not include Stalin's contribution to the death toll of World War II; see below.)

- World War II: the bloodiest in world history, causing incalculable losses to Western civilization, including the turnover of Eastern Europe to Stalin, presented with a Crusader's sword[374] at Teheran by Winston Churchill in a grotesque parody of the Crusades: 70 million dead.

- The genocides by the Nazi regime: 20 million dead.[375]

- The carpet-bombing of Dresden and Tokyo and the atomic bombing of Hiroshima and Nagasaki, all in 1945: at least 500,000 dead, combined.[376]

---

[372] The aptly named Alexander Helphand, a/k/a Parvus, who was also an advisor to the genocidal Young Turk regime, assisted the German High Command in this endeavor. Cf. Dimitri Kolgonov, *Lenin: A New Biography* (New York: Free Press/Simon and Schuster, 1994), p. 78 ff.

[373] The Soviet regime's total of 62 million dead from which we have subtracted Lenin's contribution of 6 million. Rummel cites the overall total of 62 million as "the only prudent, most probable tally in a range from a highly unlikely low figure of 28,000,000... and an equally unlikely high of 126,900,000...." Rummel, *Death by Government*, pp. 81-82.

[374] Buchanan, *The Unnecessary War*, p. 370.

[375] See Table 1.2, "20th Century Democide", in R.J. Rummel, *Death by Government* (New Brunswick, New Jersey: Transaction Publishers, 1994); availale online at http://www.hawaii.edu/powerkills/NOTE1.HTM.

[376] The A-bomb dropped on Nagasaki, the home of Japan's largest Catholic population, instantly incinerated Urakami Cathedral: "Fathers Nishida and Tamaya were hearing confessions again after the all-clear. The cathedral was only a third of a mile from where Fat Man detonated and was reduced to rubble in an instant. No one would be sure how many perished inside." Besides the A-bomb's lethal radiation, "there was its intense heat, which reached several million degrees centigrade at the explosion point. The whole mass of the huge bomb was ionized and a fireball created, making the air around it luminous, emitting ultraviolet rays and infrared rays and blistering roof tiles farther than half a mile from the epicenter. Exposed human skin was scorched up to two and a half miles away." In a concrete reinforced hospital a half-mile from ground zero "80 percent of the patients and staff perished." The surviving staff members "were shocked to find many of [the patients] dead, their bodies swollen and their skin peeled off as if they were overripe peaches." Paul Glynn, *A Song for Nagasaki* (San Francisco: Ignatius Press, 1988), pp. 19-20.

- The ethnic cleansing of Germans in the eastern provinces of Germany, delivered into the hands of Stalin by moving the Polish border westward at Yalta with the agreement of Churchill and FDR: 2 million dead in an orgy of "mass murder, rape and looting."[377]

- All the murders committed by Stalin, the monster the Allies needed to defeat the monster born at Versailles, and to whom they handed over Eastern Europe at Teheran[378] and Yalta in the name of Liberty (as mentioned above): at least 56 million dead.

And these are merely the major post-1917 bloodbaths in the Western world since the persecutions Our Lady predicted if the Consecration of Russia were not carried out. We must also include the genocides perpetrated by regimes that were the direct result of the spread of just one of Russia's errors—Communism—into other nations:

- The Red Chinese regime: 65 million dead.[379]

- The Pol Pot regime: 2 million dead.

- The North Korean regime: 1.6 million dead.

Add to these staggering tolls all the millions of lives claimed in the African civil wars and genocides that went on throughout the 20th century and continue today. For example, the Rwandan Genocide of 1994 with its estimated 500,000-1,000,000 victims, and the war in Darfur (2003-present), with its toll of 400,000 dead and 2.8 million displaced.

And there is the endless war on life in the womb. The annual death toll from abortion is more than 44 million, which is not even to consider the abortions caused by the contraceptive pill and other "contraception" methods. The death toll in the war against the unborn over the past century, when contraception and abortion spread throughout the world, could well be over a billion. *The blood of every one of those innocent children cries out to Heaven for vengeance.*

---

[377] Serhii Ploky, *Yalta: the Price of Peace* (New York: Viking, 2010), p. 216.

[378] The same Churchill who deplored the smuggling of Lenin into Russia as akin to "a culture of typhoid or of cholera… poured into the water supply of a great city," would lift his glass to Stalin in the process of preparing to turn over Eastern Europe to him at Yalta, declaring: "We regard Marshal Stalin's life as most precious to the hopes and hearts of all of us…. I walk the world with greater courage and hope when I find myself in a relation of friendship and intimacy with this great man, whose fame has gone out not only over all Russia, but the world." In Buchanan, *The Unnecessary War*, p. 376.

[379] Stephane Courtois, et al, *The Black Book of Communism*, (Cambridge, Massachusetts: Harvard University Press, 1999).

Since 1917, the nations of the world have spilled blood and wasted treasure on a scale beyond the wildest imaginings during all the centuries that preceded that pivotal year. The only exception would be the French Revolution and the French Revolutionary Wars of 1789 to 1802, claiming some three million lives. But these wars, in which the French Revolutionaries attempted to remake all of Europe in the Jacobin image, erupted precisely after *the failure to consecrate France* to the Sacred Heart of Jesus, which Our Lord requested of Saint Margaret Mary Alacoque on June 17, 1689. Successive kings of France failed to carry out the divine command. On June 17, 1789, one hundred years to the day after Our Lord made His request, the Third Estate rose up against King Louis XVI, declared itself the National Assembly of France and effectively deposed Louis. Imprisoned in the Tuileries Palace in 1791, having signed away his authority to the revolutionary government, King Louis made a vow to perform the Consecration if delivered from his plight:

> If, by an effect of the infinite kindness of God, I recover my freedom, my crown and my royal power, I promise solemnly:
>
> … To go myself in person, within three months from the day of my delivery, to the church of Notre-Dame of Paris, or in any other principal church of the place where I will be, and to pronounce, one day of Sunday or festival, at the foot of the high altar, after the offertory of the Mass, and between the hands of the celebrant, a solemn act of dedication of my person, my family and my kingdom to the Sacred Heart of Jesus, promising to give to all my subjects, the example of the worship and the devotion which are due to this adorable Heart.

But the desperate vow of the imprisoned King was too little, too late. Our Lord had waited patiently for a century to see obedience to His command, and it had never been forthcoming.

Today, as the centenary of the request for the Consecration of Russia approaches—it is only five years distant as of this writing—we are reminded of an apparition of Our Lord to Sister Lucia, recorded in her letters. At Rianjo, Spain in August 1931, Our Lord warned her that a fate paralleling that of revolutionary France and Europe awaits the whole world, including the ministers of His Church:

> Make it known to My ministers, given that they follow the example of the King of France in delaying the execution of My command, they will follow him into misfortune. It is never too late to have recourse to Jesus and Mary.

"The very future of the world is at stake." With these words of the currently reigning Roman Pontiff negates the idea that the "misfortune" of which Our Lord warned Lucia at Rianjo has already been endured in the form of World War II and the rise of Communism. The worst is yet to come. It is undeniable that Pope Benedict XVI sees unfolding today what Pope Leo XIII saw looming over the world as early as 1878, when he warned that the "evils by which the human race is oppressed on every side" were already a "deadly kind of plague which infects in its inmost recesses, allowing it no respite and foreboding ever fresh disturbances and *final disaster*."[380] Again and again Pope Benedict has made pronouncements that depart from the inexplicable "optimism" of the post-Vatican II era and return to the line of his pre-conciliar predecessors and their grave warnings for the Church and humanity:

> The darkness that poses *a real threat to mankind*, after all, is the fact that he can see and investigate tangible material things, but cannot see where the world is going or whence it comes, where our own life is going, what is good and what is evil. The darkness enshrouding God and obscuring values is *the real threat to our existence and to the world in general*.[381]

> In our days, when *in vast areas of the world the faith is in danger of dying out like a flame which no longer has fuel*, the overriding priority is to make God present in this world and to show men and women the way to God. Not just any god, but the God who spoke on Sinai; to that God whose face we recognize in a love which presses "to the end" (cf. Jn. 13:1)—in Jesus Christ, crucified and risen. The real problem at this moment of our history is that *God is disappearing from the human horizon*, and, with the dimming of the light which comes from God, *humanity is losing its bearings, with increasingly evident destructive effects*.[382]

> How many winds of doctrine we have known in recent decades, how many ideological currents, how many ways of thinking... The small boat of thought of many Christians has often been tossed about by these waves—thrown from one extreme to the other: from Marxism to liberalism, even to libertinism; from collectivism to radical individualism; from atheism to a vague religious mysticism; from agnosticism to syncretism, and so forth.... *We are moving towards a dictatorship of relativism* which does not recognize anything as certain and which has as its highest goal one's own ego and one's own desires.[383]

---

[380] *Inscrutabili Dei Consilio* (1878), n. 2.

[381] Homily for the Easter Vigil, April 7, 2012.

[382] "Letter of His Holiness Pope Benedict XVI to All the Bishops of the World", March 10, 2009.

[383] "Homily for the Pro Eligendo Romano Pontifice Mass, 18 April 2005" (as Cardinal Ratzinger).

In the Old and New Testaments, the Lord proclaims *judgment on the unfaithful* vineyard. The judgment that Isaiah foresaw is brought about in the *great wars and exiles* for which the Assyrians and Babylonians were responsible. The judgment announced by the Lord Jesus refers above all to the destruction of Jerusalem in the year 70. *Yet the threat of judgment also concerns us, the Church in Europe, Europe and the West in general.* With this Gospel, the Lord is also crying out to our ears the words that in the Book of Revelation He addresses to the Church of Ephesus: *"If you do not repent I will come to you and remove your lampstand from its place"* (2: 5).[384]

The Pope himself intimates the threat of World War III when he speaks of "a real threat to mankind" and "the real threat to our existence and to the world in general". Such a war, in a few instants of thermonuclear devastation, would produce more causalities than all the wars in human history combined. Is this not suggested (but not explained) in the vision of the "Bishop dressed in White"?

Then too there is the prospect of a financial and economic Armageddon that will affect every man, woman and child on earth. The world's paper currencies will be junked as worthless. No one will buy or sell anything with paper currency. Trade, industry, farming—everything—will grind to a halt. There will be food riots, martial law, and internment camps; chaos will descend upon the nations. And Christians will undergo outright persecution in an Islamicized Europe and even in the United States.

And yet the Consecration of Russia, which could avert these catastrophes, remains undone. True, Pope Benedict is attempting to address the crisis in the Church, which is linked to the growing civilization crisis of a once Christian West. It seems that part of him, at least, wishes to reverse the Church's course over the past forty years, to reverse its ruinous "new orientation," of which the "new" Message of Fatima is a part. The Pope has "liberated" the traditional Latin Mass, declaring that every priest in the Church is free to offer it. He has refused any longer to distribute Communion in the hand at papal Masses. He has called for a "hermeneutic of continuity" between Vatican II and the Church's constant teaching before the Council—in itself a devastating admission that something is wrong with the Council. He has lifted the "excommunication" of the bishops of the Society of Saint Pius X, initiating theological discussions with the Society's representatives precisely on the question of Vatican II's conformity with Catholic Tradition.

Tellingly, the Pope has not simply demanded that the Society's

---

[384] Pope Benedict XVI, "Homily for the opening of the 11th Ordinary General Assembly of the Synod of Bishops", Rome, October 2, 2005.

adherents "obey Vatican II," whatever that might mean, but rather has launched *discussions* about the Council and what it really teaches—a sure sign that the Council has been an enormous and unprecedented problem for the Church. This is no doubt indicated in the Third Secret with its connection to the year 1960, the year the Council preparations began in earnest—a connection between the Secret and the Council that Cardinal Bertone has most suspiciously labored to destroy.

And yet the Consecration of Russia remains undone. Pope Benedict's fears over the state of the Church and the very future of the world are hardly consistent with the Triumph of the Immaculate Heart of Mary that the Pope himself admits has yet to be seen, pointing instead to the year 2017 as a possible time of fulfillment—that fateful centenary we have just noted.

But the false friends of Fatima, both high and low, persist in the deception—the Pope's own word—that the Virgin's glorious promise has been fulfilled because the Church has done what She asked of it. But we have seen how the Pope has indicated, however obliquely, that he must try again to remove the mysterious impediment to accomplishment of the Fatima mandate. And try again he must.

Our Lady of Fatima requested such a simple thing, and Sister Lucia affirmed it again and again throughout her life: that the Pope, together with the bishops, publicly consecrate the nation of Russia—not any thing or any place else, but *Russia*—to Her Immaculate Heart. Why have they made it so complicated? Why have they done everything in their power to prevent it from happening?

The false friends of Fatima offer many pious tributes to the Message of Fatima, to the Blessed Virgin, to Sister Lucia and her truly exemplary life of selfless devotion to Christ and His Holy Mother. All of this is very good in itself. But how is it that every one of these tributes always reaches the same illogical conclusion: that the call to Marian devotion, prayer, and acts of reparation for sin in the Message must be severed from its prophetic content? In truth the two elements are inseparable parts of the one Message, delivered to earth together for the accomplishment of the whole plan the Message presents for the good of a Church and a world whose very future is indeed now at stake.

How is it that the false friends of Fatima, once their tributes are out of the way, all convey the same basic point with utter unanimity: "Fatima is finished" in its capacity as a prophecy and a warning for the Church and humanity, and now involves simply personal spiritual advancement and harmonious living with other men and their various religions and deities?

We have seen that the Pope declared at the very place of the

Fatima apparitions that "One *deceives himself* who thinks that the prophetic mission of Fatima is concluded." We have seen that His Holiness himself disclosed that the Third Secret concerns "*future realities*" of the Church which are revealing themselves "little by little" in "a really terrifying way." We have seen that after years of falsely maintaining that the events foretold in the Third Secret "belong to the past," even Cardinal Bertone has been forced to retreat to the position that the Third Secret has been fulfilled "only in part" and that we must have hope that there will be no "catastrophes." And hope there is—but only through the very means he and his fellow false friends of Fatima continue obstinately to impede.

There is no *rational* basis for the perverse refusal to mention Russia in the Consecration of Russia that the very Mother of God requested. No one can seriously maintain that the Church and the world would suffer harm if the Pope were to utter the word "Russia" during the act the Blessed Virgin requires of him. We are driven to the conclusion that only one thing can account for the bizarre decades-long campaign by Vatican bureaucrats to prevent at all costs the utterance of that single, fateful word: *they know or at least suspect that an explicit Consecration of Russia to Mary's Immaculate Heart would actually bring about Russia's conversion, and for some reason they do not wish to see this.*

We must be clear about what we are suggesting here: that the otherwise inexplicable and simply preposterous refusal to consecrate Russia by name must ultimately be diabolical in origin. This is not, of course, to say that all the churchmen involved in the refusal are conscious agents of the devil—although there are those who must know full well that they are working for the devil's ends in obstructing Russia's consecration, including the Freemasons among them. Rather, whatever their subjective intentions may be, they are lending themselves to what is objectively an evil end. The sheer irrationality of those who contrive the most nonsensical arguments in defense of a "Consecration of Russia" that refuses to mention the place is evidence of "diabolical disorientation" in the matter, to borrow Sister Lucia's famous phrase concerning the crisis in the Church. Nonsense is always a sign of the Father of Lies at work in the minds of men, even those who might be convinced they are defending truth and justice.

The Father of Lies undoubtedly has one aim in mind concerning Russia: to obfuscate the matter of its consecration and thus delay it as long as possible, thereby delaying as long as possible the consequent Triumph of the Immaculate Heart and the rout of diabolical forces that have provoked an epochal crisis in the Church and the world at large. Of course, we have it on the infallible authority of the Virgin

Herself that in the end Her Immaculate Heart will triumph, Russia will be consecrated to Her, and "that poor nation" will be converted for the good of all humanity. Yet the question before us is how long Providence will permit the Vatican Secretary of State's Party Line, and those who defend it, to obstruct what will inevitably be done in fulfillment of the divine will.

As this book reaches your hands, not just the Pope but reasonable men of all persuasions can see that the world is rushing toward "final disaster." Time grows perilously short. We cannot allow human respect to keep us any longer from opposing *publicly and without compromise* those who have, for far too long, denied our right under God to the entirety of the precious Secret the Virgin Mother of God revealed to the three seers and linked to the pivotal year 1960, and to that glorious triumph over adversity She promised if "My requests are honored." We must stand up to the false friends of Fatima, no matter how high their positions and offices in the Church or no matter how low they are in society and the Church. In doing so, we ought to affirm the following propositions, which can be considered a kind of *Magna Carta* for the liberation of the Fatima prophecies from their unjust captivity:

First, the false friends of Fatima do not own the Message of Fatima. It has not been given to them, but to the Church and the world.

Second, they have no *authority* over the Message. Only the Vicar of Christ, by a solemn and binding pronouncement, could impose upon us a due obligation with respect to the Message. Their purported dictates concerning Fatima are void and of no effect. In particular, the Vatican Secretary of State *has no competence whatsoever in the matter of Fatima*, and his attempt to assert authority over the "management" of the Fatima event is nothing but a usurpation.

Third, their opinions on what the Message means and what it requires of the Pope, the bishops, the clergy and the laity *bind no one*, as the Pope himself has made clear, and we may freely reject these mere opinions if they do not correspond to what the Message plainly states and commands. If they speak nonsense respecting the Message, we may treat it as nonsense, no matter what "official" approval they claim to possess. The Faith is always in accord with reason, and so, therefore, is the Message of Fatima.

Fourth, they have *no right* to prevent the faithful from exercising our God-given right to petition the Pope for both the Consecration of Russia to the Immaculate Heart of Mary and full disclosure of the Third Secret—*incessantly*, if necessary, like the persistent widow in Our Lord's parable, who obtained justice *only* because she did not cease to demand it until the unresponsive judge relented and did his duty. (Luke 18:5)

Fifth, their attempt to reduce the Fatima prophecies to a prescription for inter-religious brotherhood rather than Heaven's call for the Kingship of Christ and the Reign of Mary is a *mockery and a blasphemy* that we must condemn and oppose at every turn as a betrayal of the Church's irrevocable divine commission to make disciples of all nations for the salvation of souls and the glory of God.

There are no "universal Fatima intentions" for people of "all faiths," as the "World Apostolate" of Fatima blasphemously proposes with the approval of a Vatican department that has no teaching authority in the Church. The "universal intentions" of the Message of Fatima are those of the universal Church established by God, which is called Catholic precisely because the word means "universal" in Greek. The Mother of God appeared at Fatima on a *Catholic* mission to secure the salvation of souls in this one true and universal Church—through the grace of the sacraments she alone provides, and with the aid of an establishment in the world of the uniquely *Catholic* devotion to Mary's Immaculate Heart.

So much as it lies within our power—and so help us God!—*we must stop them from attempting to paganize the Fatima prophecies* in keeping with the disastrous "new orientation" of the Church since Vatican II, whose fruits are "silent apostasy," scandal and corruption, and indeed the very disaster Pope Pius XII foresaw precisely in the light of Fatima. We must secure for the Church and the world the Consecration of Russia to the Immaculate Heart.

"An ambitious program!", the skeptic might scoff. And how could common members of the Church be expected to accomplish it? But, in fact, nothing is impossible with God, and the prayers and works of the common faithful have already produced a dramatic movement in the Vatican toward fulfillment of Heaven's peace plan. We have seen on these pages the impact of the Rome conferences staged by Father Gruner's Fatima apostolate. We have seen how in this age of "social communications" so lauded by Vatican II, something as simple as a giant billboard and prominent signs, as well as publicity by a Fatima-related TV channel, brought the petition of the faithful for Italy's consecration to the Immaculate Heart to the attention of the Pope himself, who obliged only ten days after the press conference at which he had demurred from any further acts of "entrustment" to Mary.

The people of Rome, responding to social communication in the form of publicity, responded in turn to the Holy Father, and thus obtained the Consecration of their nation—whose capital is the Heart of the Catholic Church—to Mary. What the Roman people accomplished under the influence of legitimate suasion is a lesson for all the faithful of the world: *Petition the Holy Father, by every means available, to do at last what Our Lady of Fatima requested nearly a century ago. Let nothing stop you from pleading with the Pope, your earthly Father, as sons and daughters of the Father above.*

These pages have shown that the desperate condition of the Church and the world today is linked to a willful rejection of the maternal prescriptions of the Mother of God for our time by men who simply despise the Fatima prophecy while pretending to pay it homage. This travesty will end only when those responsible for it, no matter what their subjective intentions, are seen for what they are objectively: not friends, but foes of the prophetic mission of Fatima. When foe is rightly distinguished from friend, the way ahead will be clear and the mission begun at the Cova da Iria will finally reach its consummation—a consummation our worried Pope declares we have yet to see. When the prophetic mission of Fatima is returned to the command of its true friends, led by a Pope no longer constrained by the worldly-wise dictates of his manifestly errant subordinates, then every nation will witness what our heavenly Mother has promised from the beginning: "In the end, My Immaculate Heart will Triumph."

Further Suggested Reading

The author of this book has been researching, documenting, and exposing the false friends of Fatima for almost two decades. He has uncovered these false friends at every level inside the Catholic Church. In reading this book you will discover that the false friends of Fatima, like politicians, make for strange bedfellows.

This book provides in-depth analysis of the various techniques used by some of Our Lady's enemies to neutralize and bury the one and *only* solution God has given us (i.e., the Consecration of Russia) to end the life threatening problems we face. These problems include the dangers of war, famine, and the worldwide financial and economic collapse that is set to occur in the near future.

There is so much more information available for those who want to learn everything they can about the false friends of Fatima.

Below you will find a list of Articles, Manuscripts, Booklets and Reprints on the subject which the author, Christopher Ferrara, has written about over the years. Download them for free off the Internet at the address noted after the Reference — or — Order them from the Publisher for the following special Publication Fees: **Books** - $7.50 each, **Manuscripts** - $5.00 each, **Booklets** or **Reprint Packages** (**Pkgs**.) - $2.50 each. Prices include Postage and Handling to Canada and the United States. Add $2.50 Postage for Overseas Orders.

The Reports below are listed under the false friends of Fatima which they expose:

APOSTOLI, Father Andrew

"Fatima For Today: **A Response"**, May 2011, 56 pages – www. fatima.org/news/newsviews/fatima-for-today-a-response.pdf
[MANUSCRIPT #FF1]

BERTONE, Cardinal Tarcisio

Vindication: The Latest Chapter in the Story of Fatima (Fort Erie, Ontario: The Fatima Center, 2010), 64-page booklet – www. secretstillhidden.com/pdf/epilogue.pdf   [BOOKLET #BT026]

The Secret Still Hidden (Pound Ridge, New York: Good Counsel Publications, 2008), 248 pages – www.secretstillhidden.com
[BOOK #B1300]

"The Third Secret Cover-up", *The Fatima Crusader*, Issue #87, Autumn 2007, pp. 29ff – www.fatimacrusader.com/cr87/cr87 pg29.asp   [REPRINT PKG. #FF2]

"Bertone vs. Socci: Civil War Rages in Rome Over Third Secret of Fatima", *The Fatima Crusader,* Issue #86, Summer 2007, pp. 29ff – www.fatimacrusader.com/cr86/cr86pg29.asp
[REPRINT PKG. #FF2]

"Let us Hear the Witness, for Heaven's Sake", *The Fatima Crusader,* Issue #70, Spring 2002, pp. 34ff – www.fatimacrusader.com/cr70/cr70pg34.asp
[REPRINT #FF3]

BORELLI, Antonio A.

"Friendly Reflections?", April 2010, 44 pages – www.fatima.org/news/newsviews/ferraraexpose.pdf   [MANUSCRIPT #FF4]

CASAROLI, Cardinal Agostino and SODANO, Cardinal Angelo

"The Truth Breaks Out in Italy", December 2006 – www.fatimaperspectives.com/ts/perspective527.asp

"'The Party Line on Fatima' Update: Pope Sodano I", August 2002 – www.fatimaperspectives.com/pl/perspective267.asp

"The Sodano Interpretation", November 2001 – www.fatimaperspectives.com/ts/perspective123.asp

"Cardinal Sodano, Please Step Aside!", October 2001 – www.fatimaperspectives.com/ts/perspective90.asp

"Concerning Father Nicholas Gruner and Fatima Priest", December 2000 – www.fatima.org/news/newsviews/prrome.asp
[REPRINT PKG. #FF5]

A Law for One Man, Summer 2000, 32-page booklet – www.fatima.org/apostolate/defense/law1man.asp   [BOOKLET #BT006]

DOYLE, Father Thaddeus

"Setting the Record Straight: A Reply to Father Thaddeus Doyle Concerning the Consecration of Russia to the Immaculate Heart of Mary", 12-page booklet; also in *The Fatima Crusader*, Issue #98, Spring 2011, pp. 19ff – www.fatima.org/apostolate/vlarchive/strs.pdf, www.fatimacrusader.com/cr98/cr98pg19.pdf

[BOOKLET #BT027]

EVARISTO, Carlos

"Sister Lucy Betrayed", *The Fatima Crusader*, Issue #57, Spring/Summer 1998, pp. 3ff – www.fatimacrusader.com/cr57/cr57pg03.asp   [BOOKLET #FF6]

"Ambush in Fatima: October 1992", *Fatima Priest*, First Edition (Pound Ridge, New York: Good Counsel Publications, 1997), Chapter 11, pp. 119-140 – www.fatimapriest.com/ch11.html [REPRINT #FF7]

EWTN

EWTN: A Network Gone Wrong (Pound Ridge, New York: Good Counsel Publications, 2006), 276 pages – www.networkgonewrong.org [BOOK #BP036]

"More Posturing from the 'Vice President for Theology'", November 2001 – www.fatimaperspectives.com/fg/perspective103.asp

"The Art of Pious Calumny", *The Fatima Crusader*, Issue #68, Autumn 2001, pp. 29ff – www.fatimacrusader.com/cr68/cr68pg29.asp

"The Ignorant Advice of Colin Donovan", May 2001 – www.fatimaperspectives.com/fg/perspective33.asp [REPRINT PKG. #FF8]

FOX, Father Robert J.

"'Conversion of Russia' Update: Russian Spies? They're Back!", March 2005 – www.fatimaperspectives.com/cr/perspective457.asp

"Father Fox Continues to Defend the Indefensible", November 2004 – www.fatima.org/news/newsviews/1104frfox.asp

"The *New Oxford Review* Does Fatima — Badly", November 2011 – www.fatimaperspectives.com/ts/perspective612.asp
[BOOKLET #FF9]

Father Fox's Modernist Assault on Fatima, June 2004, 28-page booklet – www.fatima.org/news/newsviews/062504frfox1.asp
[BOOKLET #BT007]

GUERRA, Monsignor Luciano
"Did You or Did You Not?", *The Fatima Crusader*, Issue #76, Spring 2004, pp. 59ff – www.fatimacrusader.com/cr76/cr76pg59.asp

"A New Fatima for the New Church", *The Fatima Crusader*, Issue #75, Winter 2004, pp. 8ff – www.fatimacrusader.com/cr75/cr75pg08.asp [REPRINT PKG. #FF10]

SODANO, Cardinal Angelo
See CASAROLI, Cardinal Agostino, above.

WANDERER (The)

"Actually, Virginia, Father Gruner is Not Suspended", Autumn 2003, 16-page booklet – www.fatima.org/apostolate/defense/notsusvir.asp   [BOOKLET #I-0002]

"A New Fatima for the New Church (Part II): The Neo-Catholic Establishment Joins the Post-conciliar Revolution in Revising the Message of Fatima", *The Fatima Crusader*, Issue #76, Spring 2004, pp. 65ff – www.fatimacrusader.com/cr76/cr76pg65.asp

"Defending the Revolution", *Catholic Family News*, March 2003 – www.fatima.org/apostolate/defense/defrevolut.asp

"Pleasing Uncle Al", *Catholic Family News*, December 2001 – www.fatima.org/apostolate/defense/pleaseal1.asp

"The Neo-Catholic 'Message' of Fatima: *The Wanderer's* Recent Attack on Father Nicholas Gruner Reveals the Pathology of Neo-Catholicism", March 2001 – www.fatimaperspectives.com/nc/perspective11b.asp   [REPRINT PKG. #FF11]

For more articles about the *Blue Army, Father Fox*, and other false friends such as *Monsignor Alberto Cosme do Amaral*, we also recommend the following articles by Father Paul Kramer:

"The Plot to Silence Our Lady (Part I): Disinformation Tactics against Fatima Exposed", *The Fatima Crusader*, Issue #20, June-July 1986, pp. 9ff – www.fatimacrusader.com/cr20/cr20pg09.asp

"The Plot to Silence Our Lady (Part II): The Organization's Smear Campaign Gets Worse", *The Fatima Crusader*, Issue #20, June-July 1986, pp. 13ff – www.fatimacrusader.com/cr20/cr20pg13.asp
[REPRINT PKG. #FF12]

"The Vatican-Moscow Agreement has Silenced Our Lady", *The Fatima Crusader*, Issue #22, April-May 1987, pp. 12ff – www.fatimacrusader.com/cr22/cr22pg12.asp

"The Blue Army Leadership has followed a deliberate policy of falsifying the Fatima Message", *The Fatima Crusader*, Issue #22, April-May 1987, pp. 26ff – www.fatimacrusader.com/cr22/cr22pg26.asp   [REPRINT PKG. #FF13]

"The Plot to Silence Our Lady Continues: More Disinformation against the Message of Our Lady of Fatima", *The Fatima Crusader*, Issue #30, Winter 1989, pp. 8ff – www.fatimacrusader.com/cr30/cr30pg08.asp

"The Plot (To Silence Our Lady) Thickens", *The Fatima Crusader*, Issue #31-32, March-May 1990, pp. 4ff – www.fatimacrusader. com/cr31/cr31-32pg04.asp   [REPRINT PKG. #FF14]

"The Fatima Consecration Hoax: The Conspiracy against the Consecration of Russia Continues"**, *The Fatima Crusader*, Issue #35, Winter 1990-1991, pp. 5ff – www.fatimacrusader.com/ cr35/cr35pg5.asp

"The Fatima Consecration Hoax Continues", *The Fatima Crusader*, Issue #41, Summer 1992, pp. 18ff – www.fatimacrusader.com/ cr41/cr41pg18.asp   [REPRINT PKG. #FF15]

"Update on the Plot to Silence Our Lady", *The Fatima Crusader*, Issue #63, Spring 2000, pp. 11ff – www.fatimacrusader.com/ cr63/cr63pg11.asp   [REPRINT #FF16]

Besides the books and articles by the author, Christopher A. Ferrara, listed in this section and the articles by Father Paul Kramer, no list of readings regarding the *False Friends of Fatima* would be complete without mentioning the book – *The Devil's Final Battle*.

It is written by seven authors and edited by Father Paul Kramer and his editorial team. *The Devil's Final Battle* is a compilation of writings which expose the betrayals of a number of the above false friends of Fatima as well as others.

In this book, you will see some further documentation and discover more false rationalizations for why they attack and betray Our Lady of Fatima and Her Message.

The Devil's Final Battle (Terryville, Connecticut: The Missionary Association, 2010, Second Edition), 390 pages – www. devilsfinalbattle.com.   [BOOK #BP027V4]

One of the major obstacles in the way of the Consecration of Russia is the Vatican-Moscow Agreement which is not widely known about, and most of those who have heard of it, find it hard to believe. Inform yourself on this intrinsic evil and pass the information on to others who remain ignorant that it even exists. The following articles, by Father Nicholas Gruner and Jean Madiran and others, are all available through the publishers of this book.

"The Vatican-Moscow Agreement", by Jean Madiran, *The Fatima Crusader*, Issue #16, Sept. - Oct. 1984, pp. 5ff – www.fatimacrusader.com/cr16/cr16pg05.asp

"The Vatican Silenced by Moscow", by Jean Madiran, *The Fatima Crusader*, Issue #17, Feb. - April 1985, pp. 4ff – www.fatimacrusader.com/cr17/cr17pg04.asp

"The Catholic Church Betrayed", *The Fatima Crusader*, Issue #17, Feb. - April 1985, pp. 7ff – www.fatimacrusader.com/cr17/cr17pg07.asp

"Why the Vatican-Moscow Agreement Must Be Repudiated", by Father Nicholas Gruner, *The Fatima Crusader*, Issue #17, Feb. - April 1985, pp. 11ff – www.fatimacrusader.com/cr17/cr17pg11.asp

"Obstacle to the Consecration of Russia: The Vatican-Moscow Agreement", by Atila Sinke Guimarães, *The Fatima Crusader*, Issue #73, Spring 2003, pp. 32ff – www.fatimacrusader.com/cr73/cr73pg32.asp

"The Vatican-Moscow Agreement Has Silenced Our Lady", by Father Paul Kramer, *The Fatima Crusader*, Issue #22, April-May 1987, pp. 12ff – www.fatimacrusader.com/cr22/cr22pg12.asp (This reprint is also included in PKG. #FF13 above.)

[REPRINT PKG. #FF17]

Moscow and the Vatican, by Alexis Ulysses Floridi, S.J. (Ann Arbor, Michigan: Ardis Publishers, 1986), 279 pages. His book contains an in-depth study of the politics and evils of the agreement. Floridi's book is not available from this publisher.

For a concise explanation of the Consecration of Russia request by Our Lady of Fatima as well as a summary of the obstacles obstructing the Consecration of Russia up to 1988, read the widely acclaimed book, *World Enslavement Or Peace ... It's Up to the Pope*, written by Father Nicholas Gruner and other Fatima experts. "This book is the first and only one to fully explore the crucial issue of Our Lady's Fatima requests."... Bishop Wladyslaw Miziolek, Warsaw.

World Enslavement or Peace ... It's Up to the Pope, by Father Nicholas Gruner and other Fatima experts (Fort Erie: The Fatima Crusader, 1988), 612 pages – www.worldenslavementorpeace.com

[BOOK #BP004]